WILSONIANISM

WILSONIANISM: WOODROW WILSON AND HIS LEGACY IN AMERICAN FOREIGN RELATIONS

LLOYD E. AMBROSIUS

First published 2002 by
PALGRAVE MACMILLAN™
175 Fifth Avenue, New York, N.Y. 10010 and
Houndmills, Basingstoke, Hampshire, England RG21 6XS
Companies and representatives throughout the world

PALGRAVE MACMILLAN is the global academic imprint of the Palgrave Macmillan division of St. Martin's Press, LLC and of Palgrave Macmillan Ltd. Macmillan® is a registered trademark in the United States, United Kingdom and other countries. Palgrave is a registered trademark in the European Union and other countries.

ISBN 1–4039–6008–9 hardback
ISBN 1–4039–6009–7 paperback

Library of Congress Cataloging-in-Publication Data

Ambrosius, Lloyd E.
    Wilsonianism : Woodrow Wilson and his legacy in American foreign relations / by Lloyd Ambrosius.
        p. cm.
    Includes bibliographical references (p.).
    ISBN 1-40396-008-9 – ISBN 1-40396-009-7
        1. United States—Foreign Relations—1913-1921. 2. Wilson, Woodrow, 1856–1924—Contributions in diplomacy. 3. Wilson, Woodrow, 1856–1924—Influence. 4. World War, 1914–1918—Diplomatic history. I. Title.

E768 .A44 2002
973.91'3'092—dc21   2002074849

A catalogue record for this book is available from the British Library.

Design by Newgen Imaging Systems (P) Ltd., Chennai, India.

First edition: September, 2002
10 9 8 7 6 5 4 3 2 1

Printed in the United States of America.

To my mentor and friend
Norman A. Graebner

CONTENTS

INTRODUCTION

Woodrow Wilson and his legacy epitomized the liberal tradition in American foreign relations. The principles of Wilsonianism, which he articulated, expressed the values of democracy and capitalism, including freedom and human rights, which most Americans have lauded. Although I share these values, the chapters in this book are critical of Wilsonian ideology and statecraft. Responsible exercise of power requires more than affirmation of liberal values in the abstract; it also involves their fulfillment in practice. Good intentions are not enough. As a realist, I focus on both ends and means, both power and responsibility. It is important to scrutinize the methods used to achieve liberal goals and the often unintended negative consequences of pursuing even laudatory purposes in international relations. I do not share the liberal belief in progressive history, which has traditionally undergirded American expectations that well-intended actions will result in positive outcomes at bearable costs, at least in the long run. Like other realists, I stress the centrality of power in international relations. But power, as I understand it, is not a narrow concept; it includes culture and political economy as well as military strength. More than most realists, I emphasize pluralism in the modern world. The crosscurrents between global interdependence and pluralism limited Wilson's ability—and that of his successors—to achieve his vision of a new world order. So, too, did the inherent dilemmas and contradictions among his principles. That would not have surprised eighteenth-century founders of the American republic, who appreciated the balance of power in international relations and in a federal government with three branches. Their understanding of republicanism informs my pluralist variant of the realist tradition in international relations, and thus my critique of Wilsonianism.

My first book, *Woodrow Wilson and the American Diplomatic Tradition: The Treaty Fight in Perspective* (1987),[1] examined the origins of the League of Nations and the fight between the U.S. president and the Senate over the Versailles Treaty. Using archival sources from Germany and Great Britain as well as the United States, I placed the drafting of the League's Covenant at the Paris Peace Conference of 1919 and the fight in the United States over America's future role in world affairs within the context of international history. My subsequent book, *Wilsonian Statecraft: Theory and Practice of Liberal Internationalism during World War I* (1991),[2] focused on the president's planning for peace and his military strategy during the wartime years of 1914 to 1918, and especially on the degree of coordination between these diplomatic and military tasks. In both books, I offered critical assessments of Wilsonian diplomacy, arguing that the president failed to provide a realistic vision or legacy for the United States in world affairs.

During and after the Great War, Wilson offered his vision of a new world order, identified, in retrospect, as Wilsonianism. His liberal internationalism embraced the principles of (1) national self-determination, which affirmed both national sovereignty and democratic self-government; (2) Open Door economic globalization, which favored a competitive marketplace for trade and financial investments across national borders; (3) collective security, which found expression in the postwar League of Nations; and (4) progressive history, which undergirded the Wilsonian vision of a better future for the world. These principles—the legacy of Wilsonianism—profoundly influenced the thinking and behavior of Americans in the twentieth century. They provided the dominant ideology for the United States during this so-called American Century.[3]

Political scientists have used the categories of realism, liberalism, and socialism for the three major schools of international relations theory. Within those traditional schools of thought, they have recognized substantial variety. Some distinguished, for example, between realism and neorealism or between liberalism and neoliberalism.[4] Historians have employed similar categories, defining these as realism, liberal internationalism, and New Left revisionism. Typically not so interested in theory, their definitions of schools of thought were often less rigorous or precise.[5]

As a critic of Wilson and Wilsonianism, I have identified with the realist school, following my mentor, the historian Norman A. Graebner. His interpretation of the American diplomatic tradition profoundly affected my thinking. The theologian Reinhold Niebuhr and the political scientist Hans J. Morgenthau also influenced my understanding of ethics and international relations, and of U.S. foreign policy. The writings of George F. Kennan and Walter Lippmann, too, contributed to my perspective. Like these twentieth-century originators of realist thought in the United States, I also have learned from eighteenth-century founders of the American republic, including the political philosophy in *The Federalist Papers*. But as chapters in this book reveal, my views differ in some respects from all of them. While my critique of Wilsonianism owes much to their insights, it shifts the central focus to the paradox of global interdependence and pluralism. It emphasizes the world's diversity and the connections between integration and fragmentation in twentieth-century international history. In developing this pluralist variant of realist thought, I have benefited from Ronald Steel's critique of Wilsonianism in American foreign relations from the Vietnam War to the post-Cold War era and his biography of Lippmann.[6] I also have learned from the writings of Richard J. Barnet, David P. Calleo, Robert W. Tucker, and Stanley Hoffmann.

In agreement with other realists, I have recognized the importance of the global balance of power. Historically, all nations and empires have existed in a world they could neither control nor escape, whether or not their leaders understood or accepted this reality. Even when great powers, including the United States, pursued hegemony, they have never fully succeeded. The reality of diversity among various peoples and cultures has thwarted all such attempts. In other words, a balance of power—which is, after all, the world's only alternative to omnipotence (which no state has achieved) or impotence (which no state has sought) for any nation or empire—has defined the context in which Americans, like all others, have conducted their foreign relations.

Realism, as I understand it, does not fit some of the stereotypical definitions given by critics of this school. Political scientists, in quest of international relations theories, have sometimes distorted realist thought by reducing it to a few simple assumptions or summary statements.[7] In *Neorealism and Its Critics* (1986), Robert O. Keohane summarized the "three key assumptions" of political realism: "(1) states (or city-states) are the key units of action; (2) they seek power, either as an end in itself or as a means to other ends; and (3) they behave in ways that are, by and large, rational, and therefore comprehensible to outsiders in rational terms." This overly simplified definition of realism was similar to the one he and Joseph S. Nye had given in *Power and Interdependence* (1977). Although in that book they had offered "complex inter-dependence" as "the opposite of realism," Keohane now claimed that they had "relied on Realist theory as a basis for our structural models of international regime change."[8] He obviously was struggling with a definition of realism that was too trun-cated to express even his own political thought. Jack Donnelly experienced the same problem. In *Realism and International Relations* (2000), he defined his orientation as "undeniably non-realist" or even "anti-realist." But then he acknowledged that his position was "not all that different from that of 'realists.'" He conceded that he had "a certain sympathy for and appreciation of a heavily hedged realism as part of a pluralistic discipline of international studies."[9] Rather than rejecting realism and then acknowledging my indebtedness to this school of thought, as these political scientists did, I have identified with the realist tradition and then developed my own pluralist variant. Recognizing, moreover, the variety of particular views among those calling themselves realists, I trust that my readers will not assume that I agree with all of them—as my criticism of Henry Kissinger will show—or with stereotypical definitions of this school offered by its critics.

For political scientists and historians alike, Wilson's foreign policy epitomized liber-alism. His legacy continued to shape U.S. involvement in international affairs throughout the American Century. After World War II, the Cold War consensus embraced liberalism, but combined this tradition with tough-minded power politics. Even when U.S. leaders understood and justified their actions in terms of liberal inter-nationalism, they pursued U.S. hegemony and wielded all forms of coercion, includ-ing military force. In the practice of American statecraft, they added features that realists would expect to observe in the conduct of any great power. Ideals and self-interest thus reinforced each other in U.S. foreign relations.[10] The Vietnam War, however, shattered the Cold War consensus. In the wake of deep divisions over Vietnam, which pitted "hard" liberal cold warriors (or "hawks") against "soft" liberals (or "doves") who had turned against the war, some of the former abandoned the liberal label and became conservatives or neoconservatives.[11] But, regardless of the label, the legacy of Wilsonianism continued to find expression in American foreign relations.

World War I devastated Europe and opened a new era in global history. The geog-rapher Isaiah Bowman, who had helped the American delegation prepare for the peace conference, emphasized these changes in *The New World* (1921). "The effects of the Great War are so far-reaching that we shall have henceforth a new world," he anticipated. "Shaken violently out of their former routine, people everywhere have created or adopted new ideas and new material arrangements."[12] In his view, the course of history had changed dramatically: "The new era will date from the years of the World War just as medieval Europe dates from the fall of Rome, or as the modern democratic era dates from the Declaration of Independence."[13]

Both integration and fragmentation characterized this new world. Although Europe experienced the war's greatest impact, the consequences were global. "Even in the United States, remote though it be, the evil effects are manifold," Bowman observed. "No American, however secluded his life, however distant his home from the big cities and the coasts, is free from the consequences of the World War. The world is broken; its international life is disrupted; it is in a state of general economic disorder."[14] These were the ongoing postwar problems.

These two forces—integration and fragmentation—shaped international relations throughout the twentieth century. The political scientist Benjamin R. Barber focused on the paradoxical occurrence of both "McWorld" and "Jihad" in the post-Cold War era, and their implications for the future of democracy. The new world in the 1990s, he stressed in *Jihad vs. McWorld* (1995), was both coming together and falling apart. This was "the central paradox of human history."[15] Both Jihad and McWorld, although opposite trends, endangered democracy. "Their common thread is indifference to civil liberty," Barber noted. "Jihad forges communities of blood in exclusion and hatred, communities that slight democracy in favor of tyrannical paternalism or consensual tribalism. McWorld forges global markets in consumption and profit, leaving to an untrustworthy, if not altogether fictitious, invisible hand issues of public interest and common good that once might have been nurtured by democratic citizenries and their watchful governments."[16] Keenly aware of this dual threat to democracy, Barber eschewed the triumphalism that characterized many others in the West at the end of the Cold War. The world was still not "safe for democracy." Nor had it reached "the end of history," despite the false claims of Francis Fukuyama and others that liberal democratic ideology had become the worldwide consensus—or, in other words, that Wilsonianism had finally triumphed.[17]

The political scientist Samuel P. Huntington also recognized that modernization was generating a backlash in the post-Cold War era. "Spurred by modernization," he noted in *The Clash of Civilizations and the Remaking of World Order* (1996), "global politics is being reconfigured along cultural lines. Peoples and countries with similar cultures are coming together. Peoples and countries with different cultures are coming apart. Alignments defined by ideology and superpower relations are giving way to alignments defined by culture and civilizations. Political boundaries increasingly are redrawn to coincide with cultural ones: ethnic, religious, and civilizational. Cultural communities are replacing Cold War blocs, and the fault lines between civilizations are becoming the central lines of conflict in global politics."[18] In this new era of both integration and fragmentation, cultural differences were reshaping the world order.

The journalist Thomas L. Friedman also emphasized the combination of integration and fragmentation. In contrast to Barber or Huntington, however, he offered a much more optimistic vision of the new era of globalization. In *The Lexus and the Olive Tree* (1999), he argued that a new world order—the new system of globalization—had replaced the old Cold War system. While living in Beirut and Jerusalem, he noted: "It struck me then that the Lexus and the olive tree were actually pretty good symbols of this post-Cold War era: half the world seemed to be emerging from the Cold War intent on building a better Lexus, dedicated to modernizing, streamlining and privatizing their economies in order to thrive in the system of globalization. And half of the world—sometimes half the same country, sometimes half the same person—was still caught up in the fight over who owns which olive tree."[19] These two competing tendencies promoted both the new system of globalization and the backlash against it.

The British historian David Reynolds focused on this interaction between integration and fragmentation in global history from World War II to the end of the American Century. He understood that there were "unities—real and perceived, yet also divisions." He explained: "This was not just a divided world, therefore, but one that could apparently be almost endlessly divided. The tools of unification (from statehood to software) also served as weapons of disintegration—creating new states and sects, reinforcing old cultures and nations." The dynamics of this world involved crosscurrents, for it was characterized not only by "greater unity and keener consciousness of interconnection; but also multiple divisions and the creation of many more: to adapt the U.S. pledge of allegiance, this is a story of one world, divisible."[20]

Reynolds recognized America's extensive influence during the Cold War, but he also saw that this era involved far more than the successful Americanization of the world. He noted in *One World Divisible* (2000) that, "although this book takes seriously the impact of American power, wealth, and values on the postwar world, that does not constitute the totality, let alone the 'end,' of history." He cautioned against regarding globalization as a triumphal theme. "If stated without qualification, globalization is just cold war victor's history conceptualized in a wider frame." He emphasized that "the striking feature of recent decades has been the dialectical process of greater integration *and* greater fragmentation—the two being interrelated." He observed that "although pluralist politics and civilian rule are now more common, most of the world does not operate on American principles of liberal democracy." Nor had all people or nations benefited from the globalization system. "While the industrial economies established relationships of competitive interdependence, debt and dependence was the name of the game for much of the world. Western bailouts were conditioned on greater openness to the world economy, but the restructuring also brought misery to millions. Economic integration went hand in hand with social fragmentation."[21] Both dynamics were shaping contemporary global history.

In *Woodrow Wilson and the American Diplomatic Tradition,* I focused on the historical paradox that Barber, Huntington, Friedman, and Reynolds later stressed. I employed the concepts of interdependence and pluralism to provide the framework for interpreting the president's peacemaking in 1919 and his fight with the Senate over the Versailles Treaty.[22] I noted that he emphasized global interdependence but neglected to take into account the world's diversity. He simply failed to understand what Barber later called "the central paradox of human history." This lack of realism characterized Wilson's peacemaking. It thwarted his ability to reconcile or even comprehend the competing claims of the Allies at Paris or the Germans at Versailles. It also prevented the Democratic president from compromising with Republican senators during the treaty fight at home. He heralded the world's growing interdependence but failed to cope realistically with its pluralism. Wilsonian ideology anticipated the integration of McWorld (or the Lexus), but not the fragmentation of Jihad (or the olive tree).

Wilson's vision of a new world order did not prevail in the competition among alternatives after World War I. That era witnessed fragmentation as well as integration in international relations. By the end of the war in 1918, the Russian, Ottoman,

Austro-Hungarian, and German empires had collapsed. Several new nations emerged from the ruins. Aided by the United States, the Allies had won the war, but they, too, experienced decline. Nationalist movements in the British and French empires were asserting their rights to cast off European colonial dominance and establish their independence. From Asia and Africa came the early calls for decolonization or separation from London and Paris. Even the British dominions demanded more self-government, and Ireland claimed the same. The great powers of Europe no longer dominated world affairs as they had done throughout the past four centuries of modern history.

The collapse of the European balance of power resulted in a new alignment of global relationships. The United States and Japan were emerging as great powers on the periphery. Western European nations lost their central position as the world's leading industrial and military powers and as its net creditors. War debts and reparations changed international financial and economic connections. The United States, previously a debtor nation, now became the world's greatest creditor. Within Europe, the war also created conditions for the emergence of new ideologies and movements that challenged the existing regimes and also Wilson's vision of a new world order. Communism in Russia, Fascism in Italy, and Nazism in Germany all offered new alternatives to the Old World other than Wilsonianism.

The Great War profoundly influenced the "the generation of 1914." Even those who survived were casualties. As participants in the catastrophe that cost the lives of more than nine million soldiers and more than twelve million civilians, they witnessed the grim realities of war. No longer at home in the prewar world of their parents, this "lost generation" in Europe produced its own new culture.[23] The United States experienced a similar, if less dramatic, cultural transition. For Americans, too, the war marked the end of innocence.[24] The Southern writer Ellen Glasgow summarized this transition: "Until American idealism had been safely buried in Flanders fields, a belief in the happy end was as imperative in philosophy as it was essential in fiction. The universe, as well as a love story, must lead to romantic fulfillment." But the war had ended "the artificial glow of the past American idealism."[25]

The historian Henry F. May observed that Americans such as Woodrow Wilson had affirmed the reality of universal morality, progress, and culture. Before the war, they had shared the Victorian worldview of the nineteenth century. Younger intellectuals, however, were already beginning to revolt against those values. The war promoted this revolt. "Through the war and its outcome, through the cycle of hope, hatred and disillusion," May noted, "the credo which Wilson embodied was discredited and torn apart. The principles of moralism, progress, and culture, already linked disastrously to snobbery, racial pride, and prudery, were linked now to the Wilsonian version of the Allied cause. Inevitably, the country was to turn against both. The war brought about the victory of our intellectual rebellion, and in so doing, changed its nature."[26] Conflict between the older custodians of culture and the younger intellectual rebels affected the politics of war. This cultural clash separated crusaders from dissenters during World War I.

One young writer who contributed substantially to the intellectual revolt was the brilliant journalist Randolph Bourne. Unlike the philosopher John Dewey, with whom he had studied at Columbia University, Bourne refused to join the call for war in 1917. Despite efforts of self-styled patriots to silence him, he offered his critical analysis of the war and its intellectual advocates. He expressed profound doubts about the false promises of Wilsonianism. He criticized the government's wartime exercise of coercive powers and offered cultural pluralism as an alternative to Wilsonian ideology and statecraft. However, his radicalism remained on the margins of American politics.[27]

During the early twentieth-century era of Progressivism, traditional values continued to dominate the mainstream of American political culture. "The notion that their nation had a special mission to perfect and extend modern civilization at home and around the globe inspired patriotic allegiance in millions of voters, as similar claims had in turbulent times going back to the Revolution," the political scientist Rogers M. Smith emphasized in *Civic Ideals* (1997). "And because most voters were still middle-class white men, most found reassuring the fact that this mission justified keeping the poorer classes, the nonwhite races, and women in subordinate places for the foreseeable future, even if it promised more freedom and equality eventually to those who proved worthy."[28] Not even all U.S. citizens were entitled to benefit from the "progressive" crusade for global democracy.

Some historians also have emphasized the exclusive or restrictive character of American democracy or popular sovereignty during the Progressive era. Robert Wiebe noted in *Self-Rule* (1995) that middle-class white men, such as Wilson, continued to dominate politics during this era. In the name of reform, they sought to perpetuate the ascendancy that men of this sort had enjoyed in the nineteenth century when they had participated in democratic politics as "the People." Now they transformed political institutions and culture so as to preserve their control. This process, which they called "progressive," aimed at sinking the lower class, raising hierarchies to keep women and people of color on the margins, and dissolving the new people, particularly non-Anglo-Saxon immigrants, into an Americanized or assimilated nation. "Early in the 19th century," Wiebe concluded, "to express how individual citizens just released from hierarchical authority should recombine, white men devised the democratic People. Early in the 20th, to manage citizens now scattered by the collapse of the People, they created new hierarchies. The power to govern resided in these hierarchies."[29] Concerns of this kind led Wilson to formulate an exclusive definition of democracy and a restrictive concept of sovereignty, which he subsequently incorporated into his ideals of national self-determination and collective security during and after World War I.

Despite the radical transition away from the Victorian worldview that Henry May analyzed in *The End of American Innocence* (1959), later generations perpetuated the cultural values that Wilson epitomized. Both practitioners and students of American statecraft—politicians and intellectuals alike—continued to embrace the fundamental tenets of Wilsonianism. These provided the dominant ideology for the United States in the American Century. The intellectual revolt during World War I did not exert as great an impact in this nation as in Europe. Wilson rather than Bourne left the most influential legacy in American political culture.

Wilson's legacy seemed especially relevant to post-Cold War Americans, many of whom once more anticipated the dawn of a new world order. Numerous books and articles in the 1990s applauded his far-sighted and long-lasting contribution to the American diplomatic tradition. More than Europeans, Americans retained their belief in Wilsonianism. Scholarly controversies over Wilson's foreign policies intertwined with concerns about contemporary international relations. This nexus between U.S. policymaking and historical interpretation or political theory characterized the ongoing debate over the president's legacy.[30] Euphoria over the end of the Cold War and the apparent success of Wilsonian idealism led some historians to conclude that Wilson's foreign policies and his diplomatic legacy were fundamentally sound.[31] Even his critics acknowledged—sometimes begrudgingly—that he had played the leading role in shaping the history of U.S. foreign relations during the twentieth century. That is why a critical assessment of Wilsonianism is still important at the present time.

After the Cold War, Wilsonianism in different guises flourished as the triumphant ideology in the United States. American presidents based U.S. foreign policy on this cultural foundation. "The first two post-Cold War presidents, George Bush and Bill Clinton," observed the political scientist John Gerard Ruggie in *Winning the Peace* (1995), "articulated visions of the new era that may be characterized as broadly Wilsonian in rhetoric and aspiration."[32] Like Wilson earlier, they committed the United States to defend and promote a progressive, democratic, capitalist, and peaceful world order against its enemies. At times of crisis, they used this Wilsonian ideology to justify U.S. involvement overseas, especially when resorting to warfare.

Henry Kissinger lamented that most Americans had embraced Wilsonianism. "For three generations," the former secretary of state acknowledged in *Diplomacy* (1994), "critics have savaged Wilson's analysis and conclusions; and yet, in all this time, Wilson's principles have remained the bedrock of American foreign-policy thinking."[33] Unfortunately, in Kissinger's view, the United States had rejected realism in favor of Wilsonian liberal internationalism. Despite Wilson's failure to win the U.S. Senate's approval for the League of Nations after World War I, Kissinger concluded, "Wilson's intellectual victory proved more seminal than any political triumph could have been. For, whenever America has faced the task of constructing a new world order, it has returned in one way or another to Woodrow Wilson's precepts."[34]

Other analysts of U.S. foreign policy welcomed the triumph of Wilsonianism at the end of the Cold War. The political scientist Tony Smith applauded this resurgence and the consequent appearance of a world order of democratic states. "Since Wilson's time," he asserted in *America's Mission* (1994), "the most consistent tradition in American foreign policy with respect to this global change has been the belief that the nation's security is best protected by the expansion of democracy worldwide."[35] Because of this liberal tradition, he claimed, the United States deserved credit for the triumph of democracy. "In the mid-1990s," Smith affirmed, "Americans might well ask themselves how much the worldwide demand for democracy is the result of their century-old determination to promote this cause. Certainly the new global enthusiasm for democracy is the closest the United States had ever come to seeing its own traditional foreign policy agenda reflected on an international scale."[36]

The political scientist Amos Perlmutter agreed with Smith that Wilsonianism had made a major contribution to the defeat of totalitarianism in the twentieth century. In *Making the World Safe for Democracy* (1997), he noted: "There is no question that the Wilsonian legacy of democracy and self-determination cast a long shadow over

U.S. foreign policy concepts, and to some extent still does in the Clinton era, but it is rooted more in philosophy than in action."[37] It had provided the ideology for the United States to resist the two alternative world orders of Communism and Nazism. During World War II, President Franklin D. Roosevelt had used Wilsonianism to justify American preeminence in foreign affairs in order to defeat Adolf Hitler's Germany. But Perlmutter gave less credit to ideology alone and, like Kissinger, also emphasized military force. As a neoconservative, he regarded U.S. hegemony as a crucial contribution to world order. "In the case of both Wilson and Roosevelt," Perlmutter explained, "it was the sense of making the international system safe from rival hegemons—imperialist, revolutionary, or ideological—that were threatening the international system."[38] Likewise during the Cold War, U.S. presidents from Harry Truman to Ronald Reagan had utilized Wilsonianism against the Soviet Union, eventually defeating the totalitarian challenge of Leninism-Stalinism. Victory over Communism, Perlmutter emphasized, had required power as well as ideology.

Perlmutter did not agree with Smith's optimistic liberal version of Wilsonianism. He did not share the belief that the spread of democracy would end all wars, or at least reduce them to manageable size: "A great misconception on the part of President Wilson was that the evolution of democratic regimes would lead to a peaceful international order."[39] Wilson's vision of peace, guaranteed by democratic states through collective security, had not been realized after World War I, and Perlmutter doubted that it ever would be. In his judgment, on the contrary, the United States should recognize that peace required enforcement by great powers and that even democratic states might resort to war. He concluded: "Peace is not guaranteed by democratic systems, nor is aggression uniquely the property of totalitarians. There is no political or intellectual reason for the establishment of a new world order."[40] Thus, Perlmutter warned, the United States should not place false confidence in liberal Wilsonianism.

The historian Frank Ninkovich agreed with Kissinger, Smith, and Perlmutter that Wilsonianism had shaped U.S. foreign policy in the twentieth century. This ideology had guided the United States and molded the modern world. For him, this was not just the "American Century" but distinctively the "Wilsonian Century." In fundamental ways, however, he disagreed with other observers. He argued that realists, such as George F. Kennan, had missed the significance of Wilsonian idealism. So, too, had revisionists such as William Appleman Williams. They had offered "interest-based explanations" of U.S. foreign relations, while neglecting the vital contribution of ideology to the "real world." In *The Wilsonian Century* (1999), Ninkovich contended that: "For the United States, ideology worked. And, by that rather vulgar pragmatic standard, it was true—all of which helps to explain why Americans have been uninterested in learning from the alleged mistakes that realists and other critics continue to point out."[41]

Ninkovich combined postmodernism with neoconservatism in his triumphal history of American foreign policy during the twentieth century. Unlike Perlmutter, who emphasized material as well as cultural factors of power, he attributed U.S. victory against its totalitarian enemies to Wilsonian ideology. He claimed that the United States derived its real power from this ideology, whereas Perlmutter argued that the United States, by projecting its hegemony, had defeated Nazism and Communism in the name of Wilsonianism. Ninkovich assigned the preeminent role to ideology, while Perlmutter, more like Kissinger, gave it a subordinate place. In this respect, oddly enough, the neoconservative Ninkovich was closer to the liberal Smith in that both of them enthusiastically affirmed the ideological contributions of Wilsonianism.

So, too, did the historian Akira Iriye, who interpreted the "ideological offensive led by President Wilson" during World War I as the defining moment for the United States in the twentieth century. In *The Globalizing of America* (1993), Iriye affirmed Wilson's belief that "'democracy' was a key guiding principle precisely in such a context, for it stood for a new political order at home and, therefore, abroad." Thus, he argued, "Wilsonianism had provided the framework in which the United States redefined its external relations at a time when the age of European dominance was coming to an end. It combined America's military power, economic resources, and cultural initiatives in order to transcend traditional world affairs in which sovereign nations had pursued their interests with little regard for the welfare of the entire globe." Although "realists" might criticize Wilsonian internationalism, it had prevailed. Iriye emphasized the enduring significance of Wilsonianism for the American Century. "The emergence of the United States as an international player at the beginning of the twentieth century was significant not simply because the nation became the leading military and economic power, but also because it introduced cultural factors into world affairs," he explained. "Because the globalizing of America has been a major event of the century, Wilsonianism should be seen not as a transient phenomenon, a reflection of some abstract idealism, but as a potent definer of contemporary history." The combination of nationalism and internationalism that Wilson offered during World War I, Iriye noted, had established the foundation for American foreign relations throughout the twentieth century. "He wanted each nation to serve not only its own interests but those of the world at large. America, he said, should release its energies 'for the service of mankind.' Other countries should do likewise. The result would be the intermeshing of nationalism and international-ism, sovereign states finding meaning in their relationship to the whole."[42]

Post-Cold War presidents embraced this legacy of Wilsonianism. After Iraq invaded Kuwait on August 2, 1990, President George Bush responded to the Persian Gulf crisis by calling for a "new world order." He anticipated "a new era—freer from the threat of terror, stronger in the pursuit of justice, and more secure in the quest for peace." He wanted all nations to "prosper and live in harmony." Emphasizing global interdependence, including the West's dependence on Middle Eastern oil, he offered American leadership through the United Nations to stop Iraq's aggression and restore Kuwait's sovereignty. The United Nations, he noted, could now provide the kind of collective security its founders had envisaged.[43] When he announced the beginning of military action in the Persian Gulf on January 16, 1991, Bush reiter-ated the American commitment to "a new world order—a world where the rule of law, not the law of the jungle, governs the conduct of nations. When we are success-ful—and we will be—we have a real chance at this new world order, an order in which a credible United Nations can use its peacekeeping role to fulfill the promise and vision of the U.N.'s founders."[44] This rationale for war combined self-determi-nation for Kuwait (sovereignty, but not democracy), protection of international access to its oil (Open Door economic globalization), and collective security by the

U.N. coalition to stop aggression—all tenets of Wilsonianism. In accordance with progressive history, moreover, this new world order promised a better future.

Beyond his affirmation of these Wilsonian principles, Bush proclaimed the justice of the Persian Gulf War by demonizing Saddam Hussein and identifying the United States and its allies with God. The war, he asserted, was not between the United States and the Iraqi people. Instead, it pitted "the regime of Saddam Hussein against the rest of the world." Bush saw this conflict as a global confrontation of "good versus evil, right versus wrong, human dignity and freedom versus tyranny and oppression." Speaking to religious broadcasters, he neglected to mention oil when he avowed that "we seek nothing for ourselves" and that "U.S. forces will leave as soon as their mission is over." Under American leadership, the U.N. coalition of twenty-eight nations from six continents would pursue Operation Desert Storm to victory, reversing Iraq's aggression, restoring Kuwait's "legitimate government" and sovereignty, and establishing security and stability in the Persian Gulf.[45] It would, in other words, fulfill the promise of a new world order.

Military victory in the war against Iraq, which Bush announced on February 27, 1991, produced only limited results, however.[46] Saddam Hussein remained in power and continued to resist U.N. inspection and disarmament of Iraq's weapons of mass destruction, which the cease-fire agreement prescribed. Nevertheless, along with the end of the Cold War, the Gulf War created a sense of peace that enabled Americans to believe they could largely ignore foreign affairs. In the 1990s, they welcomed more economic globalization, which helped generate prosperity at home, but not political or military entanglement abroad in conflicts that appeared to have no direct relationship to U.S. national interests. Bill Clinton's defeat of Bush in the 1992 presidential election, in which the economy was more important than international relations, reflected this trend. In 1994, when Republicans gained control of Congress, they were even less interested in most questions of foreign policy than the Democratic president.

In this post-Cold War world, the inherent dilemmas of Wilsonianism appeared in the ambivalence and contradictions of Clinton's foreign policy. Although he appealed to Wilsonian ideals in defining America's mission overseas, he hesitated in practice to implement them. Moreover, the problems in this new era did not readily conform to the principles of Wilsonianism. It was not self-evident how to apply the principle of national self-determination to the crisis in the Balkans following the disintegration of Yugoslavia. After World War I, Wilson had favored a multinational state, but in the early 1990s Yugoslavia had fragmented into several new states. Bush had recognized these successor states, but did not want to protect them or their peoples from aggressive neighbors. Likewise, Clinton did not initially favor collective security for Bosnia or Croatia against the Serb-dominated rump-state Yugoslavia, even when Serb aggression took the form of ethnic cleansing. The United Nations attempted to stop this genocide but with little support from the United States and little success. Eventually, however, Clinton used the North Atlantic Treaty Organization (NATO) to launch air strikes against the Serbs, forcing the president of Yugoslavia, Slobodan Milosevic, who had wanted to create a Greater Serbia, into a compromise peace settlement on December 14, 1995. The Dayton Peace Accords divided Bosnia along ethnic lines, reflecting the results of ethnic cleansing as well as the ground war between the Serbs, on one side, and the Croatians and Bosnians, on the other. It stopped Serb aggression for the present. The United States now joined its European allies in the U.N. peacekeeping in Bosnia.

Peace in the Balkans remained elusive and potentially costly for the United States and its European allies. Despite the temporary setback at Dayton, Milosevic turned to the Yugoslav province of Kosovo, where Serbs began to attack the ethnic Albanian majority. Orthodox Serbs again practiced ethnic cleansing of a predominantly Muslim population. Eventually, on March 24, 1999, Clinton led NATO into a full-scale air war against Yugoslavia (Serbia) to protect the Albanian Kosovars. He justified this war by emphasizing the importance of peace in Europe: "If we've learned anything from the century drawing to a close," he affirmed, "it is that if America is going to be prosperous and secure, we need a Europe that is secure, undivided, and free. We need a Europe that is coming together, not falling apart, a Europe that shares our values and shares the burdens of leadership. That is the foundation on which the security of our children will depend."[47]

During the war, NATO celebrated its fiftieth anniversary. Poland, Hungary, and the Czech Republic, which had been under Soviet domination during the Cold War, now joined NATO as new members of this system of collective security. NATO leaders recognized that the future of this former Cold War military alliance depended on its success in the war over Kosovo. On April 23, 1999, at the NATO commemorative ceremony, Clinton explained the connection between the war and the future of NATO. "We're in Kosovo," he said, "because we want to replace ethnic cleansing with tolerance and decency, violence with security, disintegration with restoration, isolation with integration into the rest of the region and the continent. We want southeastern Europe to travel the same road as Western Europe half a century ago and Central Europe a decade ago."[48]

NATO's aims in the Balkans expressed familiar Wilsonian themes, affirming "the territorial integrity and sovereignty of all countries in the region" and "the objective of a free, prosperous, open and economically integrated Southeast Europe." The crisis in Kosovo had challenged the Western values of democracy, human rights, and the rule of law, and thus required NATO to extend its scope beyond the immediate defense of its members to stop the ethnic cleansing of Milosevic's government even within the borders of Yugoslavia.[49] On June 10, 1999, Clinton announced NATO's victory in this war. With Russia's help, collective security had worked, enabling the Kosovar people, many of whom had fled as refugees to escape ethnic cleansing, to return home. The United Nations again prepared for peace.[50]

Clinton's decisions to intervene in the Balkans evoked little public support at home. It had been easier during the Cold War when the choices had appeared to be more clear-cut. As David Halberstam observed in *War in a Time of Peace* (2001), "The questions facing a president in the post-Cold War years were more difficult to deal with than in the previous, simpler era. This time the enemy was genocide, not Communism. Because there was no direct, immediate threat to the United States during the Balkan crisis, Clinton had received few positive notices for finally using American force in both Bosnia and Kosovo .... Clearly there were no easy answers— or necessarily even right answers—in cases like this, and just as clearly there was little political upside to the intervention. Clinton and his administration had moved slowly at first, perplexed by the equation in front of them and the lack of political support at home. They had frequently stumbled but they had, however awkwardly, and belatedly, met a vital early test of post-Cold War peacekeeping."[51]

Elsewhere in the world, Clinton showed even more reluctance to intervene with military force. The terrible experience in Somalia in 1993 had made him and others in Washington very cautious. Although he deployed military force in 1994 to restore the democratically elected Jean-Bertrand Aristide to the presidency of Haiti, after a military coup had ousted him in 1991, Clinton refrained from taking action to stop the genocide in Rwanda. In the plural world of the post-Cold War era, he knew that the choices were inherently ambiguous and that the American people mostly preferred to ignore them. That indifference continued to shape the 2000 presidential election. "The nation's interest still remained inner-directed," observed Halberstam. "To much of the rest of the world, America was immensely powerful, but for a nation that powerful, it was shockingly self-absorbed. George W. Bush, the son of the former president, for whom foreign policy had been his primary political passion, appeared to have little interest in the rest of the world."[52] Not until the terrorist attacks of September 11, 2001, did this attitude dramatically change. Both the new president and the American people then discovered that the United States could not insulate itself from the outside world.

Throughout the Clinton years, the United States embraced the new system of globalization in the international economy, while seeking to minimize other obligations. On January 1, 1994, it joined Canada and Mexico in the North American Free Trade Association (NAFTA). In that same year, the United States and its major global trading partners established the World Trade Organization (WTO). Before the end of the decade, it anticipated China's entry into the WTO, giving trade a higher priority than human rights in the Sino-American relationship. Like Wilson, Clinton believed that economic freedom would promote democracy. But he also understood that the globalization system was generating a backlash that could not be ignored. He acknowledged that "the problem with the new global economy is that it is both more rewarding and more destructive." He therefore wanted to put a "human face" on the global economy by recognizing the rights of workers and protecting the environment. Clinton recognized, moreover, that the growing split between rich and poor nations should not be ignored. "The global community," he warned, "cannot survive as a tale of two cities: one modern and integrated, a cell phone in every hand, a McDonald's on every street corner; the other mired in poverty and increasingly resentful, covered with public health and environmental problems no one can manage."[53] On December 1, 1999, at a meeting of the WTO in Seattle, which attracted protesters from around the world, Clinton emphasized the benefits of global integration not only through the WTO but also the expansion of NATO and the European Union. Aware of the backlash as voiced in the protests outside, however, he acknowledged that the global economy needed to help the poorest nations as well as the wealthiest. It needed to protect the environment and the rights of workers.[54]

Crosscurrents between integration (McWorld) and fragmentation (Jihad) limited the prospects of fulfilling the promise of Wilsonianism during the post-Cold War era. Clinton recognized these limitations, which made his foreign policy frequently appear indecisive or contradictory. At the U.N. General Assembly on September 21, 1999, he reaffirmed the American commitment to Open Door economic globalization but noted the still unresolved problems, especially in the poorest nations. He also committed the United States "to strengthen the capacity of the international community to prevent and, whenever possible, to stop outbreaks of mass killing and displacement." This form of collective security was more difficult than defending a state against aggressive neighbors, however, because it blurred the distinction between internal and external threats. It raised new questions about the meaning of national sovereignty or self-determination in the interdependent, but plural world. While NATO had intervened to stop ethnic cleansing in Kosovo, giving the United Nations the opportunity to restore peace in the Balkans, Clinton warned that such action could not be undertaken everywhere. "In the real world," he conceded, "principles often collide, and tough choices must be made." The president also resolved to protect the world against nuclear, chemical, and biological weapons, noting the danger that terrorist groups might acquire these deadly weapons.[55]

In the post-Cold War world, the hopes that Wilson had expressed during World War I had still not become reality. History had not progressed to its end. Wilsonian principles of national self-determination, collective security, and Open Door economic globalization were not only difficult to implement but often inherently contradictory. Even at the end of the American Century, the world was deeply divided. As Clinton understood, powerful crosscurrents limited the fulfillment of the Wilsonian promise. Pluralism and fragmentation as well as interdependence and integration still characterized international relations. The choices for the United States, which the Cold War ideology had reduced to simple alternatives, were obviously more complex during the 1990s.

Wilsonianism continued to shape the way Americans related to the world in the twenty-first century. President George W. Bush, in his inaugural address, identified with this tradition, although he did not refer to Wilson. He saw the United States not only as a "new world" model, but also as "friend and liberator of the old." He equated the historic culture of Americanism with the world's future. "Through much of the last century," he proclaimed on January 20, 2001, "America's faith in freedom and democracy was a rock in a raging sea. Now it is a seed upon the wind, taking root in many nations. Our democratic faith is more than the creed of our country, it is the inborn hope of our humanity, an ideal we carry but do not own, a trust we bear and pass along. And even after nearly 225 years, we have a long way yet to travel." The new president, while acknowledging that American ideals were not yet universally accepted by all, cautioned potential adversaries that the United States would defend and promote them worldwide. "The enemies of liberty and our country should make no mistake," he warned: "America remains engaged in the world by history and by choice, shaping a balance of power that favors freedom. We will defend our allies and our interests. We will show purpose without arrogance. We will meet aggression and bad faith with resolve and strength. And to all nations, we will speak for the values that gave our nation birth."[56]

Terrorist attacks on September 11, 2001, against the World Trade Center in New York City and the Pentagon in Washington, DC, underscored the continuing influence of Wilsonianism. President Bush used his version of Wilsonian ideology to explain his response. To a joint session of Congress and the American people, he promised to "bring our enemies to justice, or bring justice to our enemies." Naming

Osama bin Laden and "a collection of loosely affiliated terrorist organizations known as al Qaeda" as the "enemies of freedom," he condemned their "act of war against our country." He also implicated the Taliban regime in Afghanistan, but distinguished between this government and the Afghan people. Bush denied that these enemies were true Muslims. "The terrorists are traitors to their own faith, trying, in effect, to hijack Islam itself.... Our enemy is a radical network of terrorists, and every government that supports them." The president then described their hostility toward the United States, depicting them as "the heirs of all the murderous ideologies of the 20th century." Calling for victory in this new war against terrorism, he invited all nations to join the United States, warning those who did not that they, too, would be seen as enemies. "Every nation, in every region, now has a decision to make," he announced. "Either you are with us, or you are with the terrorists. From this day forward, any nation that continues to harbor or support terrorism will be regarded by the United States as a hostile regime." While unilaterally defining the American national interest, Bush expected foreign governments to join the multilateral coalition against terrorism under U.S. leadership. He explained that "what is at stake is not just America's freedom. This is the world's fight. This is civilization's fight." In this global confrontation between good and evil, he promised victory, assuring the American people, moreover, that "God is not neutral" and "the rightness of our cause" will prevail.[57]

When Bush announced the beginning of U.S. military strikes against al Qaeda and the Taliban regime in Afghanistan on October 7, 2001, he reiterated this global theme, affirming that "the collective will of the world" supported the United States in the war against "barbaric criminals." He depicted the war as a conflict between civilization and barbarism, not between two different cultures in "the clash of civilizations" that Samuel P. Huntington had described. In this mission, the president said: "We defend not only our precious freedoms, but also the freedom of people everywhere to live and raise their children free from fear."[58] At a news conference on October 11, he assured the American people that "our war on terrorism" in response to the "attack on the heart and soul of the civilized world" would not become another "Vietnam-like quagmire in Afghanistan." Applying the lessons of the Vietnam War, Bush described this as "a different kind of war." He promised to exterminate the "parasites" without bogging down in conventional warfare. Demonizing the enemy as the "evil ones," he asserted: "We're fighting evil. And these murderers have hijacked a great religion in order to justify their evil deeds. And we cannot let it stand."[59]

Bush's rationale for the war against terrorism echoed the liberal themes that Wilson had employed during World War I. Although the president regarded himself as a conservative, not a liberal, he embraced the legacy of Wilsonianism. The political scientist Hans J. Morgenthau, who had played a leading role in developing the realist school of thought in international relations theory in the United States after World War II, had recognized Wilson's foreign policy as the epitome of liberalism or liberal internationalism. Summarizing this political perspective in *Scientific Man vs. Power Politics* (1946), Morgenthau noted that "the liberal will feel the full measure of his superiority only when he can prove to the world and to himself the righteousness of his position and the moral baseness of the enemy who must be punished for his crimes."[60] Wilson had articulated this perspective before Bush did.

Liberals, Morgenthau further observed, anticipated a new world order of peace and harmony that would end the evils of war and transform history. "When all nations are united under their own governments and all governments are subject to democratic control, war will have lost its rational justification," they believed. "Reason will reign and make wars impossible. For the reign of reason in international affairs will make impossible those fundamental conflicts for the solution of which it would be reasonable to wage war, and reason will provide instrumentalities by which the remaining conflicts can be settled peacefully. The war for national unification and for 'making the world safe for democracy' is then, as Wilson put it in his message to Congress on January 8, 1918, the 'culminating and final war for human liberty,' the 'last war,' the 'war to end war.' In the light of this analysis," Morgenthau concluded, "those Wilsonian slogans reveal themselves to be more than a clever propagandistic device; they are the expression of an eschatological hope deeply imbedded in the very foundations of liberal foreign policy."[61] Neoconservatives, whose intellectual roots went back to liberalism, voiced this hope for the "end of history" after the Cold War. Bush expressed it in his vision of a future world free from the evil of terrorism after victory in the current crusade.

Morgenthau noted that Wilson, typical of liberals, had distinguished between the people of any nation, who would choose peace if they could achieve democratic control, and the autocratic government of an enemy state such as Imperial Germany during World War I. Morgenthau summarized this liberal legacy: "Democracy is peace, autocracy war; the pacifist peoples vs. the warlike governments—such were the slogans in which the liberal attitude toward war expressed itself and in which it found its political program. Here again, Wilson is the most eloquent prophet of the new creed."[62] In conformity with this Wilsonian legacy, Bush emphasized the distinction between the Taliban regime and the people of Afghanistan. The network of Osama bin Laden and his allies in the Taliban regime, along with foreign governments that supported them, were the source of terrorism, not the people of Afghanistan or any other nation. The elimination of these terrorists or their removal from power would create the new era of peace and security.

This Wilsonian interpretation of the terrorist problem after September 11, 2001, restricted Bush's understanding of it. He acknowledged this limitation. At his news conference on October 11, he asked himself a question and then gave his answer. He asked why "in some Islamic countries there is vitriolic hatred for America?" Seeking to provide an answer, the president revealed his incapacity to comprehend why other peoples from other cultures interpreted world affairs from different perspectives. "I'm amazed," he said. "I'm amazed that there is such misunderstanding of what our country is about, that people would hate us. I am, I am—like most Americans, I just can't believe it. Because I know how good we are, and we've got to do a better job of making our case. We've got to do a better job of explaining to the people in the Middle East, for example, that we don't fight a war against Islam or Muslims. We don't hold any religion accountable. We're fighting evil."[63] Convinced that the United States was fighting a righteous war against terrorism, Bush thus acknowledged his failure to comprehend how other peoples—even those who were not terrorists—might not share this same view. Given their apparent ignorance, he sought to offer a more persuasive explanation of the American crusade.[64] Wilson had outlined his famous Fourteen Points on January 8, 1918, for this same purpose.

For Bush, as for Wilson earlier, modern American-style globalization appeared as the best, if not the only, path to the future. On November 10, 2001, he called on all "civilized nations" to join the coalition to "defend ourselves and our future against terror and lawless violence," reminding delegates in the U.N. General Assembly that "the United Nations was founded in this cause" of collective security. Bush affirmed: "There is a current in history and it runs toward freedom." Progressive history, he expected, would culminate in this outcome. He added: "We stand for the permanent hopes of humanity, and those hopes will not be denied. We're confident, too, that history has an author who fills time and eternity with his purpose. We know that evil is real, but good will prevail against it."[65] Bush, like Wilson, believed that the United States should not only provide the model for other nations but also actively encourage them to move toward its realization. Equating Americanism with internationalism, they both championed a system of globalization under U.S. leadership. But neither of them understood the backlash against it. While promoting integration, they dismissed the resulting conflicts and fragmentation as problems yet to be overcome. They saw American involvement in other countries as benevolent, and could not fathom why others elsewhere in the world might not share this view. In other words, they heralded McWorld (or the Lexus), but could not comprehend Jihad (or the olive tree).

Although Bush was, by his own admission, unable to grasp why others resented or hated the United States, some observers sought to explain this reality. *Newsweek* foreign editor Michael Hirsh did not share Bush's amazement at foreign resentment or hatred of the United States. He perceived the backlash against globalization, the pluralism and fragmentation as well as interdependence and integration in the modern world. For Hirsh, September 11, 2001, underscored "a lesson that Americans, in their complacency, had chosen not to see before but that now exploded on their doorstep: the peace they had taken for granted was not secure. The work of the American Century was not over. History had not, in fact, ended." Although U.S. hegemony had not ceased and the world had not degenerated into anarchy, "this Americanized global system nonetheless generated a great mass of discontents. And these have-nots blamed the nation they rightly identified as the shadow power behind the system. Not surprisingly," concluded Hirsh, "the deepest anger came out of the Arab world, where regimes have been, as a rule, least open to American-style globalization and political ideals."[66]

President Bush's Manichaean division of the world between allies and enemies, between those joining the United States in its righteous crusade against terrorism and those supporting the "evil ones," limited his options for dealing with the problem. It led him immediately to focus on the means of warfare. The Bush administration's misuse of the word "war" to characterize both the terrorist attacks and the American response seemed unwise to Sir Michael Howard, an eminent British historian of military and diplomatic affairs. "To 'declare war' on terrorists, or even more illiterately, on 'terrorism' is at once to accord them a status and dignity that they seek and which they do not deserve," he thought. Moreover, incorrectly using the word "war" risked "deeper and more dangerous consequences. To declare that one is 'at war' is immediately to create a war psychosis that may be totally counterproductive for the objective that we seek. It will arouse an immediate expectation, and demand, for spectacular military action against some easily identifiable adversary, preferably a hostile state; action leading to decisive results." Howard warned that the requirements for a successful campaign against terrorists might well be overlooked in "a media-stoked frenzy for immediate results." He regretted that Bush had launched "a crusade against evil" in the form of a military campaign by an American-dominated alliance, instead of a "police operation" by the international community under the auspices of the United Nations against a "criminal conspiracy." A war against terrorism might not bring victory quickly, he warned, and a prolonged war might be disastrous. It would, in any event, divert attention from the central issue: "The front line in the struggle is not Afghanistan. It is in the Islamic states where modernising governments are threatened by a traditionalist backlash: Turkey, Egypt, Pakistan, to name only the most obvious." In Howard's judgment, cultural conflicts between modern and traditional values and institutions lay at the core of the terrorist problem. Instead of focusing on the real issue, the president had launched a war against terrorism. Even a "victory" in Afghanistan would not deal with the underlying source of conflict, however. This British historian noted that "the best reasoning, and the most flawless logic, is of little value if it starts from false assumptions."[67] He did not share Bush's most recent version of Wilsonianism, and therefore doubted that the military response would achieve the expected or desired outcome of ending terrorism.

Despite probing questions from critics, whether Randolph Bourne during World War I or realists during the Vietnam War or Sir Michael Howard after September 11, 2001, Wilsonian ideology has continued to shape American political culture and statecraft. It is therefore important to understand Wilsonianism to gain insight into current affairs as well as history. When Wilson outlined his vision of a new world order, what did he really want? What kind of peace did he anticipate? The answers are not self-evident. To grasp the president's original meaning, it is essential to discern his own answers to key questions: What is a nation? What is democracy? What is sovereignty? What are the Open Door rules for the international economy? What kind of international organization could provide collective security for its members and thus enable them—without fear of external aggression—to disarm to a level required only for their internal security? What assurances might the new League of Nations give to its members—or to other nations and peoples still outside the organization—that the new world order would serve their interests and fulfill its promise? In short, how did Wilson seek to rebuild international order after victory in World War I?[68]

These are questions I have asked and sought to answer in various articles and essays as well as my previous books. I have examined the interaction between ideals and self-interest, between ideology and practice, and between internal and external factors in U.S. foreign relations, particularly in Wilsonian statecraft. By bringing several of these earlier publications together and adding some new chapters, this book offers my understanding of Woodrow Wilson[69] and of Wilsonianism. Because his legacy has continued to shape American involvement in world affairs, and is therefore important for the future as well as the past, I offer this book as my contribution to the ongoing debate over America's place in world history, its role in international affairs, and its traditions in U.S. foreign policy.

PART I
HISTORY AND IDEOLOGY

CHAPTER 1

WOODROW WILSON AND THE CULTURE OF WILSONIANISM

Revised text of the paper, "Americanism as Internationalism: Woodrow Wilson and the Culture of Wilsonianism," delivered at the Cultural History and International Relations conference, University of Paris 7, June 1999.

At the beginning of the American Century,[1] Woodrow Wilson articulated an ideology—subsequently labeled as Wilsonianism—to define a new role for the United States in world affairs.[2] Prior to his presidency, he had devoted his scholarly career to American history and politics. During World War I, he drew on his understanding of the American national experience to formulate his vision of a new world order. Wilson often noted this connection, but even when he did not explicitly relate his policies to his earlier scholarship, he used his historical knowledge as the intellectual foundation for his approach to leadership in international relations. His internationalism derived from his Americanism. Consequently, an assessment of Wilsonianism must involve an examination of both Wilson's statecraft and the American political culture from which it came. This analysis must focus on the nexus between cultural history and international relations.

While the United States was still officially neutral during World War I, Wilson developed the ideology of Wilsonianism. He articulated the principle of national self-determination and the closely related concept of collective security. On May 27, 1916, the president first announced his commitment to the idea of a postwar League of Nations. "We believe these fundamental things," he affirmed: "First, that every people has a right to choose the sovereignty under which they shall live .... Second, that the small states of the world have a right to enjoy the same integrity that great and powerful nations expect and insist upon. And, third, that the world has a right to be free from every disturbance of its peace that has its origin in aggression and disregard of the rights of peoples and nations." Wilson's vision of a new world order thus combined nationalism and internationalism.

Less than a year later, Wilson used this ideology to advocate American entry into the war against Imperial Germany. On April 2, 1917, he characterized unrestricted German submarine warfare as "a war against all nations." It was now time for the United States to participate as an active belligerent. "The world must be made safe for democracy," he told Congress. "Its peace must be planted upon the tested foundations of political liberty."[3] Wilson concluded that the United States, by intervening into the European war, should reshape the world in accordance with American ideals.

In response to the 1917 Bolshevik Revolution in Russia, Wilson decided to outline his vision of peace in more detail. He devoted most of his famous Fourteen Points on January 8, 1918, to the principle of national self-determination and the idea of collective security in an open international community as the foundation for future peace. "An evident principle runs through the whole program I have outlined," Wilson concluded. "It is the principle of justice to all peoples and nationalities, and their right to live on equal terms of liberty and safety with one another, whether they be strong or weak .... The people of the United States could act upon no other principle."[4]

When Wilson outlined his vision of national self-determination and collective security in the Fourteen Points, what did he really want? What kind of peace did he anticipate? The answers are not as self-evident as most scholars have assumed. To grasp the original Wilsonian meaning of national self-determination and its guarantee through collective security, it is necessary to discern Wilson's own understanding of several basic concepts: What is a nation? What is democracy? What is sovereignty?

All too frequently, scholars have assumed that the president's definitions of these key concepts coincided with theirs, and therefore that his rhetoric carried the same meaning they subsequently associated with his words. This has sometimes led Wilson's later critics, as well as his contemporaries, to castigate him for hypocrisy, when they were actually at fault for failing to grasp his real intent. Wilson had expressed his own understanding of apparently simple concepts such as nation, democracy, and sovereignty— all of which merged into his principle of national self-determination—in his extensive writings on American history and politics. He had devoted his academic career to the study of the modern democratic state and the style of leadership it required, focusing especially on the development of nationalism and democracy in the United States.[5]

What is a nation?[6] Wilson had answered that question in his scholarly writings. Over the years he revised and refined his views. He blended ethnoreligious and liberal elements into his interpretation of American nationalism. In *Mere Literature* (1896), he defined "our canons of Americanism." He distinguished between "American" and "un-American" qualities. Wilson affirmed that "the American spirit is something more than the old, the immemorial Saxon spirit of liberty from which it sprung. It has been bred by the conditions attending the great task which we have all the century been carrying forward: the task, at once material and ideal, of subduing a wilderness and covering all the wide stretches of a vast continent with a single free and stable polity. It is, accordingly, above all things, a hopeful and confident spirit. It is progressive, optimistically progressive, and ambitious of objects of national scope and advantage."[7] Wilson believed that great Americans, such as George Washington and Abraham Lincoln, had created the new nation and epitomized its spirit.

In his scholarship and later as president, Wilson affirmed that only mature nations should exist as separate states. He contrasted the American people, who had developed their national character over time, with other peoples who had not yet reached this stage of historical development. He did not endorse the idea, sometimes erroneously attributed to him, of fragmenting the world along ethnocultural fault lines into many new nation-states. In Wilson's view, a group of people required more than a separate racial, ethnic, or religious identity to entitle them to independent nationhood. He did not believe that all nationalities were ready to organize politically as sovereign nation-states.[8]

In his Fourteen Points, accordingly, Wilson advocated only "autonomous development" for the peoples of the Austro-Hungarian and Ottoman empires, except for the Turks. He favored restoration or creation of nation-states in Europe, including Russia, which he viewed as a single nation rather than as a multinational empire, but not in other regions of the world. He did not propose independence for German colonies, but only due attention to "the interests of the populations concerned." Wilson did not think all peoples were entitled to recognition as sovereign nations.[9]

Approaching peace after World War I from this perspective, Wilson applied the lessons he had derived from American history. He emphasized the importance of history: Historicism explained the characteristic values and institutions of the nation. A long historical process had enabled the American people to absorb their heritage from Europe and reshape it into their distinctively new nation in America. Wilson expounded this historicism in the five volumes of *A History of the American People* (1902), which he authorized for republication as ten volumes—with the addition of documents—during his presidency (1918).[10]

National development was organic and evolutionary, according to Wilson. The American people had acquired unity through their common history. This process depended on natural growth. "The constitution of a nation, though written, cannot remain a mere legal document," he proclaimed. "The life of each succeeding generation must inevitably be read into it, if only because it must be men of successive generations who read and interpret it .... It must become the vehicle of their growing thought ... [and] serve as the skeleton frame of a living organism."[11]

In Wilson's view, the American Civil War had produced organic unity in the United States. Thirty years before that war, Senator Daniel Webster of Massachusetts had articulated a conception of the Union that rejected the particularistic creed of states' rights.[12] The American people later embraced Webster's doctrine of nationalism under President Lincoln's leadership during the Civil War. This new consciousness of organic unity transformed the nation. Wilson described this fundamental change: "A Union full of new States ... a people recruited out of almost every civilized nation of the world, bound together by railway and telegraph, busy with enterprises which no State or section could imprison within local boundaries ... now at last conscious of its unity and its organic integrity, could not turn back to a particularistic creed."[13]

Although born and raised in the South, Wilson had adopted a pro-Union or nationalist view of the Civil War. He was one of the first southerners to advocate that new interpretation.[14] He believed that the historic experience of war had changed the nation: "The national consciousness, disguised, uncertain, latent until that day of sudden rally and call to arms, had been cried wide awake by the voices of battle, and acted like a passion now in the conduct of affairs."[15] Wilson concluded that "a revolution had been wrought in the consciousness and point of view of the nation."[16] This transformation, he further noted, culminated later in 1898, when the war against Spain consolidated America's national unity, ending the final remnants of sectional divisions that had lingered since "the war between the States."[17] Wilson believed that the United States, having achieved national unity by the end of the century, was now ready for a new role in world affairs.[18]

During World War I, Wilson applied the lessons he had learned from American history to international relations. His vision of the League of Nations expressed his hope that the world could achieve the same kind of organic unity that the United States had gained from the Civil War, so that it, too, could overcome its divisions. On February 14, 1919, when he presented the League Covenant to a plenary session of the Paris Peace Conference, the president expressed his expectation that the new League would grow and develop. He explained that the Covenant was "a vehicle of life. A living thing is born .... It is a definite guarantee of peace. It is a definite guarantee by word against aggression."[19] Just as the American nation operated as a living organism within the framework of the U.S. Constitution, the new League, he now hoped, would develop its new life from the Covenant. This was Americanism as internationalism.

At Johns Hopkins University in the 1880s, Wilson had learned the idea of organic historical development from two of his professors, Herbert Baxter Adams and Richard Ely. They had studied German historicism while earning their doctorates at the University of Heidelberg. For a time, Wilson embraced the germ theory of history that they taught, focusing on primordial roots to explain the nature of the modern state. Using a biological analogy, he likened society to a living organism.[20] In *The State* (1889), he traced the origins of Western European and American governments back through Greece and Rome to the Semitic and Aryan races. Wilson found the roots of these Western governments in "the primitive politics of the Teutonic races."[21] American government, he believed, had emerged from this heritage. This inheritance, "as transplanted by English colonists in the course of the two centuries which preceded our own, worked out through a fresh development to new and characteristic forms."[22] Thus, at this time, Wilson emphasized the primordial roots of the nation.

He soon shifted his focus, however, from racial origins to more recent historical development—or from heredity to environment. Along with the historian Frederick Jackson Turner, whom he befriended at Johns Hopkins, Wilson began to stress the frontier's influence on American nationalism. Before Turner delivered his famous paper on the frontier's significance in American history, Wilson published his own frontier thesis in *Division and Reunion* (1893).[23] He still viewed the nation as a living organism. But he now believed that it could embody peoples from various ethnic backgrounds. The frontier experience promoted the assimilation of various immigrants into the growing nation. Wilson's shift from the germ theory to the frontier thesis coincided with his transition from an "Anglo-conformity" to a "melting-pot" view of assimilation. There were limits to his acceptance of other nationalities, however. He restricted the melting pot to Europeans, and he never approved of "cultural pluralism."[24]

Even as he shifted from a primordial to a civic definition of the nation, Wilson had continued to believe in the hierarchy of race.[25] In writing *A History of the American People,* he revealed his racial prejudices. He depicted the New World as "a virgin continent" before the English came. Yet, the English race, which had resulted from mixing Saxon and Celtic blood, nevertheless encountered native "savages" on arrival in America. To establish and expand their settlements, the English asserted their own liberty and mastery over the New World. They removed the Indians by force. The American frontier provided a place for English self-government, but it also often provided death and sometimes enslavement for native peoples.[26] For the English, Wilson claimed, "the free life of the New World made them very democratic."[27] Yet, their "democratic" character did not prevent them from buying African slaves and establishing racial slavery in America. By the end of the seventeenth century, Wilson observed, "the shrewd New England traders were already beginning to learn how much rum would pay for ... among the savages of the African slave coast."[28] The frontier meant removal for Native Americans and enslavement for African Americans, but Wilson focused instead on the growth of liberty and democracy for English settlers.

In Wilson's account, the English colonists, augmented by Scotch-Irish and other European immigrants, had evolved into a new people. These Americans had moved naturally toward independence. Eventually they resorted to revolutionary war against England to preserve their freedom. Wilson believed that "the spirit which so angered them was natural, and not born of mere rebellion."[29] Out of their revolutionary struggle to protect their own liberty "a new nation was born."[30] Emphasizing the democratic character of the new nation, he noted that: "The war for independence had been a democratic upheaval, and its processes had seriously discredited all government which was not directly of the people."[31] George Washington, Wilson thought, had provided the critical leadership for the young republic. He deserved credit as "the maker of a nation."[32]

In Wilson's interpretation of American history, the western frontier had further contributed to the growth of democracy in the United States. As white settlers moved into the interior of the new nation, they had demanded equality. These free men, he observed, "took up land and became freeholders in that free society, and added their force to the power of the new democracy, making a nation which must be governed upon principles of equal privilege or not governed at all."[33] This democratic movement had swept the conservative Federalists, who had held power since they had drafted the Constitution in 1787, out of office, replacing them with Thomas Jefferson and his fellow Republicans. These new Republican leaders had contributed "new national principles" for the next century, Wilson asserted. "Subtly, insensibly, by an alchemy whose processes no man knew or guided, the transformations of growth were becoming also transformations of character in the young body politic of the Union."[34] As this frontier process continued in the nineteenth century, new western leaders, such as Henry Clay and Andrew Jackson, introduced an aggressively democratic style of politics.

Wilson viewed the American people in exclusive terms.[35] His concept of the nation included only white Americans of European ancestry. American Indians and African Americans were marginalized in his history. These peoples lived within the geographic borders of the United States, but he excluded them from his definition of the American people. His concept of democracy was likewise exclusive. Accordingly, he praised Jacksonian democracy, while disregarding that it had entailed both Indian removal and African American slavery. "In the new democracy which Jackson represented," Wilson noted, "the mass of common men took leave to assert themselves in all things, and use their own standards of right."[36] He thought that democracy had flourished in the antebellum South as well as the West. "In politics," he claimed, "the ruling race were as democratic as men of their kind anywhere. All white men had an equal footing of privilege there and an equal freedom."[37]

Praising white rule over people of color, Wilson used the hierarchy of race in his assessment of southern Reconstruction after the American Civil War. Despite his pro-Union interpretation of the war, he condemned the "radical" governments that had been established in the former Confederate states. He identified thoroughly with fellow white southerners who had resisted these new governments in which both black and white leaders held power. Defending white supremacy, even in its extreme forms of terror and violence by the Ku Klux Klan, Wilson lambasted Radical Republicans in Congress who had attempted to protect former slaves and promote racial equality. He deplored the role reversal that Reconstruction had brought temporarily to southern politics: "It was plain to see that the troubles in the southern States arose out of the exclusion of the better whites from the electoral suffrage no less than from the admission of the most ignorant blacks."[38]

Wilson's harsh criticism of Reconstruction in *A History of the American People* expressed his own experience in the South during this era. He concluded that the Civil War had finally shifted power from the states to the national government. The checks and balances of federalism, as originally intended by the framers of the Constitution, were finally destroyed with the Confederacy's defeat. Being, like Lincoln, pro-Union, Wilson had embraced this demise of states' rights. But he lamented the collapse of the checks and balances between the executive and legislative branches in the national government during postwar Reconstruction. Presidents Andrew Johnson and Ulysses Grant had failed to prevent the Republicans in Congress from imposing "radical" rule on the South. Wilson believed that Lincoln, if he had lived, would have pursued a moderate policy and spared the South from this terrible ordeal.[39]

Wilson's first book, *Congressional Government* (1885), which Johns Hopkins accepted as his doctoral dissertation, addressed the crisis in American government that he saw in the aftermath of the Civil War and Reconstruction. "The noble charter of fundamental law given to us by the Convention of 1787," he concluded, "is still our Constitution; but it is now our *form of government* rather in name than in reality, the form of the Constitution being one of nicely adjusted, ideal balances, whilst the actual form of our present government is simply a scheme of congressional supremacy."[40] That the federal government had used its "sovereign power" to enable African Americans to vote, while denying the franchise to white southerners, was the real problem. This had been, for Wilson, "the very ugliest side of federal supremacy."[41] He regretted that "the balances of the Constitution are for the most part only ideal. For all practical purposes the national government is supreme over the state governments, and Congress predominant over its so-called coordinate branches."[42] Henceforth, Wilson searched for a solution to this alleged problem in American government.

His idea of the modern democratic state provided the answer. He believed, as he wrote in 1885, that democracy was "the result of history, not of theory, a creation of experience rather than speculation." Democracy in America had enjoyed "a truly organic growth." Other nations could also experience the historical trend toward democracy because modern influences of popular education, the press, education, travel, and commerce, which had shaped the United States, were spreading throughout the world. He cautioned, however, that democratic institutions depended on "several all-important conditions." A democratic nation required "homogeneity of race and community of thought and purpose among the people.... The nation which is to try democracy successfully must not only feel itself an organic body, but must be accustomed to *act* as an organic body.... Not a habit of revolution, but a habit of resolution must constitute the political life of the nation."[43] In other words, only modern nations that had reached this stage in their political development were ready for democratic self-rule.

Wilson's concept of democracy, which mirrored his exclusive view of the American people, required him to define sovereignty in a restrictive way. He argued in *An Old Master and Other Political Essays* (1893) that sovereignty rested not with all citizens but with their political leadership. To be certain, the government, especially in a democracy, needed to be accountable to the people. He explained that "sovereignty, if it be a definite and separable thing at all, is not unlimited power; is not identical with the powers of the community. It is not the general vitality of the organism, but the specific originative power of certain organs."[44] Only responsible leaders, accountable to reliable voters, should exercise sovereignty on behalf of the body politic.

Wilson eventually focused on the presidency as the appropriate branch of the American government to provide democratic leadership for the nation. He had given a negative assessment of the office in *Congressional Government,* but offered a new view in *Constitutional Government in the United States* (1908).[45] As president, Wilson practiced what he had preached, creating what political scientists have called "the rhetorical presidency."[46] This modern conception, emphasizing management of public opinion, fundamentally rejected the republicanism of the Constitution's framers, who had emphasized its checks and balances. Wilson offered a new style of democratic presidency to replace the old way of republicanism. The president would thus become the real sovereign. The American people required strong executive leadership, Wilson believed. As his brother-in-law Stockton Axson noted, "His instinct for democracy involved the idea that, because a democracy is free, it is the more necessary that it be led. His faith in the people has never been a faith in the supreme wisdom of the people, but rather in the capacity of the people to be led right by those whom they elect and constitute their leaders."[47]

Wilson's concepts of nation, democracy, and sovereignty provided ideological content for his liberal internationalism during World War I. To solve the nation's and the world's problems as he understood them, he advocated the concentration of power in the presidency at home and the extension of American control abroad. His political philosophy was fundamentally different from that of eighteenth-century republicanism, which had emphasized the importance of limiting power by dividing it among different branches of government at home and of operating within the international balance of power. Wilson rejected the idea of a balance of power in international relations, just as he had abandoned the old republican concept of checks and balances in the U.S. Constitution. Wilsonianism derived from his Americanism. As he told the Senate in his "peace without victory" speech on January 22, 1917, "There must be, not a balance of power, but a community of power; not organized rivalries, but an organized common peace."[48] The new League of Nations, he anticipated, would create an international community of this kind under U.S. hegemony, although he did not openly acknowledge this power-seeking aspect of his vision of collective security. It should guarantee self-determination for nation-states, just as the American nation protected liberty for its citizens. Organic historical development should do for the democratic nations of the world what it had done for the United States, thereby overcoming sovereign divisions. Accordingly, Wilson sought to reconcile differences between nationalism and internationalism: "The greatest nationalist is the man who wants his nation to be the greatest nation, and the greatest nation is the nation which penetrates to the heart of its duty and mission among the nations of the world."[49]

Wilson refused to recognize the world's pluralism, emphasizing instead its interdependence. He expected the League to preserve world peace through collective security or international social control. Rejecting pluralism for the world, as he did for the United States, Wilson sought to escape the inherent dilemma between nationalism and internationalism. But his vision of an organic world community never overcame the diversity among nation-states. "At a more fundamental level of explanation, indeed," the historian F. H. Hinsley noted in *Sovereignty* (1986), "the League of Nations failed in its task for this other reason. It sought to solve the international problem, to avoid in particular the recurrence of war, by the suppression or the limitation by external means of the sovereignty of the individual state at a time when the outstanding development of recent history had been the increase in the power, the scope and the efficiency of the individual state—not to speak of its indispensability in the modern community."[50]

In the peacemaking after World War I, Wilson applied the principle of national self-determination as he understood it from his earlier study of American history. He recognized nation-states that he regarded as historic, but not claims for nationhood that seemed no more warranted than southern secession had been during the American Civil War. From the perspective of historicism, he welcomed Poland, Czechoslovakia, and Yugoslavia into the community of nations. Because he did not embrace the concept of ethnonationalism as the essential definition of a nation, he did not regard the inclusion of various nationalities in these new states as a violation of the principle of national self-determination. The peoples in each of these states, he believed, should all assimilate into a single nation. From his perspective, moreover, it did not violate the principle of self-determination to exclude Germans who lived in Poland, Czechoslovakia, and Austria, from the new Weimar Republic. At the end of the Great War, Wilson approved the creation of new nation-states out of the ruins of defeated European empires, but at the Paris Peace Conference of 1919 he did not favor the breakup of existing states or even the drawing of all new borders along ethnocultural fault lines. His understanding of national self-determination gave primacy to historicism, not ethnonationalism.[51]

Wilson's belief in organic historical development for nations and for the world community embraced the hierarchy of race. He recognized new nations in Europe, but not elsewhere. The mandate system of the new League provided his alternative to traditional European colonies for those peoples who, in his view, had not reached the developmental stage to become independent nations. At Paris, Wilson also applied the hierarchy of race when he rejected Japan's proposal for an affirmation of racial equality in the League Covenant.[52] Here, he was caught in the same dilemma that he had failed to resolve at home. He had endorsed the melting-pot theory of assimilation for the United States, but only for the American people of European ancestry. Native Americans and African Americans might live in the country, but not as equal citizens. Similarly, he wanted Japan in the new League, which he viewed as an organic community of nations, but he still opposed racial equality for people of color. Wilson hoped to subordinate non-Western nations, such as Japan, in the postwar world community in much the same way that he sought to dominate racial minorities in the United States. He rejected genuine pluralism or equality for all peoples around the world. In this regard, too, Wilson's internationalism derived from his Americanism.

Wilsonianism manifested Wilson's concepts of nation, democracy, and sovereignty. His ideals of national self-determination and collective security, which incorporated these concepts, were sometimes quite different from the meanings associated with them by later scholars. His ideology had emerged from his study of American history and politics. This nexus between cultural history and international relations shaped Wilson's statecraft and his legacy in the American Century.

CHAPTER 2

WOODROW WILSON AND THE QUEST FOR ORDERLY PROGRESS

Lloyd Ambrosius, "Woodrow Wilson and the Quest for Orderly Progress," in *Traditions and Values: American Diplomacy, 1865–1945,* ed. Norman A. Graebner (Lanham, MD: University Press of America, 1985), 73–100. Reprinted by permission of University Press of America.

One central theme characterized President Woodrow Wilson's leadership in world affairs. He consistently endeavored to establish his control over American foreign relations. Seeking to dominate the policy-making process in the United States and to project American influence into other countries, he intended to use the full powers of the presidency.

This search for control at home and abroad occurred within the context of a changing nation and a revolutionary world. Science and technology had enabled Americans to develop industry and build cities. Transforming the personal relationships of traditional rural communities into a bureaucratic pattern, industrialization and urbanization created a modern corporate or organizational society in the United States. These profound social and economic changes necessitated a new role for the American government in both domestic and foreign affairs.

What American democracy required, according to Wilson, was "progressive order."[1] Like other progressives, he hoped to avert uncontrollable chaos or anarchy by managing orderly change. The maintenance of the status quo no longer appeared feasible to him either in the United States or abroad. As a typical American progressive, he preferred reform to revolution. This preference shaped his attitude toward revolutions in other countries. He welcomed moderate changes, especially when these resulted in greater American influence, but opposed radical revolution. In short, under Wilson's leadership the United States searched for a dynamic form of control, not merely for order.[2]

Wilson experienced the fundamental dilemma facing American policymakers in the twentieth century. On one side, the world's growing interdependence prevented the United States from ignoring events in other places. Apparently remote developments, such as those leading to the outbreak of the European war in 1914, eventually involved the United States. On the other side, the continuing pluralism of the modern world prevented this nation from winning universal acceptance for its own ideals and practices. Foreign leaders simply refused to behave in the way the American president desired. Under these circumstances, the United States needed to define a foreign policy that would protect its own legitimate interests in an international environment it could neither avoid nor control.

Wilson ultimately failed in this task. He overestimated his ability to shape the world according to his particular vision of interdependence. Even military intervention did not give him this power. The League of Nations, which epitomized his vision, never transformed the structure of international relations as he expected. On the contrary, it generated conflict both at the Paris Peace Conference of 1919 and in the United States. The Allies as well as Germany declined to play the role Wilson assigned to them during the peacemaking after World War I, and so did the Republican senators in the United States. The persistence of pluralism prevented the Democratic president from reforming the world in accordance with his ideals. Seeking in vain for control over foreign affairs, he failed to reconcile the realities of interdependence and pluralism in his definition of American foreign policy. The fundamental dilemma created by these two contemporary features consequently continued to plague future American diplomatists. Wilson's legacy provided only inadequate guidance for them.[3]

When Wilson entered the White House in 1913, changes already occurring in the United States and around the world pointed toward a significantly different role for the president in foreign affairs. By the beginning of the twentieth century, the United States had emerged as an industrial giant. New technologies enabled its factories to produce an expanding volume of commodities for both domestic and foreign markets. Industrial development also promoted commercial agriculture. With new machinery American farmers began to produce foodstuffs for sale in cities, not only at home but also abroad. Because of abundant raw materials, both industry and agriculture were relatively self-sufficient. Although foreign trade was increasingly important, it was not absolutely essential for the prosperity of the American economy. Other countries depended more on the United States for industrial and agricultural products than this nation did on them. As a consequence, the economic basis for the emergence of the United States as a world power already existed. This reality the Spanish–American War of 1898 had clearly demonstrated. Americans had then translated their economic supremacy over Spain into military victory in Cuba as well as the acquisition of Puerto Rico, Guam, and the Philippines.

As they expanded their empire into the Caribbean and across the Pacific, Americans encountered other emerging world powers. Japan and Germany also began to challenge the traditional empires of Europe and Asia. The maritime nations of Western Europe no longer dominated global politics. The British and French empires, although still extensive, could not prevent the new rivals from staking out their claims. The Chinese and Russian empires experienced even greater difficulty as they both lost control over some of their possessions. Before it finally collapsed in 1912, the Manchu dynasty in China had made numerous territorial and economic concessions to all of the great powers, both old and new. After suffering a humiliating defeat in the Russo-Japanese War of 1904–5, the Russians acknowledged Japan's hegemony over Korea and other nearby territory. For the first time in modern history, an Asian nation militarily defeated a European empire, giving rise to fears of a "yellow peril" in Europe and the United States. Racial prejudice compounded the problems of economic and political conflict among nations.

Europe, and especially Western Europe, increasingly lost its traditional dominance in world affairs. The peace conference that ended the Russo-Japanese War was not held in London, Paris, or Berlin, but in Portsmouth, New Hampshire. Hosted by President Theodore Roosevelt, it symbolically represented the new status of the United States as a great power. Roosevelt's contribution to the peaceful resolution of the Moroccan crisis of 1905–6 between Germany, on one side, and France and Great Britain, on the other, further indicated the shift of influence in international relations away from Western Europe. The maintenance of the European balance of power no longer depended merely on the decisions and actions of the Europeans themselves. While the Japanese expanded into Eastern Asia and the Pacific, the Americans now exerted their influence not only there but also in Europe and Africa. Not confined to their own continent or even to Latin America, their involvement now extended beyond the Western Hemisphere.[4]

The potential collapse of the European balance of power and the simultaneous emergence of the United States created the conditions for Wilson's self-assigned role in world affairs. Under his leadership, for both external and internal reasons, this nation could not avoid entangling itself in the wars and politics of the Old World as it had during most of the nineteenth century. The "free security" that Americans had previously enjoyed was no longer possible.[5]

World War I engulfed the United States in 1917 despite Wilson's genuine attempt to preserve American neutrality. Global interdependence prevented this nation from escaping the war's impact. Although both the Allies and the Central Powers jeopardized America's maritime interests, Germany's submarine warfare posed the most direct threat and eventually provoked the United States to intervene. Once Wilson decided to enter the war, he began to articulate a new American foreign policy for the future peace. Summarized in the Fourteen Points, his vision of a new system of international relations provided his justification for the war's costs. At the peace conference in Paris where he sought to implement his program, the president devoted himself primarily to creating the League of Nations. This international organization, he hoped, would overcome the traditional rivalries among nations and inaugurate a new era of peace.

Ill-prepared for his new role of global leadership, Wilson drew on his own personal experience and ideas for guidance. Unable to understand the diversity of values and interests among the various peoples of the world, he typically assumed that they shared his own perspective. If foreign leaders disagreed, as they frequently did, he attributed this disagreement to their failure to represent the true interests of their own nations. He projected his conception of American nationalism onto the rest of the world, presupposing its universal validity. Viewing the United States as the vanguard, he expected other nations to follow its example and develop in the same way. His vision of the future consequently combined both universalism and unilateralism. While proclaiming a new era of internationalism, the president actually expected others to conform to his particular understanding of American ideals and practices. This paradoxical approach to foreign affairs sometimes made Wilson appear hypocritical, but the real problem was his inability to distinguish between the interests of the United States and those of other nations.

Despite his growing appreciation of the modern world's interdependence, he still failed to comprehend its pluralism. This failure appeared in his response not only to the European war but also to various revolutions during his presidency. Those in Mexico and China began before his inauguration. Others in the Russian, German, and Austro-Hungarian empires came under the impact of war and military defeat. Reacting to these revolutions without fully comprehending the forces they unleashed, Wilson lacked intellectual categories to understand them on their own terms. When he sought to influence their direction, the consequences were invariably different from his expectations. Peoples in other countries refused to behave in accordance with his own national perspective.

Wilson's search for control at home and abroad exemplified a typical impulse of progressive Americans. With the human scientific and technological conquest over nature of the nineteenth century, they now optimistically expected a similar achievement in the social, economic, and political relationships within human society itself. Social scientists at the beginning of the twentieth century began to articulate the concept of social control. The sociologist Edward A. Ross, who had studied under Wilson at Princeton, examined the various methods by which society influenced individuals in *Social Control* (1901).[6] An economist, John Bates Clark, anticipated Wilson's New Freedom with his argument for preventing the monopolistic tendencies of American corporations by preserving free competition in *The Control of Trusts* (1901).[7] Franklin H. Giddings, a leading sociologist and, like Clark, a personal friend of Wilson, offered his defense of the United States as a "democratic empire." Appealing to both Social Darwinism and the Social Gospel, he justified the American war against Spain in 1898 and the new imperialism in its wake. "My studies of theoretical sociology," he proclaimed in *Democracy and Empire* (1900), "long ago led me to believe that the combination of small states into larger political aggregates must continue until all the semi-civilized, barbarian, and savage communities of the world are brought under the protection of the larger civilized nations."[8] Convinced that the United States and Great Britain could best assume this burden, he urged his fellow Americans to undertake this new role in world affairs. Significantly, both Clark and Giddings became early and steadfast advocates of American participation in the League of Nations.

Wilson likewise welcomed the consequences of the Spanish–American War for American leadership, and especially for presidential primacy in foreign affairs. In 1900, he affirmed that the president of the United States "must utter every initial judgment, take every first step of action, supply the information upon which it is to act, suggest and in large measure control its conduct."[9] This conception of presidential control over American foreign relations continued to characterize Wilson's thought. Elaborating on it in *Constitutional Government in the United States* (1908), he asserted that the chief executive's powers in this field were "very absolute." "The initiative in foreign affairs, which the President possesses without any restriction whatever," Wilson contended, "is virtually the power to control them absolutely. The President cannot conclude a treaty with a foreign power without the consent of the Senate, but he may guide every step of diplomacy, and to guide diplomacy is to determine what treaties must be made, if the faith and prestige of the government are to be maintained. He need disclose no step of negotiation until it is virtually committed. Whatever its disinclination, the Senate may feel itself committed also."[10]

Unfortunately for Wilson, this interpretation of the Constitution failed to persuade the Republican senators under Henry Cabot Lodge's leadership after World War I.

They declined to approve the Versailles Treaty with the League of Nations Covenant exactly as he had presented it to them. The outcome of the treaty fight in 1919–20 demonstrated that the president's control over American foreign relations was considerably less absolute than he desired. Wilson's arguments persuaded other prominent political scientists such as Edward S. Corwin and Quincy Wright, but not the Senate.[11]

Like the social scientists, progressive journalists contributed to the concept of control. In *The Promise of American Life* (1909), Herbert Croly advocated "a certain measure of discipline" and "a large measure of individual subordination and self-denial" to improve the social and economic conditions of the United States, while preserving its democratic political institutions. In the name of the national interest, he urged greater executive leadership both at home and abroad. "As much in foreign as in domestic affairs must the American people seek to unite national efficiency with democratic idealism," he argued. Anticipating the end of American isolation from the Old World, he wanted the United States to prepare for its inescapable involvement in the international political economy. Reform at home would equip the nation for its new role overseas. Noting the world's growing interdependence, Croly foresaw the prospect of American intervention in a future European war to foster democracy and promote international peace. He outlined the rationale that Wilson would later use to justify the American declaration of war against Germany in 1917. In his view, American belligerency might be justified for the sake of extending this nation's control over the Old World to establish democracy and peace.[12]

Walter Lippmann agreed with Croly that progressive American leadership was essential to avoid chaos in the changing world. Because the traditional status quo was already disintegrating, the only choice for Americans was between "drift" and "mastery." He advocated rational or pragmatic control over human affairs to combine both progress and order. In *Drift and Mastery* (1914), he viewed the United States as the nation best prepared to adopt this method for dealing with the world's chaotic conditions. "Civilization, it seems to me," Lippmann concluded, "is just this constant effort to introduce plan where there has been clash, and purpose into the jungles of disordered growth."[13]

Given these attitudes, both Croly and Lippmann readily supported Wilson's foreign policy during World War I. These editors of the *New Republic* welcomed his endorsement of the idea of collective security and employed it to justify American intervention in 1917. Along with the philosopher John Dewey, they heralded American belligerency as a crusade for democracy. Reconciling their liberal idealism with pragmatism, which required them to justify the war's costs by its results, they anticipated a postwar world of democracy and peace. Lippmann even contributed directly to the preparation of Wilson's Fourteen Points as secretary of the Inquiry.[14]

Croly, Lippmann, and Dewey, like the president, wanted the United States to redeem the Old World and transform international relations through the League of Nations. But they were inevitably disappointed by the peace treaty with Germany, for their idealistic hopes could never be achieved. Their unrealistic expectation that the United States could easily impose its will on other countries resulted in their disillusionment with the Versailles Treaty. Denouncing it, these liberals now opposed American membership in the League. The bitter disappointment of Croly, Lippmann, and Dewey after the war reflected the high hopes they had earlier placed—or really misplaced—in Wilson's leadership. The problem of liberal disillusionment was theirs more than his, for no American president could accomplish the kind of universal control over foreign affairs that they all desired.[15]

Challenging the prevailing liberal attitudes of American progressives, journalist Randolph S. Bourne offered a radical critique of Wilson's foreign policy. In 1917, he asserted that "the 'liberals' who claim a realistic and pragmatic attitude in politics have disappointed us in setting up and then clinging wistfully to the belief that our war could get itself justified for an idealistic flavor, or at least for a world renovating social purpose, that they had more or less denied to the other belligerents." He understood, as they did not, that no statesman could impose rational control over the war. Warning that Wilson could never accomplish "any liberal control of events," Bourne denounced the illusion that the United States could utilize the war to regenerate the world and establish peace through a postwar League.[16]

Convinced that American progressives, including the social scientists, could never discover scientific laws of human behavior that would enable them to predict and control the future, the radical Bourne shared a fundamental premise with the conservative Henry Adams. Adams had searched for some unifying principle in history, but failed to discover it. Neither religion nor science provided him an adequate explanation of cause and effect. "Historians," he warned in *The Education of Henry Adams* (1918), "have got into far too much trouble by following schools of theology in their efforts to enlarge their synthesis, that they should willingly repeat the process in science."[17] Senator Lodge, who edited this autobiography for publication, shared Adams's skepticism. Doubting that intellectuals or statesmen could comprehend and consequently control the world's destiny as the progressives believed, the conservative senator never shared the president's attitude toward world affairs. He refused to believe the exaggerated promises of a redemptive foreign policy. For this reason, rather than merely because of partisan politics, Lodge criticized Wilson's plan for the League of Nations.[18]

Although Christianity furnished no unifying principle for Adams, it did for Wilson. His faith in God undergirded his belief in the world's universality. Combining the Social Gospel with Social Darwinism, he expected a better world to emerge from conflict. Progress would result from competition. Identifying the United States with Christianity, and patriotism with religion, he proclaimed that "America was born a Christian nation. America was born to exemplify that devotion to the elements of righteousness which are derived from the revelations of Holy Scriptures."[19] This view of the United States enabled Wilson to define the war as a crusade. "He cunningly hopes," observed the Social Gospel theologian George D. Herron, "he divinely schemes, to bring it about that America, awake at last to her national selfhood and calling, shall become as a colossal Christian apostle, shepherding the world into the kingdom of God." This motif lay behind the president's yearning for the redemption of the Old World, as Herron explained in *Woodrow Wilson and the World's Peace* (1917).[20] Praising this book, Wilson himself applauded "Herron's singular insight into all the elements of a complicated situation and into my own motives and purposes."[21] From this theological perspective, the Presbyterian president decided to call the League's constitution a Covenant and to locate its headquarters in Calvinist Geneva. Religion as well as science furnished the intellectual content of his foreign policy.[22]

Wilson's conception of the global mission of the United States emerged from his Latin American policy. In it, he combined the elements of unilateralism and universalism that would later characterize his vision of the League. In conformity with the Roosevelt Corollary to the Monroe Doctrine, he intervened unilaterally to exclude European influence from the Caribbean nations. But he hoped to achieve multilateral approval from the other nations in the Western Hemisphere for his own actions to replace European with American predominance. "The United States has nothing to seek in Central and South America," the president announced soon after his inauguration, "except the lasting interests of the people of the two continents, the security of governments, intended for the people, and for no special group or interest, and the development of personal and trade relationships between the two continents, which shall redound to the profit and advantage of both and interfere with the rights and liberties of neither."[23] The fulfillment of this goal depended on Wilson's ability to win universal acceptance of his own ideals and practices by the nations of Latin America. He anticipated resistance from some of their leaders, but deluded himself into believing that the peoples shared his aspirations. He ignored the pluralism of the region.

Announcing his new Latin American policy in 1913, the president emphasized "the development of constitutional liberty in the world." He thought the new Panama Canal, linking the Atlantic and Pacific oceans, would foster closer ties between North and South America. When it opened in 1914, it would unite the two continents with common political and military as well as commercial interests. From this perspective he stressed the idea of Pan-Americanism. At the suggestion of his friend, Edward M. House, Wilson attempted to negotiate a Pan-American treaty of nonaggression and political cooperation with the ABC countries, Argentina, Brazil, and Chile. While he saw this multilateral treaty as an extension of the Monroe Doctrine to guarantee the territorial integrity and republican political institutions of these countries, they saw the danger of American hegemony. Despite their resistance throughout 1915, the president continued to hope for the Pan-American treaty's successful conclusion. "Our concern for the independence and prosperity of the states of Central and South America is not altered," he affirmed in his annual message to Congress. "We retain unabated the spirit that has inspired us throughout the whole life of our government and which was so frankly put into words by President [James] Monroe. We still mean always to make a common cause of national independence and of political liberty in America. But that purpose is now better understood so far as it concerns ourselves. It is known not to be a selfish purpose. It is known to have in it no thought of taking advantage of any government in this hemisphere or playing its political fortunes for our own benefit. All the governments of America stand, so far as we are concerned, upon a footing of genuine equality and unquestioned independence."[24]

Wilson believed that the United States, unlike other great powers, played an exceptional role in world politics. It served the common welfare of mankind rather than its own imperial ends. "This is Pan-Americanism," he explained. "It has none of the spirit of empire in it. It is the embodiment, the effectual embodiment, of the spirit of law and independence and liberty and mutual service." Denying the similarity between the hegemony of the United States over its weaker neighbors and that of other empires, the president presupposed that his view of progressive American politics coincided with the interests of Latin American nations. Addressing the Pan-American Scientific Congress in Washington early in 1916, he reiterated his vision of Pan-Americanism: "For politics I conceive to be nothing more than the science of the ordered progress of society along the lines of greatest usefulness and convenience to itself." As he had earlier for the United States, Wilson now prescribed "progressive order" for Latin America to avoid uncontrollable chaos. The Latin Americans, however, were no more eager to submit to American than to European control. After more than two years of fruitless effort, by early 1917 the president quietly dropped his proposal for a Pan-American treaty.[25]

At the same time that he promoted his multilateral conception of Pan-Americanism, Wilson intervened unilaterally in Latin America. He dispatched American troops to more countries there than any of his predecessors in the White House. Despite his denunciation of "dollar diplomacy," he fully intended to protect American economic and commercial interests in the region. He also appreciated the strategic importance of the Caribbean as a vital seaway to the Panama Canal. Fearful that the European powers, and especially Germany, might establish a naval base that could threaten this seaway, he sought to counter this prospect by preventive action. By fostering governments in the Latin American countries around the Caribbean that were friendly to the United States, and if necessary by imposing them through military intervention, the president sought to guard against any threatening European influence.

In practice, however, the distinction between defensive and offensive acts disappeared as he asserted American control over weak Latin American nations. The occupation of Haiti in 1915 and the Dominican Republic in 1916 exemplified this pattern. Wilson sent the American navy to these island nations to force them to establish governments acceptable to him and to control their finances. Although he spoke about constitutional liberty, the military intervention that he practiced in these countries overrode their own constitutions. His real objective was American control rather than democracy or merely order. Facing internal resistance, the American marines in Haiti and the Dominican Republic trained local police forces to crush it. The United States ensured the election of its own clients to the top political offices or simply established its own military government. While preventing Germany or any other European power from interfering, the president consolidated American hegemony in the Caribbean.[26]

Mexico gave Wilson more difficulty than any other country in the Western Hemisphere. Here the American–European rivalry in Latin America became most intense. Great Britain and Germany enjoyed considerable political as well as economic influence in that country. Like the United States, these European powers endeavored to protect their interests during Mexico's revolution by playing off one faction against another. Early in 1913, through a successful coup against the revolutionary government of Francisco Madero, General Victoriano Huerta established himself in Mexico City. Although the American ambassador had participated in planning this counterrevolutionary coup, which resulted in Madero's murder, the new American president refused to recognize the Huerta government. For over a year, Wilson attempted various methods, ranging from diplomatic mediation to military intervention, to replace it with an acceptable alternative. As he once remarked, "I am going to teach the South American Republics to elect good men!"[27]

The president desired neither to annex any of Mexico's territory nor to establish a formal protectorate over the country, but he nevertheless intended to impose his will. To counter the United States, Huerta turned to Europe and especially to Great Britain. He resisted Wilson's plan to replace him through a democratic election.

The failure of the United States to shape Mexico's political institutions by peaceful methods led the president to resort to military intervention. The occupation of Veracruz in April 1914, although timed to prevent the landing of a German ship with munitions and justified by the brief detainment of American sailors at the port of Tampico, resulted from his determination to remove Huerta. Unexpected Mexican resistance and consequent American casualties induced Wilson to accept mediation by the ABC countries as a face-saving way to extricate the United States from a dangerous situation. He could not control Mexico as easily as he had originally anticipated.[28]

Venustiano Carranza, leader of the Constitutionalists, eventually succeeded Huerta as president of Mexico. Wilson recognized his government. Yet, Carranza, too, endeavored to protect his country's independence from American paternalism. On occasion, he collaborated with the United States to strengthen his position against his internal foes, notably Francisco "Pancho" Villa. But when Wilson sent General John J. Pershing's punitive expedition into Mexico in March 1916, the Mexican president saw it as a threat. Villa had raided Columbus, New Mexico, to provoke American military intervention, and succeeded in accomplishing his objective. While Pershing vainly attempted to capture him, Villa recruited more troops and waged guerilla warfare against both the Americans and Carranza's government.

Pershing's troops clashed not only with Villa's but also with Carranza's. Under these circumstances, the Mexican government turned to Berlin for military assistance. In January 1917, Germany's foreign secretary, Arthur Zimmermann, responded by proposing an alliance against the United States. Although the German government never intended to give Mexico much support to reconquer Texas, New Mexico, and Arizona, it hoped to divert the United States from Europe by embroiling it in a war with Mexico. This plan failed disastrously as British intelligence intercepted the Zimmermann telegram and gave it to Washington. Releasing it to the press, the president used the Zimmermann telegram as dramatic evidence of Germany's threat to the United States. As the United States moved toward war against Germany, he ordered Pershing to withdraw from Mexico despite the punitive expedition's failure to achieve its objective. This withdrawal improved Mexican–American relations but left a legacy of distrust. Carranza continued to oppose Wilson's vision of regional interdependence as he denounced the Monroe Doctrine. He did not welcome the endorsement of this doctrine in the League of Nations Covenant.[29]

Disclosure of the Zimmermann telegram contributed to the already deteriorating German–American relationship. Germany's submarine warfare had moved the United States to the brink of war by the spring of 1917. At the beginning of the European war in 1914, Wilson had proclaimed a policy of impartial neutrality. The sinking of the British passenger liner *Lusitania* on May 7, 1915, by a German submarine prompted him to condemn this new form of warfare. "The rights of neutrals in time of war," he protested with reference to the American passengers who lost their lives, "are based upon principles, not upon expediency, and the principles are immutable." Because the president refused to make a comparable protest against

British maritime practices, Secretary of State William Jennings Bryan resigned during this crisis. He wanted to continue impartial neutrality. Yet, Wilson himself, despite his moral condemnation of Germany, intended to keep the United States out of the war. "The example of America," he explained, "must be the example not merely of peace because it will not fight, but of peace because peace is the healing and elevating influence of the world and strife is not. There is such a thing as a man being too proud to fight. There is such a thing as a nation being so right that it does not need to convince others by force that it is right."[30]

The *Lusitania* incident convinced Robert Lansing, Bryan's successor at the State Department, that "the German ambition for world dominion" threatened all democracies, including the United States. He thought that "the military oligarchy which rules Germany is a bitter enemy of democracy in every form; that, if that oligarchy triumphs over the liberal governments of Great Britain and France, it will then turn upon us as its next obstacle to imperial rule over the world; and that it is safer and surer and wiser for us to be one of many enemies than to be in the future alone against a victorious Germany."[31]

Yet, even Lansing still wanted to maintain American neutrality. In October 1915, the president approved his recommendation to protest against Great Britain's offshore blockade and definition of contraband. Continuing to criticize British maritime practices, the secretary of state proposed, in January 1916, a modus vivendi between the Allies and the Central Powers. With Wilson's endorsement, he attempted to convince the Allies to disarm their merchant ships in exchange for a pledge from the Central Powers that their submarines would follow the rules of cruiser warfare under international law. The purpose of this modus vivendi was to keep the United States out of the war.

Wilson endeavored both to protect American rights on the high seas and to avoid war. "No matter what military or naval force the United States might develop," he proclaimed in 1915 as he launched his plans for enlarging the American armed forces, "statesmen throughout the whole world might rest assured that we were gathering that force, not for attack in any quarter, not for aggression of any kind, not for the satisfaction of any political or international ambition, but merely to make sure of our own security.... The mission of America in the world is essentially a mission of peace and good will among men."[32]

During his campaign for preparedness early in 1916, he reiterated this theme. Wilson contended that "there is a moral obligation laid upon us to keep out of this war if possible. But by the same token there is a moral obligation laid upon us to keep free the courses of our commerce and of our finance, and I believe that America stands ready to vindicate those rights." Moreover, he thought the defense of North and South America might require the United States to enter the war. Pan-Americanism might justify American belligerency. "We have," he announced, "made ourselves the guarantors of the rights of national sovereignty and of popular sovereignty on this side of the water in both the continents of the Western Hemisphere."[33]

To prevent Germany's submarines from drawing the United States into the war, Wilson offered American mediation. He sent Colonel House to Europe during the spring of 1915 and again in 1916. Neither Germany nor the Allies welcomed House's vague proposals for ending the war without victory. To divert him from the divisive issues of the current war, the British foreign secretary Edward Grey encouraged him to think about the methods for guaranteeing future peace. In response, House and later Wilson began to formulate the idea of a postwar League of Nations. They hoped somehow to transcend the bitter rivalries of the war by promising American participation in the future preservation of peace. The president first publicly endorsed this idea of collective security in a speech to the League to Enforce Peace on May 27, 1916. He announced "that henceforth alliance must not be set up against alliance, understanding against understanding, but that there must be a common agreement for a common object, and that at the heart of the common object must lie the inviolable rights of peoples and of mankind."[34] This proclamation of universal human rights offered no guidelines for resolving the territorial and economic issues separating the Central Powers from the Allies. Wilson turned his attention to these issues for the first time in December 1916, when he sent peace notes to the belligerents. Having abandoned House's earlier plan for American mediation through the convening of an international peace conference, he now requested both sides in the war to state their aims. The German government, which had recently proposed direct negotiations with the Allies, refused to fulfill Wilson's request for a statement of war aims, while the Allied governments rejected Germany's proposal.

In the context of this stalemate, the president delivered his famous "peace without victory" address to the Senate on January 22, 1917. Blaming the European balance of power and alliances for the Old World's problems, he called for a new system of collective security. "There must be," he said, "not a balance of power, but a community of power; not organized rivalries, but an organized common peace." His vision of a future League of Nations represented the worldwide expansion of the Monroe Doctrine. "I am proposing, as it were," Wilson explained, "that the nations should with one accord adopt the doctrine of President Monroe as the doctrine of the world: that no nation should seek to extend its polity over any other nation or people, but that every people should be left free to determine its own polity, its own way of development, unhindered, unthreatened, unafraid, the little along with the great and powerful."[35] Thus, the president sought world peace through international control—that is, a global Monroe Doctrine—instead of a balance of power.

Wilson's policy of American neutrality collapsed with the beginning of Germany's unrestricted submarine warfare in February 1917. Prior to this time, the Germans had hesitated to use their submarines for fear of provoking the United States. After sinking the British freighter *Arabic* in August 1915, and torpedoing the French channel steamer *Sussex* in March 1916, they had promised not to attack merchant or passenger ships without giving a warning and rescuing the victims. This pledge to abide by the rules of cruiser warfare had effectively prevented Germany from using its submarines. As long as this condition prevailed, the United States experienced greater difficulty with British maritime practices. In July 1916, after Great Britain published a discriminatory list of American firms that traded with the Central Powers, Wilson had vigorously protested against the continuing British violations of American rights. But these grievances now appeared relatively unimportant as the Germans broke their pledge and resumed submarine warfare.

After the sinking of American ships in mid-March 1917, Wilson called the Congress into session and recommended a declaration of war. Referring to his "peace

without victory" address, he told the Congress: "Our object now, as then, is to vindicate the principles of peace and justice in the life of the world as against selfish and
autocratic power and to set up amongst the really free and self-governed peoples of
the world such a concert of purpose and of action as will henceforth insure the
observance of those principles." Denouncing the autocratic government of Imperial
Germany, he called for the liberation of the German people. "The world," he
concluded, "must be made safe for democracy. Its peace must be planted upon the
tested foundations of political liberty."[36] The Congress apparently agreed as it voted
four days later, on April 6, 1917, to declare war against Germany.[37]

Revolution in Russia seemed to justify Wilson's wartime crusade for democracy.
The new provisional government, which replaced the Romanov monarchy after the
abdication of Czar Nicholas II in mid-March, promised to establish constitutional
liberty and to keep Russia in the war. It immediately received diplomatic recognition
from the United States. In his war message, the president affirmed that "Russia was
known by those who knew it best to have been always in fact democratic at heart, in
all the vital habits of her thought, in all the intimate relationships of her people that
spoke their natural instinct, their habitual attitude towards life. The autocracy that
crowned the summit of her political structure, long as it had stood and terrible as was
the reality of its power, was not in fact Russian in origin, character, or purpose; and
now it has been shaken off and the great, generous Russian people have been added
in all their naive majesty and might to the forces that are fighting for freedom in the
world, for justice, and for peace."[38] Wilson promptly extended credits to the provisional government and sent a special mission led by the Republican elder statesman
Elihu Root to encourage it.

Naively assuming that the Russian people shared his own ideals and his current
enthusiasm for the war, the president was totally unprepared for the Bolshevik revolution in November 1917. He refused to recognize the radical Soviet regime of
Vladimir I. Lenin. Nor did he welcome its appeal for the opening of peace negotiations. His hopes for democracy in Russia and victory in the war against Germany
were now directly threatened by the Bolsheviks. Wilson thought these adverse developments in Russia resulted from a misunderstanding of American and Allied war
aims by the Russian people. Responding to the Bolsheviks, he decided to clarify these
aims in a major address to Congress on January 8, 1918. "Whether their present
leaders believe it or not," he proclaimed, "it is our heartfelt desire and hope that some
way may be opened whereby we may be privileged to assist the people of Russia to
attain their utmost hope of liberty and ordered peace."

The president went on to outline the Fourteen Points of his peace program.
Calling for open diplomacy and freedom of navigation and commerce, for disarmament and national self-determination, he concluded by advocating a postwar organization of collective security. Although quite general, this statement offered the most
explicit definition of a European policy that any president had ever made. For the
first time, the American government was outlining its view of peace conditions for
the continent of Europe. One central theme characterized this program, Wilson
stressed: "It is the principle of justice to all peoples and nationalities, and their right
to live on equal terms of liberty and safety with one another, whether they be strong
or weak."[39]

Despite American efforts to foster democratic institutions in Russia and keep it in the war, the Bolsheviks remained in power and negotiated a separate peace with Germany in March 1918. The Treaty of Brest-Litovsk, by ending the war on the Eastern Front, created a crisis in Western Europe. During the summer of 1918, the Central Powers threatened to defeat the Allies before the United States could provide decisive relief. The American Expeditionary Forces (AEF) under General Pershing were only beginning to appear on the Western Front. Because the United States had previously prepared for only a defensive war against Germany, it required a year after the American declaration of war before Pershing's troops were ready to make a sizable contribution. Meanwhile, the British and French forces encountered the German spring offensive.[40]

Under these circumstances, Wilson finally agreed in July 1918 to American military intervention in Russia. Although neither he nor his military advisers shared the British and French hopes for restoring the Eastern Front, he now relented to repeated Allied requests to send American troops into Siberia as well as northern Russia. Their mission, as he defined it, was strictly limited. In Siberia he allowed the American army to assist a Czecho-Slovak corps, which had earlier fought on the Eastern Front, to leave Russia by proceeding along the Trans-Siberian Railway to the port at Vladivostok. From there they could depart for the Western Front. Both at Vladivostok and in the northern Russian ports of Murmansk and Archangel were supplies that he did not want to fall into hostile hands. He also hoped that the presence of American troops in Siberia would contain Japanese ambitions there and in northern Manchuria.

Although Wilson wanted to avoid American military interference in the internal affairs of Russia, that was impossible. Despite his intentions, the American forces unavoidably participated in the Russian civil war against the Bolsheviks. The president limited this involvement as he had during the Mexican revolution. "My policy regarding Russia," he explained, "is very similar to my Mexican policy. I believe in letting them work out their own salvation, even though they wallow in anarchy for a while."[41] He attempted to influence both revolutions by encouraging constitutional governments favorable to the United States and even by intervening with American troops, but refrained from an all-out effort to use military power to replace undesirable regimes with American-made alternatives. That degree of control he restricted to the weak Caribbean nations.

Throughout the war, Wilson maintained an aloofness from the Old World. The United States became an Associated rather than an Allied Power. Instead of merging with the Allied armies, the AEF preserved its separate identity under Pershing's command. The president never endorsed the secret treaties of the Allies or their desire to crush the new Soviet government by intervening on the side of anti-Bolshevik factions in Russia. When he failed to secure Allied approval of his own peace program, Wilson proclaimed it unilaterally in his Fourteen Points. He wanted other nations to embrace American ideals and practices, but he did not intend to sacrifice American independence. Expressing this paradoxical attitude in a major address in late September 1918, he affirmed: "We still read [George] Washington's immortal warning against 'entangling alliances' with full comprehension and an answering purpose. But only special and limited alliances entangle; and we recognize and accept the duty of a new day in which we are permitted to hope for a general alliance which will avoid entanglements and clear the air of the world for common understandings and the maintenance of common rights."[42]

Wilson identified with the American diplomatic tradition of isolation from the Old World as he heralded American participation in the future League of Nations. Both unilateralism and universalism characterized his diplomatic style. When Germany, after the failure of its summer offensive, turned to him for an armistice in October 1918, he did not hesitate to handle the negotiations largely by himself. Experiencing military defeat, the Germans now appealed for peace on the basis of the Fourteen Points. Sending House to Paris to deal with the Allies, the president succeeded in gaining their approval as well for most of his peace program. The Armistice on November 11, 1918, ended the war with commitments by the Allies and Germany to base the peace treaty on his Fourteen Points.

Wilson's detachment from the Allies worried Republican leaders, including Roosevelt. "Above all," the ex-president stated, "we feel that at the Peace Conference, America should act, not as an umpire between our allies and our enemies, but as one of the allies bound to come to an agreement with them, and then to impose this common agreement upon our vanquished enemies."[43]

Wilson decided to participate personally in the negotiations at the Paris Peace Conference of 1919. This summit conference reflected the global character of world politics as delegates from every continent attended it. Of the five great powers, only three—Great Britain, France, and Italy—were European. The United States and Japan were the other two. Russia was conspicuously absent as the victorious powers invited neither the Soviet government nor any of its rivals to Paris. The problems of the Russian civil war and of Bolshevism nevertheless intruded onto the proceedings. Other empires had followed Russia into revolution, creating the specter of the westward expansion of Bolshevism. On the eve of the Armistice, the Hohenzollern and Hapsburg monarchies in Germany and Austria-Hungary collapsed under the impact of military defeat. So did the Ottoman Empire of Turkey.

Throughout Central and Eastern Europe and also the Middle East, new states emerged to supplant the previous empires. Some of them, such as Poland and Czechoslovakia, found immediate acceptance in Paris, but others waited on the outside. A delegation from the new Weimar Republic, which had replaced Kaiser Wilhelm II in Germany, arrived there only after Wilson and the Allied leaders had prepared the peace treaty for it to sign. Others were totally excluded. Representatives from the recently proclaimed Irish republic failed to receive a hearing of their case for independence from Great Britain. So did the revolutionary Ho Chi Minh, who wanted to emancipate Vietnam from French colonial rule. The Allies, with Wilson's concurrence, intended to exclude the internal affairs of their empires from the agenda.[44]

At the beginning of the peace conference, the president reiterated the redemptive theme of his foreign policy. He called on the Allies to join the United States in a new international order to achieve universal justice and liberty. "In coming into this war," he proclaimed, "the United States never thought for a moment that she was intervening in the politics of Europe, or the politics of Asia, or the politics of any part of the world. Her thought was that all the world had now become conscious that there was a single cause which turned upon issues of this war. That was the cause of justice and liberty for men of every kind and place. Therefore, the United States would feel that her part in this war had been played in vain if there ensued upon it merely a body of European settlements."[45] The heart of Wilson's peace program was the League of Nations. He made the drafting of the Covenant for this postwar international organization his first priority in Paris. But before he could succeed in this task, he needed to accommodate the various interests of the principal Allies, for they did not share his particular conception of global interdependence.

Although the British delegates generally cooperated with Wilson in drafting the Covenant, Prime Minister David Lloyd George forced him to approve a colonial settlement and a naval agreement favorable to the British Empire. The president approved the British idea for a system of mandates under the League because he, too, believed that backward peoples needed the supervision of civilized nations. The mandates for the former German colonies in Africa and the Pacific barely disguised their acquisition by the British, French, Belgian, and Japanese empires. He also agreed not to expand the American navy without consulting the British.

The French premier Georges Clemenceau, who wanted to restore the European balance of power, hoped to transform the League into an anti-German alliance. Although the French delegates failed in that endeavor, Lloyd George and Wilson offered France separate treaties guaranteeing its security against German aggression. Clemenceau also gained their consent for continuing the temporary occupation of the Rhineland under the peace treaty with Germany. Not willing to depend on Wilson's League or German disarmament for French security, Clemenceau preferred these more traditional methods. Rather than relying on the vague promises of Article 10 of the Covenant, which would obligate all nations in the League to respect and preserve the territorial integrity and political independence of each other, the French wanted to establish alliances and strategic frontiers for themselves and also for Poland and Czechoslovakia so as to prevent a resurgent Germany from again threatening its neighbors.

Wilson also made concessions to Italy, although he rejected Premier Vittorio Orlando's claim to the Adriatic city of Fiume. "The whole question," he asserted, "resolved itself into this: we were trying to make peace on an entirely new basis and to establish a new order of international relations. . . . To put Fiume inside Italy would be absolutely inconsistent with the new order of international relations."[46] Failing to persuade Orlando, Wilson appealed over his head to the Italian people. The Italian delegation then left the peace conference.

The unity that Wilson sought on the basis of universal ideals obviously did not exist. The Italians eventually returned to Paris, but only after Orlando had received a vote of confidence from the Italian parliament to demonstrate that he, not Wilson, accurately represented public opinion in his own country. Their temporary absence threatened the president's hopes for the League and consequently prompted him to compromise with the Japanese over the Shantung province of China. He did not want to risk the prospect that Japan as well as Italy might refuse to sign the peace treaty and remain outside the League, for that would shatter even the illusion of its universal character.

Wilson finally succeeded in creating the postwar League, but only by accommodating the national interests of the Allies. Although in theory he emphasized the world's interdependence, in practice he acknowledged its pluralism as well. He could not escape from the dilemma that these two features created.[47]

The Shantung controversy at Paris reflected the ambiguity in Wilson's attitude toward China and Japan. He wanted to protect the political independence and territorial integrity of the Chinese republic and to maintain the Open Door policy of the United States. Although critical of President William Howard Taft's earlier "dollar diplomacy," he, too, endeavored to preserve equal economic opportunities for American merchants and investors in China. Yet, Wilson also sought to avoid conflict with Japan over China. He did not want to pay too high a price to protect American interests there.

At the beginning of the European war in 1914, Japan had declared war against Germany and sent its troops into China to seize the German concessions in Shantung. The United States could not prevent the Japanese from taking advantage of the war to expand their empire at Germany's—and also China's—expense. After consolidating their control over Shantung, the Japanese in January 1915 asked the Chinese government to concede Twenty-one Demands. They wanted its approval not only for the transfer of German rights in Shantung to Japan but also for the previously established Japanese dominance in Manchuria and Inner Mongolia, the concession of new mining and industrial rights in central China, the prohibition of future leaseholds for other powers along the Chinese coast, and the establishment of a virtual Japanese protectorate throughout China. In March, Secretary Bryan expressed American opposition to the Twenty-one Demands, but he also acknowledged a special Japanese interest in northeastern China. After Japan delivered an ultimatum to the Chinese in May, Bryan reminded it of American interests. The United States, he affirmed, would not recognize any Sino-Japanese agreement that violated the rights of American citizens in China, the political and territorial integrity of the Chinese republic, or the Open Door policy. Nevertheless, the Japanese forced the Chinese to concede all of the Twenty-one Demands except for the protectorate. Whether the Wilson administration would acquiesce in these gains, regarding them as Japan's special interests, or oppose them as infringements on American rights in China, remained undetermined. The Lansing-Ishii agreement in November 1917, which encompassed both possible positions, perpetuated this ambiguity.

Wilson began to take a harder line toward Japan as he reacted to its extensive intervention in Siberia. At the peace conference, he attempted to deny its claim to succeed Germany in Shantung. In Paris, the Japanese also demanded the affirmation of racial equality in the League of Nations Covenant. On this issue, the Chinese agreed. But racial prejudice in the British Empire and the United States surfaced as Wilson supported the British in rejecting this principle. After defeating this Japanese proposal, he finally conceded on Shantung. He feared that otherwise Japan might not join the League. This compromise deeply disappointed the Chinese and resulted in their refusal to sign the Versailles Treaty. Clearly, Wilson's vision of a new international order failed to produce harmony in Eastern Asia.[48]

By adjusting to the realities of global politics at the peace conference, the president succeeded in creating the League of Nations. But it did not inaugurate the new era of peace he had promised. Foreign nations still served their own interests rather than accept his particular vision of interdependence. The world's pluralism continued to produce conflict. Germany's strenuous objections to the peace treaty as a breach of the Fourteen Points provided only one example of the perpetual rivalry among nations, which the League did not overcome. The Germans naturally understood the Fourteen Points differently from the Allies or Wilson himself. The Versailles Treaty failed to fulfill their hopes for a "Wilson peace." They signed it on June 28, 1919, only under duress.[49]

Like all statesmen, the president lacked the capacity to redeem the world. He could not control it. There was no universal consensus among nations. Not even all Americans shared his perspective. The peace treaty inevitably resulted in disappointment at home as well as abroad. By his exalted rhetoric, he had fostered false expectations and thereby contributed to postwar disillusionment. In the United States, the Senate, especially critical of the League, rejected the treaty with Germany. Wilson's search for control at home and abroad ended in partial failure. He had extended American influence throughout the world, but never adequately defined a foreign policy for dealing with pluralism as well as interdependence. In a diverse international environment, the United States could not win universal acceptance for its own ideals and practices. It lacked the power to impose them on all nations. Yet it could not ignore foreign threats to its own legitimate interests. In the final analysis, Wilson failed to resolve this fundamental dilemma of American foreign relations in the interdependent and plural world. His legacy included no realistic definition of foreign policy for the United States in the twentieth century.

Part II

Collective Security and the German Problem

CHAPTER 3

WILSON'S LEAGUE OF NATIONS: COLLECTIVE SECURITY AND NATIONAL INDEPENDENCE

Lloyd E. Ambrosius, "Wilson's League of Nations," *Maryland Historical Magazine* 65 (Winter 1970): 369–93. Reprinted by permission of *Maryland Historical Magazine*.

Historians of President Woodrow Wilson's role in the creation of the League of Nations generally have agreed that he sought to revolutionize American foreign policy. They have argued that he abandoned the tradition of isolationism in favor of active participation in world affairs. Noting the system of collective security that he attempted to establish through the League, they have concluded that the president departed radically from the historic policy of the United States.[1] This widely held interpretation has overemphasized Wilson's departure from traditional American diplomacy. He abandoned American isolationism in part—but only in part. By his personal participation in the Paris Peace Conference of 1919 and by his vision of future American participation in the League of Nations, the president obviously altered the traditional policy. Never before had the American government shown such direct and extensive concern for the political and military situation in Europe and elsewhere in the world.

Yet, far more than historians have recognized, Wilson's conception of the League of Nations and of the American role in world affairs continued to reflect the isolationist heritage of the American diplomatic tradition. This interpretation of Wilson is not new. Walter Lippmann, who as the secretary of the Inquiry helped to formulate Wilson's peace program, recognized "the instinctive American isolationist view of Woodrow Wilson." Even while involving the nation in the war and while anticipating the creation of the League, the president retained the isolationist aversion to commitments in Europe. "Wilson," wrote Lippmann, "in spite of the complexity of his character and his mind, was moved by the old American feeling that America is a new land which must not be entangled with Europe."[2] The isolationist heritage continued to influence Wilson's view of the American role in world affairs during the drafting of the Covenant of the League at Paris. His conception of the League of Nations marked only the first, cautious step from traditional isolationism to the military and political commitments that the United States would later assume in NATO.

Wilson believed that American membership in the League would not entangle the United States in European politics because it represented a general commitment rather than a particular obligation. Paying homage to the American isolationist tradition, the president said in New York City on September 27, 1918, that "we still read Washington's immortal warning against "entangling alliances" with full comprehension and an answering purpose. But only special and limited alliances entangle; and we recognize and accept the duty of a new day in which we are permitted to hope for a general alliance which will avoid entanglements and clear the air of the world for common understandings and the maintenance of common rights."[3]

Wilson's belief that the League could guarantee the peace settlement without entangling the United States in European affairs rested in part on his conception of impartial justice for all nations. If the principle of national self-determination, as outlined in his Fourteen Points, was embodied in the peace settlement, Wilson assumed that the problem of enforcement would be minimal. Since such a settlement would render justice to vanquished as well as victor, the League could guarantee it without involving excessive commitments.

In the event that conflicts arose despite the fairness of the settlement, the president thought that moral suasion would most likely suffice to prevent aggression. At the University of Paris on December 21, 1918, he reviewed his position, saying:

> My conception of the league of nations is just this, that it shall operate as the organized moral force of men throughout the world, and that whenever or wherever wrong and aggression are planned or contemplated, this searching light of conscience will be turned upon them and men everywhere will ask, "What are the purposes that you hold in your heart against the fortunes of the world?" Just a little exposure will settle most questions. If the Central powers had dared to discuss the purposes of this war for a single fortnight, it never would have happened, and if, as should be, they were forced to discuss it for a year, war would have been inconceivable.[4]

This exaggerated estimate of the power of moral suasion, as well as Wilson's conception of impartial justice, contributed to his belief that the League could guarantee the peace settlement without entangling the United States in European affairs.

Premier Georges Clemenceau and the French delegates on the League Commission at the peace conference looked with skepticism at Wilson's belief in the efficacy of justice and moral suasion as the principal foundation for an enduring peace. They wanted instead to create a league that would continue the wartime coalition against Germany. Desiring the League to be more than a superparliament that could make decisions without the power to implement them, the French premier wanted to delegate executive authority to the organization and make it capable of action in the event of aggression.[5] Within the French Foreign Office, Léon Bourgeois had headed a commission that formulated plans for such a league. On February 4, 1919, the French foreign minister Stéphen Pichon wrote to Wilson, endorsing the recommendation of the Bourgeois commission. "The French Foreign Office Commission," he explained, "envisioned a League capable of applying effective military as well as diplomatic, juridical, and economic sanctions. That is, the League would be not merely a debating society but against aggression an effective alliance."[6] France, in short, sought to make the League into an anti-German alliance prepared for immediate military action at the direction of its executive.

Despite their differences over methods, Wilson shared with the French leaders the objective of making the League an effective guarantee against aggression. Having expressed that goal as the last of his Fourteen Points, the president pressed for its adoption at Paris as Article 10 of the Covenant. This provision, which Wilson regarded as "the key to the whole Covenant," was his most important contribution to that document. When the League Commission considered this article on February 6, he urged its acceptance despite British opposition and French skepticism.

Under the provisions of Article 10, the members of the League would "undertake to respect and preserve as against external aggression the territorial integrity and existing political independence of all Members of the League." Robert Cecil, a British delegate, attempted to transform this article from a positive into a negative guarantee by an amendment that would remove the obligation for the mutual preservation of territorial integrity and political independence. As he had earlier when Secretary of State Robert Lansing had advanced the same idea, Wilson now rejected this proposal. With the failure of Cecil's amendment, Ferdinand Larnaude, a French delegate, proceeded to criticize Article 10 from the opposite side as "only a principle." He wanted the Covenant to stipulate some method for the implementation of the objective should that become necessary. In response to his demand, the Commission ultimately agreed that in the event of aggression the Council of the League of Nations should recommend the means for the fulfillment of the obligation. In accordance with other parts of the Covenant, however, the Council could offer advice only with the unanimous approval of its members and even then the Council's decision would not bind the members of the League. In other words, if the United States had joined the League as Wilson planned, Article 10 would have imposed no definite obligations except those approved by the American government in the Council and then accepted by it as a recommendation from the Council. Even that kind of a commitment had seemed too strong for Cecil, while it appeared too weak for Larnaude. Wilson's position lay between those two extremes.[7]

Wilson never disclosed the precise degree to which he felt Article 10 would have obligated the United States to use military force to protect the members of the League against aggression. David Hunter Miller, who served as the legal adviser to the president during the drafting of the Covenant, wrote that "the very general notion that Article 10 of the Covenant is a guarantee against invasion is entirely erroneous."[8]

Yet, Wilson apparently regarded Article 10 as sufficiently binding to commit the United States to the employment of military force should that become necessary to prevent a repetition of the experience of World War I. He made his most explicit assertions in response to statements by Larnaude and Bourgeois expressing concern for French security. The president affirmed, at a meeting of the League Commission on February 11, that: "It must not be supposed that any of the members of the league will remain isolated if it is attacked, that is the direct contrary of the thought of all of us. We are ready to fly to the assistance of those who are attacked, but we cannot offer more than the condition of the world enables us to give." He further asserted that: "All that we can promise, and we do promise it, is to maintain our military forces in such a condition that the world will feel itself in safety. When danger comes, we too will come, and we will help you, but you must trust us. We must all depend on our mutual good faith."[9] This latter statement, in which Wilson specifically mentioned military force with particular reference to France, doubtless explained his later willingness to join with David Lloyd George in offering France a security treaty. The president had broken from the isolationist tradition at least so far as Western Europe was concerned.[10]

Although anticipating the possible future use of American military power in a situation similar to that of World War I, Wilson remained vague and indefinite with regard to other circumstances and other parts of the world. During an address in Salt Lake City on September 23, 1919, when explaining the obligations the United States would assume under Article 10, he declared:

> If you want to put out a fire in Utah, you do not send to Oklahoma for the fire engine. If you want to put out a fire in the Balkans, if you want to stamp out the smoldering flame in some part of central Europe, you do not send to the United States for troops. The council of the League selects the powers which are most ready, most available, most suitable, and selects them only at their own consent so that the United States would in no such circumstances conceivably be drawn in unless the flame spread to the world. And would they then be left out, even if they were not members of the League?[11]

The president, in other words, anticipated no greater American military involvement in Central and Eastern Europe under Article 10 than if the Covenant had not been drafted.

Wilson hoped that the League could guarantee the national self-determination of its members through peaceful means rather than military force. In accordance with his view, which he shared with the British government, Articles 12–15 of the Covenant provided methods for the pacific settlement of disputes between the members of the League. Article 12 obligated them to refrain from war until after one of three methods for a peaceful resolution of the conflict had been attempted. The League members might submit the issue to arbitration or to an international court (Article 13), or they might refer it to the Council (Article 15). These provisions did not provide for the compulsory settlement of disputes. The only obligation on the League members was that they attempt a settlement through one of the three pacific methods before resorting to war. As Cecil noted, "All that the Covenant proposed was that the members of the League, before going to war, should try all pacific means of settling the quarrel."[12] If the dispute were submitted to arbitration or to judicial settlement and one of the parties refused to accept the decision, the responsibility for implementing it devolved on the Council of the League. From the perspective of the British and American representatives, however, this obligation for the implementation of a decision appeared minimal. They assumed that the most serious disputes would not be submitted to arbitration or to an international court but instead would go directly to the Council in accordance with Article 15. And the commitments under that article were strictly limited.[13]

On February 6 and 7, when the League Commission considered the provisions for the pacific settlement of disputes, the Belgian delegate, Paul Hymans, offered some substantial amendments to the Anglo-American draft of the Covenant. He wanted to empower the Council to recommend the settlement of a dispute by a majority rather than a unanimous decision. He thus hoped to avert the possibility that the opposition of a single member of the Council—in addition to the parties to the dispute since they were prohibited from voting—could prevent it from even recommending a settlement, for in that case the peace machinery of the League would break down. As his second amendment, the Belgian delegate sought to obligate the League members to accept a unanimous recommendation of the Council. In essence, he proposed compulsory arbitration in all cases in which the Council reached unanimous agreement on the terms of the settlement.[14]

Both of the Belgian amendments received the support of the French delegates, who shared with Hymans the desire to strengthen the League Council. But neither Wilson nor Cecil conceded the American or British right of veto within the Council or accepted the principle of compulsory arbitration. The League Commission, failing to reach a final decision on the Belgian amendments, referred them to a subcommittee for further consideration. Prior to the meeting of the subcommittee, David Hunter Miller of the United States met with Eustace Percy of Great Britain to discuss the Belgian proposals and to coordinate the Anglo-American opposition. On the subcommittee, which included no American members, Robert Cecil represented the Anglo-American position with a fair degree of success. The report of the subcommittee, which was presented to the League Commission on February 10, excluded the provision for a majority recommendation by the Council. In response to the second Belgian amendment, however, the report made a minor concession in the form of an addition to Article 15. This article already provided that in the event the Council rendered a unanimous recommendation for the settlement of a dispute, the members of the League should not go to war against any nation that complied with that decision. The subcommittee now added to this negative obligation the positive obligation that "if any party shall refuse so to comply [with a unanimous Council decision], the Council shall consider what steps can best be taken to give effect to their recommendation." At its meeting on the tenth, the League Commission adopted this part of the subcommittee's report for incorporation in Article 15 of the Covenant.[15]

Although temporarily accepting this positive obligation, President Wilson later moved to extract it from the Covenant. He wanted the Council to assume no responsibility for the enforcement of even a unanimous recommendation for the settlement of a dispute. His aversion to the enforcement of even a decision in which the United States would necessarily concur revealed the isolationist heritage in Wilson's conception of the League of Nations. At a private meeting with Cecil on March 18, with House and Miller also attending, the president proposed a revision of Article 15 to remove the positive obligation for enforcement that the League Commission had adopted on February 10. After securing the support of the British delegate, Wilson introduced this revision in the League Commission on March 24 and obtained its acceptance. Although the French delegates raised no issue on this point, the president's aversion to any obligations for the implementation of even a unanimous Council recommendation brought into question the extent to which he felt committed under Article 10. His position on Article 15 certainly showed that Wilson hoped to limit American obligations within the League.[16]

Hymans offered a third amendment that further clarified the limits of the obligations under Article 10. The Anglo-American draft had provided for sanctions by members of the League against any nation that resorted to war before attempting a settlement through one of the three pacific methods under Articles 12–15. The Belgian delegate now proposed the extension of these sanctions under Article 16 to cover a breach of Article 10 as well. President Wilson led the opposition to this amendment. He did not want the sanctions of Article 16, including the severance of commercial and financial relations and the prohibition of personal contacts, to apply to Article 10. He approved the employment of sanctions, including possible military force, for the limited purpose of requiring the parties to a dispute to submit it to arbitration, to an international court, or to the Council of the League. But he absolutely opposed any automatic sanctions against violators of Article 10, for he thought that guarantee might be fulfilled without the necessity of sanctions. The president succeeded in defeating the third Belgian amendment, thereby limiting the application of sanctions. Accordingly, the provisions for sanctions under Article 16 referred only to Articles 12–15, not to Article 10.[17]

During the drafting of the Covenant in February 1919, the issue of disarmament revealed the sharpest divergence between the French and the Anglo-American conceptions of the League of Nations. President Wilson had, in the fourth of the Fourteen Points, called for the reduction of national military forces to "the lowest point consistent with domestic safety." The League and disarmament were complementary features of his peace program. With the guarantee of their political independence and territorial integrity under Article 10, Wilson believed the League members could reduce the size of their armed forces. Rather than facing the possible necessity of defending itself, each member would need a military force only for the maintenance of internal order and for the fulfillment of joint obligations under the Covenant. The establishment of the League would thus facilitate disarmament.[18] Lloyd George shared the president's view of the close relationship between the League and disarmament. At a meeting of the Imperial War Cabinet on December 25, 1918, the British prime minister had said that "if the League of Nations did not include some provision for disarmament it would be regarded as a sham." He further asserted that "disarmament would be regarded as the real test of whether the League of Nations was a farce, or whether business was meant." The British as well as the American government thus anticipated disarmament as a consequence of the formation of the League of Nations.[19]

While the American and British leaders looked toward disarmament under the League of Nations, the French government hoped to transform it into a military alliance. Clemenceau and the French members of the League Commission sought to maintain the effectiveness of the wartime coalition against Germany rather than to reduce the armed forces of the League members. The divergence between the Anglo-American and the French standards for measuring the success of the League became apparent during the consideration of Article 8 of the Covenant. On February 11, Bourgeois introduced two amendments that would have radically changed this disarmament article. In accordance with the French conception of the League as an alliance, he proposed the maintenance of an international force prepared for immediate military action. Second, he called for international control under the League of the military establishments of its members. This second amendment possessed the dual purpose of empowering the League to inspect disarmament and to require a nation to maintain adequate armed forces for the fulfillment of its obligations under the Covenant. The French thus desired the League to place minimum as well as maximum limits on the strength of national military forces.[20]

Within the League Commission, the French amendments encountered the hostile criticism of the American and British delegates. Although asserting the determination of the United States to fulfill its obligations under the Covenant, President Wilson strongly opposed either an international force or any international control of the military forces of the League members. He did not want to substitute "international militarism for national militarism." Nor did he wish to permit the control of any American armed forces by the League or to assume any responsibility for the inspection of the military establishments of other League members. In opposing the French amendments, Wilson sought to minimize the definite commitments for enforcement under the Covenant. Like Lloyd George, he identified the League with disarmament rather than with extensive military obligations for the enforcement of the peace settlement.

This Anglo-American conception ran directly counter to the French view. "The idea of an international force," asserted Larnaude in defense of the French amendments, "is bound up with the very idea of the League of Nations, unless one is content that the League should be a screen of false security." The French government cared little whether the League permitted or required its members to disarm as long as it afforded security to them. From the French perspective, the enforcement of the peace settlement, not disarmament, should serve as the standard for measuring the success of the League. And to achieve that purpose, the French leaders believed the League needed a military force ready for immediate action.[21]

Failing to reach agreement on February 11, the League Commission referred the French amendments to the drafting committee, which met on the following day. At that time Cecil frankly told Larnaude that France should drop its amendments and appreciate the more limited commitments that the United States and Great Britain were prepared to offer. He warned the French delegate that the American—and, to a lesser extent, the British—government might ignore altogether the problems of Europe unless France accepted the assistance of the United States and Great Britain on their own terms. As a partial concession, Cecil renewed the proposal, which he had made in the League Commission on the previous day, to create a permanent commission under the League to advise on military questions. That commission would possess no power either to effect disarmament or to coordinate military planning by the members of the League; it could only offer advice. This British proposal fell so far short of the French desire for international supervision of the military forces of the League members that Larnaude refused to accept it.[22]

Since the drafting committee failed to resolve the issue, the French amendments again came before the League Commission on February 13. At this session, the French delegates continued to press their amendments, while Cecil urged the acceptance of his limited proposal of a permanent commission. In the absence of Wilson, Colonel House supported the British position but without taking an active part in the discussion. Bourgeois and Larnaude, advocating the amendment that provided for the control or verification of the military establishments of the League members, noted that the provisions for the pacific settlement of disputes and for sanctions assumed that even the League members might violate the Covenant. To guard against that danger, Bourgeois urged the adoption of international inspection. He said that "by a thorough-going supervision of armaments the League of Nations would discourage any attempt at war. On the other hand, if such verification were not established every ambitious State, or State of imperialistic leanings, would have plenty of time to organise itself secretly and to proceed with a sudden attack. War would be encouraged by the lack of such verification."[23] The League Commission, however, rejected this French amendment in favor of Cecil's proposal for a permanent commission. In accordance with this decision, Article 9 of the Covenant provided for the creation of a permanent commission to advise the Council concerning disarmament and military questions generally.[24]

After their initial failure, the French delegates next urged the formation of an international force. Reviewing the proposal, Bourgeois said that because of "the risk of sudden aggressions," the French government "insisted upon the necessity of having certainly and constantly not only an international army, but national contingents of the different associated nations ready to act because if we wait until concerted action be established between various military authorities ... it is certain that very much time will elapse before the associated contingents become effective."[25] In support of this amendment, Larnaude argued that the effectiveness of the League as a deterrent against war depended on its preparation for military action. If the League was to guarantee the political independence and territorial integrity of its members, it needed to be an effective military alliance. "Unfortunately," he said, "right by itself can do nothing but enhance great injustices."

Accordingly, the French delegates advocated the establishment of at least a general staff under the League to prepare for immediate military operations in the event of aggression. This French amendment for military preparedness, and the conception of the League that it assumed, conflicted directly with the Anglo-American view. "The League of Nations," asserted Cecil, "could not be considered as an alliance against Germany. Nothing would more quickly imperil peace." Again, the Anglo-American conception of the League prevailed. The League Commission voted to reject the French amendment, thereby excluding any military planning by the League in advance of a crisis. In harmony with Wilson's view, the League Commission relegated military force to a distinctly secondary position in the maintenance of the peace settlement.[26]

After the completion of the drafting of the Covenant, President Wilson, as chairman of the League Commission, presented it to the plenary session of the peace conference on February 14, 1919. Describing the general character of the League, he noted that "throughout this instrument we are depending primarily and chiefly upon one great force, and that is the moral force of the public opinion of the world." Moral suasion, in accordance with the Anglo-American conception, would serve as the principal method for the enforcement of the Covenant. Yet, he observed that military force might play a role in the League. "Armed force," said the president, "is in the background in this programme, but it is in the background, and if the moral force of the world will not suffice, the physical force of the world shall. But that is the last resort, because this is intended as a constitution of peace, not as a League of War." Despite the lack of emphasis on military force and the indefinite character of the obligations of the Covenant, Wilson thought the League would maintain peace and prevent aggression. Referring to the Covenant, he said that "while it is elastic, while it is general in its terms, it is definite in the one thing that we were called upon to make definite. It is a definite guarantee of peace. It is a definite guarantee by word against aggression."[27]

The president had still not convinced the French leaders that the League would fulfill the goals that he proclaimed. At the plenary session, Bourgeois observed that

France shared the principles of political independence and territorial integrity. "If, however, we wish these principles to triumph, if we wish them to be guarded by effective guarantees," he asserted, "it is not enough to proclaim them—we must further organize a system of jurisdiction and action alike in order to defend them." Accordingly, he reiterated the French arguments in favor of the verification of disarmament, and he renewed the French plea for the establishment of an international force. To achieve its goals, the French leaders thought the League needed to become an effective alliance with the capacity to take immediate military action. Yet, this advice failed to convince either Wilson or Lloyd George that the Covenant needed revisions.[28]

Later that month, André Tardieu, Clemenceau's closest associate and adviser at the peace conference, drafted a memorandum on the problem of French security. In this memorandum, dated February 25, Tardieu offered an explicit criticism of the League as outlined in the Covenant. He noted that the methods for the pacific settlement of disputes and for sanctions applied only to the members of the League. Although other nations such as Germany might, under Article 17 of the Covenant, assume the responsibilities of membership for the purpose of settling a particular controversy, they had no obligation to do so. The cooling-off period, during which Wilson thought moral suasion could effect a settlement, might therefore never begin. But even if Germany became a League member, the French leaders feared the possibility of a sudden attack.

Although granting that the League would ensure final victory in the event of future German aggression, Tardieu pointed to the failure of the Covenant to provide methods for an immediate military response. He warned that before any American troops could be sent to aid France, the Council of the League would need to reach a decision, the president must concur in the recommendation and deliver a message to the Congress, the Congress must then declare war, and finally the United States would have to mobilize a military force and transport it to Europe. This delay would place a premium on a sudden attack. Tardieu here touched on a most devastating criticism of the Anglo-American conception of the League of Nations. Wilson and Cecil argued that the League would maintain peace and prevent aggression primarily by providing for a cooling-off period during which moral suasion could operate. Yet, by making no provision for an immediate military response, the Covenant encouraged a potential aggressor to mount a sudden attack.

In short, the provisions for the pacific settlement of a dispute through a delay and the operation of moral suasion would work as long as nations adhered to the Covenant, but this would break down as soon as the nations defied the League. The League would then fail as "a definite guarantee of peace" and "against aggression" at the very moment when its guarantees were most needed. Tardieu consequently called for the separation of the Rhineland from Germany and for the occupation of this territory by Allied troops, but he failed to convince the American and British governments of the necessity for these military measures.[29]

Following the presentation of the Covenant to the plenary session on February 14, President Wilson returned to the United States for a month. Here, he encountered criticism of the League from members of the Senate. In the hope of overcoming this opposition, the president, on his return to Paris, sought revisions of the Covenant. He hoped to clarify the terms of that document without making any basic changes in the character of the League. Accordingly, he secured provisions that permitted the members of the League to withdraw on two years' notice and that prohibited the League from interfering in the domestic affairs of its members.

As the most important revision, Wilson called for the explicit recognition of the Monroe Doctrine. Before the League Commission, he defended this change by saying that "the Covenant provides that the members of the League will mutually defend each other in respect of their political and their territorial integrity. This Covenant is therefore the highest tribute to the Monroe Doctrine, for it is an international extension of that principle by which the United States said that it would protect the political independence and territorial integrity of other American States."[30] On April 10, the president introduced an amendment to Article 10 that mentioned the Monroe Doctrine by name and stated that nothing in the Covenant conflicted with its validity.

This proposal provoked criticism especially from the French delegates, who feared that the recognition of the Monroe Doctrine would justify traditional American isolationism. "It would certainly be very unfortunate," said Larnaude, "if the Monroe Doctrine should be interpreted to mean that the United States could not participate in any settlement of European affairs decided upon by the League." Wilson sought to convince the French delegates that the specific recognition of the Monroe Doctrine would not result in American indifference toward European affairs. Although he maintained the distinction between the Old and New Worlds, the president had departed from the isolationist tradition to the extent that he recognized a relationship between American and French security. "I again assure M. Larnaude," he pledged, "that if the United States signs this document it is solemnly obliged to render aid in European troubles when the territorial integrity of European States is threatened by external aggression." Robert Cecil, recognizing that a part of the French objection to the amendment stemmed from its connection with Article 10, suggested that the reference to the Monroe Doctrine be made in a separate article. The amendment would then avoid the appearance of weakening Article 10. In accordance with Cecil's recommendation, the League Commission, on the following day, adopted Wilson's amendment as Article 21 of the Covenant.[31]

During March and April 1919, while Wilson sought revisions of the Covenant to meet the Senate objections, the French delegates renewed their pleas for military preparedness under the League. Having retreated from their earlier demand for an international force, they wanted now at least the formation of a general staff. Even if the League could not take military action on its own initiative, the French leaders hoped it at least could prepare advance plans. The American members of the League Commission continued to react strongly against this proposal. Following a private meeting with Bourgeois, Colonel House expressed his opposition in his diary. "What he wants," recorded House, "that is what the French want, is to make the League an instrument for war instead of an instrument for peace. Also to make it a league against Germany and for the benefit of France. They desire to create a general staff with authority to plan all sorts of military defenses, invasions and whatnot."[32]

Although opposing the French conception of the League as an alliance, House envisioned some future American participation in European affairs through the League. Indeed, he said, "the only excuse we could give for meddling in European or world affairs was a league of nations through which we hope to prevent wars. If that was not to be, then we would not care to mix again in their difficulties."[33] This conception of the League revealed an instinctive isolationism, for it assumed that the United States could refrain from participation in European or world affairs. House reflected Wilson's view of the League. The president opposed any obligations beyond those that had been incorporated in the Covenant before February 14. With the support of House and Cecil, he rejected the French proposal for a general staff.[34]

On April 28, the League Commission reported the Covenant to the plenary session of the peace conference for final action. At this time, Bourgeois continued to criticize the Covenant, which incorporated the Anglo-American rather than the French conception of the League. He said that advocates of the League such as Wilson

> asked that the most complete liberty should be left to each nation; according to them the settlement of conflicts by pacific methods did not become obligatory, nor was any operative penalty to be imposed on a State which failed in the obligations which it had undertaken; they relied essentially on the moral influence which opinion throughout the world would exercise, thanks to the public deliberations of the International Council, in order to insure the free consent of each State to the execution of the measures recommended on behalf of them all. There were grounds for fearing that a conception of this kind could only lead to ineffective results.[35]

To increase the effectiveness of the League in the enforcement of the peace settlement, Bourgeois once again introduced the French amendments for the verification of disarmament and for the establishment of a general staff. But the plenary session, like the League Commission earlier, rejected these proposals. The Covenant of the League of Nations, as finally adopted, remained substantially that of February 14, except for the revisions that Wilson had introduced. And even those changes had not altered the basic character of the League.[36]

Within the American Commission, President Wilson had failed to convince all of the delegates of the efficacy of his League. Henry White, a career diplomat and the one Republican member of the delegation, doubted that the League would become an effective deterrent against aggression and war. Although always loyal to the president and distrustful of French motives, he shared the French skepticism about the League. White believed Wilson had failed at the Paris Peace Conference "because he is a one-idea man, and thought the League of Nations would be the sovereign panacea for the world's tragedy which he could not prevent, but a repetition of which he hoped might be thereby prevented; and he staked everything on its establishment."[37]

Secretary of State Robert Lansing shared White's conviction that the president attached too much importance to the League. Yet, his criticism, unlike White's, showed no appreciation for the French position. Rather than opposing the potential ineffectiveness of the League, Lansing denounced it as an alliance. Especially critical of Article 10, he thought the Covenant provided for the continuation of the wartime coalition of the major powers in violation of the principle of equality of all nations, small as well as great. He opposed a League in which the major powers would play the leading roles. Lansing believed Wilson had betrayed his earlier vision of the League and had fallen into the snare of European diplomacy. On May 6, 1919, the secretary of state recorded his objections to Wilson's League. "Even the measure of idealism, with which the League of Nations was at first impregnated," wrote Lansing,

> has, under the influence and intrigue of ambitious statesmen of the Old World, been supplanted by an open recognition that force and selfishness are primary elements in international cooperation. The League has succumbed to this reversion to a cynical materialism. It is no longer a creature of idealism. Its very source and reason have been dried up and have almost disappeared. The danger is that it will become a bulwark of the old order, a check upon all efforts to bring man again under the influence of idealism, which he has lost.[38]

In his account of *The Peace Negotiations,* Lansing summarized the differences between his and Wilson's conceptions of the League of Nations. "The mutual guaranty" of Article 10, he wrote,

> from its affirmative nature compelled in fact, though not in form, the establishment of a ruling group, a coalition of the Great Powers, and denied, though not in terms, the equality of nations. The oligarchy was the logical result of entering into the guaranty or the guaranty was the logical result of the creation of the oligarchy through the perpetuation of the basic idea of the Supreme War Council. No distinction was made as to a state of war and a state of peace. Strongly opposed to the abandonment of the principle of the equality of nations in times of peace I naturally opposed the affirmative guaranty and endeavored to persuade the President to accept as a substitute for it a self-denying or negative covenant which amounted to a promise of "hands-off" and in no way required the formation of an international oligarchy to make it effective.[39]

By his distrust of Old World diplomacy and by his opposition to Article 10, Secretary Lansing adhered to traditional American isolationism more resolutely than the president himself. Although White and Lansing privately expressed disapproval of Wilson's conception of the League, neither of them offered constructive alternatives.

General Tasker H. Bliss, the fifth member of the American Commission, generally approved Wilson's League and consequently offered neither criticism nor alternatives. Although recognizing the lack of confidence among French leaders in the League of Nations, Bliss merely advised them to strengthen their faith. He explained: "One can only say to them to have faith in a League of Nations and to heartily work for the establishment of such a League, which will put the power of the world behind every state that is threatened with wanton aggression. But to this they only shrug their shoulders. They do not seem to have the slightest real faith in the efficacy of a League of Nations."[40] When referring to "the power of the world," Bliss, although a four-star general, thought no more in military terms than Wilson. He had earlier written that "I am of those who believe that disarmament and a League of Nations go hand in hand. There can be no fair and free discussion of anything till that is settled .... The American principle, I am inclined to think, is a League of Nations with equal representation. How can you give equal representation with some nations weak and other with millions of trained soldiers or fleets of battleships or both?"[41] General Bliss thus shared the president's conviction that the League could achieve its purpose without relying heavily on military power.

A fundamental dichotomy characterized Wilson's conception of the League of Nations. On the one hand, he stressed the goals that he thought the League would achieve, while, on the other, he emphasized the lack of any definite obligation for the use of military force to achieve such goals. In reporting the Versailles Treaty, including the Covenant, to the Senate on July 10, 1919, the president said that the League would create "such a continuing concert of free nations as would make wars of aggression and spoilation [*sic*] such as this that has just ended forever impossible."[42] Yet, in a subsequent report to the Senate on July 29, Wilson noted that "the Covenant of the League of Nations provides for military action for the protection of its members only upon advice of the Council of the League—advice given, it is to be presumed, only upon deliberation and acted upon by each of the governments of the member States only if its own judgment justifies such action."[43]

Wilson attempted to escape from the dichotomy inherent in the League by resorting to the distinction between a moral and a legal commitment. At a conference with the Senate Foreign Relations Committee on August 19, he asserted that

> the United States will, indeed, undertake under article 10 to "respect and preserve as against external aggression the territorial integrity and existing political independence of all members of the league," and that engagement constitutes a very grave and solemn moral obligation. But it is a moral, not a legal, obligation, and leaves our Congress absolutely free to put its own interpretation upon it in all cases that call for action. It is binding in conscience only, not in law.[44]

Republican Senators William Borah, Philander Knox, and Warren G. Harding focused the attention of the committee on the discrepancy between the goals and the methods of Wilson's League. They recognized that as a matter of policy the United States and other members of the League either would or would not be obligated to take military action in the event of external aggression against a League member. If they were obligated, as Wilson claimed when he spoke of the moral commitment, then the United States would not enjoy the freedom of choice that the president asserted when he referred to legal commitments. By contrast, if the League members were not obligated to use military force, then the League would not possess the value of a deterrent that Wilson claimed for it. In short, they recognized that the League could not guarantee the objectives that Wilson proclaimed without involving more obligations than the Covenant specified. For them, the president's compromise between the departure from and the adherence to the American isolationist tradition was inadequate, for the League would either involve more obligations than they desired or fail to guarantee the national self-determination of all its members.[45]

At the Paris Peace Conference of 1919, President Wilson had obviously modified the American isolationist tradition. His concern for the political and military affairs of Europe and his plan for American participation in the League of Nations documented that fact. But the departure was not complete, for the Covenant lacked precise commitments except of a limited nature. The president retained an instinctive isolationist aversion to involvement in the politics of the Old World. During the drafting of the Covenant, he succeeded in limiting the legal obligations that the United States would have assumed in becoming a member of the League. He reserved in particular the complete freedom of choice in the use of military force. Although he had abandoned the isolationist tradition to the extent that he endorsed a separate treaty guaranteeing French security against German aggression, Wilson avoided similar commitments elsewhere in the world. The Covenant of the League included no such definite obligation.

During the conference with the Senate Foreign Relations Committee, the president acknowledged his instinctively isolationist attitude toward Europe. Senator Harry New asked, "Was it the policy of the American delegates to avoid participation by the United States in strictly European questions and their settlement?" In response, Wilson affirmed that "it certainly was our endeavor to keep free from European affairs."[46] His conception of collective security constituted only the first stage in the transition of American thought. With respect to military and political commitments in Europe, Wilson's League of Nations went beyond the total aversion of traditional isolationism but stopped far short of the definite obligations later assumed in NATO.

CHAPTER 4

WILSON, CLEMENCEAU, AND THE GERMAN
PROBLEM AT THE PARIS PEACE
CONFERENCE OF 1919

Lloyd E. Ambrosius, "Wilson, Clemenceau, and the German Problem at the Paris Peace Conference of 1919," *The Rocky Mountain Social Science Journal* 12 (April 1975): 69–79. Reprinted by permission of the Western Social Science Association.

At the Paris Peace Conference of 1919, President Woodrow Wilson and Premier Georges Clemenceau approached the German problem from fundamentally different perspectives. The French premier recognized that despite its recent defeat, Germany possessed the potential capacity to reemerge as a dominant European power. Although Germany did not immediately threaten French security, Clemenceau wanted to draft a peace treaty designed to protect France in the future and to provide for its enforcement. Wilson, seeing a defeated Germany, failed to appreciate Clemenceau's concern for the future security of France. Confusing ends and means, he considered the French emphasis on the necessity for adequate methods of enforcing the peace settlement as evidence of punitive aims. What Clemenceau saw as a requirement for future security, Wilson viewed as an act of revenge and a violation of the liberal world order he hoped to establish under the League of Nations. The president failed to recognize that he and Clemenceau disagreed more fundamentally over the methods for achieving their shared goals than over the goals themselves. They both hoped to achieve a permanent peace with Germany but advocated different means to accomplish that end.

American and German historians have shared Wilson's misperception of his controversy with Clemenceau over the German problem at the peace conference. They, too, have ignored Germany's potential threat to French security after World War I. Underestimating this problem, they have invariably seen Clemenceau as the villain of the peacemaking. The authorized biographers of Wilson, William E. Dodd and Ray Stannard Baker, first offered the interpretation that subsequent American historians have followed. According to Dodd, Clemenceau represented "the old diplomacy, the old balance of power and sharp political bargaining. He swore eternal enmity to everything German; he vowed anew that France should have her reparation, that no illusions of a better world order, no league of nations should swerve him an inch from his course." Dodd viewed the president, in contrast, as the advocate of a liberal peace designed to protect the integrity of Germany and to avoid the provocation of a future world war. From this perspective, the drama of the Paris Peace Conference of 1919 resulted from the confrontation between the French premier and the American president. "It was Wilson versus Clemenceau," wrote Dodd, "with Italy on the side of Clemenceau, and Lloyd George wavering."[1]

Offering the same interpretation, Baker drew a sharp distinction between the Old Diplomacy of Europe and the New Diplomacy of the United States. In his view, Clemenceau epitomized the evils of the former and Wilson the virtues of the latter. To achieve an enduring peace, Baker assumed, the United States needed to moderate the extravagant French demands and to preserve a stable, prosperous, and, hence, powerful Germany.[2]

Subsequent historians have refined the arguments, but they have not escaped the framework of New versus Old Diplomacy. They have continued to interpret the peace conference as a contest between Wilson's liberal and Clemenceau's Carthaginian peace. George B. Noble, although far more sensitive to France's concern for security than most American historians, noted the limiting influence of French public opinion on Clemenceau's freedom to approve "a bonafide application of Wilsonism." He argued:

> The "problem of Germany" could not be solved by halting, halfway measures, whether applied to armistice terms, food and raw materials policy or military provisions. Yet an overwrought, highly suspicious and ill-informed French public would scarcely permit its government to pursue a far-sighted policy with regard to any of these. Nor could a policy acceptable to patriotic French opinion be fitted into the context of policies acceptable to France's war-time allies and associates. The "problem" was therefore destined to drag on throughout the Conference and into the post-war world.

Because of the "antagonistic Allied policies" in Paris and the isolationist tradition and "partisan politics at home," Noble concluded that "the Wilsonian ideology suffered a double defeat."[3]

Developing this theme, Paul Birdsall viewed the Versailles Treaty as "the outcome of the struggle between Wilsonian principles of a new world order and the principles of reactionary nationalism."[4] Even Thomas A. Bailey criticized only the president's methods, not his frame of reference. "Wilson had a noble vision," he concluded, "but he made the tragic mistake of thinking that mankind, without the proper preparation and education, could attain a kind of international millennium at a single bound."[5] Arthur S. Link likewise emphasized the conflict between "Wilsonian idealism" and "Allied ambitions."[6] Arthur Walworth similarly contrasted the altruistic Wilsonian goals with those of the Allies by interpreting Wilson's participation in the peace conference as the New World returning to redeem the Old.[7] Clemenceau remained the villain for Seth P. Tillman as he concluded that "Britain and the United States were responsible for the most enlightened, most progressive, and most moral features of the treaties of peace."[8]

More than he recognized, Arno J. Mayer adhered to the traditional perspective. He contrasted Wilson, "who was religiously dedicated to the New Diplomacy," with the conservative adherents of the Old Diplomacy. Instead of a Carthaginian or "punitive peace" espoused by the European Allies, especially France, the president pursued "a middle, reformist solution" to peacemaking. Yet, he failed in this pursuit, Mayer asserted, because of his growing apprehension of Bolshevism. "It now appeared that Lenin's indictment of Wilson and Wilsonianism was not altogether without merit."

Mayer concluded: "However reluctantly, the President was one of the chief movers of the counterrevolutionary enterprise." Although depicting Wilson's betrayal during the peace conference of the principles he had earlier articulated, Mayer continued to view the wartime and postwar diplomacy from the perspective—which Wilson as well as the European socialists had shared—of New versus Old Diplomacy.[9]

Adopting a similar dichotomy for his interpretation, N. Gordon Levin, Jr., contrasted "the progressive values of liberal-internationalism," which Wilson epitomized, with "the atavistic values of traditional European imperialism." Especially critical of Clemenceau, Levin denounced "the French position of an extremely punitive peace." He thought it was necessary for the United States to moderate the "extreme French demands," including "extorting the largest possible reparations from Germany." The president's "crucial" task at the peace conference was "to check Allied imperialism" and to reintegrate Germany into "a new world order." Like previous American historians, and like Wilson himself, Levin saw a "reintegrationist" or a "punitive approach" as the only options open to the peacemakers of 1919.[10]

From a similar viewpoint, the German historian Klaus Schwabe believed that there was a "Wilson peace" that could have been realized after World War I. If the Armistice had not reduced Germany to impotence, and if the United States had cooperated with Germany to thwart the extreme demands of the European Allies, he contended, the peace conference could have drafted a "Wilson peace" instead of the Versailles Treaty.[11] By interpreting the peacemaking within the framework of New versus Old Diplomacy, all of these historians have accepted the basic assumptions of Wilson's own perspective.

Recent scholarship on German diplomacy during the war has pointed toward a different conclusion. Hans W. Gatzke and Fritz Fischer argued persuasively that Germany, because of the combination of its war aims and its power, seriously jeopardized the security of France.[12] Despite the disagreements among European historians over the details of this interpretation, they have generally agreed that Germany threatened to destroy the balance of power and to establish its hegemony in Europe.[13] Moreover, as Gerhard L. Weinberg has demonstrated, the defeat of Germany in 1918 did not destroy its potential for endangering French security in the future.[14] Contrary to the assumption of President Wilson and of the American and German historians who have adhered to the Wilsonian framework of New versus Old Diplomacy, that problem continued after the war.

Because of their contrasting perceptions of the German problem, Wilson and Clemenceau approached the peace conference from different perspectives. The president assumed that his major task was to moderate the extravagant claims of the Allies. He failed to recognize that the United States needed, in addition, to provide France with a definite guarantee against the resurgence of Germany. Wilson, of course, never denied the importance of French security but simply attached little urgency to this question. Clemenceau, by contrast, devoted his attention single-mindedly to the German problem. Wanting to ensure the permanence of the victory, he focused on the methods for the enforcement of the Versailles Treaty. American and German historians, interpreting the peacemaking of 1919 from a dualistic perspective and accepting the dichotomy of New versus Old Diplomacy, have contrasted the goals of Wilson and Clemenceau. They have failed to recognize that the central differences between the American president and the French premier concerned the methods of enforcing the Versailles Treaty. Even their disagreements over the terms of the peace settlement reflected their more fundamental differences over its enforcement. The contest between Wilson and Clemenceau at the peace conference was real but not, as historians have previously assumed, that of a farsighted American statesman versus a paranoid French nationalist. The problem of French security was genuine, not Clemenceau's fabrication to justify revenge against a weak and defeated Germany.

Wilson and Clemenceau, because of their divergent views on the question of enforcement, advocated contrasting conceptions of the League of Nations. Under his vision of world organization, the president hoped that moral suasion would prevent future aggression and preserve peace. On the eve of the peace conference, he announced, "My conception of the league of nations is just this, that it shall operate as the organized moral force of men throughout the world, and that whenever or wherever wrong and aggression are planned or contemplated, this searching light of conscience will be turned upon them .... Just a little exposure will settle most questions."[15]

Wilson succeeded, with British assistance, in writing his conception of collective security into the Covenant of the League of Nations. As he presented that document to the plenary session of the peace conference on February 14, 1919, he summarized its general character, observing that "throughout this instrument we are depending primarily and chiefly upon one great force, and that is the moral force of the public opinion of the world." At the same time, he acknowledged that the League might resort to military power. "Armed force is in the background in this programme," he said, "but it is in the background, and if the moral force of the world will not suffice, the physical force of the world shall. But that is the last resort, because this is intended as a constitution of peace, not as a League of War."[16]

Wilson regarded Article 10 as "the key to the whole Covenant." Yet, he emphasized that it imposed no definite military obligation on the United States. Attempting to explain to the Senate Foreign Relations Committee how the League of Nations could guarantee the collective security of its members while each of them retained complete freedom to interpret its military commitments, Wilson resorted to the dubious distinction between moral and legal obligations. He asserted:

> The United States will, indeed, undertake under article 10 to "respect and preserve as against external aggression the territorial integrity and existing political independence of all members of the league," and that engagement constitutes a very grave and solemn moral obligation. But it is a moral, not a legal, obligation, and leaves our Congress absolutely free to put its own interpretation upon it in all cases that call for action. It is binding in conscience only, not in law.[17]

The president had earlier assured the Senate that, under Article 10, the United States would retain the right unilaterally to decide whether or not to participate in any joint military action. "The Covenant of the League," he explained, "provides for military action for the protection of its members only upon advice of the Council of the League—advice given, it is to be presumed, only upon deliberation and acted upon by each of the governments of the member States only if its own judgment justifies such action."[18] Although Wilson advocated the League of Nations as the principal method for the enforcement of the Versailles Treaty, he strongly opposed making it into a military alliance. Wanting it to rely on moral suasion, he refused to accept any definite military obligation for the Unites States under the Covenant.

Clemenceau recognized the inadequacy of the League of Nations as a guarantee of French security. Completely skeptical about the power of moral suasion, he wanted to maintain the wartime coalition as a military alliance against Germany. He urged Lloyd George and Wilson to accept the definite obligation for Great Britain and the United States to protect France and to join in military planning for that purpose. During the drafting of the Covenant, the French delegation accordingly proposed the creation of an international military force under the League of Nations. Wilson, joined by the British delegation, absolutely rejected this proposal. He even refused to consider the creation of a general staff under the League, a proposal that the French leaders offered as a compromise. Even planning for military preparedness, without the organization of an actual international force, seemed unnecessary to Wilson for the success of the League. His close friend and adviser Edward M. House, reflecting the president's attitude, recorded his reaction in his diary. "What the French want," he wrote, "is to make the League an instrument for war instead of an instrument for peace. Also to make it a league against Germany and for the benefit of France. They desire to create a general staff with authority to plan all sorts of military defenses, invasions and whatnot."[19] Both Wilson and House, underestimating the problem of French security, failed to appreciate Clemenceau's argument that a League of Nations that neglected military considerations and depended primarily on moral suasion would be utopian.[20]

Although Wilson and Clemenceau shared the goal of German disarmament, this question further revealed their differences over enforcement. The president wanted to restrict the size of Germany's armed forces but refused any permanent American commitment to prevent German rearmament. His chief military and naval advisers shared this attitude. Admiral William S. Benson reported to Wilson that during the drafting of the naval terms of the Versailles Treaty he had steadfastly opposed any enforcement of disarmament. He thought that permanent restrictions on Germany's navy would violate its sovereignty and thereby provoke, rather than prevent, a future war. He hoped at least that the United States would not agree to participate in such permanent enforcement.[21] General Tasker H. Bliss offered the same advice. "My personal opinion," he informed Wilson, "is that it would be wiser if our colleagues would put a little more trust in the growing democratic feeling of [Germany] and in a League of Nations, both of which will be a better protection for France and the rest of Europe, than the harassing control which they propose to maintain. You will note that I am opposed to this continuing military control, so far as the United States is concerned." On this issue, Bliss enjoyed the support of his colleagues in the American Commission to Negotiate Peace.[22]

During the consideration of the military terms in March 1919, the president opposed the permanent enforcement of German disarmament. He approved the creation of control commissions only for the purpose of supervising the initial reduction of Germany's army, navy, and air force. Calling for their abolition after approximately three months on the completion of that task, he demanded that "the Allies should agree among themselves that these Commissions would cease to function when the terms had once been carried out; for example, as soon as the army had been actually reduced to 100,000 men." At Wilson's insistence, the military terms of the Versailles Treaty included no provisions for the continued supervision of Germany's armed forces. They provided for the disarmament of Germany but without any guarantee against its subsequent rearmament. Only later did Wilson reluctantly agree to authorize the League of Nations to inspect Germany's permanent compliance with the disarmament conditions.[23]

Clemenceau clearly recognized the inadequacy of German disarmament as well as the League of Nations for French security. Refusing to rely on these methods, he advocated the separation of the Rhineland from Germany and its continued occupation by American and Allied troops, hoping in this way to enforce the peace settlement. Yet, because he deemed the maintenance of the wartime coalition even more critical for French security, Clemenceau faced the difficult task of convincing President Wilson and the British prime minister David Lloyd George to accept the French policy. He dared not proceed unilaterally with action they opposed.

André Tardieu, Clemenceau's closest associate at the peace conference, outlined the French attitude toward the Rhineland in a major memorandum on February 25, 1919. Critical of the League and of German disarmament because of their inherent limitations, he urged the maintenance of the military control of the Rhine. He urged that France needed the Rhineland as a buffer in case Germany repeated its aggression of 1914.[24] The American and British leaders strongly opposed this method of enforcing the Versailles Treaty, regarding it as an unnecessary violation of the territorial integrity and sovereignty of Germany. In view of the deadlock that resulted over the Rhineland question, Lloyd George began to grope for an alternative guarantee of French security. He now originated the idea of a security treaty under which Great Britain and the United States would promise immediate military assistance to France in the event of unprovoked German aggression. Wilson endorsed this proposal, believing that it involved no greater American commitment to France than Article 10 of the League Covenant.[25]

On March 14, Wilson and Lloyd George confronted Clemenceau with the very choice he had hoped to escape. They promised a special guarantee of French security, but only if he abandoned his proposal for the permanent occupation and separation of the Rhineland. For Clemenceau the dilemma was acute because he believed the security of France required both the continuation of the wartime coalition, which the security treaty would clearly symbolize, and the maintenance of military control of the Rhine. The French premier welcomed the security treaty but refused to abandon the Rhineland. He argued that neither the League of Nations nor the disarmament of Germany provided an adequate guarantee of French security. Nevertheless, he offered to modify his earlier position by conceding that the peace treaty might stipulate a time for the evacuation of American and Allied troops from the Rhineland. In exchange for this concession, he proposed the demilitarization of the left bank of the Rhine and a 50-kilometer zone on the right bank. As a method of enforcement, he demanded the creation of a permanent commission to inspect the demilitarized zone and asserted the right to send troops back into the Rhineland if Germany violated the demilitarized zone or began to rearm. In case of German violations, he wanted the right to resort to the initial strategy of the military control of the Rhine. He also requested the British and American leaders to agree that the entry of German troops into the Rhineland would constitute an act of aggression, thereby obligating their governments to respond under the security treaty.[26]

Clemenceau still failed to convince either Wilson or Lloyd George of the importance of the Rhineland to French security. Responding in his Fontainebleau Memorandum of March 25, the British prime minister opposed both temporary and permanent occupation of the Rhineland as well as its separation from Germany. Although approving the demilitarization of the left bank, he absolutely opposed the maintenance of any troops in the Rhineland as a method of enforcement. He wanted France to rely exclusively on the security treaty.[27] Wilson, endorsing the Fontainebleau Memorandum, joined with Lloyd George in condemning the French policy toward the Rhineland as a gross injustice that would provoke Germany into a future war. Although he accepted Clemenceau's proposal for demilitarization, the president rejected any method for its enforcement. He opposed both the creation of a permanent commission for inspection and the reentry of troops into the Rhineland in case of German violations. He even felt that German violations of the demilitarized zone would not require any British or American reaction under the security treaty. Clemenceau sharply criticized Wilson and Lloyd George for attempting to appease Germany at the expense of France. Recognizing that Germany's conception of justice differed from that of the Allied and Associated Powers, he argued that the hope of achieving a durable peace through a just settlement was an illusion and, consequently, that enforcement was essential. "We must not compromise the results of our victory," he pleaded. "The League of Nations is offered to us as a means of providing the security we need: I accept this method; but if the League of Nations cannot enforce its orders with military sanctions, we must find this sanction some other way."[28]

On March 28, Wilson submitted a proposal to Clemenceau that summarized his views. He approved the demilitarization of the left and right banks of the Rhine and nominally agreed to consider the introduction of German troops into this zone as a hostile act. He also offered the first draft of the security treaty. In it, the president tied the guarantee against unprovoked German aggression to the League of Nations by stipulating that the security treaty would terminate as soon as the League itself could provide for French security. In his response, Clemenceau urged the importance of enforcing the demilitarization and disarmament terms and requested a clarification of British and American obligations under the security treaty. He wanted to authorize the League of Nations to investigate any alleged German violations of the military terms of the peace treaty. Since Wilson had prevented the creation of permanent commissions for this purpose, the French premier hoped at least to impose this responsibility on the League. In the event of German violations, moreover, he expected immediate American and British military assistance under the security treaty. In addition to these long-term methods of enforcement, he called for at least the temporary occupation of the Rhineland.[29]

Clemenceau's arguments for enforcement failed to convince Wilson, who refused to alter his proposal of March 28. The president still opposed inspection even by the League of Germany's compliance with the military terms. He wanted the United States to assume no additional responsibility for the defense of France merely because Germany began to rearm or to send troops into the Rhineland, and he consequently refused to consider such violations as hostile acts.[30] When House delivered this negative response, he "read the riot act to Clemenceau" and demanded acceptance of the president's proposal. The French premier now realized that he needed to offer further concessions to prevent the disruption of the wartime coalition. He informed House that he would accept the March 28 proposal if Wilson would approve the temporary occupation of the Rhineland. Clemenceau wanted to continue the occupation for 15 years as a guarantee of Germany's execution of the peace treaty, including especially the payment of reparations. Since Clemenceau had by now abandoned his demand for the permanent occupation and separation of the Rhineland from Germany, the president reluctantly consented to the temporary occupation for 15 years.[31]

Lloyd George, who was temporarily absent from the peace conference, returned to discover that the Anglo-American cooperation against France over the Rhineland question had collapsed. Despite his earlier opposition to even the temporary occupation of the Rhineland, he now had no alternative but to approve the compromise that Wilson and Clemenceau had worked out in mid-April. He also accepted their draft of the security treaty with France.[32] As these leaders prepared a public announcement of the security treaty, Wilson revealed the limited interpretation that he placed on it. Although at Clemenceau's insistence this treaty stipulated that the rearmament of Germany or the introduction of its armed forces into the demilitarized zone would constitute hostile acts, the president refused to mention these provisions in the public statement because "it would look as though, if Germany should do so, the United States would have at once to send troops. This was not what was intended. Troops were only to be sent in the event of an act of aggression." Wilson anticipated the use of American troops to defend France only if Germany again invaded France.

He proposed and the other leaders finally approved an announcement that merely stated that he and Lloyd George would seek the approval, respectively, of the Senate and the Parliament for the French security treaty. The reservation in this announcement was significant. Wilson had earlier written to Henry White: "All that I promised is to try to get it."[33] He never spoke in that manner about parts of the peace settlement, such as the League of Nations, which he firmly supported. After finally sending the French security treaty to the Senate on July 29, he exerted no further effort to gain its acceptance. When he defended the Covenant and other parts of the Versailles Treaty during his western tour in September 1919, Wilson made no attempt to arouse public opinion in favor of the French security treaty. Within the Senate, moreover, he refused to use his influence to obtain the approval of its ratification. Obviously, he placed little value on this method to achieve France's security.[34]

Historians, adhering to the dualistic Wilsonian framework of New versus Old Diplomacy, have assumed that the alternatives open to the peace conference were a liberal or a Carthaginian peace. As solutions to the German problem, they have recognized both "reintegrationist" and "punitive" approaches to peacemaking and have generally regarded the result as an unhappy compromise between them. From this perspective, for example, Thomas A. Bailey concluded that "the Treaty of Versailles fell between two stools. It was neither a thorough-going victor's peace nor a peace of accommodation."[35]

Neither the president nor subsequent historians recognized the opportunity in 1919 of granting Clemenceau's essential requests for French security without endorsing a

Carthaginian peace. He—and they—failed to perceive the distinction between the imposition of a punitive peace on Germany and the enforcement of moderate terms. By refusing to support the effective maintenance of the wartime coalition, which was Clemenceau's principal solution to the German problem, Wilson sacrificed the possibility of providing security to France without forcing a Carthaginian peace on Germany. Confusing ends and means, he never recognized the possibility of seeking to reintegrate Germany into a peaceful Europe while also offering definite methods for the protection of France. Instead, underestimating Germany's potential threat and overestimating the power of moral suasion, the president offered a utopian League of Nations without a feasible system for enforcing the Versailles Treaty. The Paris Peace Conference of 1919, failing to solve the German problem, provided neither security for France nor a permanent peace.

CHAPTER 5

SECRET GERMAN–AMERICAN NEGOTIATIONS
DURING THE PARIS PEACE CONFERENCE

Lloyd E. Ambrosius, "Secret German–American Negotiations during the Paris Peace Conference," *Amerikastudien/American Studies* 24 (Number 2, 1979): 288–309.

Politicians, journalists, and scholars have recently drawn attention to the role of intelligence operations in American foreign relations. Although they have concentrated on the Central Intelligence Agency (CIA) and similar organizations during the Cold War, the issues that they have raised were not unique to this era. After World War I, General John J. Pershing's staff, and especially his intelligence officers, initiated and pursued negotiations with the military and civilian leaders in Germany despite the absence of authorization from President Woodrow Wilson. Like the more recent activities of the so-called intelligence community of the United States, these secret German–American negotiations during the Paris Peace Conference of 1919 posed fundamental questions for a democratic government. At issue was the relationship between the clandestine operations and the official diplomacy of the United States. Within this context arose the problem of responsible control over intelligence activities or, where military intelligence officers were involved, of the appropriate form of civil–military relations.

Questions about intelligence activities have constituted part of the broader consideration of the organization of American foreign relations. Recent disclosures by congressional investigations of some operations of the American intelligence community at home and abroad have demonstrated the importance of these questions. After examining this evidence of the abuse of power, Morton Halperin and others discerned the specter of "the lawless state." In their comprehensive study on remaking foreign policy, Graham Allison and Peter Szanton emphasized the organizational connection with reference to intelligence activities. In his earlier book on the Cuban missile crisis, Graham Allison offered three models or approaches to the study of foreign policy. He demonstrated the impact not only of the rational actor but also of the organizational process and intragovernmental or bureaucratic politics on the international conduct of the United States. Morton Halperin employed similar categories in his analysis of bureaucratic politics and foreign policy. Despite the importance of the rational approach to American national security, he stressed the influence of various organizational interests and of politics within the government on the formation and implementation of foreign policy.[1] In common with the New Left historians, Allison and Halperin concentrated on the internal origins of American foreign relations. Yet, in contrast to the recent revisionists' focus on socioeconomic issues and ideological consensus, Allison and Halperin emphasized the diversity among American policymakers over the primarily politico-military questions of national security. For them, the essence of decision making involved compromise among the powerful personalities and bureaucracies in the American government.[2]

Organizational problems and bureaucratic politics have characterized civil–military relations during the twentieth century. The emergence of the military profession in the United States required a new form of civilian control. The industrial and managerial revolutions of the nineteenth century rendered obsolete the earlier "subjective civilian control" embodied in the citizen–soldier. As Samuel Huntington observed, the mass armies of this new era of total war needed responsible institutional management. The failure of the United States to establish and maintain what he called "objective civilian control" produced "the crisis of American civil–military relations" during and after World War II. The delineation between political and military issues became obscure and, as a consequence, both civilian control and military professionalism suffered. The professional soldier, as Morris Janowitz demonstrated, increasingly involved himself in the political technique of pressure group tactics. He could not avoid the organizational realities of the contemporary era.[3] Although the problems associated with these developments became more apparent during World War II and the Cold War, they were not altogether new. The secret German–American negotiations during the Paris Peace Conference anticipated the later crisis in civil–military relations and exemplified a similar breakdown in civilian control and military professionalism.

After World War II, George F. Kennan observed the inability of the State Department to control American policy during the occupation of Japan. In Tokyo, General Douglas MacArthur avoided civilian control. Kennan warned:

> Whoever in Washington takes responsibility for placing a major American armed establishment anywhere beyond our borders, particularly when it is given extensive powers with relation to civil affairs in the area where it is stationed, should remember that he is not thereby creating just an instrument of American policy—he is committing himself seriously to the insights, interests, and decisions of a new bureaucratic power structure situated far from our shores and endowed with its own specific perspective on all problems of world policy; and to this extent he is resigning his own power of control over the use to be made of America's resources in the process of international life.[4]

What Kennan observed with reference to MacArthur and Japan applied as well to Pershing and Germany.

After the Armistice on November 11, 1918, General Pershing moved the advance headquarters of the American Expeditionary Forces to Trier in Germany. Colonel Arthur L. Conger, chief of the intelligence section at Trier, and other members of the AEF general staff soon established direct contact with the top military and civilian leaders in the new German republic. President Wilson had not authorized, and was only partially informed about, their activities. He and other members of the American Commission to Negotiate Peace received only abridged military intelligence reports, which did not reveal that the American officers were engaged in negotiations designed to influence the outcome of the peace conference. Although largely unsuccessful, this military diplomacy encouraged the German leaders to expect a treaty more in accordance with their interpretation of the Fourteen Points than with Wilson's. Thus was fostered the German conviction that the president betrayed Germany to the Allies by eventually approving conditions of peace that violated his Fourteen Points. By attempting to influence the proceedings of the Allied and Associated Powers and by misleading the Germans, Conger and his military colleagues interfered with the official diplomacy of the peace conference.

In 1955, Fritz T. Epstein first disclosed the role of Colonel Conger in the secret American military diplomacy during the period of the Armistice. In his article, "Zwischen Compiègne und Versailles," Epstein used the limited sources that were then available. He focused especially on the negotiations in May 1919, which he regarded as the "high point" in the episode, but that were actually the anticlimax. In 1971, Klaus Schwabe further examined the secret German–American negotiations within the context of the peace conference. His book, *Deutsche Revolution und Wilson-Frieden,* provided considerably more information than Epstein's earlier article about the negotiations, and particularly on their significance for Germany. Schwabe neglected, however, the organizational problems of the military intelligence activities of Pershing's general staff and their implications for American civil–military relations.[5]

Colonel Conger initiated the secret negotiations in Bingen on December 4, 1918, with Walter Loeb, who was affiliated with the intelligence department of the workers' and soldiers' council in Frankfurt, one of many such councils in the new German republic. At Conger's invitation, Loeb came on December 13 to the AEF advance headquarters in Trier, where the ranking officer, Brigadier General Preston Brown, an assistant chief of staff from Pershing's General Headquarters, joined the discussion. The American officers began to encourage false expectations of a rift between the United States and the Allies. Stressing the American commitment to Wilson's Fourteen Points, they made a fundamental distinction between these conditions for peace and the harsher terms of the Armistice. Critical of France, they expressed the desire for reconciliation with Germany. Both Brown and Conger emphasized the importance of convening a National Assembly and establishing a legitimate government in Germany, suggesting that these political developments would facilitate the supply of food for Germany from the United States. Loeb reported these meetings to Carl Giebel, who represented Germany's revolutionary government, the Council of People's Commissars, at the Supreme Command of the German Army.[6]

On learning of the American initiative, General Wilhelm Groener, who had replaced Erich Ludendorff as first quartermaster general in the Supreme Command, seized the opportunity to pursue the direct contact with the United States. Baron Paul von Eltz Rübenach, whom he sent to Trier on December 30 to deliver a statement to Conger, explained that the Supreme Command had formed an "alliance" with Friedrich Ebert to prevent a radical revolution in Germany. Refusing to recognize the legitimacy of Germany's revolutionary government, the Supreme Command supported the majority Social Democrats in their desire for an early election of a National Assembly. Emphasizing the "danger of Bolshevism," Eltz expressed strong disapproval of the soldiers' councils and accused Hugo Haase and Emil Barth, two of the Independent Social Democrats in the Council of People's Commissars, of flirting or collaborating with this Russian threat. He proposed especially an alliance between Germany and the United States to "fight against Bolshevists" and for this purpose urged the inclusion of Germany in the future League of Nations.[7] At a subsequent meeting in Trier with Loeb and his colleague, Dr. Norbert Einstein, on January 4–5, 1919, Conger responded favorably to Groener's message. Sharing Groener's fear of Bolshevism, he criticized the workers' and soldiers' councils and warned that a socialist Germany could anticipate no financial credit from the United States. Conger again urged the creation of a democratic government through a National Assembly, which would enable the United States to demobilize its troops and adopt a favorable attitude toward Germany's economic needs.[8]

Groener sought a special shipping agreement with the United States. At his instigation, three German shipping company executives—the North German Lloyd's general director Philipp Heineken and director Carl Stapelfeldt, and the Hamburg American Line's director Richard F. Peltzer—came to Trier on January 13 and 14 to meet with Colonel Conger, General Brown, and Brigadier General Dennis E. Nolan, the assistant chief of staff in charge of the intelligence section at Pershing's General Headquarters in Chaumont. The representatives of Germany's leading steamship companies submitted a proposal to provide passenger ships for the purpose of transporting American troops via Bremen and Hamburg to the United States. They expected these steamers to bring cargoes on their return trips, thereby reviving trade between Germany and the United States. To the shipping company executives, Brown and Nolan gave political advice, emphasizing the merits of the American constitution and the advantages to Germany of adopting this model. Especially critical of France and the French constitution, Conger added that under the American rather than a parliamentary system of government it was much easier to keep military secrets.[9]

Germany's shipping proposal, which was submitted to General Pershing, came too late to influence the proceedings of the Armistice Commission. Although Brown and Conger, with Nolan's concurrence, shared the proposal with Admiral William Benson, an American naval adviser, it did not result in a special agreement between Germany and the United States. As a condition for renewing the Armistice, the Allied and Associated Powers instead required Germany to agree to provide ships to them jointly in return for food. Nevertheless, Heineken informed Conger that the steamship companies still hoped to reach a special agreement with the United States in connection with the next renewal of the Armistice in mid-February. Conger relayed this information through Nolan to Pershing's chief of staff, General James W. McAndrew, so that the AEF commander-in-chief could inform Edward M. House, Wilson's intimate adviser and a delegate in the American Commission to Negotiate Peace.[10]

General Groener sought not only a special shipping agreement and American influence over political developments in Germany but also more favorable peace terms. He sent Baron von Eltz to Trier on January 26 to warn Conger against the consequences of extreme Allied demands. "We are convinced," stated Eltz, "that France as well as England want our complete destruction." Suggesting that the loss of substantial territory to France and Poland would result in the triumph of Bolshevism in Germany, Groener's spokesman urged German–American collaboration against both the Allies and Bolshevism. As Conger passed Eltz's statement through Nolan to Chief of Staff McAndrew, Groener's proposals reached the highest level in Pershing's general staff.[11]

American officers continued to intervene in German politics. In Trier on January 25 to 26, Conger once more impressed on Loeb the advantages to Germany of adopting a republican constitution like that of the United States. Loeb reported this conversation to the German foreign minister, Count Ulrich von Brockdorff-Rantzau, informing him that Ebert was fully aware of the connection with Conger. President Wilson was not equally well informed by Pershing's staff. Loeb's report included the prediction that the next American president would be a Republican, a prediction about the election of 1920 that Wilson had obviously not instructed Conger to make.[12] Nevertheless, Germany's confidential agents gave Conger the response that the American officers desired. Loeb and Einstein assured him on February 2 that the new constitution of the Weimar Republic would create the "United States of Germany." Although the constitution would provide for a parliamentary system, it would establish a new republican government of the various German states, while preventing Prussian domination. From the peace conference, and especially from Wilson, the Germans expected a settlement within the limits of their interpretation of his Fourteen Points. Loeb warned Conger that "Germany will not sign a peace going over the fourteen points of President Wilson." Nolan included this warning and news about the plans at Weimar to draft "a constitution in general similar to that of the United States of America" in his report to Pershing. He identified Loeb only as an emissary from Ebert, Philipp Scheidemann, and Matthias Erzberger, chairman of Germany's delegation at the Armistice Commission. Pershing edited this report by deleting Conger's and Nolan's names before sending it on to House on February 10. In this form, the report did not reveal to Wilson's close adviser the sources of the American military intelligence.[13]

The American military diplomacy continued to encourage the Germans to expect Wilson's support in the Armistice renewal and peace negotiations. In Trier on February 8 to 9, Loeb and Einstein asked Conger why the United States had permitted the Allies to require Germany to surrender ships in return for food as a condition for the mid-January renewal of the Armistice. Rejecting the American distinction between the Armistice and the future peace, they expressed the German fear that concessions made now would become part of the eventual settlement. While defending the earlier agreements regarding ships and food, Conger assured the German agents that Wilson and the American army officers would oppose any efforts in the Armistice Commission to require additional economic concessions as a condition for the mid-February renewal. He gave this assurance despite the lack of presidential instructions. On other issues, Conger told Loeb and Einstein about the differences between the Allies and the United States over the League of Nations and raised the possibility of eventual German membership. He left them with the impression that he spoke with the authority of General Pershing, and presumably of President Wilson as well. In their reports, both Conger and Loeb gave more details about what they heard than what they said. Conger's report, which expressed Germany's concerns as questions without full information on his answers, passed from Nolan to Pershing. Before submitting it to House, the AEF commander-in-chief edited the report. In this extracted version, Pershing did not reveal that the information came from Conger's interview with Loeb and Einstein. Nor did he disclose, although he especially noted in the original report, the willingness of the German government to supply the

United States with any information it desired. Pershing obviously did not wish to inform House fully about the secret German–American negotiations.[14]

Representatives of Germany's steamship companies maintained their contact with the AEF advance headquarters. In Trier on February 11 and 13, North German Lloyd and Hamburg American Line executives pursued the question of the Armistice renewal. Heineken and Wilhelm Cuno, anticipating the possibility that the Armistice Commission would impose new conditions, discussed the disadvantages of either accepting or rejecting them. When they raised the prospect of speaking directly with American civilians, Conger refused to arrange such talks. He assured them that he would relay all messages—even those strictly political—through Brown to Pershing. He obviously did not wish to relinquish the military control over these negotiations. Without revealing the absence of civilian authorization, Conger expressed his preference for a separate peace with Germany. Strongly condemning the Allies, he referred twice to "the stupid governments of England and France." Yet, he began to discourage Germany from expecting too much from the United States by explaining that American public opinion prevented Wilson from making an open break with the Allies. He implied that the president was privately inclined toward such a break. Anticipating a possible disruption of the Armistice Commission, Conger wrote Nolan that "in that event the lines we have established into Germany will become of increasing importance to us."[15] The expected rupture did not occur as the Armistice Commission renewed the Armistice for an indefinite period without imposing new conditions. With Conger's encouragement, Erzberger approved this renewal.[16]

Political developments in Germany followed the course that the American officers had encouraged. After elections in January, the National Assembly convened in Weimar early in February and chose Ebert as the first president of the republic. Scheidemann, whom he selected as chancellor, organized a cabinet of Social Democratic, Center, and Democratic parties. This moderate coalition excluded the Independent Social Democrats from the government. When Conger met Loeb and Einstein again in Trier on February 23, although lacking instructions from the responsible American civil officials, he expressed on behalf of the United States complete satisfaction with this new German government. Reviewing the negotiations leading to the recent Armistice renewal, he credited Wilson with successfully preventing France from requiring new economic and military concessions. Conger voiced optimism that the president would also prevail in the peace conference and force France to adhere to his Fourteen Points. He stated that Germany could anticipate lenient military and naval conditions and noted that the League of Nations Covenant opened the possibility of future German membership. As Conger's information was less than totally accurate, these secret negotiations continued to encourage the German leaders to expect a peace treaty more in accordance with their conception of Wilson's Fourteen Points than with the official position of the Allied and Associated Powers.[17]

This secret military diplomacy conflicted with the activities of the official American delegation in Paris. Earlier in February, the American Commission to Negotiate Peace had sent Captain William R. Gherardi of the U.S. Navy on a mission to Berlin to collect information. He learned from the German Foreign Office about Conger and Loeb. A member of the Foreign Office, which was not yet fully informed about their relationship, mistakenly identified Loeb as Conger's confidential agent.

Reporting to the American delegation, Gherardi noted his own as well as the Foreign Office's embarrassment over this American connection with the German Supreme Command.[18] This complaint was referred to Brigadier General Marlborough Churchill, chief of the War Department's Military Intelligence Division, who was currently in Paris to provide liaison between Pershing's general staff and the American Commission. Sending a copy of Gherardi's report to Nolan, Churchill advised him to handle it with extreme delicacy and warned that, if informed, Wilson as well as the American Commission might disapprove of the American military intelligence operations. "Under present conditions," he cautioned Nolan, "the Peace Commission has constituted itself, to all intents and purposes, the Government of the United States, and if we handle this thing in writing, they might issue instructions which would cripple your work. These instructions would probably be backed up by the President."[19] Although his assignment was that of liaison with the American delegates in Paris, Churchill obviously had not informed them about and did not welcome their interference with the secret negotiations.

Pershing's general staff preserved the secrecy of its intelligence activities by providing only partial information to the American Commission. At General Nolan's request, Conger supplied a deceptively accurate answer to Gherardi's complaint. Taking advantage of the mistaken identification of Loeb, Conger replied: "I have never employed anyone named Loeb as confidential agent, and I have never asked anyone of that name to request any information for me from the military authorities." Although less than the total truth, this answer was what Nolan desired. Incorporating it into his own response to Churchill on March 1, Nolan affirmed as well his belief that Pershing, even more than the American Commission, needed accurate information on internal developments in Germany. Nolan asserted that

the [AEF] Commander-in-Chief's duty to keep informed as to the internal situation in Germany, until the Treaty of Peace is signed, is almost as great as it was during the period of active operations. While it is highly desirable that the Peace Commission know what is going on in the interior of Germany, it is absolutely essential that the Commander-in-Chief here should know. That necessitates that we have a few high-class, dependable agents who can keep in touch with the existing government officials in Germany as well as with the people who may throw them out of power.

With this assertion of military supremacy in the intelligence field, Nolan opposed any civilian interference with Conger's activities. In accordance with Nolan's response, Churchill informed Joseph C. Grew, secretary general of the American Commission to Negotiate Peace, that neither Conger nor any other AEF intelligence officer had employed anyone named Loeb or requested him to obtain military information for them. Churchill was confident that this deceptive denial would close the matter. This was mastery in bureaucratic politics.[20]

These attitudes and practices of the American military intelligence officers after World War I foreshadowed the later operations of the American intelligence community during the Cold War. As the Senate Select Committee to Study Governmental Operations with Respect to Intelligence Activities, under the chairmanship of Frank Church, reported in 1976, "The fact that government intelligence agencies resist any examination of their secret activities even by another part of the same government should not be minimized. The intelligence agencies are a sector of American government set apart." The conditions of the Cold War, like those in 1918 and 1919, fostered a penchant for secrecy. The Church committee observed that "the fear of war, and its attendant uncertainties and doubts, has fostered a series of secret practices that have eroded the processes of open democratic government."[21] This erosion was occurring in civil–military relations during the Paris Peace Conference.

Undaunted by the American Commission's obvious disapproval, Conger met Loeb again in Trier on March 8 and 9. This time he cautioned Germany against giving its own interpretation to the Fourteen Points while overlooking the fact of military defeat. In the name of the American government, Conger warned that the United States would take into consideration the interests of its Allies while implementing the Fourteen Points. He explained that the situation in Paris had changed since Wilson's return to the United States. When Loeb asked whether this statement was an official communication, Conger answered only that it was made in accordance with his instructions. Yet, these instructions had come neither from the president nor the American delegation in Paris, a fact that Conger did not share with Loeb. As evidence of the new situation, Conger noted that the German army would be permitted fewer troops than he had earlier indicated. He mentioned Wilson's difficulties in the United States concerning the League of Nations because of the American tradition of avoiding entanglement in European affairs. Conger also reported that the Allies were divided over whether Bolshevism was a real threat in Germany or merely a bogus issue fabricated by the German military leaders to retain their power and influence. To assess the validity of these views, Loeb invited American—but not Allied—officers to visit Germany.[22]

Accepting this invitation, which Erzberger also extended, Conger traveled through Germany between March 15 and 21. Accompanied by Major Frederick Henrotin of Pershing's general staff, he sought to investigate particularly the strength and condition of the German army. During this trip, German military and civilian leaders exploited the American fear of Bolshevism. In Koblenz, Baron von Eltz gave Conger and Henrotin a memorandum from General Groener that the German general staff had prepared, stressing the danger of Bolshevism and the urgency of Allied and especially American support. Groener warned that harsh peace terms would promote the conditions for revolution in Germany. For its part, he stated, "Germany is employing all the force left her to quash the terrible danger. She is fighting a brave but desperate fight to gain a respite for Europe and the world. Germany, broken down in war, holds the fate of the civilized world in her hands." Eltz also supplied Conger with some prewar documents to counter Allied propaganda about Germany's responsibility for starting the war. These documents from the German general staff purportedly would "prove our innocence and the guilt of the Entente."[23]

German leaders used the threat of Bolshevism to justify the maintenance of their army. In Berlin on March 18, the Social Democratic defense minister, Gustav Noske, stressed the importance of Germany's army, whose strength he placed at only 220,000 active troops, for defense against Poland. On the following day, Conger and Henrotin went to Kolberg to meet officers of the German general staff. General Groener assured them that "the German army was incapable of resuming military operations of any nature whatsoever." He, too, noted the importance of protecting

Germany's eastern border and justified the role of the Freikorps in preventing Bolshevism in Berlin and the Ruhr district. Field Marshal Paul von Hindenburg addressed the Allied charge that Germany's military leaders were exploiting the issue of Bolshevism to restore their power. He stated that Ludendorff shared his concern with "the peril threatening from the East. People who pretend that we are conspiring to put on foot a new army are completely in error." Before returning to Trier, Conger discussed the current situation with Professor Hans Delbrück, under whom he had studied history before the war at the University of Berlin. Delbrück told him that despite its weakness Germany would not tolerate the loss of the Saar to France or of Danzig and Posen to Poland. He warned "that the world was faced by a great crisis and the form of a great war which had not yet begun, between Bolshevism and Civilization, and that on the peace terms would depend whether Germany would fight in that war with or against Bolshevism."[24]

Conger and Henrotin were overwhelmingly convinced by the German Supreme Command and Professor Delbrück. On March 21, they reported their "General Conclusions" that the German army was incapable and its general staff had no intentions of resuming the war against the Allied and Associated Powers. Although Germany would offer no military resistance on the Western Front, the American officers warned that "it must be expected that the members of the present German government, backed by the General Staff, will fight to the end against any alteration of the former eastern boundary, for military reasons." Noting the German anxiety over the possible loss of territory, they echoed Delbrück's warning that Germany must receive acceptable terms from the peace conference or it would turn to Bolshevism. On March 22, Conger went to Paris to brief General Pershing, thus providing a direct link between the top German military and civilian leaders and the AEF commander-in-chief.[25]

On the same day that Conger briefed Pershing, the American Commission to Negotiate Peace considered sending another mission to Germany. Obviously unaware of Conger's and Henrotin's trip, the American delegates to the peace conference discussed the desirability of sending a civilian, Ellis Loring Dresel, to continue the work of Captain Gherardi's earlier mission. Concluding that it was inadvisable at this time to send anyone into Germany, the American Commission, with Secretary of State Robert Lansing, Henry White, and General Tasker H. Bliss attending this session, instead authorized Bliss to request political reports from General George H. Harries, who was stationed in Berlin.[26] Bliss asked Pershing to instruct Harries to submit such reports. Rather than providing the requested information, Nolan sent Bliss a copy of Conger's and Henrotin's "General Conclusions," but without disclosing the source of this document. At a conference on March 27, Bliss and Nolan arranged for Pershing's general staff to provide the American Commission with daily summaries of information about Germany. The American delegates in Paris welcomed military information, but remained unaware of the secret negotiations with Germany.[27]

With its unauthorized military diplomacy, Pershing's general staff continued to foster false German expectations. At Conger's request, Loeb came to Limburg on March 27 and 28 to learn the results of his trips to Germany and subsequently to Paris. Conger informed the German agent that Pershing and his general staff were pleased with his report. He related—although there is no evidence to support this claim—that the AEF commander-in-chief had passed the report directly to President Wilson, who was also quite satisfied with it. Conger said he was convinced that Hindenburg, Groener, and the German general staff were absolutely loyal to the new republican government and were not exploiting the issue of Bolshevism for their own advantage. He felt they were justified in using troops to maintain internal order as well as protect the eastern frontier against Poland, Czechoslovakia, and Bolshevism. Specifically repudiating his earlier statement at their March 8 and 9 meeting, Conger now assured Loeb that Wilson had the upper hand at the peace conference. Since his return to Paris, the president was determined to force the Allies to adhere to his Fourteen Points. Obviously pleased with this news, Loeb shared a message from Erzberger that no German statesman would sign a peace treaty that exceeded the terms of the Fourteen Points. He also told Conger about the anxiety in Germany over the possible landing of General Joseph Haller's army in Danzig because these Polish troops might stimulate or engage in anti-German activities. Above all, this conversation convinced Loeb of the importance of the direct connection through Conger to Pershing and, so he thought, ultimately to Wilson himself.[28]

Loeb's report persuaded the German government to pursue the secret negotiations with the United States. He immediately notified Erzberger and Brockdorff-Rantzau about his encouraging discussion with Conger, and they informed President Ebert and Chancellor Scheidemann.[29] After consideration by the German cabinet on March 28, Erzberger and Brockdorff-Rantzau gave instructions to Loeb, who was scheduled to meet Conger in Trier. On March 30, Loeb submitted a statement of "Peace Conditions Acceptable to Germany." This document, which was probably drafted in Trier and was given to Conger with the understanding that it was unofficial, explained Germany's interpretation of the Fourteen Points and pledged its willingness to accept such peace conditions. In addition, Loeb proposed that Germany and the United States cooperate in dealing with the situation in Russia.[30]

This summary of "Peace Conditions Acceptable to Germany" reached President Wilson only indirectly and without the identification of its source. Although Conger sent it immediately to Nolan and on to Pershing, the AEF commander-in-chief did not furnish a copy directly to Wilson. Instead, Nolan supplied the document to Bliss after removing the reference to German–American collaboration in dealing with Russia. Bliss distributed this edited version to the American Commission to Negotiate Peace on March 31 as the fifth in the series of daily summaries of information about Germany. Rather than revealing its special origins, Nolan merely attributed the document to "an authoritative and very confidential source." In another memorandum to Bliss, Nolan conveyed a German proposal to transport General Haller's army to Poland directly through Germany rather than via Danzig. Loeb had submitted this offer to Conger in Trier. On April 1, Bliss passed both of Nolan's memoranda on to the president, recommending a favorable response.[31] Wilson immediately brought them to the attention of the Allied leaders in the Council of Four. Because it was unofficial, he saw little value in the statement of "Peace Conditions Acceptable to Germany," but welcomed the German proposal regarding Haller's army. On this issue, the secret negotiations directly influenced the official diplomacy of the peace conference. With the concurrence of the British prime minister David Lloyd George and the French premier Georges Clemenceau, the Council of Four instructed Marshal Ferdinand Foch to accept the German proposal, but without surrendering their right to use the port of Danzig. In the Armistice Commission at Spa on April 3 and 4, Foch reached an agreement with Erzberger. Following his instructions, Foch arranged the transportation of Haller's army by train across Germany to Poland.[32]

Conger exaggerated the benefits of the military diplomacy for Germany at the peace conference. Meeting with Loeb on April 5–6 in Trier, he noted the favorable compromise concerning Haller's army. He erroneously claimed that the summary of "Peace Conditions Acceptable to Germany" had strengthened Wilson's ability to secure favorable terms for Germany in the Council of Four. Although acknowledging that he had transmitted this summary only as information, he again assured Loeb that the German prospects were better than he had stated on March 8–9. Despite the omission of the reference to German–American collaboration in dealing with Russia from Nolan's edited version, Conger discussed this question with Loeb. Without instructions from Wilson or the American Commission, Conger nevertheless answered that the United States would not supply troops for action in Russia and Eastern Europe because of the American attitude that Europe should solve its own problems. Yet, Conger thought the United States would, if necessary, furnish troops to maintain order in Germany. The German leaders did not welcome this suggestion. When Erzberger raised the question in Weimar on April 8, the cabinet decided that American and Allied soldiers were not needed to preserve order in Germany.[33]

Continuing to discuss the future peace treaty in Trier on April 12 and 13, Conger and Loeb focused on some of the differences between the American and German interpretations of the Fourteen Points. Adhering to the "Peace Conditions Acceptable to Germany," Loeb opposed the payment of damages resulting from submarine warfare. Conger warned him that, if Wilson decided such damages were covered by the Fourteen Points, Germany should pay. He told Loeb to expect the continuation of French military occupation and economic control of the Saar, but that Germany would not lose this district. In Weimar on April 14, the cabinet discussed the procedure for resolving these differences over reparations and the Saar. Although opposing concessions beyond the "Peace Conditions Acceptable to Germany," Erzberger proposed the continuation of negotiations with the United States through Conger. The cabinet rejected this proposal, refusing to authorize such instructions to Loeb. This decision accorded with the position of the Foreign Office. Erzberger and Brockdorff-Rantzau represented contrasting approaches to peacemaking, as Conger observed in a report prepared for Nolan's submission to Chief of Staff McAndrew.[34]

Conger's analysis of German politics overestimated the possibility of American influence. In late April, Brockdorff-Rantzau told Ellis Loring Dresel, whom the American Commission had sent to Berlin, that Germany would reject peace conditions that violated the Fourteen Points. The foreign minister stated specifically that he would not sign, and the cabinet would not approve, a treaty requiring even the temporary surrender of the Saar or Upper Silesia. When Dresel's report arrived in Paris, Wilson shared it in the Council of Four on April 24.[35] In contrast to Dresel's report, and to Henrotin's growing concern about military influence in Germany, Conger remained optimistic. He informed Nolan on April 14 that "the German Government is absolutely in a mood to be guided by the advice of the United States on matters of difficulty which may arise." To provide this guidance, he recommended the continuation of direct German–American communication after the German delegation's arrival in Paris. Loeb, too, wanted to continue the direct contact with the United States.[36]

Pershing's general staff maintained its connection with the German cabinet, but without fully informing President Wilson. On board the German delegation's train from Berlin to Paris late in the night of April 28 to 29, Conger informed Brockdorff-Rantzau that he could contact him directly by a special telephone line from Paris or through Major Royal Tyler, chief American intelligence officer for liaison with the Allies in Paris. Despite the lack of civilian authorization, he told the foreign minister that Wilson was striving in a difficult situation to achieve a peace acceptable to Germany and urged him to sign the treaty when it became obvious that further negotiation would not improve it. According to his notes, Brockdorff-Rantzau responded that he would not sign a treaty that included terms for the Saar and Danzig as Conger had described. He warned that such harsh terms would bring Bolshevism to Germany. Conger's version was much more optimistic. In a short statement sent to Bliss for submission to Wilson, he opined that Brockdorff-Rantzau "will sign when told that the time has arrived." He revealed the arrangement for communication with the foreign minister in Paris, but indicated that it was through Berlin rather than direct. Conger remarked that his conversation with Brockdorff-Rantzau was especially interesting within the context of earlier interviews on April 26 and 27 in Berlin. During one of these interviews with members of the German cabinet, the foreign minister had expressed his willingness to sign the peace treaty if at all possible. This view was shared by Ebert, Scheidemann, Erzberger, and Johann von Bernstorff, the former German ambassador to the United States who was currently in charge of the Foreign Office's planning for the peace negotiations. Yet, they expected the treaty to conform to their interpretation of the Fourteen Points as outlined in the March 30 statement of "Peace Conditions Acceptable to Germany." Wilson shared the reports of these interviews with the Council of Four on May 1. He was not pursuing secret negotiations with Germany behind the backs of the Allied leaders, but lacked full information about the American military intelligence operations. Conger did not disclose to him the possibility of direct communication with Brockdorff-Rantzau in Paris. Nor did he report to the president about his continuing meetings with Loeb. In response to the German agent's earlier inquiry, Conger informed him in Trier on May 4 that he, too, wanted to maintain their connection during the peace conference.[37]

On behalf of the Allied and Associated Powers, Clemenceau presented the peace treaty to Brockdorff-Rantzau at Versailles on May 7, 1919. Three days later, at Conger's invitation, Loeb and Einstein came to Limburg to discuss its terms with him and Major Henrotin. Comparing the treaty with the "Peace Conditions Acceptable to Germany," Loeb asserted that the entire German cabinet found it unacceptable. He warned that these terms would endanger the Weimar Republic by strengthening the German nationalists and Bolshevists. Admitting that he and his colleagues also were greatly surprised by the Versailles Treaty, Conger exposed himself to some very penetrating questions about the nature of these secret negotiations. Because the German government had viewed Conger as Pershing's agent and had naturally assumed that he represented the official American position, Loeb wanted to know why he had misled Germany into expecting more favorable conditions of peace. When Conger attempted to explain that Pershing had never represented the State Department, but instead consulted directly with the president, Loeb then asked why Wilson had provided Pershing with false information. Conger declined to answer. When he reminded the German agents of his warning on March 8–9 that the United States and the Allies would interpret the Fourteen Points in the context of Germany's defeat, Loeb countered that twice since then Conger had expressly repudiated that statement. Loeb concluded that either Germany had misunderstood Wilson's role in the negotiations or the president had fallen under the mastery of Clemenceau. Given these alternatives, he was unconvinced by Conger's argument that the German delegation should sign the treaty with the expectation of eventual revision of its worst features. Loeb now doubted Wilson's assistance in the future.[38]

Despite this bleak prospect, Erzberger and Bernstorff wanted to preserve the contact with the United States. At Erzberger's request, Conger and Henrotin returned to Berlin on May 18 and 19. They attempted to convince Erzberger and Bernstorff that Germany must sign the treaty. Warning that Wilson favored it and that American public opinion would support his use of the army to impose it, they now belatedly discouraged any expectations of a rift between the United States and the Allies. Urging the Germans not to interpret the treaty too literally, they encouraged them to anticipate its moderate implementation. To Professor Delbrück, who was planning to leave immediately for Versailles, Conger similarly promised revision in practice, while Henrotin delivered the same message to the Foreign Office for Brockdorff-Rantzau. This combination of threats and promises failed to convince Delbrück and Bernstorff, who continued to oppose the treaty. After the German cabinet discussed its response to the Versailles Treaty, Erzberger adopted a more conciliatory attitude. Wanting Germany to sign the treaty, but only if it did not depart too far from the Fourteen Points, he submitted some proposals to Conger. President Ebert, who seemed to occupy an intermediate position between Bernstorff and Erzberger, nevertheless sent a message to Conger and Henrotin that Germany might offer active resistance against the treaty. Yet, this warning was contradicted by General Groener's spokesman, Major Otto Kroeger, who revealed Germany's inability to resume fighting on the Western Front. Reiterating a familiar anti-Bolshevik theme, Kroeger appealed for a larger army to preserve internal order and protect Germany's eastern frontier.[39]

Conger and Henrotin submitted their reports immediately to the American Commission to Negotiate Peace. Secretary Lansing relayed them to Wilson on May 21, noting their "extremely valuable" information and especially Erzberger's proposals. This time, the president did not bother to share the American intelligence with the Allied leaders in the Council of Four. As earlier, when he received the March 30 summary of "Peace Conditions Acceptable to Germany," Wilson chose not to pursue separate or secret negotiations with the German government through the American intelligence officers. Conger also went personally to Paris on May 22 to brief General Pershing, who found the information "very interesting." Through the reports of Conger and Henrotin, the American Commission now learned that the American military officers were directly in contact with the German cabinet. This news revived the question, which Captain Gherardi's letter had raised in February, of military interference in the peacemaking. Yet, at their meeting on May 23, Lansing, White, and Bliss decided not to pursue this issue. The American Commission concluded that "this was a matter in which they could not interfere at all. These two officers were entirely under the control of General Pershing and any information which they had submitted to the Commission had been offered by General Nolan merely as a matter of courtesy with a desire to facilitate the work of the Commission."[40]

The deference of these official American delegates toward Pershing prevented them from asserting civilian control. His immense prestige after the war gave Pershing the advantage in intragovernmental politics. Indeed, until Congress and President Gerald Ford celebrated the American Bicentennial in 1976 by promoting George Washington to a six-star General of the Armies above all other past and present ranks, Pershing had since 1919 enjoyed the premier position among American military heroes. The civil-military relations between the American Commission to Negotiate Peace and the American Expeditionary Forces exemplified a general pattern in the twentieth century. As Morris Janowitz observed, "Civilian control of military affairs remains intact and fundamentally acceptable to the military; any imbalance in military contributions to politico-military affairs—domestic or international—is therefore often the result of default by civilian political leadership."[41]

With the acquiescence but not the authorization of the American Commission, Pershing's general staff continued the secret negotiations. At General Brown's invitation, Loeb and Einstein returned to Trier on May 24 and 25 to discuss with Conger and Henrotin the results of their reports in Paris. The American officers once more combined threats and promises. While noting the American army's preparation for a military advance into Germany, Conger offered the hope of negotiations on the basis of Erzberger's proposals. He attempted to persuade Loeb of the accuracy of this information with the reminder that he had done more for Germany than had Dresel. Claiming to have spoken with a prominent member of the American delegation in Paris, Conger offered that conversation as the basis for his expectation of negotiations. Although skeptical, Loeb accepted his invitation to meet again in order to gain further information about the American and Allied response to the German counterproposals. As he reported to Scheidemann, Loeb recalled that this military connection had achieved some favorable results, notably the compromise for the transportation of General Haller's army to Poland. Yet, he agreed with Brockdorff-Rantzau that Conger offered little hope. The foreign minister had concluded that Germany could not rely on Wilson for revision of the treaty, since he had already failed to fulfill his promise of the Fourteen Points.[42]

For their final meeting with Conger and Henrotin on June 3 and 4, Loeb and Einstein again traveled to the AEF advance headquarters in Trier. Affirming that the German attitude toward signing the treaty had not changed since the American officers visited Berlin, Loeb explained that its unfulfillable terms would cause the economic ruin of Germany and, by violating the right of self-determination, would produce another war. He wanted to know the American reaction to the German counterproposals. Conger merely promised to relay this question, admitting for the first time that he could not speak for the American delegation in Paris. He said that, while the American Commission appreciated Germany's difficulties, it expected the

Germans to sign the treaty. Warning of the terrible consequences of rejection, Conger urged the Germans to accept the treaty and then join with the United States to provide world leadership in the League of Nations. Despite the fantastic character of this proposal for German–American collaboration, Loeb saw some basis for hope and recommended further negotiations. Brockdorff-Rantzau disagreed. He instructed Bernstorff, after consulting Scheidemann and Erzberger, to end all contacts with Conger. Having separately reached the same conclusion, Bernstorff and Erzberger readily endorsed this action. With the chancellor's concurrence, these members of the German cabinet decided by June 13 to halt the secret negotiations with the United States.[43]

Conger's efforts on behalf of Germany failed because he lacked presidential authority. Despite the American military intelligence activities, Wilson as well as the Allied leaders refused to make the concessions that Brockdorff-Rantzau demanded at Versailles. Conger and his colleagues in Pershing's general staff had misrepresented the official American position during the peace conference. By encouraging the German leaders to expect a treaty more in accordance with their interpretation of the Fourteen Points than with Wilson's, these secret negotiations provided a substantial basis for the German conviction that the president betrayed them to the Allies at Paris. The Germans did not know that the American officers operated without instructions from the responsible civilians. Indeed, neither Conger nor any other member of Pershing's general staff even informed Wilson or the American Commission about their numerous meetings with Loeb, Einstein, and Baron von Eltz. The reports to them from Pershing and his staff included only Conger's interviews with Brockdorff-Rantzau, Erzberger, and Bernstorff, and other edited information. None of these reports revealed that the American officers negotiated secretly to influence the Armistice renewal and peace conditions for Germany.

Although obviously lacking presidential authority through the American Commission, Conger claimed that Pershing dealt directly with Wilson. This claim was inaccurate. The most important information the president received from the secret negotiations—the summary of "Peace Conditions Acceptable to Germany," the proposal for transporting General Haller's army through Germany, and the reports of Conger's and Henrotin's two trips to Berlin—reached him indirectly through General Bliss and Secretary Lansing. If Pershing ever discussed his intelligence officers' activities with Wilson, neither he nor the president left any record in their personal or official papers. Nor did Pershing communicate with the president through the War Department. Contrary to his standing orders from Secretary of War Newton D. Baker to "keep the Department fully advised of all that concerns your command," Pershing sent no information to Washington and received no instructions about the secret negotiations.[44]

In retrospect, Loeb questioned whether Conger had exceeded his instructions from Pershing. That was a possibility, for Loeb's reports contained considerably more detail than the existing AEF records on Conger's statements during their meetings. Although perhaps operating somewhat on his own, Conger probably did not depart very far from his instructions. Too many officers from the AEF General Headquarters were personally involved in the secret negotiations for their activities to have escaped Pershing's attention. Their frequent reports to Chief of Staff

McAndrew and to Pershing, as well as his numerous personal meetings with Conger and Nolan, offered the AEF commander-in-chief ample opportunity to curtail unauthorized activities.[45]

The secret German–American negotiations represented a significant breakdown in civilian control and military professionalism. Although, as Richard D. Challener noted, "the climax of civil supremacy" over military affairs occurred during his administration, President Wilson delegated extensive responsibility for military operations to the American Expeditionary Forces. "In the actual conduct of operations," General Pershing recalled, "I was given entire freedom and in this respect was to enjoy an experience unique in our history."[46] This practice, which had become the normal organizational process by the end of the war, permitted Pershing's general staff to abuse its power by exceeding the limits of strictly military affairs. As Fritz Epstein earlier observed, and contrary to Klaus Schwabe's later argument, Colonel Conger engaged in military diplomacy without civilian authorization. Pershing's general staff operated without the approval or supervision of the president either directly or through the American Commission to Negotiate Peace. These secret negotiations with Germany, for which Pershing was primarily responsible as AEF commander-in-chief, constituted a major interference with the official diplomacy of the Allied and Associated Powers during the Paris Peace Conference. Anticipating the later crisis in American civil–military relations, this episode epitomized the fundamental problem for a democratic government of maintaining responsible control over its intelligence activities.

CHAPTER 6

WILSON, THE REPUBLICANS, AND FRENCH SECURITY AFTER WORLD WAR I

Lloyd E. Ambrosius, "Wilson, the Republicans, and French Security after World War I," *The Journal of American History* 59 (September 1972): 341–52. Reprinted by permission of *The Journal of American History.*

Historians of the fight between Woodrow Wilson and the Senate over the Versailles Treaty have generally shared the president's perspective. From Denna Frank Fleming and W. Stull Holt through Ruhl J. Bartlett and Thomas A. Bailey to Selig Adler and John Chalmers Vinson, they have regarded the League of Nations as a valuable contribution to international relations, while viewing its Republican critics as negative and partisan politicians. Arno J. Mayer, who recently offered a significant account of the politics of peacemaking after World War I, adhered to this traditional interpretation. If the Republicans rather than Wilson had drafted the peace treaty with Germany, he concluded, "it would hardly have fostered a healthier international climate for the United States, for Europe, and for the world."[1] Vinson pictured the controversy over the League of Nations and the election of 1920 as a "referendum for isolation," while Adler interpreted the defeat of the Versailles Treaty and the victory of Warren G. Harding as evidence of "the isolationist impulse." John Milton Cooper, Jr., examined the origins of postwar American isolationism during the period of neutrality before 1917. He argued that before the United States intervened in World War I the Republicans had begun to coalesce around an isolationist position in opposition to Wilson's internationalism.[2]

By emphasizing the negative, partisan, and isolationist role of the Republicans during the treaty fight, historians have ignored the extent to which that party supported a positive alternative to Wilson's League of Nations. Many of the top Republican leaders—including Henry Cabot Lodge, Elihu Root, and Philander Knox—advocated the maintenance of the wartime coalition against Germany during the postwar years. They favored a military alliance limited to Western Europe, although they opposed the indefinite commitments of a universal League of Nations. Apprehensive of the resurgence of Germany, they wanted the United States to continue its wartime cooperation with the European Allies. Although examining the extensive support of these Republicans for the codification of international law, a world court, and arbitration, Warren F. Kuehl and Sondra R. Herman overlooked their interest in such a postwar guarantee of French security. Like the other historians, they viewed Wilson's League of Nations as the culmination of American internation-alism.[3] Even the biographers of leading Republicans have virtually ignored their posi-tive alternative to Wilson's League and their concern for the security of France.[4] The differences between the president and the Senate were more complex than historians have generally recognized. The treaty fight was not simply a contest between Democratic internationalism and Republican isolationism.

Lodge, the Republican leader and chairman of the Senate Foreign Relations Committee, outlined his recommendations for the peace settlement in an address to the Senate on December 21, 1918, and in a detailed memorandum that he gave to Henry White on December 2. Wilson had selected White, a career diplomat, as the only Republican member of the American delegation to the Paris Peace Conference. In the private communication, Lodge emphasized that "the first and controlling purpose of the peace must be to put Germany in such a position that it will be phys-ically impossible for her to break out again upon other nations with a war for world conquest." To achieve that objective, the senator called for the restoration of France and Belgium and for the establishment of a series of barrier states in Eastern Europe between Germany and Russia. As compensation for the wartime destruction, he wanted Germany to pay the maximum indemnity that it could afford. While demanding the postponement of the organization of the League of Nations, he stressed the continuing importance of unity between the United States and the Allies. By proposing these measures, Lodge supported the essential features of the peace program of the French premier Georges Clemenceau.[5]

Wilson ignored this advice and successfully urged the Allied leaders to proceed with the drafting of the Covenant for the League of Nations. Instead of an alliance limited to the victorious powers of World War I, the president envisaged a global system of collective security that would ultimately encompass all nations, including Germany. Article 10 of the Covenant, which Wilson regarded as the heart of that document, obligated each League member to respect and preserve the territorial integrity and political independence of every other member.

The publication of the preliminary draft of the Covenant on February 14, 1919, prompted the Republican leaders to clarify their attitudes toward the peacemaking in Paris. Henry L. Stimson, former secretary of war, immediately expressed his views to Will H. Hays, chairman of the Republican National Committee. Although criti-cal of Article 10 as a violation of the Monroe Doctrine, Stimson wanted Hays to avoid a negative response to the League of Nations. After consultations with Stimson, Hays turned to Root for a policy that could unify the party.[6] Root, former secretary of war and secretary of state in Theodore Roosevelt's cabinet, outlined his position in a public letter to Hays on March 29, 1919. Instead of the global system of collective security that Wilson advocated, the Republican elder statesman preferred a specific alliance. He wanted to avoid the indefinite commitments that Article 10 might entail. Nevertheless, since the League would initially consist only of the victorious powers and would amount in practice to the maintenance of the wartime coalition, Root announced his qualified support. "It is primarily not a provision for a permanent League of Nations," he briefly explained in another letter, "but for a continuance of the present alliance against the Central Powers for the purpose of the reconstruction which must necessarily follow the War." Before giving his full endorsement to American membership in the League, Root called on the peace conference to amend the Covenant to authorize the right of withdrawal.[7]

After the peace conference adopted the final Covenant with amendments on April 28, Lodge called on Root to evaluate the revised document. The majority leader hoped to unify the Republicans in the Senate behind Root's policy. In consultation with Senator Knox, who had served as William Howard Taft's secretary of state, Lodge and Root drafted a letter that Root sent to Lodge on June 19. As in the letter to Hays, Root noted the distinction between the League and an alliance. Hoping to avoid the indefinite commitments of Article 10, which would make the United States the world's policeman for an unlimited time, he nevertheless favored a specific alliance for the security of France. He explained that: "If it is necessity for the security of western Europe that we should agree to go to the support say of France if attacked, let us agree to do that particular thing plainly, so that every man and woman in the country will understand the honorable obligation we are assuming. I am in favor of that. But let us not wrap up such a purpose in a vague universal obligation, under the impression that it really does not mean anything likely to happen."[8]

Wilson failed to appreciate the distinction that Root and other Republicans made between a global system of collective security and an alliance limited to Western Europe. At the peace conference, to break the deadlock over the Rhineland question, the president had accepted the British prime minister David Lloyd George's proposal for Great Britain and the United States to protect France against unprovoked German aggression. In return for Clemenceau's abandonment of the French demand for the permanent occupation and separation of the Rhineland from Germany, the American and British leaders signed security treaties pledging their countries to defend France against a future German attack. When the president submitted the French security treaty to the Senate on July 29, 1919, he defended it as thoroughly consistent with the Covenant of the League of Nations. He viewed this alliance as a particular instance of the action that the League might take under Article 10 rather than as an alternative to it. The French security treaty, which Wilson had linked to the Covenant at Paris, stipulated in Article 3 that it would become and remain effective only with the approval of the League Council.[9]

By refusing to consider the alliance as an alternative to the League, Wilson jeopardized the support of Republican senators for the French security treaty. Albert J. Beveridge, who absolutely opposed any commitment in postwar Europe, urged Lodge to reject this treaty. Refusing to accept Beveridge's advice, the Republican leader from Massachusetts detailed his position. Writing on August 11, 1919, Lodge affirmed:

> If there had been no proposition such as is included in Article 10, but a simple proposition that it would be our intention to aid France, which is our barrier and outpost, when attacked without provocation by Germany, I should have strongly favored it for I feel very keenly the sacrifices of France and the immense value her gallant defense was to the whole world. But they have made the French treaty subject to the authority of the League, which is not to be tolerated. If we ever are called upon to go to the assistance of France as we were two years ago, we will go without asking anybody's leave. It is humiliating to be put in such an attitude and not the least of the mischief done by the League is that Article 10 will probably make it impossible to do anything for France as Root recommends and as many of our Senators desire.

Explaining his preference for an alliance with France unconnected with the League, Lodge said: "That would be a distinct and separate thing which we could well afford to do. When it is already wrapped up in that unending promise [of Article 10] to go to the assistance of anybody it becomes intolerable."[10]

During the struggle between Wilson and the Senate over the Versailles Treaty, a majority of the Republican senators demonstrated their willingness to join with Root and Lodge in favor of American membership in the League with reservations. But even some of the Republican senators who were irreconcilably opposed to Wilson's system of collective security revealed their concern for French security. As Ralph A. Stone noted, half of the irreconcilables favored the maintenance of the wartime coalition.[11] The most prominent member of this group, Knox, clearly expressed his desire for the United States to play a significant role in postwar Europe. He believed that any major shift in the European balance of power such as Germany had threatened during the World War should concern the United States.

On December 18, 1918, Knox summarized his "new American doctrine" in a major Senate address: "If a situation should arise in which any power or combination of powers should, directly or indirectly, menace the freedom and peace of Europe, the United States would regard such situation with grave concern as a menace to its own freedom and peace and would consult with other powers affected with a view to concerted action for the removal of such menace." Although uncompromising in his opposition to the League, Knox indicated his willingness to endorse a specific alliance. "If it prove wise for the United States to enter some definite entente," he asserted, "well and good, provided it be a small and natural one, bringing only limited and appropriate obligations." He left no cause for doubt about his attitude toward French security against Germany. On March 1, 1919, in the Senate, he declared that "our cobelligerents need have no anxiety, for so surely as the sun rises if the Hun flood again threatened to engulf the world, we shall again be found fighting for the right, with the same complete accord and cooperation as in the past, all for the defense of civilization." Knox, who wanted to avoid both Wilson's League and traditional isolationism, introduced a resolution on June 10 that embodied his "new American doctrine." In addition to separating the League Covenant from the Versailles Treaty, the resolution provided in Section 5 that

> it shall be the declared policy of our Government, in order to meet fully and fairly our obligations to ourselves and to the world, that the freedom and peace of Europe being again threatened by any power or combination of powers the United States will regard such a situation with grave concern as a menace to its own peace and freedom, will consult with other powers affected with a view to devising means for the removal of such menace, and will, the necessity arising in the future, carry out the same complete accord and cooperation with our chief cobelligerents for the defense of civilization.[12]

Another irreconcilable Republican, Frank B. Brandegee of Connecticut, shared Knox's perspective. On November 19, 1919, he suggested that the Senate should pass Section 5 of the Knox resolution rather than approve the ratification of the Versailles Treaty. "France will be satisfied with that," he declared. "All they want to know is that they will be secure. I think we ought to do something for France." Brandegee had earlier shown his interest in the French security treaty. When

President Wilson had neglected to send it to the Senate at the same time as the Versailles Treaty, he demanded its immediate submission. The senator criticized the president for violating a provision of the treaty with France that required him to submit it simultaneously with the Versailles Treaty. Brandegee asserted that the Senate should refuse to consider the treaty with Germany until it received the French security treaty. After repeated criticism from Brandegee on July 24 and 28, Wilson delivered this treaty to the Senate on the following day. When the Senate Foreign Relations Committee conferred with the president on August 19, Brandegee again raised the subject of the French security treaty. He voiced his opposition to the link between it and the League of Nations. He failed, however, to convince Wilson that the American government should not permit the League Council to determine whether or not the United States would protect France against German aggression.[13]

Senators George H. Moses of New Hampshire and Joseph Medill McCormick of Illinois, two of the seven Republican irreconcilables who generally agreed with Knox, expressed their willingness to support the French security treaty. Shortly after the announcement of this treaty in Paris, Moses, according to a report of the *New York Times* on May 9, stated his preference for the alliance with France and Great Britain instead of the Covenant. McCormick stated similar views in private correspondence, including a letter to William Jennings Bryan on November 22, 1919. Albert B. Fall of New Mexico, another member of the Knox group, refrained from giving an express endorsement to the French security treaty although he defended its constitutionality. In contrast, he criticized the Covenant for violating the Constitution by delegating to the League Council the authority to determine when aggression had taken place. The delegation of this authority, according to Fall, would mean the surrender of the power of Congress to decide whether or not to declare war. Under the French security treaty, the Congress would retain this power.[14] The attitudes of Moses and Fall were particularly significant because they, along with Lodge, Knox, and Brandegee, were members of the Senate Foreign Relations Committee. The votes of the seven Democrats in addition to those of any two of these five Republicans would have sufficed to report the French security treaty to the Senate.

The other two Republican irreconcilables who were members of the Senate Foreign Relations Committee did not share the views of the Knox group. Hiram W. Johnson of California and William E. Borah of Idaho opposed the French security treaty as well as the League of Nations. Johnson used Wilson's justification of the alliance as a criticism of the Covenant. If the American commitment to France represented nothing more than a particular instance of the obligations under Article 10, he argued, then the acceptance of membership in the League would make the United States the world's policeman. He doubted that the American people were prepared to assume such unlimited responsibilities. He feared, however, that the Senate might approve the French security treaty even if it rejected the League. Johnson informed Beveridge on November 24, 1919, that "very many of the Senators have been carried away with the idea, first, of doing this for France, and secondly, with adopting a course, which they foolishly thought might avoid a league of nations."[15]

Earlier that year, when the first reports of the French security treaty reached the United States, Beveridge encouraged Borah to oppose it as well as the League. Borah agreed. He noted, moreover, that the Allied leaders apparently lacked confidence in the League or the French security treaty would not be necessary.[16] Borah opposed both the League and the alliance because he wanted in no way to curtail the future independence of the United States. However, he never argued that German aggression against France would not concern the United States. During debate in the Senate on July 25, although explicitly opposing the French security treaty, Borah stated: "I do not say that we should not go to the rescue of France in case Germany assaults her. I am not arguing that question at all; but I do say that if that condition ever arose the people of that particular time, judging all the facts as they should then exist, should have the right to determine whether or not they should go to war, free of any obligation whatever to take anyone else's construction."[17] James M. Beck, a leading Republican foe of the League outside of the Senate, had recently suggested to Borah that the United States might enter an alliance with the European Allies. The senator responded by reaffirming his opposition to a "political combination with European powers," although he expressed a preference for "leaving aside the question of the special alliance." By emphasizing the League rather than the alliance and by linking the two together, President Wilson made it easier for Borah to oppose the French security treaty.[18]

Within the Republican ranks, the mild reservationists rather than the irreconcilables gave the least support to the balance-of-power policy of Senator Knox. Except for George W. Norris of Nebraska, the eleven senators listed by Knox as opponents of his resolution included those who were most willing to endorse Wilson's League. The remaining 38 Republicans, numbering more than one-third of the Senate, undoubtedly favored the Knox resolution for a variety of reasons. Some, such as Johnson and Borah, probably supported it as a method of killing the League; probably for the opposite reason, the mild reservationists refused their support. But apparently many of the Republican senators agreed with Knox's "new American doctrine," even though they insisted on strong reservations before approving American membership in the League of Nations.[19]

Wilson, by subordinating the French security treaty to the League, sacrificed the possibility of agreement with the Republicans on a policy for the protection of France against German aggression. The president, the Democratic senators, and the mild reservationist Republicans undoubtedly hoped to achieve that objective through the League. Other Republicans, who were just as concerned with French security, preferred an alliance limited to Western Europe. Wilson's action, which split the ranks of the Republican senators, caused Lodge to fear the defeat of the French security treaty. On May 20, 1919, shortly after the publication of this treaty in Paris, the majority leader informed White that "if there had been no Article 10, I think it would have stood a very good chance. What its future will be now, I cannot say." He reiterated this assessment of the Senate a month later. Lodge reported that "Article 10 has created hostility ... particularly to giving a specific support to France in case of German invasion, which, if it had not been for Article 10 of the League or for the League itself, would I think have unquestionably been granted."[20]

During the midst of the League fight in the Senate, Lodge continued his interest in the ratification of the French security treaty. In mid-October he expressed his intention to call for action on this alliance as soon as the Senate finished with the Versailles Treaty.[21] Before taking this action, however, he expected to sever the link between the French security treaty and the League. On November 1, Root urged

Lodge to proceed with the ratification of the French security treaty. He explained that "it is desirable to accompany the opposition which you are making to the vague and indefinite commitments of the League Covenant with an exhibition of willingness to do the definite certain specific things which are a proper part of the true American policy, and which are necessary to secure the results of the War upon which America has expended so much life and treasure."[22] Like Lodge, Root expected the Senate first to remove Article 3 of the treaty that subordinated this guarantee of French security to the action of the League Council. In his reply, the senator reiterated his support for the French security treaty and his determination to achieve its ratification. He reported, however, that Senator Irvine Lenroot of Wisconsin doubted that the Senate would give its consent even with the removal of Article 3.[23]

By the end of the session on November 19, Lodge despaired of the possibility of gaining the Senate's approval of the French security treaty. The Republicans alone lacked the votes necessary for ratification, and the Democrats refused to join them. Explaining the predicament, he said: "I am anxious to get the treaty through but I cannot hope to pass it unless the Democrats, or the bulk of them, will go with those of us who favor the treaty and I have not been able to find out, although I have been at work on it since the session began, what they are going to do in regard to it or what the President wants to have them do. That is the difficulty of the situation."[24] Brandegee as well as Lodge noted the failure of the president to support the French security treaty. Speculating on the reason for this neglect, Brandegee wrote Beveridge that "Wilson is doing nothing whatever to urge the Senate to pass the French–American Treaty which he promised to France. I do not believe he will raise his finger in behalf of this Treaty because he will think that the passage of this Treaty would tend to relieve the pressure by France for the ratification of the German Peace Treaty. Therefore he will abandon the only thing which France cares about and sacrifice it to his Covenant."[25]

Since the Republicans refused to consider the French security treaty connected with the League and the Democrats refused to consider it aside from the League, no agreement was possible. Although the president and members of the Senate from both parties hoped to protect France from future German aggression, the conflict over methods prevented a clear statement of that policy. Referring to this situation, Lodge described the fate of the French security treaty in *The Senate and the League of Nations:*

> The treaty was duly referred to the Committee on Foreign Relations. It was never taken up and never reported out. It would have been quite useless to do so, even if the Committee had favored it, for I do not think there was the slightest chance that the Senate would ever have voted to accept it. There was no desire on the part of Senators of either Party at that stage to bind the United States irrevocably with agreements to go to war again under certain prescribed conditions.[26]

This account, published in 1925, gave an excessively negative picture of the situation in 1919, for Lodge neglected to explain the disagreement over Article 3, the failure of the president to lend his support, and the extent to which the fight over Article 10 contributed to opposition to any commitment in postwar Europe. His book, moreover, reflected Lodge's own increasing disillusionment with postwar France.[27]

White, who held the best position for mediating between Wilson and the Republican leaders, failed in this task. During the peace conference, he carried on an extensive correspondence with Lodge and Root. Yet, he seemed unable to comprehend the criticism that Republican senators leveled against the League. It puzzled White that the president's critics seemed to favor an alliance with France, for he could not imagine that the Senate might approve the treaty with France while rejecting the League. Because of his inability to appreciate the position of the Republican leaders, White failed in the basic task of a good diplomat—the accurate communication of information. No meaningful dialogue between the president and the Senate could take place through White.[28]

Former President Taft, like White and Wilson, hoped to guarantee the security of France through the League of Nations. As president of the League to Enforce Peace, he was the most prominent Republican advocate of collective security. During the treaty fight, he attempted to bridge the gap between the president and the Republicans by working with the mild reservationists. In his frequent correspondence with Frank B. Kellogg of Minnesota, Porter J. McCumber of North Dakota, Charles L. McNary of Oregon, and LeBaron B. Colt of Rhode Island, neither the former president nor these Republican senators indicated any interest in the French security treaty. Apparently indifferent, they evidenced neither the hostility of Borah and Johnson nor the support of Root and Lodge for the alliance with France.[29]

A wide variety of attitudes on the problem of French security existed within the Republican party after World War I. Root and Lodge, the important leaders outside and within the Senate, supported the French security treaty. According to the estimates of Lodge and Johnson, "many" or "very many" of the senators favored this alliance. The Knox group of irreconcilables, even if all of them did not advocate the ratification of the treaty with France, at least favored the maintenance of the wartime coalition with the European Allies. Taft and the mild reservationists hoped to achieve the same goal through the League of Nations.

Wilson, by subordinating the French security treaty to the League, sacrificed the potential support of Republicans for an alliance limited to Western Europe. By forcing a choice between a global system of collective security and a total abdication of responsibility, he unwittingly strengthened the position of irreconcilables such as Borah and Johnson, who opposed both the League and the French security treaty. The responsibility for the failure of the United States to adopt a constructive policy toward the problem of French security therefore rested at least as much with Wilson as with the Republicans. To the extent that any party in opposition in the United States can, the Republicans offered a viable alternative to the president's peace program. The rigidity of Wilson's thought, as he refused to consider any alternative to the League of Nations, prevented him from recognizing this opportunity for agreement with the Republicans in the Senate.

Historians who have shared the president's perspective have failed to recognize the complexity of the controversy in the Senate. Interpreting the treaty fight as a contest between Democratic internationalism and Republican isolationism, they have necessarily ignored the extensive support among Republicans for an alliance with France. The Republicans have consequently appeared to play a negative and partisan role by opposing Wilson's League of Nations. Only a few scholars, such as the realists after World War II, have adopted the ideas that various Republican leaders expressed after World War I. George F. Kennan, Hans J. Morgenthau, and Robert E. Osgood shared their skepticism about Wilson's utopian plan for permanent peace as well as their emphasis on close cooperation between the United States and the European Allies. The realists similarly favored an alliance limited to Western Europe rather than a universal system of collective security. They regarded a German invasion of France, whether in 1914 or 1940, as a threat to the European balance of power and consequently to the United States. Like the top Republican leaders, they identified French security as an American national interest. Yet, even the realists have overlooked the affinity between their position and the views of earlier Republicans.[30] Thus, the critics as well as the defenders of Wilson's perspective have neglected to examine the differences between the president and the Republicans over the question of French security after World War I. They have alike ignored the importance of this issue for the reinterpretation of the treaty fight in 1919.

CHAPTER 7

THE UNITED STATES AND THE WEIMAR REPUBLIC: AMERICA'S RESPONSE TO THE GERMAN PROBLEM

Lloyd E. Ambrosius, "The United States and the Weimar Republic: America's Response to the German Problem," in *Perspectives in American Diplomacy: Essays on Europe, Latin America, China, and the Cold War,* ed. Jules Davids (New York: Arno Press, 1976), 78–104.

America's response to the German problem after World War I occurred within the intellectual framework that Woodrow Wilson articulated and epitomized. In the Fourteen Points and subsequent wartime addresses that became the basis for the Armistice with Germany, he promised a liberal peace of "impartial justice" to victor and vanquished alike.[1] He wanted the United States to play the leading role in the League of Nations to preserve such a peace. Wilson's conception of the League emphasized both the functions of enforcing and revising the Versailles Treaty. Article 10 of the League Covenant provided for enforcement by promising the preservation of territorial integrity and political independence "against external aggression." Article 19 outlined the procedure for revision of outmoded treaty provisions and for "consideration of international conditions whose continuance might endanger the peace of the world."[2] Wilson saw no contradiction between these two functions of enforcement and revision because he assumed that his peace program would reconcile the differences between Germany and the Allies. He viewed himself as the spokesman for the people of all countries.

At the Paris Peace Conference of 1919 during a dispute with the French premier Georges Clemenceau over the Saar Valley, the president requested permission to take his case directly to the French people. "If you will permit me to explain to them candidly my own feeling," he asserted to Clemenceau, "I have no fear of their judgment."[3] Wilson's supreme confidence that his peace would satisfy both victor and vanquished led him to underestimate the difficulty of enforcing the Versailles Treaty. Voicing the president's perspective, Secretary of State Robert Lansing rejected strategic considerations in the determination of Germany's eastern border. He contended that "the fixing of frontier lines with a view to their military strength and in contemplation of war was directly contrary to the whole spirit of the League of Nations, of international disarmament, and of the policy of the United States as set forth in the declarations of President Wilson."[4] No such methods for the enforcement of the treaty appeared necessary to American leaders because of their belief in the possibility of reconciliation between Germany and the Allies.

This belief, or what might be called the myth of a Wilson peace, characterized the president's vision of the League of Nations. Convinced that a liberal peace would require minimal enforcement or revision, he advocated American leadership in the world organization without anticipating major burdens for the United States. He wanted the American government to play the key role in deciding when to enforce and when to revise the peace settlement, while avoiding entanglement in the affairs of the Old World.[5]

The fundamental difficulty with Wilson's solution to the German problem was that his definition of justice differed substantially from Germany's. Early in 1919, Friedrich Ebert, president of the new Weimar Republic, affirmed his nation's commitment to the Fourteen Points. "Germany laid down her arms trusting in President Wilson's principles," he reminded the American and Allied leaders in Paris. "Let them now give us the Wilson peace to which we lay claim. Our free and popular republic, the whole German people, asks only to be allowed to enter the League of Nations as an equal, and through industry and ability to earn a respected position."[6] As the peace conference proceeded with the drafting of the treaty, German leaders became increasingly disillusioned with the results. By late April, Ellis Loring Dresel, a specialist on German affairs in the American Commission to Negotiate Peace, was surprised by the "unexpectedly bitter and aggressive attitude of people" in Berlin.[7]

Before the presentation of the treaty to the German delegation at Versailles on May 7, 1919, Chancellor Philipp Scheidemann and Foreign Minister Ulrich von Brockdorff-Rantzau prepared to resist what they regarded as a harsh and unjust peace. They felt that the treaty violated the American and Allied commitment to the Fourteen Points. "The entire German Government," Dresel's assistant reported, "is overwhelmed by the severity of the peace terms .... No one can account for the entire failure to realize Wilson's principles."[8] Rather than sign the Versailles Treaty, the German delegation demanded its revision. Prime Minister David Lloyd George and other delegates from the British Empire were somewhat sympathetic, but Clemenceau and other French leaders opposed any substantial concessions. Wilson joined with the Allied premiers in rejecting most of the German demands. They chose instead to impose their conditions of peace on Germany, requiring its endorsement of their definition of justice.[9]

Wilson's obvious failure to satisfy Germany as well as the Allies revealed the inadequacy of his European policy. His interpretation of the Fourteen Points was unacceptable in the Weimar Republic. He had assumed that Germany's new representative government would share his conception of a liberal peace, but its unanimity of opposition challenged this illusion. The Democratic party in Germany, which most nearly conformed to Wilson's ideal, withdrew from the Weimar coalition in protest against the Versailles Treaty, leaving the onerous task of signing and ratifying it to the Social Democratic and Center parties. The implications of these political developments were ignored by the president. Because of the continuing estrangement between Germany and the West, the treaty would require more extensive enforcement or revision than he anticipated. Yet, Wilson pursued neither alternative.

The failure of the Versailles peace to reconcile the former enemies was not merely the result of extreme Allied, and especially French, claims against a defeated

Germany. If the Allies had accepted Wilson's position on every disputed point at the peace conference, the treaty would still have failed to meet the German demands for revision. The only other alternative was enforcement, but the president steadfastly refused any continuing American obligations for this purpose except through the League of Nations.[10] Although minimal enforcement or revision would not achieve the desired accommodation, Wilson continued to place his hopes in the League for the resolution of European conflicts. He called on his countrymen to accept his vision of America's "destiny" as a leading world power. "It has come about," the president proclaimed as he officially presented the Versailles Treaty to the Senate, "by no plan of our conceiving, but by the hand of God who led us into this way. We cannot turn back. We can only go forward, with lifted eyes and freshened spirit, to follow the vision."[11]

Seeking to cope with the unresolved conflicts between Germany and the West, the British and French governments adopted divergent policies during the interwar years. British policymakers from Lloyd George to Neville Chamberlain sought peace through appeasement. Except for Austin Chamberlain, they pressed for revision of the Versailles Treaty without special regard for French interests. In contrast, the French solution to the German problem emphasized enforcement. Although French leaders such as Clemenceau and Aristide Briand and even Raymond Poincaré were not inflexible, they generally favored the maintenance of the status quo as defined by the peace treaty.[12]

These differences, and Wilson's indecisiveness, were apparent in the first major postwar crisis that resulted from the Kapp Putsch. General Walther von Lüttwitz and other military officers in the Reichswehr, who opposed the disarmament required by the Versailles Treaty, attempted to destroy the Weimar Republic and create a new government under Wolfgang Kapp. When this new military government was proclaimed on March 13, 1920, workers and civil servants in Berlin and throughout Germany engaged in a general strike to prevent its success. Within a few days the coup failed and the legitimate government of President Ebert and Chancellor Gustav Bauer resumed power in Berlin. Radical workers in the Ruhr industrial region, however, refused to disband their Red Army, while demanding disarmament of the Reichswehr and punishment of the supporters of the Kapp regime. This challenge to the authority of the legitimate government gave the Reichswehr, whose top officers had remained neutral during the Kapp Putsch, the opportunity to restore its prestige as the defender of the republic against Bolshevism.

The crisis assumed international dimensions because much of the Ruhr Valley lay within the demilitarized zone. To restore order, the German government requested permission to send troops into that area. But before the Allies approved this request, the new cabinet of Chancellor Hermann Müller ordered the Reichswehr into the demilitarized zone. Although this fait accompli violated precisely those provisions of the Versailles Treaty that were emphasized in the abortive French security treaties with Great Britain and the United States, the British government approved the German action and opposed any retaliatory measures. The French government, in contrast, sought to enforce the treaty by occupying German towns along the Main River pending the withdrawal of the Reichswehr from the demilitarized zone. The Lloyd George government protested against Premier Alexandre Millerand's independent effort at enforcement. The United States adopted a fairly passive position during the crisis. President Wilson and Secretary of State Bainbridge Colby shared the British attitude and approved the German action, despite the violation of the Versailles Treaty and the French security treaty. Their protests against the independent French response, however, were less vigorous than those of the British. The Wilson administration thus avoided major responsibility for either revising or enforcing the peace settlement.[13]

Although unwilling to enforce the Versailles peace, President Wilson refused to abandon it. When the Senate rejected the treaty without reservations, he declined to compromise or to consider a separate peace with Germany. This impasse between the executive and legislative branches of the American government was resolved by the new Republican administration. President Warren G. Harding accepted the Congressional Peace Resolution as the basis for a settlement with Germany. During the negotiations that culminated in the German–American Treaty of Berlin on August 25, 1921, the American officials demanded that Germany recognize all of the rights and privileges that the United States would have gained under the Versailles Treaty. Avoiding the obligations of that treaty, the Harding administration excluded the unacceptable provisions such as the Covenant of the League of Nations.[14]

Despite their differences over the separate peace, there was substantial continuity from Wilson to Harding in American policy toward Europe. The exclusion from the Berlin Treaty of those sections of the Versailles Treaty relating to European political and territorial questions followed the same priorities that Wilson had earlier outlined. During the Armistice negotiations in October 1918, the president had omitted these same conditions from his list of "essentially American terms" in the Fourteen Points. Except for the League of Nations, which in itself offered no solution to the German problem, both the Republicans and the Democrats agreed on the basic definition of American interests in Europe.[15]

During the early 1920s, the issue of reparations became the focal point of tension between Germany and the West. This issue was politically explosive because reparations were justified in Article 231 by the assertion of Germany's responsibility for the war. This war-guilt clause was the special contribution of John Foster Dulles, who later became President Dwight D. Eisenhower's secretary of state in the 1950s, to the Versailles Treaty.[16] By May 1921, when the Allies forced Germany to accept the London Schedule of Payments, the British began to heed the arguments of economists such as John Maynard Keynes in favor of revision. So, too, did the French. The London Schedule for the payment of reparations actually imposed less of a burden on Germany than appeared on the surface. The British and French governments, however, did not publicize their concessions for fear of political repercussions at home. The German government naturally ignored them because it hoped for still further revision. Chancellor Joseph Wirth and the key member of his cabinet, Walther Rathenau, developed the policy of "fulfillment" for the purpose not really of fulfilling the terms of the Versailles Treaty in the strictest sense, but merely to the extent necessary to avoid harsher terms while gaining time for more extensive revision.[17]

The American government shunned entanglement in the controversy over reparations, wanting to avoid responsibility for both enforcement and revision. Throughout the decade it refused to acknowledge any link between war debts and reparations. "The position of this Government," Secretary of State Charles Evans

Hughes explained, "has always been that the question of debts is irrelevant to the question of German reparations. Germany can not pay more or less because of what France may owe and France can not collect what Germany can not pay."[18] With this attitude, the Harding administration remained aloof from the developing European crisis over reparations. When Germany defaulted on its payments and Premier Poincaré retaliated by sending French troops into the Ruhr in January 1923, the United States responded by withdrawing the remaining American troops from the Rhineland. This termination of American participation in the Rhineland occupation, which had continued since the Armistice, removed the last symbol of American commitment to the enforcement of the Versailles Treaty.[19]

The conclusion of a separate peace with Germany and the withdrawal of American troops from the Rhineland marked the resurgence of traditional American isolation from Europe. After 1923, the United States avoided political and military commitments in the Old World but continued its close financial and commercial relations with Europe. Because of its overwhelming economic power, the United States exercised a tremendous influence on European affairs, despite the attitude of aloofness on the part of American policymakers. This combination of aloofness and involvement was aptly labeled by Joan Hoff Wilson as "independent internationalism."[20] The policies of the American government exemplified this stance toward Europe. The United States played a decisive role in the revision of the reparations settlement through the Dawes and Young plans of 1924 and 1929, but without sacrificing its tariff and debt policies. Americans refused to acknowledge any link between war debts and reparations or that the Fordney-McCumber Tariff of 1922 and the Hawley-Smoot Tariff of 1930 hindered the payment of both these obligations. To achieve the desired revision of the reparations settlement without assuming responsibility for the results, the Harding and Coolidge administrations encouraged the formation of committees of experts, which were not officially linked with the American or Allied governments. Although two Americans, Charles Dawes and Owen Young, chaired the committees that drafted the plans that bore their names, the United States avoided any direct responsibility for these major revisions of the Versailles Treaty.[21]

President Calvin Coolidge emphasized the American economic interest in Europe. "We have the interest of our debt," he stated in reference to the American involvement in the committees of experts that formulated the Dawes plan, "and our interest in the economic recovery of Europe." Although desirous of contributing toward European prosperity, the president wanted to avoid political entanglement. He hoped for the success in August 1924 of the London Conference, which would adopt the Dawes plan and arrange for the withdrawal of French troops from the Ruhr, but refused to play a direct role in these European affairs. "We wouldn't want to take a part in their political discussions over there," said Coolidge, "and on the other hand we want to do everything we possibly can to assist in any way we can without getting into their political difficulties."[22]

This attitude of political isolation from Europe continued to shape American policy in the 1920s. When the European governments began to consider the appointment of new committees of experts for the purpose of replacing the Dawes plan with a final reparations settlement, the Coolidge administration declined to nominate American members. As Secretary of State Frank Kellogg explained in

October 1928, "The American interest in reparations is entirely too small to justify this Government's assumption, either directly or indirectly, of any responsibility respecting settlement of the whole problem of reparations."[23] Like Charles Dawes earlier, Owen Young would serve in a private rather than official capacity.

Even in pursuit of the Open Door for American commerce, the American government sought to avoid political entanglement. Writing to President Coolidge in November 1923, Secretary of State Hughes summarized the Open Door policy of the United States. "Our position," he explained, "is that we are always ready to give appropriate support to our nationals in seeking opportunities for business enterprise abroad, but we do not undertake to make the government a party to the business negotiations or use political pressure for the benefit of private interests in order to obtain particular concessions, or intervene in favor of one American interest as against another. We are persistent in our efforts to maintain the Open Door policy, or equality of commercial opportunity, but we do not attempt to assume obligations for the government, expressed or implied, which under our system we could not undertake to discharge."[24] One month later, in December 1923, this conception of the Open Door was written into the German–American Commercial Treaty, which served as the model for subsequent treaty negotiations during the Republican era.[25] In the perspective of American policymakers, there was no contradiction between political isolation from Europe and the pursuit of the Open Door.

William Appleman Williams ignored this American attitude of aloofness, while emphasizing the involvement of the United States in European economic affairs and the consequent political impact on Europe of that American involvement. He dismissed too readily the so-called legend of isolationism in the 1920s.[26] Williams's interpretation was embraced by a German scholar, Werner Link, in his book on the American stabilization policy in Germany. In this comprehensive study of German–American relations from 1921 to 1932, Link stressed the role of the United States in the recovery of Germany. Focusing particularly on reparations, he, like Williams, explored the interrelationship between economic and political affairs. What Williams and Link failed to appreciate, however, was that American leaders in the 1920s made a sharp distinction between politics and economics, and that these categories—however artificial—influenced their policies. Link and Williams also neglected political and military issues that were not directly involved in financial and commercial relations.[27]

American political and military isolation from Europe contributed to the success of German revisionism. Without the support of the United States, the Allies began to remove their control over the Weimar Republic. With considerable mastery, Gustav Stresemann, the chief architect of German foreign policy from 1923 to 1929, pursued the goal of ending the enforcement of the Versailles Treaty. Continuing the policy that Wirth and Rathenau had started when they signed the Rapallo Treaty in April 1922, which normalized diplomatic and commercial relations between Germany and the Soviet Union, he played Russia off against the West to gain concessions from both sides. Soviet–German collaboration, which facilitated the rearmament of Germany, weakened the position of Poland and consequently helped to undermine the French system of alliances. Stresemann further eroded the French alliances with Poland and Czechoslovakia with his proposal for a multinational guarantee against aggression in

Western Europe. Written into the Locarno Treaty in October 1925, this guarantee satisfied the immediate French requirements for security, but at the expense of France's eastern allies. The Locarno Treaty also ended the prospect that Great Britain might conclude a new alliance with France to replace the earlier security treaty, which had been nullified by the American refusal to ratify its counterpart. In the spirit of Locarno, the French and British welcomed Germany into the League of Nations in September 1926. With a seat on the Council, the German government could now veto any effort by the League to enforce the peace treaty. When the British and French governments agreed to remove the Inter-Allied Military Control Commission from Germany in January 1927, Stresemann succeeded in ending their surveillance over the German armed forces. Although the Weimar Republic had never fully complied with the conditions of disarmament of the Versailles Treaty, the Allied governments ignored the violations and ceased their attempt at enforcement. Stresemann's final effort to remove Allied control over Germany culminated after his death in the complete withdrawal of British and French troops from the Rhineland by June 1930.[28]

The revision of the Versailles Treaty during the 1920s failed to achieve the desired reconciliation between Germany and the West. The spirit of Locarno, like the myth of a Wilson peace, proved to be an illusion. Ignoring the implications of these developments in European diplomacy, American officials maintained policies toward Europe that had lost touch with reality. The outlawing of aggressive war with the 1928 Kellogg-Briand Pact and American proposals for disarmament provided no solution to the German problem.[29]

Nevertheless, President Herbert Hoover continued to pursue peace and prosperity through revision. Epitomizing the American stance of "independent internationalism," he wanted the United States to play an influential role in Europe without assuming responsibility for the enforcement of the Versailles Treaty. Hoover's policies as president followed his earlier views. During the Paris Peace Conference in 1919, he had encouraged Wilson to avoid postwar commitments and preserve American independence. "It grows upon me daily," wrote Hoover, "that the United States is the one great moral reserve in the world today and that we cannot maintain the independence of action through which this reserve is to be sustained if we allow ourselves to be dragged into the detailed European entanglements over a period of years."[30] He supported Wilson's peace program, including the League of Nations, but deemphasized Article 10 of the Covenant. Hoover saw the League primarily as an instrument of appeasement and revision rather than enforcement. As he later wrote, "The major purpose of the League was to serve as a medium of pacific settlement of controversies among free nations."[31] Along with John Maynard Keynes, he criticized the excessive reparations claims of the Allies. He feared that such harsh terms would undermine the moderate parties of the Weimar Republic and strengthen the militarist and Bolshevik extremists, thereby destroying the hope of democracy in Germany. Hoover, consequently, opposed what he regarded as a Carthaginian peace, and he advocated revision of the Versailles Treaty.[32]

President Hoover's policies supported German revisionism during the last years of the Weimar Republic. Once the Allies adopted the Young plan and withdrew their last troops from the Rhineland, the authoritarian government of Chancellor Heinrich Brüning and Foreign Minister Julius Curtius abandoned the policy of "fulfillment." They adopted a more active foreign policy designed to gain political support at home and to remove some of the remaining restrictions of the Versailles Treaty. They set out to achieve a German–Austrian customs union as a first step toward an eventual Anschluss between these two German-speaking countries, to secure a moratorium on reparations payments under the Young plan, and to obtain recognition of the principle of equality of armaments for Germany in relation to the Western powers. Hoover welcomed the announcement in March 1931 of a customs union between Germany and Austria. "Evidently you don't approve of the Versailles Treaty," Secretary of State Henry Stimson said in surprise upon hearing the president's position. "Of course I don't," answered Hoover, "I never did."[33] Ignoring the political implications of the customs union, he shared none of the French fears arising from this unilateral German violation of the peace treaty. French opposition would ultimately force the governments of Austria and consequently Germany to abandon their plans for the customs union, but this French triumph owed nothing to the United States. During this controversy, the financial crisis in Europe and the United States substantially worsened.

In May 1931, the Kreditanstalt, Austria's largest bank, collapsed, sending shock waves through Germany to the United States. The prospect of major bank failures in both these countries mounted as private American banks increasingly curtailed their loans to Germany. When Hoover became aware that leading New York banks, which had loaned substantial shares of their reserves to Germany, might fail in the event of a financial collapse there, he intervened dramatically. He proposed a one-year moratorium beginning July 1, 1931, on intergovernmental payments of reparations and war debts. Hoover thereby implicitly recognized the link between these two, although he still officially refused to acknowledge it. As an outstanding example of "independent internationalism," the Hoover moratorium was announced unilaterally by the American government without adequate consultation with the Allies or with Germany. Hoover soon became aware that the moratorium alone would not avert the threatened financial collapse. A few weeks later he urged the adoption of a standstill agreement that would prevent the withdrawal of private credit from Germany. By halting intergovernmental payments and restriction of private loans, the Hoover moratorium and the standstill agreement eased the financial crisis of 1931. During the negotiations over these financial concessions to Germany, the French government suggested the idea of a political moratorium. Such a limitation on Germany's rights under Article 19 of the Covenant to request further revision, however, was unacceptable in both Berlin and Washington. At the end of the one-year moratorium, the Lausanne agreement effectively ended all efforts by the Allies to collect reparations from Germany. They expected the United States to adopt a similarly lenient policy on war debts, which Hoover still hoped to avoid because he wanted to shift the burden from the United States. He preferred to pursue peace and prosperity through revision rather than enforcement of the Versailles Treaty, and preferably at the expense of the Allies instead of the United States or Germany.[34]

Before the final revision or cancellation of the reparations settlement, President Paul von Hindenburg replaced Brüning with Franz von Papen, who represented Germany at the Lausanne Conference. His new government, closely linked with the Reichswehr, also continued the previous cabinet's demand for equality of armaments. At the World

Disarmament Conference in Geneva, the American delegation supported Germany's claim by urging the adoption of the Hoover plan for disarmament. Although his plan for the reduction of offensive weapons was not approved, Hoover endorsed a major concession to the Weimar Republic in order to prevent the failure of the conference. On December 11, 1932, shortly before Adolf Hitler's seizure of power, the United States joined with the Allies in recognizing the principle of equality for German armaments. The Disarmament Conference adopted a convention that affirmed Germany's "equality of rights in a system which would provide security for all nations."[35] The Hoover administration's revisionist solution to the German problem, however, failed to enable the more moderate parties to retain control in the Weimar Republic.

During the 1930s, the alternatives of enforcement and revision, which President Wilson had combined in his conception of the League of Nations, became increasingly divergent. Hugh R. Wilson, the last American ambassador to Nazi Germany, continued to argue the wisdom of revision and appeasement even after the beginning of World War II.[36] In contrast, the historian William E. Dodd, who had served as President Franklin D. Roosevelt's ambassador to Germany from 1933 to 1937, abandoned that alternative after the Munich Conference. He now claimed that if only the Republicans in the Senate had accepted the Wilson peace and the United States had joined the League of Nations, the world would not be facing its present situation in 1938. Although as ambassador he had experienced considerable difficulty in recommending policies for coping with Hitler's Germany, Dodd skipped over the interwar years to reaffirm the myth of a Wilson peace.[37] He thus made an early contribution to the campaign for liberal internationalism, which was now identified with collective security rather than appeasement. With the triumph of this campaign during World War II, Wilson's vision of American leadership in world affairs would enjoy a "second chance" and would become an integral part of American ideology during the Cold War. America's response to the German problem after World War I would thus continue to influence the foreign relations of the United States well beyond the era of the Weimar Republic.[38]

The myth of a Wilson peace shaped a variety of responses to the German problem after World War I. The president's search for "impartial justice" at Paris in 1919 continued in the form of the revisionism and appeasement of Herbert Hoover and Hugh R. Wilson as well as in the liberal internationalism of William E. Dodd. Belief in the feasibility of Wilson's peace program has characterized a half-century of historical writing by his defenders from Dodd and Ray Stannard Baker to Arthur S. Link.[39] Even the president's critics have often endorsed a mythical Wilson peace. John Maynard Keynes criticized the Carthaginian character of the Versailles Treaty. He claimed that Lloyd George and Clemenceau bamboozled Wilson into abandoning his Fourteen Points in favor of a harsh settlement. Keynes assumed that if only the president had not been bamboozled, he could have achieved a peace of reconciliation between Germany and the Allies. Keynes's critique influenced both British and American revisionists. During the postwar years, Americans such as Harry Elmer Barnes raised the war-guilt question and advocated changes in the treaty to achieve an elusive Wilson peace.[40]

British and American criticism of the war-guilt clause and reparations settlement coincided with the German appeal for revision. Yet, while Keynes attributed the failure at Paris to the bamboozlement of Wilson, German nationalists condemned the president for betraying his commitment to their country by abandoning the Fourteen Points. Demanding what they regarded as a genuine Wilson peace—instead of the Versailles Treaty—they, too, fostered the illusion of its feasibility. Like Stresemann during the Locarno era, German nationalists refused to acknowledge that they and Wilson had never interpreted his Fourteen Points in the same way.

In recent years, New Left historians have offered still another explanation for Wilson's failure at the peace conference. Arno J. Mayer and N. Gordon Levin, Jr., attributed it to his fear of Bolshevism rather than to the success of Clemenceau and Lloyd George in bamboozling the president or to his willful betrayal of Germany. Reacting to the Russian Revolution, Wilson appeared to these historians to sacrifice his liberal peace program and to join the Allied leaders in a counterrevolutionary front against the Bolshevik threat. Mayer and Levin assumed that by reacting so negatively to radical revolution and by endorsing the punitive Allied claims, the president had abandoned the real hope for a just peace.[41]

In the most outstanding study of German–American relations in 1918–1919, the German historian Klaus Schwabe provided a different version of the myth of a Wilson peace. He renounced both the betrayal thesis of the German nationalists and the counterrevolutionary thesis of the New Left. Rejecting as well Keynes's caricature of the "bamboozled" Wilson and the traditional American defense of him as a largely successful diplomatist at Paris, Schwabe instead accounted for the president's failure to write the Fourteen Points into the Versailles Treaty by emphasizing the weakness of postwar Germany. Despite his good intentions and clear perception, Schwabe concluded, the president could not compel the Allies to implement the Fourteen Points because of German impotence resulting from the Armistice. In this interpretation of the peacemaking, Schwabe presupposed that a more powerful Germany might have enabled the American president to achieve a mutually acceptable "Wilson peace."[42] Such an accomplishment, however, remained beyond the capabilities of the statesmen of the United States and the Weimar Republic.

In its various forms, the myth of a Wilson peace thus continued to characterize the historiography on German–American relations as well as the official American response to the German problem after World War I.

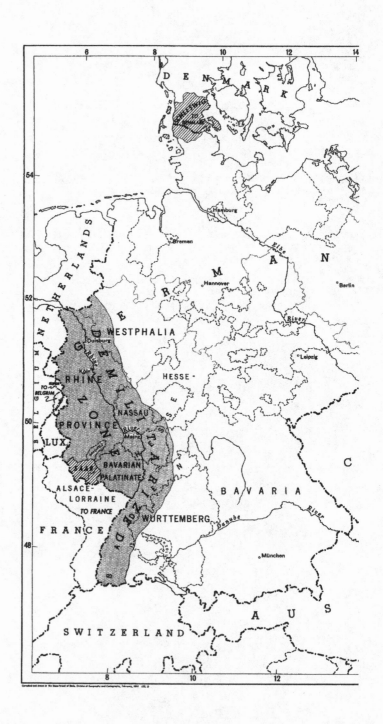

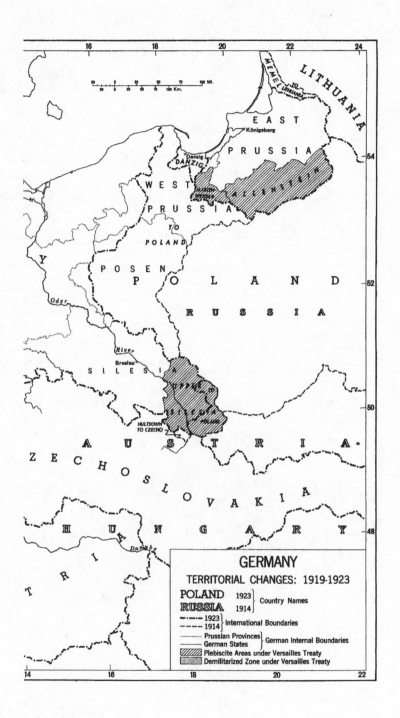

LITHUANIA

MEMEL
TO
LITHUANIA

EAST
PRUSSIA
Königsberg

DANZIG
Danzig

WEST
PRUSSIA
MARIEN-
WERDER
ALLENSTEIN

54

TO
POLAND

POSEN
P O L A N D

Oder

R U S S I A

52

River
Breslau
S I L E S I A
UPPER
SILESIA
POLAND
HULTSCHIN
TO CZECHO

A U S T R I A -

50

Z E C H O S L O V A K I A

H U N G A R Y
Danube

48

T R I A

GERMANY
TERRITORIAL CHANGES: 1919-1923

POLAND 1923 } Country Names
RUSSIA 1914

— · — 1923 } International Boundaries
— — — 1914

.... Prussian Provinces } German Internal Boundaries
.... German States

▨ Plebiscite Areas under Versailles Treaty
▦ Demilitarized Zone under Versailles Treaty

PART III
NATIONAL SELF-DETERMINATION AND ETHNIC POLITICS

CHAPTER 8

ETHNIC POLITICS AND GERMAN–AMERICAN RELATIONS AFTER WORLD WAR I: THE FIGHT OVER THE VERSAILLES TREATY IN THE UNITED STATES

Lloyd E. Ambrosius, "Ethnic Politics and German–American Relations after World War I: The Fight over the Versailles Treaty in the United States," in *Germany and America: Essays on Problems of International Relations and Immigration,* ed. Hans L. Trefousse (New York: Brooklyn College Press, 1980), 29–40. Copyright 1981, Brooklyn College of The City University of New York. Reprinted by permission of Brooklyn College.

President Woodrow Wilson and the critics of his foreign policy in the United States engaged in a bitter confrontation over the Versailles Treaty, including the League of Nations Covenant. This political fight revealed fundamental disagreement over American involvement in postwar international affairs. In 1919 and again in 1920, the Senate rejected the peace treaty with Germany and opposed American membership in the new League of Nations. The country apparently endorsed this repudiation of Wilson's diplomacy in the presidential election of 1920. Various participants in the treaty fight offered sharply conflicting explanations for this outcome. Yet, there was a remarkable consensus regarding the crucial importance of ethnic politics. Wilson blamed professional ethnic leaders for successfully organizing against the treaty; they claimed credit for its defeat. Historians have subsequently adopted this interpretation. Endorsing Wilson's vision of American leadership in world affairs, some historians have echoed his criticism of the hyphenates for their obstructive role in the peacemaking. To other historians who have identified with the ethnic groups he denounced, the president appeared as the chief culprit. Still others have taken a more balanced view of the impact of ethnicity on the treaty fight. But most historians have accepted and repeated the common interpretation that ethnic politics vitally affected German–American relations after World War I.

President Wilson carried his crusade for the League of Nations to the American people during his western tour in September 1919. In St. Paul, Minnesota, he began to attack hyphenated Americans for their opposition to the peace treaty, asserting that "the most un-American thing in the world is a hyphen." He was not objecting to the "affectionate memories" of ancestral countries. Indeed, he was proud of his own Scotch-Irish and English heritage. But he expected immigrants and their descendants to give their first loyalty to the United States or to American purposes as he defined them. The president charged in Cheyenne, Wyoming, that "it is the pro-German forces and the other forces that showed their hyphen during the war that are now organized against this treaty." In Denver, Wilson repeated his condemnation of the hyphenates as its foremost opponents outside the halls of Congress. He asserted, "There is no organized opposition to this treaty except among the people who tried to defeat the purpose of this Government in the war. Hyphens are the knives that are being stuck into this document." In his last address before his collapse in Pueblo, Colorado, the president denounced these critics for "disloyalty," charging that "any man with a hyphen in this great contest" was "an enemy of the Republic."[1]

George Creel, Wilson's official wartime propagandist, developed this thesis. In *The War, the World, and Wilson,* Creel blamed the hyphenates for undermining the president's efforts at the Paris Peace Conference. He noted that "the draft of the League constitution was denounced even before its contents were known or explained. The bare fact that the document had proved acceptable to the British Empire aroused the instant antagonism of the 'professional' Irish–Americans, the 'professional' German–Americans, the 'professional' Italian–Americans, and all those others whose political fortunes depended upon the persistence and accentuation of racial prejudices." These ethnic groups were responsible, according to Creel, for "the stab in the back" of Wilson. Explaining how the treaty was killed, Creel maintained that "the forces of hyphenation were boldly called into being and no effort was spared to revive and exaggerate the divisive prejudices of American life." In cooperation with the Republican party, professional ethnic leaders destroyed the national unity that Wilson sought. Concluding that "the unity that was our pride has been torn into tatters by the pull and haul of a revived and multiplied hyphenation," Creel lamented that this disunity at home prevented the American government from playing its leading role in the postwar world.[2]

Others closely associated with Wilson offered the same interpretation of the treaty fight. Joseph Tumulty, the president's secretary, repeated Creel's accusation against the professional ethnic opponents of the Versailles Treaty. This was an old theme for Tumulty, who, in 1916, had persuaded Wilson to request the "Irish agitator" Jeremiah O'Leary and other "disloyal Americans" not to vote for him in the presidential election. In 1920, Tumulty persuaded the Democratic presidential candidate James M. Cox to employ this same divisive tactic, but without the same apparent success.[3] The historian William E. Dodd, who entered government service during World War I, shared the president's views of his ethnic critics. In his biography of Wilson, Dodd especially castigated the German–Americans and Irish–Americans for obstructing the peacemaking. Assuming that the process of assimilation would produce national unity, he regretted that "the 'melting pot' had not done its work."[4]

British government officials recognized the ethnic foundation of Wilson's foreign policy. William Wiseman, the influential chief of the British intelligence service in the United States, accused the American Irish and Germans of plotting together for the independence of Ireland and a German victory in the war. He reported that Wilson deplored this German–Irish collaboration and that the American people seemed increasingly to awaken to the danger of "the Sein [*sic*] Fein dealings with the

Germans in America." Similar allegations were published in London, although the British government possessed no substantial evidence for the period after the United States entered the war. Wiseman predicted that, despite German propaganda and overwhelming American sympathy for Ireland, the British and American ideals of the League of Nations would triumph. His reports, based on interviews with Wilson, reflected the common understanding that the success of an Anglo-American peace required playing off one ethnic group against another in the United States. Accusations of a German–Irish plot were designed to prevent any such collaboration not only between Germany and Ireland but also between German–Americans and Irish–Americans.[5]

Wiseman reported the Senate's overwhelming 60-to-1 vote in June 1919 for William E. Borah's resolution urging the American delegation at the peace conference to secure a hearing for representatives of the Irish republic in Paris. He considered this encouragement of Irish rebels as "deeply significant" because it revealed that "all politicians in this country regard it as matter of course that they must support any Irish movement." The president, however, ignored this senatorial advice. After returning to the United States, Wilson told Wiseman that Irish extremists were trying to kill the treaty and prevent American membership in the League of Nations on the false and "devilish theory" that this country then would eventually resort to war against Great Britain to liberate Ireland. The president informed the British intelligence chief that, if necessary, he would tour the country to defend the treaty against such critics.[6]

The British government, like Wilson, refused to recognize Irish independence as a means of gaining support in the United States for the League of Nations. On his mission as special ambassador to the United States in the fall and winter of 1919 and 1920, Viscount Edward Grey observed the impact of the Irish question on the treaty fight. To divide radical from moderate Irish–Americans and so lessen their influence in American politics, he recommended a British policy of self-government, but not independence, for Ireland. He opposed any concessions to the Sinn Fein in Ireland even for the sake of American ratification of the Versailles Treaty. Grey's successor as ambassador, Sir Auckland Geddes, continued to stress the importance of playing ethnic groups against one another in the interest of Anglo-American friendship. He observed that the Anglo-Saxons were a minority in the American population, but that these English and Scotch-Irish elements were nevertheless determined to retain their traditional control by keeping other ethnic groups divided. To assist President Wilson in his pursuit of good Anglo-American relations, Geddes advised the British prime minister David Lloyd George in June 1920 to identify the Sinn Fein rebellion in Ireland with Bolshevism, hoping thereby to discredit the Irish nationalists and maintain the loyalty of the American Irish to the Democratic party. Geddes further recommended that the British government announce its desire for cooperation with Germany in order to gain the support of German–Americans for good relations between the United States and Great Britain.[7]

George Sylvester Viereck, one of the most prominent of the professional German–Americans, agreed with Wilson that "the hyphen is the real danger." But from his perspective, the dangerous hyphenates were the Anglo-Saxons who collaborated with Viscount Grey. In November 1919 and again in March 1920, when the Senate voted on the Versailles Treaty, Viereck urged its rejection in editorials in *The American Monthly:*

> If the Allies had accepted Mr. Wilson's fourteen points, now fourteen scraps of paper, a new world would have arisen out of the ruins of Europe. Now we have secret treaties, blackmail and a League of Damnations.... We trust that the Senate of the United States will repudiate the peace treaty and the covenant, for we should blush to see our country united in any manner, no matter how transitory, with the sinister forces of national oppression and international blackmail.

In direct contrast to Wilson, Viereck praised Jeremiah O'Leary for "his gospel of Americanism." He thought O'Leary deserved the gratitude of Americans of German as well as Irish descent because he had withstood "the Reign of Terror initiated by the Wilson Administration."

As his own courage increased during the postwar era, Viereck condemned even the advocacy of the League of Nations as "moral treason to the United States." During the election of 1920, he joined with the German American National Conference in endorsing the Republican candidate Warren G. Harding for the presidency. Although not his first choice, Viereck saw Harding's election as offering the best opportunity to keep the United States out of the League of Nations, which he regarded as "simply a mutual covenant to guarantee to each of the various thieves the possession of his stolen property." When Harding defeated Cox, Viereck claimed that "the decisive part played by German Americans is plainly written in the results and freely admitted by victors and vanquished. The Irish–Americans added their weight to the terrific blow against Wilsonism." In a message to the president-elect, Viereck congratulated Harding on "the victory of your Americanism over Woodrow Wilson and all his works, including his League of Nations and the infamous Peace Pact of Versailles."[8]

Despite his prominence, Viereck was not a typical German–American. Senator John Sharp Williams of Mississippi, one of Wilson's most faithful supporters among Southern Democrats during the treaty fight and the only senator to vote against Borah's pro-Irish resolution, pointedly questioned Viereck's wartime loyalty to the United States, but not that of the vast majority of German–Americans. The senator repeated his demand after the war for the undivided loyalty of all Americans of German ancestry. Despite his own ethnic prejudices, Williams was correct in noting the contrast between professional German–Americans, such as Viereck, and most members of that ethnic group.[9]

Advocates of the Versailles Treaty employed divide-and-conquer tactics; its opponents recruited the support of hyphenated Americans. Republican Senator William E. Borah of Idaho, an irreconcilable foe of the League of Nations, worked closely with New York's Judge Daniel F. Cohalan and the Friends of Irish Freedom during the treaty fight. In collaboration with the old Fenian John Devoy, Cohalan converted this Irish–American organization into an anti-League lobby. Although aware that the Fourteen Points referred only to the Central Powers and not to the British Empire, they hoped the president would somehow apply the principle of national self-determination to the Irish question. When it became apparent early in 1919 that the peace conference would not endorse the cause of Ireland, they turned against

Wilson and his policy of Anglo-American cooperation. In *The Gaelic American,* Devoy denounced the League of Nations as "a British conspiracy against the very existence of these United States as a free, independent, self-governing Nation." Noting the significance for Ireland, Cohalan deplored that under Article 10 of the Covenant "the territorial integrity and existing political independence of the British Empire should be preserved by all the great signatories to the League of Nations." That meant, he further observed, that "no country outside the British Empire, if there were a Rising or Rebellion in Ireland, would be permitted to come to the assistance of Ireland." On the contrary, as Devoy warned, "the continuance of British rule in Ireland will be guaranteed and the United States will be pledged to come to England's aid if England demands it."[10]

The Gaelic American reported the Senate's rejection of the peace treaty in November 1919 as "the greatest victory for Americanism" since the American Civil War and "the greatest defeat of English diplomacy that it has ever sustained." Irreconcilable senators achieved this triumph, according to this Irish–American newspaper, because "Irish citizens stood in a solid phalanx behind them." Senator Borah agreed. "You have rendered in this fight a service which no other man has rendered or could have rendered," he wrote to Judge Cohalan. "Your country will always be under a debt of gratitude to you. In addition to that too much cannot be said in honor of the Irish people who have helped to make this great fight." Although Borah praised these professional Irish–Americans for their "love of America," their response to the League of Nations was essentially anti-British. Devoy saw Viscount Grey's desire for American ratification of the treaty as a good reason for opposing it. When the Senate voted against Wilson for a second time in March 1920, the editor of *The Gaelic American* announced that "Irish citizens of the United States have every reason to be gratified at the defeat of the rotten Treaty and dishonest Covenant. Theirs was the first voice raised in warning to the American people against the League of Nations. They were the first to see the perils for America involved in the infamous Article X."[11]

Irreconcilable opponents of the Versailles Treaty were just as convinced that hyphenated Americans played a key role in defeating it as were President Wilson and his associates. This remarkable consensus on the importance of ethnic politics has also characterized the historiography of the treaty fight. Some historians, such as Louis L. Gerson, have disapproved of ethnic influences on American foreign policy, including "the hyphenate challenge to internationalism" after World War I.[12] With the revival of Wilsonian internationalism during and after World War II came other negative assessments of ethnic involvement in the peacemaking. Thomas A. Bailey advised that "politics, in so far as possible, should be kept out of foreign affairs." Adhering to the ideal of the "great melting pot," he criticized the hyphenates for participating in "the parade of prejudice" against the peace treaty. Selig Adler saw "help from the hyphenates" as a major factor in "the isolationist impulse." Viewing "Americanization" and "hyphenization" as opposite trends, he considered the advocacy of "America First" by hyphenated Americans as "a perverted nationalism." Although devoting less attention to ethnic politics, Julius Pratt attributed "the renunciation of world leadership" partly to "the prejudices of dissatisfied racial minorities." Arthur S. Link similarly noted the negative contributions of the German–Americans, Irish–Americans, and Italian–Americans to the great debate over the League of Nations.[13]

These historians who have embraced Wilsonian internationalism also have accepted Wilson's prejudices with respect to ethnic politics. For them, the assimilation of immigrants in the American "melting pot" was a domestic prerequisite for successful American leadership in international affairs. The process of "Americanization" applied both to the hyphenates in the United States and to foreign countries in the League of Nations. A few historians, such as Charles C. Tansill, have attacked Wilson's Anglo-conformity conception of American nationalism and his corresponding vision of internationalism. From their perspective, the professional ethnic opponents of the peace treaty, especially the Irish–Americans, made a valuable contribution by resisting American membership in the League of Nations.[14] But they, too, have accepted the common interpretation that ethnic politics vitally affected the treaty fight. Even historians who have offered a more balanced view of the influence of hyphenates on American foreign policy after World War I have shared this consensus.[15]

There are, however, major difficulties with this common interpretation. Contrary to Wilson's charge, the principal organized opposition to the Versailles Treaty throughout the country, as in the Senate, came from the Republican party. And its leader in the treaty fight, Senator Henry Cabot Lodge of Massachusetts, shared the president's attitude toward immigrants. "One of our greatest objects in this country," Lodge asserted, "must be thoroughly to Americanize the people who come to us from other lands. The effect of the League [of Nations] is absolutely hostile to this purpose. These foreign questions are dividing our citizens of foreign birth or foreign parentage upon questions outside those concerning the United States . . . . I regard this as one of the most serious objections to the covenant of the League." From the same ethnic perspective as Wilson's, Lodge reached the opposite conclusion regarding the League of Nations.[16] During his presidential campaign, Senator Harding repeated this Republican theme: "How can we have American concord; how can we expect American unity; how can we escape strife, if we in America attempt to meddle in the affairs of Europe and Asia and Africa . . . ? It is not alone the menace which lies in involvement abroad; it is the greater danger which lies in conflict among adopted Americans." This criticism of Wilson's foreign policy led to Viereck's endorsement of the Republican candidate and, in turn, to Cox's unsuccessful effort to discredit Harding by association with allegedly disloyal hyphenated Americans.[17]

The common interpretation of ethnic politics in the treaty fight paradoxically ignored the ethnic diversity in the United States. Joseph Tumulty, who advised the divide-and-conquer tactic, was himself one of the most prominent of American Irish Catholics. Of the five senators of Irish ancestry, all Democrats, only three—John K. Shields of Tennessee, Thomas P. Gore of Oklahoma, and David L. Walsh of Massachusetts—won the approval of *The Gaelic American*. The other two—James D. Phelan of California and Thomas J. Walsh of Montana—were condemned for faithfully supporting Wilson.[18] President Eamon de Valera of the Irish republic, who was in the United States during the treaty fight, challenged the Devoy-Cohalan leadership. He and his supporters among Irish–Americans were not primarily interested in defeating the treaty, but wanted to keep open the option of gaining recognition of Ireland through membership in the League of Nations.[19] Tammany Hall also vied with Cohalan and Devoy. In the 1920 presidential election, only one out of every four or five Irish–American voters in New York City who had supported Wilson in

1916 rejected Cox. The defections among other ethnic groups were significantly higher.[20] The vociferous opposition to the peace treaty of the Friends of Irish Freedom under the leadership of Cohalan and Devoy was not nearly as politically significant as they claimed or as Wilson and Cox feared.

In a very real sense, the influence of ethnic politics did stop at the water's edge. There was no correlation between roll-call votes in the Senate on the numerous amendments and reservations to the Versailles Treaty and votes on domestic issues, such as women's suffrage, prohibition, and compulsory English-language instruction for aliens. As they voted, senators distinguished between these social or ethnocultural issues at home and foreign-policy questions abroad. Although senators from states with substantial German–American populations tended somewhat to favor amendments or reservations, there was no uniform pattern. Wisconsin's Robert M. La Follette was the most extreme of the irreconcilable Republicans, but Nebraska's Gilbert M. Hitchcock led the Democratic senators in supporting Wilson during the treaty fight. Although many German–Americans would reject Cox in 1920, their disillusionment with Wilson did not directly influence senatorial votes against the peace treaty.[21]

The controversy between Wilson and the professional hyphenates, although of marginal importance to the outcome of the treaty fight, was an expression of their different ethnocentric attitudes. They used each other as scapegoats. Historians who have likewise rejected the legitimacy of ethnic diversity in the politics of American foreign policy have repeated these charges and countercharges. For a new interpretation of the fight over the Versailles Treaty in the United States, historians need to reassess this episode in German–American relations from the perspective of cultural pluralism.[22]

CHAPTER 9

DILEMMAS OF NATIONAL SELF-DETERMINATION: WOODROW WILSON'S LEGACY

Lloyd E. Ambrosius, "Dilemmas of National Self-Determination: Woodrow Wilson's Legacy," in *The Establishment of European Frontiers after the Two World Wars,* eds. Christian Baechler and Carole Fink (Bern: Peter Lang, 1996), 21–36. Reprinted by permission of Peter Lang AG.

President Woodrow Wilson's legacy once more seemed highly relevant in the post-Cold War world. The principle of national self-determination, at the core of his vision of a new world order, appeared to offer guidance in the international politics of the 1990s. Dilemmas of national self-determination that had plagued Wilson also troubled Presidents George Bush and Bill Clinton. The resurgence of nationalism after the Cold War raised ethnocultural questions, along with strategic and economic problems, like those that Wilson had faced during World War I and at the Paris Peace Conference of 1919. Recent U.S. presidents, like Wilson earlier, attempted with their European partners to resolve these dilemmas at an acceptable cost to the great powers. Conflicts that nationalism spawned, both within and among states, still thwarted the creation of a new world order in conformity with Wilson's ideals.

As a modern principle in international politics, national self-determination combined the earlier concepts of sovereignty and democracy. Alfred Cobban, the pioneering historian of national self-determination, defined it as "the right of a nation to constitute an independent state and determine its own government for itself."[1] Affirming both a state's sovereignty over certain territory and a people's right to self-government, the principle justified popular sovereignty within nation-states. Development of this principle coincided with the emergence of modern nationalism.

Daniel Patrick Moynihan credited Wilson with placing the principle of national self-determination at the top of the international agenda. "Wilson did not create nationalism," Moynihan noted, "nothing of the sort. But he did respond to it with the doctrine of self-determination."[2] Moynihan welcomed Wilson's legacy in international law as a typically American amalgam of idealism and self-interest. He criticized Henry Kissinger's "realist" perspective for exaggerating geopolitical or military factors in international politics. In contrast, Moynihan emphasized the continuing potency of ethnicity, or what Walker Connor called "ethnonationalism."[3] He understood nationalism as an ethnocultural phenomenon.

Moynihan attributed Wilson's decision to lead the United States into World War I to his pro-British bias. He concluded that "Woodrow Wilson, Scotch-Irish that he was, believed that Americans were of the 'Anglo-Saxon race' and need come to the rescue of their brethren in Britain."[4] Wilson did identify himself as Scotch-Irish and English in ancestry, and with the "Anglo-Saxon" racial heritage, but Moynihan's simplistic conclusion ignored the president's fiercely independent American nationalism.[5] More perceptive than Moynihan, British officials in Washington and London during Wilson's presidency recognized the limited influence of ethnicity on his diplomacy. They understood that, despite his racial and ethnic prejudices, Wilson would not follow British leadership during and after World War I. He pursued his own independent course in international politics.[6]

Henry Kissinger shared Moynihan's appreciation of Wilson's legacy in U.S. foreign relations, however much he deplored it. Kissinger observed that "Wilsonianism has survived while history has bypassed the reservations of his contemporaries. Wilson was the originator of the vision of a universal world organization, the League of Nations, which would keep the peace through collective security rather than alliances.... It is above all to the drumbeat of Wilsonian idealism that American foreign policy has marched since his watershed presidency, and continues to march to this day." Kissinger added that "whenever America has faced the task of constructing a new world order, it has returned in one way or another to Woodrow Wilson's precepts."[7]

Tony Smith praised Wilson's statecraft for seeking to promote democracy worldwide and thereby tame nationalism, "the chief political problem of the twentieth century." He noted with approval that the president committed the United States to a peace settlement that could make the world safe for democracy. "His ambition at the Paris Peace Conference of 1919 to create a European order of democratically constituted, nationally self-determining states associated in the League of Nations, was the direct fulfillment of his pledge." Moreover, Smith asserted: "Whatever his illusions as to the ease with which 'right-minded men' might come to agreement, Wilson was the first world leader to respect the power of nationalism and to try to channel its great strength in the direction of democracy and international cooperation, beginning in Central and Eastern Europe but incorporating the rest of the world thereafter." In Smith's judgment, Wilson deserved primary credit for establishing the American diplomatic tradition of promoting world order by fostering democratic nation-states in the twentieth century.[8]

Moynihan, Kissinger, and Smith agreed that the principle of national self-determination formed the core of Wilson's new world order. Although he did not state this principle explicitly in his Fourteen Points address, they all regarded it as his guiding concept. Moreover, all of them presupposed that Wilson was thinking primarily in terms of ethnicity or ethnonationalism. Oddly enough, like Moynihan, Kissinger claimed that Wilson offered "ethnic self-determination" as the basis for a new international system to replace the old European balance of power.[9] Smith, too, affirmed that "Wilson respected the power of nationalism and favored national self-determination. States were presumed to be legitimate when they were democratically constituted, and it was expected that in most instances ethnic boundaries would make for the frontiers of countries."[10]

Derek Heater, Cobban's former student, contributed an important book on national self-determination. In substantial agreement with Moynihan, Kissinger, and

Smith, he noted the president's long-range influence on international politics. Although Wilson had failed to realize his ideals at the Paris Peace Conference of 1919, Heater applauded his efforts. Despite the inability of the League of Nations to keep the peace after World War I, or the United Nations in recent years, Wilson at least had suggested a solution to endemic problems of twentieth-century international politics. Heater regarded Wilson's insight into international institutions to ameliorate nationalism's evil effects as "his greatest relevance for our own age."[11]

Heater joined Moynihan, Kissinger, and Smith in acknowledging Wilson's pivotal role in making national self-determination a key principle in international politics. All these authors agreed that, for better or worse, Wilson's legacy was still relevant in the post-Cold War era. National self-determination, according to Heater, combined both national consciousness and self-government by emphasizing popular sovereignty within democratic nation-states. To clarify which people should constitute a particular nation and deserve self-government, Heater claimed that Wilson had regarded language as "the best test of nationality."[12]

In contrast to the focus on ethnonationalism in all these recent studies, the president himself had understood the principle of national self-determination from the perspective of historicism. Wilson regarded language as only one factor, and not the controlling one, in defining a nation. Nor was race or ethnicity the determining factor in national identity for him, although Wilson's own racial and ethnic prejudices certainly influenced his decisions.[13] Instead of attributing primacy to ethnocultural factors, he understood nationalism as the consequence of historical development. A people's national consciousness, Wilson believed, was shaped by the historical process, and this process involved political leadership. Civic affinities were more important than primordial ones.

Long before World War I, Wilson had formed his historicist perspective, which was at once conservative and progressive. He summarized his view of the historical process in 1889. Wilson emphasized the "historical causes" of American nationalism and democracy. He stressed "the growth of the national idea, which is coincident with the conscious development of the national experience and life." Elaborating this crucial point, Wilson explained that "no people can be a nation before its time, and its time has not come until the national thought and feeling have been developed and have become prevalent. Until a people thinks its government national it is not national." For Wilson, the American Civil War, "a final contest between nationalism and sectionalism," not only preserved the Union but also fixed the "national idea" in this country. Through a process of "organic development" or "natural history," the United States had become a democratic nation. This lesson of American history, he believed, was applicable in other countries.[14]

The American Civil War shaped Wilson's view of the United States as a nation-state. His definition of national self-determination and its application in international politics during his presidency expressed his understanding of this pivotal experience in American history. During the Civil War, President Abraham Lincoln had preserved the national Union and prevented the secession of the South. By war, he denied the right of southern states to withdraw from the Union and form their own Confederacy. As Garry Wills brilliantly argued, Lincoln redefined the American nation in his famous Gettysburg address. Denying a states-rights' or secessionist interpretation of self-determination, he reaffirmed the national unity of the United States and renewed its historic affirmation of equality in the Declaration of Independence. Lincoln dedicated all Americans to the proposition "that this nation, under God, shall have a new birth of freedom—and that government of the people, by the people, for the people, shall not perish from the earth."[15]

Wilson, although himself a southerner from Virginia and Georgia, embraced Lincoln's view of the American Civil War. He became the first prominent scholar from the South to adopt a nationalist, pro-Union interpretation of the war. In 1880, he explained that, "*because* I love the South, I rejoice in the failure of the Confederacy." In agreement with John Bright, who had seen the Union as "one people, and one language, and one law, and one faith over all that wide continent, the home of freedom, and a refuge for the oppressed of every race and of every clime," Wilson thanked God that "this happy vision has been realized" and that "union *still* binds us together."[16] Postwar reconstruction of the southern states consolidated "an indestructible Union of indestructible states," destroying forever "the doctrine of the right of secession." Wilson further explained that "the real revolution was not so much in the form as in the spirit of affairs. The spirit and temper and method of a federal Union had given place ... by the merciless winds of war, to a spirit which was consciously national and of a new age."[17]

Wilson followed historical precedents not only of Lincoln in the Civil War but also of William McKinley, Theodore Roosevelt, and William Howard Taft at the turn of the century. After the Spanish–American War of 1898, these U.S. presidents denied independence to the Philippines. Preferring to rule the islands as a U.S. colony, they postponed the Filipino people's right to national self-determination. Significantly, Wilson agreed that the Filipino people were not yet ready for self-government. He justified delaying their independence by distinguishing between mere self-government and democratic self-government. Wilson thought that the United States, before granting independence to the Filipino people, should serve as their tutor in democracy, just as the British imperial rulers had instructed the American colonists in representative government before their revolutionary "War for Independence."[18]

Wilson believed that not all people who claimed the right of self-government actually constituted a nation. "You cannot call a miscellaneous people, unknit, scattered, diverse of race and speech and habit, a nation, a community," he explained. "That, at least, we got by serving under kings; we got the feeling and the organic structure of a community. No people can form a community or be wisely subjected to common forms of government who are as diverse and as heterogeneous as the people of the Philippine Islands. They are in no wise knit together."[19] In Wilson's view, a people needed to develop an organic community, with a distinctive historical consciousness, before they qualified as a nation. Moreover, the state played a crucial role in nation-building. Political leadership was essential for the development of a nation. That had been the contribution of the British government to the American colonies before 1776 and of Lincoln's government during the Civil War, and it should be the role of the United States in the Philippines in the twentieth century.

Both with regard to the Philippines and later in Paris in 1919, Wilson viewed the creation of a new nation as a progressive process of historical development. It required far more than a common ethnicity or language. He emphasized the state's role—that is, political leadership—in this process, although his concept of a nation as a living organism combined both primordial and civic attachments. Above all, he emphasized the distinctive historical consciousness of any people who might be identified as a separate nation. In his view, national identity developed out of the total heritage and experience of a given people over a long period of time. Moreover, good political leadership might enable that process of historical development to assimilate new immigrants from foreign lands as they came to share the nation's distinctive historical consciousness. Peoples from various racial or ethnic origins, and with different languages and cultural habits, might eventually join together in the same nation if, but only if, they embraced its communal sense of historical identity.[20]

During World War I, Wilson the historian, who was now the U.S. president, consciously drew on his understanding of the American past to proclaim his ideals for the future. He used American nationalism as the norm for the world. Hoping to create a League of Nations to replace alliances and rivalries among the empires of the past, Wilson envisioned a new global community of democratic nation-states living in peace with each other. On May 27, 1916, he proclaimed that "every people has a right to choose the sovereignty under which they shall live." He thought that "small states" as well as "great and powerful nations" should enjoy sovereignty and territorial integrity free from aggression.[21] The Monroe Doctrine had affirmed this right of self-determination in the New World long before Wilson transformed it into a global principle in the twentieth century. In his "peace without victory" address on January 22, 1917, Wilson proclaimed that "the nations should with one accord adopt the doctrine of President Monroe as the doctrine of the world: that no nation should seek to extend its polity over any other nation or people, but that every people should be left free to determine its own polity, its own way of development."[22] The postwar League of Nations, he hoped, would become the worldwide extension of the Monroe Doctrine.

Wilson led the United States into the European war against Imperial Germany in 1917 with this promise. German submarine warfare, he now argued, posed a universal threat "against all nations." In his global crusade for political liberty, he proclaimed that "the world must be made safe for democracy." Embracing nationalism as the dominant force in the modern world, he expected democratic values and institutions to prevent one nation's sovereign claims from endangering those of other nations. All democratic nations, he hoped, would eventually join together for mutual security in a new League of Nations.[23]

The Russian Revolution posed an acute dilemma for Wilson. In 1917, he welcomed the new government that replaced the czar, but refused to recognize the subsequent Bolshevik regime that overturned this provisional democracy. He ordered U.S. troops into northern Russia and Siberia in 1918, although this intervention inevitably resulted in fighting between these troops and the Bolsheviks. He denied diplomatic recognition to the Soviet government, believing that the Russian people would never accept communist rule. Wilson's policy of nonrecognition and his decision to intervene in Russia apparently violated the principle of national self-determination, however much he tried to justify his anti-Bolshevik policies as essential strategic actions in the war against Imperial Germany.[24]

Within Wilson's perspective, however, his response to the Russian Revolution actually expressed the principle of national self-determination inasmuch as it required both sovereignty and democracy. Paradoxically, U.S. officials attempted to foster democracy through diplomatic and military intervention in the former Russian empire. Believing that Bolshevism and democracy were opposing forces, Wilson wanted to encourage democratic alternatives to the Soviet regime. To honor Russian sovereignty, he sought to preserve the former empire's territorial integrity as much as possible. Assuming, as he did, that the Russian people would never accept Bolshevism and would want to align themselves with the United States and the Allies, the president saw limited U.S. military intervention in Russia as a method to help the Russians achieve their self-determination against the common enemies, the Germans and the Bolsheviks. Strategic and ideological factors thus coincided in America's secret war against Bolshevism. The president, however, preferred patience and diplomacy rather than extensive military intervention by the United States or the Allies. He hoped to allow time for democratic government to emerge within the former Russian empire. In other words, he was waiting for the process of historical development to remedy the problem of Bolshevism, albeit with a little assistance from the United States. The president's attitudes and policies toward Bolshevism in Russia thus evidenced his progressive historicist understanding of national self-determination.[25]

Given his historicism, Wilson never expected to realize his ideals immediately. He refrained from promising national self-determination—that is, sovereignty and democracy—to all peoples. The guiding principle of his Fourteen Points offered less than the right of all peoples to live in their own nation-states. He announced on January 8, 1918, that the "evident principle" in his "whole program" was "the principle of justice to all peoples and nationalities, and their right to live on equal terms of liberty and safety with one another, whether they be strong or weak." Wilson did not promise that postwar Germany should include all Germans or that other peoples of the same ethnicity or language should all inhabit their own nation-states. Notably, he did not advocate the destruction of the Habsburg empire.[26]

During World War I and at the Paris Peace Conference of 1919, Wilson hesitated to recognize new nations, especially outside of Europe. As in the Philippines earlier, he applied the principle of national self-determination with great caution. He did not undermine British rule in Ireland, Egypt, and India, or French rule in Indochina. Wilson recognized only new nations that emerged from the collapse of the Russian, German, Austro-Hungarian, and Ottoman empires. He applied the principle of national self-determination only to the defeated empires. Even there, he hesitated to recognize the governments of new nations until he was certain they possessed the historical qualities of nationality that he witnessed in the American experience.[27]

Wilson cautiously applied the principle of national self-determination, especially in the defeated empires beyond Europe. David Steigerwald correctly observed that "Wilson supported national aspirations when the people in question seemed to conform to, or have some promise of conforming to, his idea of the 'organic' state and when the given issue was necessary to a restoration of political order and coherence. All other questions, he believed, could be left to the League of Nations."[28] This latter category included the extra-European territories of the defeated empires that would be placed under League of Nations mandates. Wilson approved the distribution of Germany's former colonies in Africa and the Pacific to the British Empire, France, Belgium, and Japan under League mandates, an alternative to colonialism that was essentially colonialism in all but name. It was different, he thought, because those governments would exercise mandatory instead of sovereign rights. He expected them to fulfill the same mission in their League mandates that the United States had assigned itself in the Philippines.[29]

Throughout the Paris negotiations, Wilson demonstrated his great reluctance to change historical boundaries. That was not required by his principle of national self-determination. He had not come to the peace conference to redraw the historical map of the Old World. The United States, he reminded his colleagues in the Council of Four, had no direct interest in European territorial questions. When, however, changes were necessary to accommodate new nation-states, such as Poland, Czechoslovakia, and Yugoslavia, he wanted the new boundaries to coincide with "ethnographic affinities" to the greatest extent possible. Yet, even in those cases Wilson's diplomacy expressed his historicism. From his perspective, the historical process of nation-building should incorporate ethnocultural factors such as race, ethnicity, or language into a new civic consciousness, thereby creating a new nationality. It therefore seemed appropriate to him that the new nations of Poland, Czechoslovakia, and Yugoslavia all included a variety of peoples.[30]

During the negotiations of the Versailles Treaty, Wilson sought to minimize Germany's territorial losses, except those outlined in his Fourteen Points. He approved the annexation of Alsace-Lorraine by France and the creation of the Polish corridor to the Baltic sea, but he opposed other extensive changes in Germany's historical boundaries, at least without plebiscites. As Wilson and Allied premiers debated the conditions of peace, he stressed "moderation and fairness." In the Council of Four on March 27, 1919, he explained his great reluctance to redraw Europe's map: "Everywhere we are compelled to change boundaries and national sovereignties. Nothing involves greater danger, for these changes run contrary to long-established customs and change the very life of populations whilst, at the same time, they affect their feelings. We must avoid giving our enemies even the impression of injustice."[31]

Wilson approved changes in Germany's historical boundaries only when he regarded these as essential to the peace settlement. The French government of Premier Georges Clemenceau advanced both historical and economic reasons for annexing the Saar. Although sympathetic toward France's claims for economic compensation from the Saar coal mines, Wilson rejected the historical argument. "The annexation of these regions to France," he responded, "does not have a sufficient historical foundation. One part of these territories was French for only twenty-two years; the remainder has been separated from France for over one hundred years." As a compromise, the British prime minister David Lloyd George suggested that the Saar be detached from Germany and established as a separate state, but not annexed to France. Wilson rejected that proposal as well, explaining that "I believe that we violate the principle of self-determination as much by giving one people an independence it does not request as by making them pass under the sovereignty of another. The sole principle I recognize is the one of the consent of the governed."[32] Unlike Luxembourg, "a small historical entity," the Saar lacked the qualities that Wilson associated with an independent state. He and the Allied premiers finally settled their differences by placing the Saar under the League of Nations for 15 years, but actually under French administration, until the local people determined their national affiliation in a plebiscite. Meanwhile, the Saar remained nominally under German sovereignty.[33]

Minor changes in Germany's boundaries were acceptable to Wilson, sometimes without a plebiscite. On the Belgian–German border, he approved Belgium's direct annexation of the Eupen-Malmedy region. On the Danish–German border, however, he favored a plebiscite to resolve the question of Schleswig. He thought the Council of Four should not involve itself in possible changes in the Dutch–German border. He approved a new boundary between Germany and Lithuania without a plebiscite, after Lloyd George assured the Council of Four that the proposed border followed "the ethnographic line."[34] Wilson resisted extensive changes in Germany's boundaries, however, even for the sake of European security. He absolutely declined to consider the separation of the Rhineland from Germany, although he acquiesced in its temporary occupation by the United States and the Allies for fifteen years. Rejecting strategic arguments for detaching the Rhineland from German sovereignty, he said, "I insist on maintaining the right of self-determination."[35]

Wilson readily agreed with the European premiers to give Poland access to the sea and establish Danzig as a free city. He also supported Poland's claim to Upper Silesia. However, he wanted to "respect ethnographic lines as much as possible" in drawing Polish boundaries with Germany. "My great concern is to avoid putting too many Germans in Poland," he said. Beyond the Polish corridor, he thought that the people of East Prussia's provinces of Marienwerder and Allenstein should decide by plebiscite whether to remain in Germany or join Poland.[36] At first, Wilson concurred with the transfer of Upper Silesia to Poland without a plebiscite. He saw no contradiction between this territorial change and his Fourteen Points. Because of the dominant influence of German capitalists and civil servants in Upper Silesia, he did not believe that a plebiscite could fairly determine the will of the local population, which he thought was largely Polish. Once the German delegation at Versailles vigorously protested against the loss of Upper Silesia, Lloyd George began to advocate a plebiscite, suggesting that the principle of national self-determination required it. Wilson retorted: "I cannot allow you to say that I am not for the right of self-determination. That is absurd. What I want is the true expression of popular sentiment." He eventually agreed to settle the dispute over Upper Silesia with a plebiscite in one or two years. A plebiscite would determine whether the inhabitants of Upper Silesia wanted to remain in Germany, as the Germans claimed, or to unite with Poland.[37]

Seeking to draft the Versailles Treaty in accordance with his principle of national self-determination, Wilson preferred historical boundaries. This approach to peacemaking favored Germany by minimizing its territorial losses, but it also worked against Germany in some instances. He never believed that Germany had a rightful claim to incorporate all Germans into one nation-state. Accordingly, he approved the old frontier between the German and Austro-Hungarian empires as the new border between Germany and Czechoslovakia, except for transferring the small Ratisbor district of Upper Silesia to Czechoslovakia without a plebiscite.[38] He also agreed to forbid Germany from annexing what remained of Austria. While denying this right to Germany, he sought to protect Austria's self-determination by recognizing its right to unite voluntarily with Germany, subject to approval by the League of Nations.[39]

Problems of national and religious minorities in postwar Europe induced Wilson to clarify his principle of national self-determination. Typical of the peace settlement, the Versailles Treaty left some Germans outside of Germany's postwar borders, notably in Austria, Czechoslovakia, and Poland. The Jews, without their own homeland, also lived in the new nations of Central and Eastern Europe. The mixture of peoples in this area produced serious ethnocultural conflict both within and among states, posing the question of the rights of ethnic and religious minorities. "We liberated the Poles, the Czechoslovaks, the Yugoslavs," Lloyd George told his colleagues in the Council of Four, "and today we have all the trouble in the world preventing them from oppressing other races."[40]

Wilson wanted the historical process of nation-building to resolve these problems by integrating minorities into the new nations of Europe. His attitude toward the rights of minorities expressed an American-style, assimilationist view of nationalism. The Council of Four agonized over the rights of minorities in Poland, where anti-Semitism was especially evident. Wilson rejected the idea of autonomy for the Jewish community, hoping instead that the Poles would assimilate the Jews into their new nation. He expressed this same idea toward the Germans in postwar Poland. As their land was transferred to Poland, he hoped their loyalty would be as well. He affirmed that "we don't want them to remain German forever."[41] Although desiring to protect the rights of Jews and Germans, Wilson did not want to interfere with Poland's internal affairs. At his insistence, the treaty that the United States and the Allies required Poland to sign for the protection of ethnic and religious minorities gave no right to the Jews or other minority communities to appeal for protection to the League of Nations. Wilson wanted to reserve the right of intervention to the members of the League Council. Unless the great powers decided to act through the League to protect minorities, he did not want it to infringe on Poland's self-determination.[42]

Wilson summarized his view of national self-determination in the Council of Four on May 26, 1919. He reminded his colleagues that the United States had entered the European war in 1917 because of Imperial Germany's threat to "political liberty and national independence of all the countries of the world." He explained that "nations completely disinterested in European territorial questions" had participated in the war "as in a crusade, not for territorial changes, but for the destruction of the intolerable danger of a political and ethnic tyranny which would have held back the progress of the world for a century or more." In the ensuing peace negotiations, Wilson opposed territorial changes that violated the principle of national self-determination, stating that "it is impossible for me to agree that a people can be handed over to foreign domination without their consent."[43]

Wilson understood national self-determination within his perspective of historicism. Where the collapse of defeated empires required the drawing of new borders to replace historical boundaries, he wanted to follow ethnographic lines. For him, "ethnographic affinities" were more important than either strategic or economic considerations in redrawing boundaries for the peace settlement. "Except where nearly impassable frontiers forced themselves upon us, such as the one drawn by the crests of the Alps," he affirmed, "we have followed the boundaries traced by ethnographic affinities, according to the right to self-determination."[44] Because he rejected the doctrine of secession and favored an American-style, progressive assimilation of various peoples into a homogeneous nation, however, he never thought that all people of a particular race or ethnicity or language should inhabit their own nation-state.

Moynihan, Kissinger, Smith, and Heater neglected Wilson's historicism when they identified his principle of national self-determination with ethnonationalism. That primordial factor was undoubtedly present in Wilson's thinking, but it was qualified by the civic factor of the state's role in nation-building. Both factors were subsumed by the progressive historical process of forming national consciousness. Wilson understood nationalism and interpreted the principle of national self-determination from his historicist perspective.

Overlooking this crucial point, Heater thought that Wilson had too readily compromised his ideals to accommodate the postwar realities and the Allies. Contrasting idealistic and practical aspects of Wilsonian statecraft, Heater criticized the peace treaties with Germany, Austria, and Hungary for denying the promise of national self-determination. Heater's severe criticism expressed his unsubstantiated claim that Wilson defined nationality primarily in terms of language and his presumption that Wilson's ideals promised all people of the same nationality, such as the Germans, the right to live in one nation-state.[45]

This common misinterpretation—made by Moynihan, Kissinger, and Smith, as well as Heater—exaggerated ethnocultural factors in Wilson's ideals. Like the president's contemporary critics who expected him to help a particular nationality achieve statehood, and then enable that nation-state to acquire all territories with inhabitants of the same ethnicity or language, these writers ignored that Wilson had made no such general commitment in his Fourteen Points or elsewhere. As a consequence, they overstated the extent of his failure to write the principle of national self-determination into the peace treaties in 1919.

Ironically, this distortion of Wilson's ideals also obscured the fundamental reason for his ultimate failure in international politics: Wilson's vision of a new world order never adequately confronted the inherent dilemmas of national self-determination. That was his unfortunate legacy. When he combined the concepts of sovereignty and democracy into the principle of national self-determination, he obscured the fact that democratic theory had traditionally assumed the existence of the political unit. As Robert A. Dahl stressed, "The criteria of the democratic process presupposes the rightfulness of the unit itself."[46] But that was the very presupposition that old empires and new nations refused to accept during World War I and at the Paris Peace Conference. In other words, contrary to Wilson's hope, democratic methods were inadequate to resolve all the conflicts that erupted in this new age of nationalism. The League of Nations could guarantee world peace only if all nations and peoples shared a common interest, but obviously they did not. Nationalist conflicts, both within and among states, continued to cause war in the years ahead. The dilemmas of national self-determination prevented Wilson's vision of a new world order from being realized after World War I or later in the twentieth century.

Part IV
Historiography and Wilsonian Statecraft

Chapter 10
Woodrow Wilson's Health and the Treaty Fight, 1919–1920

Lloyd E. Ambrosius, "Woodrow Wilson's Health and the Treaty Fight, 1919–1920," *The International History Review* 9 (February 1987): 73–84. Reprinted by permission of *The International History Review.*

Confusion and controversy have surrounded both the state of Woodrow Wilson's health and the reasons for U.S. rejection of the Versailles Treaty. Scholars have reached no consensus on either of these questions, and certainly not on the nexus between them. Specialists in medicine and psychology, as well as historians and political scientists, have entered into this scholarly controversy, offering conflicting interpretations of the president's physical and psychological condition, and especially its impact on his political leadership in 1919 and 1920. Anyone seeking to understand the politics of peacemaking in the United States after World War I must, therefore, take into account the condition of Wilson's mind and body. His political personality—however it was shaped—was a significant factor in the fight over the League of Nations.

Internal contradictions marked Thomas A. Bailey's interpretation of the treaty fight. In *Woodrow Wilson and the Great Betrayal* (1945), he placed primary responsibility on Wilson and the Democrats, rather than Senator Henry Cabot Lodge and the Republicans, for defeating the League. Bailey concluded that "the treaty was slain in the house of its friends rather than in the house of its enemies. In the final analysis it was not the two-thirds rule, or the 'irreconcilables,' or Lodge, or the 'strong' and 'mild reservationists,' but Wilson and his docile following who delivered the fatal stab.... This was the supreme act of infanticide. With his own sickly hands Wilson slew his own brain child." In another passage, Bailey summarized more explicitly the effect of the president's illness on this act of infanticide, asserting that "Wilson's physical and mental condition had a profoundly important bearing on the final defeat of the treaty." Bailey seemed to agree with the retrospective judgment of Senator Gilbert M. Hitchcock, the Democratic minority leader during the treaty fight, who had concluded that "I shall always believe ratification would have been possible if Wilson's health had not given way; when that tragedy occurred, not even his best friends could exercise any considerable influence on him." Hitchcock thus attributed the treaty's failure to the president's intransigence, the tragic consequences of his stroke in 1919. Bailey, elsewhere in his book, however, repudiated the logic of Hitchcock's argument and, in so doing, contradicted himself. He stated: "Some apologists for Wilson claim that if he had not collapsed he would have compromised with Lodge. Perhaps so, but there is nothing to support such a view in his public utterances, in his private papers, or in his character."[1]

Bailey thus offered the contradictory conclusions that Wilson's health vitally affected the outcome of the treaty fight, and that it did not. The only way he might have reconciled these two conclusions would have been to argue that a healthy Wilson could have forced Lodge and the Republicans to accept the League without their reservations. If they had acquiesced in his demand for unqualified ratification, then he could have achieved his goal without compromising with Lodge. But Bailey did not present this case, and there is no evidence to warrant it.[2]

Sigmund Freud and William C. Bullitt enlivened the controversy with their psychological study of *Thomas Woodrow Wilson* (1966). Collaboration during the early 1930s between the Viennese founder of psychoanalysis and the U.S. diplomat produced this critical study, a crude application of psychoanalysis to history: Freud contributed his theory, and Bullitt offered his experience and knowledge of Wilson. They argued that during the treaty fight he was suffering from "an extraordinary mental disintegration," the consequence of unresolved conflicts in his personal life. One conflict originated in his childhood, emerging from his ambivalent relationship with his domineering father, Joseph Ruggles Wilson, a Presbyterian clergyman. Freud and Bullitt claimed that Wilson was afflicted throughout his life by "the conflict between his passivity to his father and his aggressive activity against his father, and that his mental equilibrium depended on his ability to beat Lodge into submission and to repress his knowledge of the truth about the Peace Conference." During the treaty fight, the Republican senator was "a father representative." The president's need to repress his knowledge about the negotiations in Paris, in the Freud-Bullitt view, arose from his tremendous guilt over the concessions he had made to the Allies. Wilson was, in other words, desperately seeking "to escape the scourgings of his Super-Ego." This was the other internal conflict that afflicted him. Suffering from a "father fixation" and a guilty conscience, he sought release in 1919 by offering himself as a sacrifice, identifying himself unconsciously with Jesus Christ as "the Savior of the World." He preferred death to compromise with Lodge. According to Freud and Bullitt, Wilson's neurosis—which was now "very close to psychosis"—accounted for his political failure during the treaty fight.[3]

This interpretation presupposed the accuracy of Bullitt's view of the peace conference. He claimed, in his letter of resignation from the U.S. delegation on May 17, 1919, that Wilson could have achieved his vision of "a new world order" if he had openly appealed to world public opinion rather than secretly surrendering the Fourteen Points. "That you personally opposed most of the unjust settlements, and that you accepted them only under great pressure, is well known," Bullitt wrote to the president. "Nevertheless, it is my conviction that if you had made your fight in the open, instead of behind closed doors, you would have carried with you the public opinion of the world, which was yours; you would have been able to resist the pressure and might have established the 'new international order based upon broad and universal principles of right and justice' of which you used to speak." This view of Wilson's failure in Paris undergirded the analysis of Freud and Bullitt, who saw the president's acute psychological problems in 1919 as the consequence of his "moral collapse" during the peace conference, especially since he denied this reality even to himself. "His mental life from April to September 1919, when he collapsed completely and permanently, was a wild flight from fact," they claimed.[4] Underlying this dubious interpretation was the assumption that the Versailles Treaty substantially violated the Fourteen Points and that Wilson could have forced the Allies to accept his own position. But the reality of the peace conference was otherwise, as he recognized more clearly than either of them. The psychological interpretation of Freud and Bullitt therefore rested on an inaccurate historical foundation.[5]

Before publication of the Freud-Bullitt study, Alexander L. George and Juliette L. George had offered a similar, but more sophisticated, analysis of Wilson's political personality. They employed Freudian psychology, following the lead of the political scientist Harold D. Lasswell. They, too, traced the president's psychological problems to his childhood, emphasizing his father's negative contribution to his low self-esteem. "At the root of Wilson's numerous blunders, both in negotiating the Treaty and later in attempting to secure its ratification," argued the Georges in *Woodrow Wilson and Colonel House* (1956), "was his complicated personal involvement in the objective of an idealistic peace and a new world order." His inner needs drove him to attempt immortal work and to seek domination. He could not compromise with Lodge, another father figure, during the treaty fight. Because power provided compensation for his low self-esteem, the president sought political domination over the Senate. "So now," the Georges concluded, "he did not want to reach a compromise agreement with the Senate. He wanted to defeat the Senate, and especially Lodge. If he could not overcome his enemies, it would be less painful to him to sacrifice the Treaty than to make concessions. He could relieve his sense of guilt for having provoked his own defeat by picturing himself martyred in a great cause and by seeking vindication from 'the people'—a vindication for which he strove to his dying day."[6] Thus, according to the Georges, Wilson's psychological problems explained his refusal to compromise with Lodge, and the consequent failure of the United States to ratify the treaty and join the League.

Another political scientist, James David Barber, embraced the Georges' interpretation, giving it a new label. In his book on *The Presidential Character* (1972), he grouped Wilson with Herbert Hoover and Lyndon Johnson as active-negative presidents. They were all energetic and active leaders who did not enjoy political life. With grim determination, they pursued power to the point of their own destruction. Like the Georges, Barber traced the origins of presidential compulsion to early experiences of childhood, adolescence, and young adulthood, agreeing with them that "Wilson attempted to compensate for low self-esteem by dominating his social environment with moralistic rhetoric." This search for power and perfection, Barber concluded, created within Wilson "the psychological context for his stubborn, self-defeating behavior in the League fight."[7]

The neurologist Edwin A. Weinstein offered an alternative to these Freudian interpretations of Wilson's personality, but on one point agreed with the Georges and Barber as well as with Freud and Bullitt: They all concurred that, for Wilson, the pursuit of victory was more important than success. His power motive was greater than his desire for any particular achievement.[8] But Weinstein rejected the Freudian conclusion that Wilson's yearning for power arose from his troubled relationship with his father; instead, he argued that the president's Calvinist ethic furnished the source of his hard work and self-confidence. "This orientation," Weinstein nevertheless conceded, "sometimes led to overconfidence and rigidity, and to greater concern for success and victory than for the nature of the achievement itself." But he did not regard this as a pathological condition in the Freudian sense. In Weinstein's diagnosis, Wilson's neurological illness caused the negative changes in his personality after 1906, and especially in 1919 and 1920. He had suffered a series of little strokes before his massive stroke on October 2, 1919, and denial of his disability further contributed to Wilson's abnormal behavior. "Following his stroke," Weinstein observed, "the outstanding feature of the President's behavior was his denial of his incapacity."[9] In other words, the psychological consequences of brain damage accounted for his inability to function normally during the treaty fight.

The historian Arthur S. Link immediately noted the implication of the neurologist's diagnosis for reinterpreting the treaty fight. Answering the question of whether he thought Wilson's stroke might explain his uncompromising stubbornness, Link wrote:

I do. A few years ago one could have argued both ways. But Dr. Edwin A. Weinstein's broad-gauged medical history of Wilson argues persuasively that his 1919 stroke was a massive one, caused by the occlusion of the main artery on the left side of his face. According to Weinstein, Wilson's behavior during the Treaty fights [sic] was typical of the behavior of a person who had undergone such an experience. He became irritable, proud, defensive, rigid, dogmatic, unyielding. Wilson was different after the stroke; his refusal to compromise, his stubborn insistence upon having the whole or nothing even though he might have got two-thirds is altogether typical of a stroke victim.[10]

Thus, Link joined the controversy over the president's health on Weinstein's side. Weinstein and Link, with the clinical psychologist James William Anderson, launched a direct attack on Freudian interpretations of Wilson in the *Political Science Quarterly*. Criticizing particularly the Georges' book, they presented a positive image of Wilson's relationship with his father and added the dimension of his relationship with his mother. They offered the diagnosis of developmental dyslexia as an alternative explanation for his slowness in learning to read—that is, a physical rather than emotional explanation for this childhood problem. Reiterating that Wilson suffered from a series of strokes in 1896, 1900, 1904, and 1907, they claimed that these contributed to his rigidity as president of Princeton during the controversies over the quad plan and the graduate college. Wilson's behavior after his later massive stroke followed the same pattern. Weinstein, Anderson, and Link thus concluded: "In October 1919 he had a massive stroke that completely paralyzed the left side of his body and produced mental attitudes and personality changes which were important factors in his failure to obtain ratification of the Treaty of Versailles."[11]

In his medical and psychological biography of *Woodrow Wilson* (1981), Weinstein elaborated his findings. "It is the author's opinion," he wrote, "that the cerebral dysfunction which resulted from Wilson's devastating strokes prevented the ratification of the Treaty. It is almost certain that had Wilson not been so afflicted, his political skills and his facility with language would have bridged the gap between the Hitchcock and Lodge resolutions, much as he had reconciled opposing views of the

Federal Reserve bill in 1913, for example, or had accepted the modifications of the Treaty suggested in February, 1919."[12] Not only Link, but other historians, including Charles E. Neu and John Milton Cooper, Jr., found in Weinstein's argument a persuasive explanation for the president's behavior during the treaty fight.[13]

But Weinstein and his collaborators failed to persuade the Georges. In reply, they questioned his diagnosis of developmental dyslexia and of little strokes, noting quite correctly the dearth of credible evidence. Dr Michael F. Marmor, an ophthalmologist from whom they had obtained an opinion, challenged Weinstein's thesis that Wilson had suffered a series of little strokes over the years. In his judgment, there was insufficient medical evidence to prove this hypothesis. In *The New England Journal of Medicine,* he accused Weinstein of violating the adage that physicians should not think of zebras when they hear hoofbeats, that is, that they should use common sense rather than imagine the most far-fetched diagnosis of a patient's illness. Marmor buttressed the Georges' conclusion that Wilson's political personality was not caused by long-term neurological illness. Adhering to their original interpretation, the Georges rejected Weinstein's explanation of Wilson's intransigence during the treaty fight. They acknowledged that his October 1919 stroke undoubtedly affected Wilson's behavior, but discounted its political significance:

> Whatever the nature of the brain damage he sustained in the fall of 1919, it altered neither his grasp of his problem with the Senate nor his strategy to deal with it. He had struck his unyielding position long before October 1919—a position that anguished practically everyone who cared personally about him or supported U.S. entry into the League of Nations. Wilson's conduct in this respect after the stroke was entirely consistent with his behavior before it. Both before and after, ample warnings were conveyed to him of the all but inevitable consequences of his refusal at every turn to compromise. Both before and after the stroke, he rejected these warnings, using the same arguments against compromise and cogently communicating them from his sick-bed. The stroke seemed not to modify his behavior one whit in this respect.[14]

On this crucial point, the Georges reached the correct conclusion: Wilson maintained his inflexible position from the beginning of the treaty fight to the bitter end. Long before he suffered his stroke in October 1919, he had decided to take an all-or-nothing stance in dealing with the Senate. When he returned to the United States in February during the middle of the peace conference, he called on the Democrats to turn the League into a partisan issue. He was in no mood to make any substantial concessions, and showed no inclination to compromise with the Republicans even after they signed the round robin. Although he called for some modifications in the Covenant after returning to Paris, the president did not accept all of the changes that Republicans had suggested in February 1919, or at any other time. By the end of the peace conference, he had also firmly resisted the most substantial demands for revision that the Germans and the British presented. He was strongly committed to the treaty, including the Covenant, without further revision. In his official presentation of the treaty to the Senate, he claimed that it represented God's will. Making that assertion hardly indicated flexibility on Wilson's part. In his meetings with individual senators and with the Senate Foreign Relations Committee during July and August 1919, he rejected all requests for significant compromise. He maintained this uncompromising stance during his speaking tour of western states before his collapse. This clearly established pattern of Wilson's behavior before the October 1919 stroke provided no basis for expecting that he would have compromised on any significant point with the Republicans.

As an opinion, Weinstein's view cannot be refuted, nor does it need to be. No historian can disprove a counterfactual statement of opinion. No evidence is available to prove that Wilson, if he had not suffered a massive stroke in 1919, would not have compromised with the Republicans; however, the whole pattern of the president's leadership revealed his inflexibility. At no time, either before or after his stroke, did he show any willingness to accept either amendments or reservations to the Versailles Treaty in the resolution of ratification. He was willing only to consider a separate interpretative resolution. As long as Wilson persisted in rejecting reservations in the legally binding resolution of ratification, there was no prospect of bridging the gulf between his position and that of Republican senators. The issues were far more fundamental than the particular words in the different reservations. No facility with language could resolve them. At stake was the balance between the executive and legislative branches of the U.S. government in determining its foreign policy, as well as the policy itself. These were real issues on which even a healthy Wilson could not, in all probability, have convinced the Senate to surrender in 1919 and 1920.[15]

None of the psychological and medical explanations of the president's political behavior is fully satisfactory. Wilson and Lodge recognized that real differences divided them, and neither was willing to compromise his basic position. These differences had emerged long before the peace conference or the president's massive stroke.[16] Freud and Bullitt as well as Weinstein and Link neglected to account for this element of continuity throughout the postwar years. Because the president had adopted his all-or-nothing stance before April 1919, his so-called moral collapse could hardly explain his rigidity during the remainder of the treaty fight. Freud and Bullitt overlooked this fundamental problem. Nor could Wilson's massive stroke sufficiently account for the failure of his political leadership after October 1919. Weinstein and Link ignored that his subsequent public behavior followed the same pattern as before. A Freudian interpretation of Wilson's childhood might help explain his presidential character, but the historical evidence is inconclusive, and Link and Weinstein correctly noted this deficiency in the Freud-Bullitt study as well as the Georges' book. Fortunately, for an understanding of Wilson's role during the treaty fight, it is largely irrelevant whether childhood experiences with his father or mother, or other formative influences, shaped his political personality. It is, however, essential to comprehend the interaction between the president and other leaders, such as Lodge, and to place this personal dimension within the larger historical context. As Bernard Brodie observed in a review of the Georges' book, "It is one thing to observe compulsive behavior and identify it for what it is; it is quite another to find the original causes."[17]

While Link and Weinstein, on one side, and the Georges and Marmor, on the other, continued their dispute, the psychiatrist Jerrold M. Post offered the most persuasive synthesis. He agreed with the Georges and Marmor that the evidence is insufficient to support Weinstein's unequivocal diagnosis of developmental dyslexia and of a series of little strokes. But he also criticized the Georges for overemphasizing Wilson's father and neglecting his mother, for both parents had contributed significantly to his character. From Wilson's relationship with both parents, he had acquired not only high aspirations but also his self-defeating behavior. His massive stroke in 1919 magnified this negative propensity, but did not create it. Post thus correctly emphasized the element of continuity in the president's political behavior throughout the treaty fight.[18]

An accurate analysis of Wilson's personality requires an understanding of the historical context in which he operated. While the treaty fight cannot be comprehended without regard for his psychological and physical condition, neither can his presidential character be explained without regard for the external environment of American progressivism. One of the most important features of this context for Wilson was the emergence of the Social Gospel in the United States, as he interpreted U.S. participation in the World War within the framework of his Christian faith. A Social Gospel theologian, George D. Herron, published a book entitled *Woodrow Wilson and the World's Peace* (1917), proclaiming the kingdom of God on earth as the ultimate goal of the president's foreign policy. After reading the book, Wilson applauded "Herron's singular insight into all the elements of a complicated situation and into my own motives and purposes."[19] As a good Presbyterian, the president called the League's constitution a Covenant and located its headquarters in Calvinist Geneva.[20] From this perspective, while officially submitting the Versailles Treaty to the Senate, he proclaimed that it fulfilled God's progressive destiny for the United States.[21] Given his understanding of the U.S. mission, Wilson naturally suffered from despair as he realized that neither the Old World nor the U.S. Senate would conform to his vision of internationalism. In this context, he entrusted the League's fate to God. In a speech during his western tour in September 1919, the president reaffirmed his belief in Divine Providence and confided that, if it were not for his faith, he would go crazy.[22] Link and Weinstein, the Georges, and Freud and Bullitt all quoted these presidential statements as evidence for their various interpretations, yet it is not necessary to accept their medical or psychological analyses to understand Wilson's hope and despair: These were the normal consequences of his religious convictions, not the pathological results of "moral collapse" or neurological illness. His theology misled the president into a false understanding of international relations, as Reinhold Niebuhr would later argue, but this was not a uniquely personal failure.

Another important feature of the historical context during this era of American progressivism was the pervasive search for control. Science and technology had enabled Americans to conquer nature by the beginning of the twentieth century, and they now hoped to achieve the same success in human relations. Industrialization and urbanization had created a new society, which required the government to play a more active role both at home and abroad; within a changing nation and a revolutionary world, progressive Americans hoped to avoid uncontrollable chaos or anarchy. They wanted control of the trusts, or social control, at home as well as collective security abroad. Seeking orderly progress, they preferred reform to revolution, and it was in this spirit that Wilson created the League of Nations. He epitomized the American search for control, but he was not unique. Other Americans shared this progressive perspective.[23] Perhaps his personal experiences as a child, resulting in low self-esteem and a strong power motive, contributed to the president's desire to dominate the Senate during the treaty fight, but this Freudian explanation is, at best, insufficient and, at worst, inaccurate. It failed to account for the pervasive striving for control that characterized progressive Americans, not all of whom, surely, had domineering fathers. In Wilson's case, moreover, recognition of the failure of American progressivism to transform the world undoubtedly contributed to his inflexibility during the treaty fight.[24] These were social, not merely personal, responses to the external environment of the modern world.

For a comprehensive understanding of the treaty fight, historians of U.S. foreign relations must take into account Wilson's health. The condition of his mind and body undoubtedly influenced his political leadership, but other factors in the historical context after World War I contributed even more to the president's failure to achieve U.S. ratification of the Versailles Treaty. The leading protagonists in the scholarly controversy over his health, focusing too narrowly on psychological or medical problems, neglected the external environment of American progressivism and the realities of international affairs. As a consequence, their explanations for the treaty's defeat in the Senate are inaccurate, and even their interpretations of Wilson's personality are inadequate. It is time for scholars to view the president as a whole person within the historical context of the modern world.

CHAPTER 11

THE ORTHODOXY OF REVISIONISM:
WOODROW WILSON AND THE NEW LEFT

Lloyd E. Ambrosius, "The Orthodoxy of Revisionism: Woodrow Wilson and the New Left," *Diplomatic History* 1 (Summer 1977): 199–214. Reprinted by permission of *Diplomatic History.*

The Vietnam War fostered a vigorous debate over American foreign policy in which the New Left played a prominent role. Critical of American involvement in Southeast Asia, these recent revisionists began to reinterpret the origins of the Cold War. They searched for the historical roots of the prevailing Cold War policies that culminated in the war. The parameters of this reassessment, however, were narrower than generally recognized in the heat of the debate. There was an orthodoxy to the revisionism of the New Left. The revisionist critique was less radical than either the New Left or cold warriors appreciated. In both orthodox and revisionist interpretations, Woodrow Wilson was a central figure. The contemporary and historical debate over American foreign policy focused on his conception of liberal internationalism.

To American statesmen, World War II afforded a "second chance" to realize Wilson's vision of liberal internationalism.[1] President Harry S. Truman, addressing the closing session of the United Nations Conference in San Francisco, praised it for creating "a great instrument for peace and security and human progress in the world." He expected the approval of the U.N. Charter by the U.S. Senate, despite its earlier rejection of Wilson's League of Nations. "By this Charter," Truman told the delegates, "you have given reality to the ideal of that great statesman of a generation ago— Woodrow Wilson." He thought it was the duty of the United States, along with the other world powers, "to assume the responsibility for leadership toward a world of peace." Heralding the emergence of a "new structure of peace," he urged the delegates: "Let us not fail to grasp this supreme chance to establish a worldwide rule of reason— to create an enduring peace under the guidance of God."[2]

This Wilsonian vision of American leadership in world affairs provided the intellectual framework of the Cold War. Despite obvious differences, there was more constancy than change in the foreign policy of the United States from Truman to Henry Kissinger. From the Truman Doctrine, through those of Dwight Eisenhower and Lyndon Johnson, to that of Richard Nixon, presidential doctrines expressed the Wilsonian worldview in the context of the Cold War. A generation of American statesmen, convinced that the refusal of the United States to join the League of Nations led directly to the Munich Conference and to World War II, wanted to avoid even the appearance of appeasement in response to aggression. For them the Munich analogy, or the domino theory with reference to Southeast Asia, was the crucial lesson of recent history.[3] Typical of the Cold War era, Nixon affirmed that "Wilson had the greatest vision of America's world role. But he wasn't practical enough." He regarded Wilson as a personal hero and as "our greatest President of this century."[4] Secretary of State John Foster Dulles likewise epitomized at once the Wilsonian legacy and the American involvement in the Cold War.[5]

Reacting against this prevailing Wilsonian internationalism, the realists advocated a foreign policy based on the national interest. This limitation on the purpose of foreign policy expressed their pessimistic view of human nature. The theologian Reinhold Niebuhr, rejecting the optimistic liberal faith of the Social Gospel, warned against the confusion of the relative with the absolute, or the identification of the United States with the kingdom of God. Challenging the assumption of American innocence, he contributed an appreciation of the importance of power and irony in organized human relations.[6] Following Niebuhr, one group of realists such as Hans J. Morgenthau, George F. Kennan, and Norman A. Graebner directly attacked the Wilsonian premises of contemporary American foreign policy. They questioned the belief in progress and in universal moral principles, and thought, in any case, that these ideals provided inadequate, if not disastrous, guidelines for American leadership in the world. Critical of the moralistic and legalistic character of American diplomacy, they urged instead the pursuit of the national interest. For them such a policy was neither immoral nor amoral, but simply realistic. Because the United States was not omnipotent, it lacked the power to impose its ideals throughout the world. Rather than enlist in a liberal crusade, these realists thought a sound American policy should take into account the existing balance of power and limit its goals to national defense.[7]

While these realists fundamentally criticized Wilsonian idealism, their views never gained wide acceptance in the American foreign-policy community. Instead, the advocates of ultrarealism—to use David Halberstam's term—prevailed. Ultrarealists such as McGeorge Bundy and Walt W. Rostow accepted the progressive goals of Wilson's liberal internationalism, but hoped to achieve these in a more practical and hard-headed fashion. Like the realists, they emphasized the crucial link between political and military affairs and the importance of the balance of power. In defining the national interest of the United States, however, they combined these considerations of power politics with an affirmation of Wilson's conception of the American mission in the world. This combination of Wilsonian idealism and ruthless power politics characterized the prevailing Cold War attitude. Secretary of State Dean Acheson was a chief architect of this view. "Acheson," as Halberstam noted, "was always the true interventionist who deeply believed that the totalitarians might exploit the democracies. He was not soft, Acheson, he never was. He was Wilsonian, but new-generation Wilsonian, Wilson flexing old ideals with new industrial and technological might, Wilson with a longer reach." This perspective continued to shape American policy as the United States intervened in Southeast Asia. Bundy and Rostow, among "the best and the brightest" of American policymakers in the administrations of John F. Kennedy and Lyndon Johnson, epitomized this Cold War attitude during the Vietnam War.[8]

The New Left, protesting against the war and the entire shape of American foreign policy, attacked what they considered to be a Cold War consensus. Holding the realists responsible as the intellectual spokesmen for American foreign policy, they rejected their perspective. The recent revisionists, however, failed to distinguish between various groups of realists. They blurred, for example, the basic differences between Kennan and Acheson.[9] While some realists questioned the American involvement in Vietnam, revisionists uniformly criticized them as architects of the Cold War. Ironically, while rejecting the consequences of ultrarealism in Southeast Asia, the New Left offered a remarkably similar appraisal of Woodrow Wilson.[10]

Denna Frank Fleming clearly exemplified the link between the Wilsonian tradition in American diplomacy and the New Left. A partisan defender of Wilson's foreign policy, Fleming provided one of the first revisionist interpretations of *The Cold War and Its Origins*. He believed that World War II provided a "second chance" for the creation of a "world community." Like the ultrarealists, he assumed "the indivisibility of peace." Viewing the League of Nations as an excellent instrument for preventing aggression, Fleming criticized the appeasement of Munich as a futile attempt to preserve peace. During the subsequent war with Nazi Germany, the hope for a peaceful future lay with the maintenance of the alliance of the Soviet Union, the United Kingdom, and the United States. President Franklin D. Roosevelt clearly appreciated and pursued a policy of continuing collective security. "The abrupt reversal of Woodrow Wilson's policy after 1918," wrote Fleming, "had let us in for World War II. This time we would not about face the moment the fighting ended." As isolationists were converted to internationalism, the United States joined with its allies at the San Francisco Conference in creating the United Nations. From Fleming's perspective, however, President Truman soon tragically reversed the direction of Roosevelt's policy of collective security. Adopting Winston Churchill's anti-Communist attitude, he led the United States into confrontation with Soviet Russia, summarizing his new policy of containment in the Truman Doctrine. Therefore, in Fleming's interpretation, Truman bore major responsibility for originating the Cold War. Because the president's actions produced the Cold War, by implication the United States possessed the power to avoid it. Fleming shared with the ultrarealists the illusion of American omnipotence, believing in the possible creation of a Wilsonian world.[11]

Other New Left historians found it equally difficult to offer a genuinely radical interpretation of American foreign relations. Revisionists such as William Appleman Williams expressed a favorable view of Herbert Hoover, despite his service in the Wilson administration during World War I and his lifelong admiration of the Democratic president. Compared to Wilson, Hoover's more obvious aversion to noneconomic involvement in Europe apparently attracted the New Left.[12] Like the historiography on Hoover's foreign policy, that on Wilson's exemplified the orthodoxy of recent revisionism. The New Left experienced the same limitation as Senator William E. Borah in criticizing Wilson's diplomacy. Although they apparently represented opposite poles in the debate over foreign policy after World War I, the senator and the president viewed the American role in world affairs from a common national perspective.[13] Revisionist historians similarly shared many of Wilson's presuppositions, while attempting to present a radical critique of his conduct of American foreign relations. The substance of their criticism was not as radical as their tone.

N. Gordon Levin, Jr.'s *Woodrow Wilson and World Politics* exemplified the limited parameters of the New Left historiography. Although acknowledging his intellectual indebtedness not only to his mentor Louis Hartz but also to New Left historians William Appleman Williams and Arno J. Mayer, Levin interpreted America's response to war and revolution within the framework of Wilson's ideology. His book appropriately received the praise of Wilson's foremost and sympathetic biographer, Arthur S. Link. In a review Link affirmed that "the author has described brilliantly and perceptively both the dynamics and the long-range purposes of Wilson's foreign policies.... Levin has such respect for the evidence that he never distorts the record or uses it merely to prove his point.... What else can one say about the result except that it is judicious, balanced, and as detached as it is humanly possible to be?"[14]

Like Louis Hartz, Levin emphasized the exceptionalism or uniqueness of the liberal tradition in America. In his view, it was out of this tradition that Wilson developed his conception of "a stable world order of liberal-capitalist internationalism," which became the basis for American foreign policy in the twentieth century. Because "the President never doubted that American liberal values were the wave of the future in world politics," he saw no conflict between American national interests and internationalism. "For Wilson, then," wrote Levin, "American national values were identical with universal progressive liberal values, and an exceptionalist America had a mission to lead mankind toward the orderly international society of the future." From his centrist perspective, Wilson opposed "the atavistic values of traditional European imperialism" on the Right and "the values of Leninist revolutionary-socialism" on the Left. Levin developed this theme by emphasizing that the American involvement in World War I was at once antagonistic toward autocratic Imperial Germany and revolutionary Bolshevism. After Germany and Soviet Russia concluded a separate peace in the spring of 1918, their apparent collaboration against liberal-capitalist internationalism moved Wilson toward intervention in the Russian Revolution. By intervening in Siberia, Levin contended, the United States could fulfill "a Wilsonian desire to oppose both Bolshevism and German imperialism on behalf of a pro-Allied and liberal-nationalist Russia." Yet, the same ideology led the president after the war to oppose full-scale Allied intervention in Russia. According to Levin, Wilson feared that such interference in Russia's internal affairs would rally even anti-Bolshevik Russians to support the Soviet regime. By opposing British or French intervention, the United States would at once thwart Allied imperialism and weaken Bolshevism in Russia.[15]

Levin viewed the Paris Peace Conference of 1919 as the culmination of Wilson's search for a liberal-capitalist world order. Stressing his ambivalence toward postwar Germany, he examined the contradictory "reintegrationist" and "punitive" tendencies in the president's peacemaking. Levin felt that "a crucial Wilsonian task at Paris would be to check Allied imperialism and construct a new world order of liberal-capitalist stability into which a reformed Germany could be reintegrated." The successful reintegration of Germany promised also "to check the expansion of Bolshevism in the immediate postwar period." Within the American delegation, leading proponents of the reintegrationist approach, which Levin preferred, were Secretary of State Robert Lansing, General Tasker H. Bliss, Henry White, and Herbert Hoover. Wilson, however, never fully accepted their advice or "the newly democratized Germany." Succumbing to "his sense of punitive righteousness" and the demands of the Allies, he departed from the reintegrationist policy. In so doing, the president caught himself on the horns of a dilemma. "In short," Levin concluded, "the central contradiction of Wilsonian policy at Paris was reflected in the tension between the President's desire to reintegrate a liberal Germany into a peaceful and non-revolutionary world order and his almost equally strong punitive determination to avoid any appeasement of Germany." Levin saw the Allies, and especially the French, as the chief protagonists of a punitive peace. "The French were primarily concerned with extorting the largest possible reparations from Germany," he asserted. Their position on territorial and security questions likewise reflected "the French anti-reintegrationist view." In contrast, Levin observed, "Wilsonians were concerned with moderating these extreme French demands in the interests both of a fair, lasting peace and of Germany's liberal political order and unity."[16]

In Levin's interpretation, Wilson attempted to resolve the contradiction between the reintegrationist and punitive approaches to peace with his conception of the League of Nations. The League, which would initially exclude Weimar Germany from membership, would provide the method for enforcing the Versailles Treaty. Yet, after a probationary period under American and Allied control, Germany could earn the right to join the League. Levin accordingly argued "that, for Wilson himself, the League of Nations served the function of resolving whatever contradictions were inherent in his efforts to create a European settlement which would control and punish Germany and which would, at the same time, also insure against war or revolution." The League of Nations in Wilson's vision of a liberal world provided the means of transcending a punitive peace. "In sum, then," Levin concluded, "the basic Wilsonian reintegrationist conception of the League, as an inclusive community of liberal states mutually pledged to defend international law and one another's territorial integrity, had the potential of ideologically transcending the actual anti-German context from within which the League emerged at Paris."[17]

This dualistic interpretation of Wilson's policy toward Germany, or what Levin called the "reintegrationist-punitive dialectic," was hardly a radical departure in American historiography; nor was the casting of France in the role of the president's principal antagonist at the peace conference. William E. Dodd expressed similar themes in 1920. In his biography of Wilson, Dodd viewed the French premier Georges Clemenceau as the epitome of "the old diplomacy, the old balance of power and sharp political bargaining." The reactionary Clemenceau opposed the progressive liberalism of the American president. "If there was ever a clear case of short-sighted social reaction against a far-sighted liberalism," Dodd claimed, "it was just this intense struggle between Clemenceau the realist and Wilson the idealist."[18] Dodd enjoyed Wilson's encouragement in writing his biography. Ray Stannard Baker, the president's authorized biographer, adopted the same perspective. He contrasted Wilson's peace program with both German and Allied militarism. Criticizing the French demands along the Rhine, Baker affirmed: "At bottom, then, the whole trouble was militarism—whether German or allied—the military point of view, the idea of force as the antidote to fear. Instead of seeing in these military sanctions a way to safety as the French did, the President saw in them just the opposite—more insecurity, more fear, more war." In contrast to this punitive European approach to peace, Wilson proposed the transformation of international relations through the creation of a new world order with the League of Nations. "He was offering the world—and the French!—the only substitute for the old equilibrium of forces—which was a new order of international relations, based upon moral principles, mutual trust, and common guarantees: the League of Nations."[19]

Other historians maintained the dualistic framework that had characterized Dodd's and Baker's interpretations. Paul Birdsall ardently defended Wilson's diplomacy by contrasting the American and Allied peace programs. He saw the Versailles Treaty as "the outcome of the struggle between Wilsonian principles of a new world order and the principles of reactionary nationalism."[20] Although critical of Wilson for his share in the "lost peace," Thomas A. Bailey likewise viewed the alternative solutions to the German problem as—in Levin's terminology—either reintegrationist or punitive. In his study of the peace conference, Bailey concluded that "the Treaty of Versailles fell between two stools. It was neither a thoroughgoing victor's peace nor a peace of accommodation."[21] During the Cold War, this progressive dualism characterized the favorable assessments of Wilson's diplomacy. Seth P. Tillman contrasted the Anglo-American and French positions on most major issues of postwar policy. Compared to France, he argued, "Britain and the United States were responsible for the most enlightened, most progressive, and most moral features of the treaties of peace." Unlike Bailey's view of the "lost peace," Tillman considered the Versailles Treaty a feasible basis for postwar peace. Like Birdsall, he saw it as a reasonable facsimile of the Fourteen Points. Moreover, anticipating Levin's later interpretation, Tillman viewed the League of Nations as the potential means of transforming international relations from the old system characterized by the punitive French approach to peacemaking into a new world order based on democratic principles. He concluded that "the loss of the opportunity which so briefly presented itself to the democratic world was the work not of the statesmen of 1919 but of their successors, who lost it completely."[22]

Levin adhered to Wilson's perspective, not only in his dualistic reintegrationist-punitive framework and his critical attitude toward France but also in his more basic presupposition of the primacy of domestic politics. Rather than examine the complex relationships between American and foreign affairs, he interpreted the response of the president and his advisers to the European war and the Russian Revolution as the outward projection of American liberal-capitalist values. Wilson, too, presupposed the primacy of domestic politics in his interpretation of American foreign relations. Having been the first prominent scholar to endorse Frederick Jackson Turner's frontier thesis, he used it to explain the emergence of the United States as a world power. "It is not by accident," Wilson proclaimed in 1916, "... that only eight years elapsed [after the closing of the frontier in 1890] before we got into the politics of the world." The Spanish–American War of 1898 was the result, and it in turn expanded the American involvement in world affairs. "Ever since then we have been caught inevitably in the net of the politics of the world." As a consequence of the frontier's closing, the president concluded that the United States should help create and join a league of nations. "What disturbs the life of the whole world is the concern of the whole world," he affirmed, "and it is our duty to lend the full force of this nation, moral and physical, to a league of nations which shall see to it that nobody disturbs the peace of the world without submitting his case first to the opinion of mankind."[23] Wilson thus presupposed the primacy of domestic politics, although his book on *The State* had been a pioneering work in the field of comparative politics. Similarly, by interpreting Wilson's foreign policy as the international expression of the internal American ideology, Levin eschewed the comparative approach that distinguished the historical studies of Louis Hartz.[24]

Levin's presupposition of the primacy of domestic politics accounted not only for his focus on Wilsonian ideology but also for his neglect of foreign sources. He ignored the foreign policy of Germany and the German delegation at Versailles. Like Birdsall, whose book suffered from the same omission, Levin judged the Paris negotiations against a Wilsonian standard of an ideal peace rather than relative to the real situation in postwar Europe. Naively assuming that the complete adoption of the reintegrationist approach to peacemaking would have achieved its desired result, he asserted that by succumbing to the punitive approach the president contributed to "the creation of a self-fulfilling prophecy about the character of the postwar German state." Levin's misunderstanding of the Weimar Republic matched that of Wilson himself. Without naming "those postwar German leaders who most completely adhered to Wilsonian values," Levin presumed their existence and their readiness to reintegrate Germany into the American liberal-capitalist world order.[25] Wilson was shocked when they failed to appear at Versailles, but Levin never confronted this problem.

For Levin and other New Left historians, domestic politics provided the sources of foreign policy. A radical young historian in the Weimar Republic, Eckart Kehr, originated the non-Marxist thesis of "the primacy of internal politics" in international relations. Reversing the Rankean and Bismarckian tradition of the primacy of foreign policy, Kehr emphasized the social and economic determinants in the politics and, consequently, foreign policy of Germany. Although ostracized by the German historical profession, Kehr gained some recognition in the United States. Charles A. Beard supported him and praised his work. Similarly critical of American foreign relations, Beard incorporated Kehr's approach and conclusions into *The Idea of National Interest* and *The Open Door at Home*. Despite its radical implications for German historiography, the analysis of social and economic factors in politics was not new in the United States. Indeed, as Kehr himself noted, both Beard and William E. Dodd would have appeared as socialists beyond the pale of respectability in Germany, but not so in the United States.[26] Beard bequeathed this analytical framework to recent American revisionists, such as William Appleman Williams. Although apparently unaware of Kehr's influence on Beard, Williams accepted Kehr's contention of the primacy of domestic politics and Beard's version of it in the Open Door thesis, including its social and economic bias.[27] These ideas have characterized the New Left critiques of American foreign relations, including that of Levin.[28]

Arno J. Mayer, more directly influenced by Kehr, emphasized the primacy of domestic politics in his volumes on the *Political Origins of the New Diplomacy* and the *Politics and Diplomacy of Peacemaking*. Like Levin, he offered a more orthodox interpretation than he thought. His categories of Old and New Diplomacy were introduced much earlier by Ray Stannard Baker. Significantly, Baker served as a principal source for Mayer.[29] Mayer redefined Baker's dichotomy between Old and New Diplomacy. Whereas Baker had emphasized the national differences between

American and European diplomacy, Mayer examined the international implications of the socioeconomic differences between the "parties of order" and the "parties of movement" in the United States and Europe. He accordingly focused on the New Diplomacy not only of Wilson but also of Lenin. In his first volume, Mayer viewed the American president as a brilliant and realistic statesman, who refused to endorse the reactionary war aims of the Allies and who heralded instead a new world order. "Wilson's analysis of the crisis which led him to formulate and practice the New Diplomacy," he concluded, "was hardly that of a political idealist or a nonconformist minister whose thought and temperament were 'essentially theological, not intellectual.' In the course of the war the president developed either a dormant or a new historical acumen which enabled him to make an unusually perspicacious assessment of both the domestic and the international tensions generated by the simultaneous waning of an old era and the birth of a New World."[30]

Like Levin, Mayer depicted Wilson as the proponent of "a middle, reformist solution" instead of a Carthaginian or "punitive peace" as desired by the Allies. Yet, in his second volume, Mayer became increasingly critical of the president for his failure at the Paris Peace Conference and especially for his negative response to the Bolshevik Revolution. He criticized Wilson for compromising with the Allies and betraying his vision of New Diplomacy when confronted with Lenin's revolutionary variety of New Diplomacy. "However reluctantly," wrote Mayer, "the President was one of the chief movers of the counterrevolutionary enterprise."[31] This criticism of Wilson was expressed by Levin as the sacrifice of the reintegrationist in favor of the punitive approach to peacemaking.

Mayer's division of American and European politicians between the "parties of movement" and the "parties of order" resulted in distortion. These categories, which were more appropriate for Europe than the United States, failed to account for the link between progress and order in American thought and practice. Wilson had long affirmed the ideal of "progressive order" for democracy in the United States.[32] During the peacemaking, he maintained this perspective.

In his formal presentation of the Versailles Treaty to the Senate, Wilson justified the new role of the United States in world politics in the name of progress. "It has come about," he said, "by no plan of our conceiving, but by the hand of God who led us into this way. We cannot turn back. We can only go forward, with lifted eyes and freshened spirit, to follow the vision. It was of this that we dreamed at our birth. America shall in truth show the way. The light streams on the path ahead and nowhere else."[33] This progressive faith was fundamental in the thought of Wilson and his apologists, as radically disillusioned critics such as Carl Becker recognized. After reading Dodd's biography of Wilson, Becker responded that "the war is inexplicable on any ground of reason, or common sense, or decent aspiration, or even of intelligent self-interest; on the contrary it was as a whole the most futile and aimless, the most desolating and repulsive exhibition of human power and cruelty without compensating advantage that has ever been on earth. This is the result of some thousands of years of what men like to speak of as 'political, economic, intellectual, and moral Progress.' If this is progress, what in Heaven's name would retardation be!"[34]

While proclaiming his vision of American-led progress in world affairs, Wilson also stressed order. During the Red Scare, which his administration fostered and which coincided with his fight with the Republican-controlled Senate over the League of Nations, the president applauded the reelection of the Republican incumbent Calvin Coolidge to the Massachusetts governorship. He called it "a victory for law and order. When that is the issue all Americans stand together."[35] This yearning for order was fundamental in Wilson's conception of the League, as Warren F. Kuehl emphasized.[36] Progress and order were inextricably bound together in Wilson's thought. From his own progressive perspective, Mayer ignored this link. Accordingly, in his view, Wilson shifted from the "parties of movement" to the "parties of order" as he betrayed his progressive New Diplomacy to the counterrevolutionary Old Diplomacy. Unlike Becker, who saw this process as inevitable failure rather than betrayal, Mayer failed to appreciate the impossibility that World War I could culminate in the creation of a new world order. His dualistic progressive interpretation contrasted with that of Becker, who anticipated the post-World War II realism of Morgenthau, Kennan, and Graebner. By rejecting the traditional progressive framework, Becker was more fundamentally radical than recent revisionists who maintained this perspective.

Viewing the debate over foreign policy in the United States from Wilson's perspective, Mayer categorized Senator Henry Cabot Lodge as a reactionary proponent of the Old Diplomacy. "The keynote," he observed, "was struck by Senator Lodge, whose broadsides against the President's peace program and strategy were identical with those of the most ardent bitter-enders in Britain, France, and Italy."[37] Levin offered a similar interpretation as he asserted that "Lodge was an outspoken protagonist for the French position of an extremely punitive peace."[38] This negative identification between Lodge and the French was not a new theme. Dodd voiced it while Wilson still resided in the White House: "The challenge of Clemenceau, the prince of the European reactionaries, was proof of the sweeping momentum of the President's purposes. The heated anger of the Bourbon groups in the United States, increasing in temperature with every succeeding wave of enthusiasm that broke at the feet of the President, was still clearer proof."[39] Denna Frank Fleming developed this theme in his study of the treaty fight, observing that the partisan and obstructionist Lodge "stood for as harsh a peace as any European chauvinist could desire."[40] Thomas A. Bailey adopted an equally critical view of Lodge, although he attributed to the president the principal responsibility for the "great betrayal" of the Versailles peace, the Allies and Germany, and the American people.[41] In their interpretations of the politics of peacemaking in the United States, Mayer and Levin perpetuated these traditional views.[42]

Emphasizing the primacy of domestic politics over foreign policy, and especially its social and economic determinants, Mayer and Levin neglected other factors. They devoted little attention to the vitally important influence of evangelical Christianity on Wilson's foreign policy. The major contribution of the president's religious beliefs to his foreign policy was recognized and explored far more thoroughly by Alexander L. and Juliette L. George in their personality study of Wilson and Edward M. House.[43] In their highly rational reconstructions of Wilsonian ideology, Mayer and Levin also excluded the misperception, confusion, error, and irrationality of American diplomacy. These factors, which Becker had observed, were described by Walter Millis in his analysis of American entry into the war and most perceptively by George F. Kennan in his studies of Soviet–American relations during the Russian Revolution.[44] Mayer and Levin, however, stressed the consistently anti-Bolshevik character of the American response to the Russian Revolution. Attributing the American and Allied intervention in Russia to this antipathy toward Bolshevism, they rejected Kennan's perspective and followed instead that of Williams.[45]

By focusing intently on the domestic origins of American foreign relations, Mayer and Levin avoided the mistake of superimposing an intellectual framework onto Wilson's foreign policy that was alien to his ideology. They recognized that the president did not operate within the realistic perspective of a balance of power. In this regard, their interpretations differed markedly from those of Edward H. Buehrig, Ernest R. May, Arthur S. Link, and Daniel M. Smith. Writing during the Cold War, these historians viewed Wilson as a balance-of-power statesman, who realistically responded to the European war by leading the United States toward intervention and by developing the postwar League of Nations. They adopted the terminology of the realists, but rejected the Morgenthau-Kennan critique of Wilson's diplomacy. Like the ultrarealists, these scholars combined an affirmation of Wilson's ideals with an emphasis on power politics.[46] This combination of idealism and practicality was labeled by Link as Wilson's "higher realism."[47]

Praising Wilson for his leadership during the period of American neutrality, May offered a different conception of realism from that of Morgenthau, Kennan, and Graebner.

> It is hard, indeed, to find fault with Wilson's statesmanship. Retrospective analysts have contended that he was unrealistic. He should, it is suggested, have thrown America into the war to prevent German victory, preserve Anglo-American control of the seas, and overturn authoritarian and militarist ideologies. But this criticism supposes that Wilson should have acted against a German menace that might never have materialized. Although the President's dreams could look to the eternal future, his diplomacy conformed to Bismarck's rule: it assumed any contingency more than six months away to be out of calculation. Dealing with both Britain and Germany, Wilson concerned himself with the immediate interests of his country. America's security was not threatened in the predictable future. Her economic power and her prestige were in danger. His policy fended off present threats.[48]

Adopting a similar conception of realism, Buehrig approved the president's combination of idealism and practicality in the American response to the European war. "Underlying Wilson's whole policy of peace without victory," he argued, "was an appreciation of the balance of power point of view: namely, that stability is to be found in an equilibrium of forces no less than in moral excellence."[49]

Rejecting this interpretation of Wilson, Mayer and Levin rightly appreciated that he did not define the American national interest in the context of a realistic assessment of the international balance of power. Yet, because of their restricted focus on the domestic origins of foreign policy, Mayer and Levin reduced the complexity of world politics to more manageable categories than was possible for Wilson at the time.[50]

The New Left critique of Wilson's foreign policy during World War I embraced much of the progressive Wilsonian ideology. In the dualistic framework of the "reintegrationist-punitive dialectic" or New versus Old Diplomacy, the negative view of the French and American opponents of Wilson as reactionaries, and the presupposition of the primacy of domestic politics, Levin and Mayer shared the president's attitudes. Especially emphasizing the internal origins of foreign policy, Levin and Mayer, like Williams, failed to escape from the traditional American perspective sufficiently to offer a genuinely radical interpretation of it. Their viewpoint was more orthodox than that of Becker or the realists, who rejected the Wilsonian faith in progress toward the ideal world of liberal internationalism. Although obviously adopting a more favorable attitude toward the Bolshevik Revolution—and more radical in that sense—the recent revisionists substantially retained Wilson's presuppositions in their interpretations.

In the context of the American diplomatic tradition, the pluralist critique of the Cold War was more radical than that of the New Left. Developing the perspective of realists such as Morgenthau, Kennan, and Graebner, critics such as Ronald Steel, David Calleo, Richard J. Barnet, and Robert W. Tucker urged the United States to abandon the Wilsonian mission of *Pax Americana* and to accept the plural world. They rejected the idea of "one world" and distinguished between areas where the United States had vital interests (e.g., Western Europe) and where it did not (e.g., Vietnam). Contrasting imperial and national interests, they criticized the American empire of the Cold War. Recognizing the limits of American power, these pluralists advocated the curtailment of American involvement in world affairs or the acceptance of a "new isolationism." Although they, too, emphasized the domestic origins of foreign policy, their criticism of American intervention in the Cold War took into account the external conditions. They believed that the reality of a plural world, which no major power could control, prevented not only the United States from achieving the Wilsonian ideals of liberal internationalism but also the Soviet Union from a similar communist triumph. In such a world, the pluralists understood that the United States could protect its interests without engaging in liberal crusades. This pluralist critique of the Wilsonian legacy in the Cold War questioned the fundamental premises of American foreign policy.[51]

There was, in contrast, an orthodoxy to the revisionism of the New Left. Like the ultrarealistic American cold warriors, recent revisionists affirmed many of the tenets of Wilson's liberal internationalism. Their contributions to the contemporary and historical debate over American foreign policy failed to challenge his progressive vision of a new world order. The New Left historians instead maintained the basic Wilsonian perspective of the American diplomatic tradition.

CHAPTER 12

VIETNAM REVISITED: WILSON'S GHOST

Revised text of the Herbert S. Schell lecture, "Vietnam Revisited: Wilson's Ghost," delivered at the University of South Dakota, October 2001.

During the 1990s, Robert S. McNamara joined others in celebrating Wilson's legacy by offering his reinterpretation of the Vietnam War and his lessons for the twenty-first century. He identified himself with Wilsonianism and criticized the realist school of thought in international relations. It was perhaps significant that the former secretary of defense waited for the end of the Cold War before offering his revisionist history of the Vietnam tragedy and his Wilsonian advice for the future. His books, although badly flawed, deserved serious attention because of what they revealed, however unwittingly, not only about America's longest war but also about U.S. political culture and foreign relations in the post-Cold War era.

In *Argument Without End* (1999), with coauthors James G. Blight and Robert K. Brigham, McNamara attempted to answer difficult and important questions about the Vietnam War. He believed he had finally found the answers. "The thesis of this book," McNamara asserted, "is that the war was a tragedy for both sides. Both Washington and Hanoi could have accomplished their purposes without the appalling loss of life. There were missed opportunities, either for avoiding the war before it started or for terminating it before it had run its course."[1] McNamara claimed that both sides in the protracted conflict could have achieved their goals without the war. Unfortunately, the evidence in this book did not support that conclusion. His thesis about "missed opportunities" suffered from the same preconceived judgments and mistaken assessments that had characterized his tenure in office. McNamara's revisionist history of the Vietnam tragedy was as badly flawed as his earlier statecraft.

As one of the chief architects of American military escalation in Vietnam during the 1960s, McNamara was directly responsible for the terrible consequences of the war. Along with his colleagues in the administrations of Presidents John F. Kennedy and Lyndon B. Johnson, he hoped to achieve U.S. goals in Vietnam either through a military victory or a diplomatic settlement. But he never devised a military strategy to win the war or a diplomatic solution to end it through negotiations. McNamara was still dealing with that terrible dilemma, which he could not escape then and could not resolve afterward. *Argument Without End,* while not fulfilling his avowed intent to disclose "missed opportunities," nevertheless revealed a great deal about the reasons for America's longest war.

McNamara included a picture of Woodrow Wilson opposite the first page of this book. In the caption under the picture, McNamara expressed his hope that lessons from the Vietnam War will enable the world in the twenty-first century to live in peace, thus achieving what Wilson had promised but failed to attain. "At the end of World War I," McNamara observed, "President Wilson believed, as did many other Americans, that we had won a war to end all wars. How wrong they were. The twentieth century has become the bloodiest in all human history. Must we repeat that carnage in the twenty-first century? This book will draw lessons from the Vietnam War to reduce that risk."[2]

McNamara hoped to succeed where Wilson had failed. In the Wilsonian tradition, he claimed the moral high ground for himself and suggested that others who might disagree with his lessons of history were amoral, if not immoral. He focused his criticism on the "realists." He stated: "I am aware that the majority of political scientists, particularly those of the realist school, believe morality—as compared with a careful calculation of national interests based on balance-of-power considerations—is a dangerous guide for establishing foreign policy. They would say that a foreign policy driven by moral considerations promotes zealousness and a crusading spirit, with potentially dangerous results. But the United States has defined itself in highly idealistic and moral terms through its history." Claiming that realists were—and still are—indifferent to issues of morality, he sought to discredit their political theories or historical judgments by suggesting that they were unconcerned about the high level of killing throughout the past century. "But surely," he affirmed, "in the most basic sense, one can apply a moral judgment to the level of killing that has occurred in the twentieth century. *There is no justification for it today, and there can be no justification for its continuation into the twenty-first century!*"[3]

In *Wilson's Ghost* (2001), McNamara and his coauthor James G. Blight elaborated their prescriptions for reducing the risk of conflict, killing, and catastrophe in the twenty-first century.[4] Likening "the ghost of Woodrow Wilson" to that of Jacob Marley in Charles Dickens's *A Christmas Carol,* they urged U.S. policymakers to heed the moral and multilateral imperatives, which they identified as the essence of Wilson's message or legacy. In their so-called radical agenda, they advocated "a new foreign and defense policy for America and the world based on a moral imperative to reduce deaths from war, and a U.S. commitment to lead the world toward that objective but never to apply its political, economic, or military force unilaterally."[5] This Wilsonian orientation, they argued, would be the opposite of a "realist" foreign policy.

It is not surprising that McNamara would focus his criticism on realists, for several leading proponents of realism in the 1960s were among the first and most incisive critics of U.S. policy toward Vietnam. I noted this realist dissent in *Woodrow Wilson and the American Diplomatic Tradition.*[6] The realism of Reinhold Niebuhr, Walter Lippmann, Hans J. Morgenthau, George F. Kennan, and Norman A. Graebner enabled them to recognize the fundamental errors in judgment of the Kennedy and Johnson administrations that were responsible for American military escalation and diplomatic failure in Vietnam. These realists spoke out against the war in meetings with President Johnson and other U.S. officials, in hearings before the Senate Foreign Relations Committee, and in teach-ins on university campuses at a time when most Americans, including most intellectuals as well as politicians, still supported the war. They were certainly not indifferent to the moral issues arising from that war in the 1960s, although they defined morality in a radically different way from McNamara.[7]

At the core of realist thought was the moral conviction that responsibility and power must go together. If a person or government exercises the power of war and peace, then that same person or government must bear the moral as well as political responsibility for either action or inaction. Those with political power are morally responsible for their decisions and for the consequences of those decisions. Good intentions are not enough. Kennan later explained the integral "connection between power and responsibility." He did not believe that the United States should pursue the mission of expanding democracy worldwide. "Democracy, as Americans understand it, is not necessarily the future for all mankind," he affirmed, "nor is it the duty of the U.S. government to assure that it becomes that. Despite frequent assertions to the contrary, not everyone in this world is responsible, after all, for the actions of everyone else, everywhere. Without the power to compel change, there is no responsibility for its absence. In the case of governments, it is important for purely practical reasons that the lines of responsibility be kept straight, and that there be, in particular, a clear association of the power to act with the consequences of action or inaction."[8]

In the judgment of realists during the 1960s, McNamara failed this crucial test of political and moral responsibility. Hans J. Morgenthau, often incorrectly regarded as the realist least concerned about morality, made this point in very explicit terms with reference to McNamara. In June 1966, he wrote:

> The President is personally in charge of the war in Vietnam, and he cannot escape either blame or praise for what we are doing there. Furthermore, we can pinpoint the sources of advice upon which the President has based certain fateful decisions. We know, for instance, who, from the beginning of President Johnson's tenure in office, has consistently urged the bombing of North Vietnam as a means of bringing the war to a quick, victorious conclusion. We know that this man is today one of the President's principal advisers. We know that if the Secretary of Defense had been as consistently wrong in his calculations as president of the Ford Motor Company as he has been in the conduct of the war in Vietnam, either the Ford Motor Company would have gone broke or he would have been fired.[9]

That was a moral judgment of McNamara's leadership as well as a strategic assessment of his advice. In August 1966, Morgenthau emphasized this point when he called the present U.S. policy in Vietnam "morally dubious, militarily hopeless and risky, [and] politically aimless and counterproductive."[10]

In *Argument Without End*, McNamara still defined morality in a way that might allow himself to escape responsibility for his exercise of power and for consequences of his advice. He claimed the moral high ground for himself without ever addressing fundamental issues that realists raised during the war. Even when he acknowledged some personal responsibility for "missed opportunities" during the Vietnam War, he sought to shift most of the blame to the Vietnamese. He did not acknowledge that the pursuit of unrealistic U.S. goals in Vietnam had prolonged the war and increased the casualties. He did not admit that the United States could never have achieved its goals in Vietnam so long as the Vietnamese remained willing and able to resist.

Instead, McNamara sought to narrow the discussion to "missed opportunities," which he defined in such a way as largely to exonerate himself of moral responsibility for the war and its consequences. His failures, or so he would have readers of *Argument Without End* believe, were only in the realm of inadequate information and misperception. McNamara concluded: "The fundamental enemy—the root cause of the agony over the Vietnam War—was mutual ignorance, the inability of Washington and Hanoi to penetrate the outlook of the other side."[11] He still hoped to evade criticism, such as Morgenthau's, of the political incompetence and moral bankruptcy of his statecraft.

Like President Wilson earlier, McNamara appealed to American exceptionalism as the foundation for his claim of moral superiority. When he went to Hanoi to initiate the conversations that are recorded in *Argument Without End,* he was most concerned about whether the Vietnamese would acquiesce in his definition of the project. His arrogance and moral certitude appeared in his questions about that first anticipated meeting: "Will the Vietnamese really want to play this game by our rules? Would they agree to take a critical look at their own mindset, which labeled the Kennedy and Johnson administrations as 'neocolonialists' and 'neoimperialists' whose primary motive was to destroy the Hanoi government? I knew—without question—that if this was their mindset they were *dead wrong!* But would these committed communists in Hanoi really agree to reexamine not only Washington's mindsets, in search of mistakes, but also their own?"[12] It did not take long during the first meeting for McNamara to get his answer. After he asserted that both Hanoi and Washington had misunderstood each other, General Vo Nguyen Giap responded: "I don't believe we misunderstood you. You were the enemy; you wished to defeat us—to destroy us. So we were forced to fight you—to fight a 'people's war' to reclaim our country from your neoimperialist ally in Saigon—we used the word 'puppet,' of course, back then—and to reunify our country."[13]

McNamara denied that Americans had played an imperial role in Vietnam. He asked the Vietnamese a rhetorical question and then told them his answer: "Were we—was I, was Kennedy, was Johnson—a 'neoimperialist' in the sense you are using the word? I would say *absolutely not!*" Americans had harbored no such motives toward Vietnam, he claimed: "There was no such intent." But while McNamara focused on America's good motives, Vo Nguyen Giap assessed the consequences of its behavior. Good intentions were not enough to exonerate the United States of its moral or political responsibility. The Vietnamese general refused to narrow the discussion to "missed opportunities."

> Lessons are important. I agree. However, you are wrong to call the war a "tragedy"—to say that it came from missed opportunities. Maybe it was a tragedy for you, because yours was a war of aggression, in the neocolonialist "style," or fashion, of the day for the Americans. You wanted to replace the French; you failed; men died; so, yes, it was tragic because they died for a bad cause. But for us, the war was a noble sacrifice. We did not want to fight the U.S. We did not. But you gave us no choice. Our people sacrificed tremendously for our cause of freedom and independence. There were no missed opportunities for us.[14]

General Giap refused to accept even part of the blame for the protracted war.

Expressing his belief in American exceptionalism, McNamara rejected the label of imperialism for the United States. He argued that the American role in Vietnam was fundamentally different from that of other great powers. In his summary of the "major forces" that the Vietnamese people had faced during the twentieth century, he listed "European imperialism, Japanese militarism, American global containment, Maoist internationalism, and Soviet hegemonism."[15] In contrast to the others, he asserted, the United States had pursued a defensive role in Vietnam. He thought "the motives driving U.S. foreign policy" were "almost entirely *defensive*."[16] He acknowledged that, if he had been a Vietnamese communist in the 1960s, he might not have understood this. "However," McNamara insisted, "if I had been a Vietnamese communist and had held those views, I would have been totally mistaken."[17]

According to McNamara, Kennedy and Johnson, like President Dwight D. Eisenhower, had feared that there would be "falling dominoes" throughout Southeast Asia if South Vietnam fell to Communism. In line with its strategy of global containment, the United States had therefore pursued a defensive policy in Vietnam. "Throughout the Kennedy and Johnson administrations," McNamara explained to the Vietnamese, "we operated on the premise that the loss of South Vietnam to North Vietnam would result in all of Southeast Asia being overrun by communism and that this would threaten the security of both the United States and the entire noncommunist world." This apparent global threat had required a global response. "Like most Americans," he continued, "we saw communism as monolithic. We believed that the Soviets and the Chinese were cooperating and trying to extend their hegemony."[18] Hence, the U.S. involvement in Vietnam had originated from fears and defensive motives.

McNamara claimed that, in sharp contrast to France, the United States had never sought to create a colonial empire in Vietnam. He criticized the Vietnamese for failing to understand this crucial distinction and blamed them for projecting their image of France onto the United States: "Hanoi, in effect, projected onto the United States a kind of colonial mode of operation not significantly different from that of the French, who had occupied the country for more than a century. However, unlike the French, Americans were ambivalent about their global role and were not colonialists in the way that the French could be characterized. Had Hanoi understood this—had it achieved a more empathetic understanding of U.S. fears and motivations—it could have appealed to a strong set of American motives emphasizing self-determination and anticolonialism. But Hanoi did *not* understand this."[19] Thus the Vietnamese were responsible for "missed opportunities" resulting from their misperception. They should have seen that the United States was committed to the Wilsonian ideals of national self-determination and anticolonialism, not a new imperial or colonial threat seeking to replace France.

During discussions with McNamara in the 1990s, the Vietnamese acknowledged only one mistake in their earlier view of Americans. It was this: In 1945, they had erred in believing that Americans were different from the Japanese or the French. In other words, the Vietnamese had naively accepted the idea of American exceptionalism. They had mistakenly thought that the United States would fulfill its Wilsonian ideals of national self-determination and anticolonialism. Tran Quang Co, former first deputy foreign minister of Vietnam, acknowledged this mistake. "Prior to

September 1945," he said, "the Vietnamese people perceived the U.S. to be a world leader in the fight against fascism. At that time, the Vietnamese people considered the U.S. to be the only powerful Western country that opposed colonialism. Because of this, Vietnam had hoped that the U.S. would sympathize with the Vietnamese people's legitimate struggle for independence, freedom, and happiness. Unfortunately, reality proved that it was not so."[20] After the disillusioning experience in 1945, when the United States failed to promote Vietnamese independence at the expense of French colonialism, Vietnamese leaders such as Ho Chi Minh had changed their erroneous view of Americans, no longer seeing them as fundamentally different from the French.

Henceforth, Tran Quang Co told McNamara, the Vietnamese had viewed the Americans, like the French, as intent on establishing their dominance in Southeast Asia. The Americans might have thought they were fulfilling the Wilsonian ideal of national self-determination, but they were actually pursuing hegemony. "From the Vietnamese perspective," he recounted, "the outbreak of the war was not due to any Vietnamese misunderstanding of France or the United States. Instead, we believe war was brought to Vietnam by outside countries, in spite of the fact that Vietnam wanted to obtain national independence through peaceful means. I stress 'through peaceful means.' Vietnam did not want war." Rejecting McNamara's assertion that the war had resulted from "misjudgments, miscalculations, and misinformation" on both sides, Tran Quang Co insisted that it originated from "a serious conflict of basic interests."[21] U.S. involvement threatened Vietnamese independence. He outlined the only two ways the Vietnamese saw for terminating the war: Either one side might win a military victory over the other and "successfully achieve its desired goals" or both sides might "change their objectives sufficiently to reach a mutually acceptable compromise."[22] The war had resulted from this fundamental conflict between Hanoi's and Washington's goals in Vietnam. Consequently, Tran Quang Co and his colleagues saw no "missed opportunities" of the kind McNamara claimed to see. In short, the Vietnamese rejected the central thesis of *Argument Without End.* But McNamara insisted that they were wrong. He reiterated his thesis, claiming, moreover, that the discussions documented his original idea about "missed opportunities."

Stanley Hoffmann, viewing American involvement in Vietnam during the 1960s from a realist perspective, had rejected the distinction between France and the United States that McNamara still asserted in the 1990s. In May 1966, Hoffmann recognized: "Differences are more apparent than real. France, a colonial power, was the target of the rebellion from the start. But the United States support for Saigon's rulers is finally making it the target of all South Vietnamese nationalists—Communist or not."[23] Given this reality, Hoffmann concluded that the United States should abandon its pursuit of military victory and seek a political settlement, which would involve sacrificing the current U.S. goals in South Vietnam. "For our part," Hoffman advised, "we must shift from the unsuccessful manipulation of domestic Vietnamese affairs to the determination of the external conditions, thanks to which a South Vietnam in which the Vietcong would play an important role, or even a reunified Vietnam under Communist rule, would not be a threat to peace in Southeast Asia; i.e., neutralization with various international guarantees under U.N. or Geneva Conference controls."[24] The Johnson administration, including McNamara, rejected any such diplomatic settlement. Instead, its conduct of American foreign policy continued to exemplify what Hoffmann called "the Wilsonian syndrome."[25]

In the 1990s, McNamara still sought to obfuscate what Hoffmann, Morgenthau, and other realists had clearly understood at the time of the Vietnam War. In November 1968, analyzing an address by McGeorge Bundy, who had served as Kennedy's and Johnson's national security adviser during the American escalation of the war in Vietnam, Morgenthau observed that

> the crucial question has always been: Who shall govern South Vietnam, the Communists or their opponents? This issue can be interpreted in two different ways, one narrow and short-range, the other broad and long-range. It can mean the prevention of a Communist takeover, or it can mean, in the words of President Johnson, favorably quoted by Mr. Bundy on another occasion, "the independence of South Vietnam and its freedom from attack," that is, the defeat of the Viet Cong and of North Vietnam.... The whole conduct of the war—search and destroy, pacification, the massive bombing of Vietnam, North and South—is of course intelligible only if one assumes the broad interpretation of our goal. That interpretation was indeed the one supported by our policy-makers, Mr. Bundy included, who in 1965 spoke of "victory" and not the mere prevention of defeat, before the inevitability of failure had become obvious, albeit not acceptable, even to President Johnson.[26]

As secretary of defense, McNamara had supported the broad interpretation of U.S. goals. On January 27, 1965, he and Bundy presented to President Johnson the "fork in the road" memorandum, in which they advised U.S. military escalation rather than diplomatic concessions.[27] As a revisionist historian, however, McNamara tried to present himself as the chief advocate for the narrow interpretation. He even sought, moreover, to convey the impression that Presidents Kennedy and Johnson had also been willing to accept the narrow interpretation, or possibly even less, and therefore that Hanoi had missed the opportunity to negotiate peace with Washington on mutually acceptable terms. During the discussions in Hanoi in the 1990s, McNamara told the Vietnamese: "I think I can speak for Presidents Kennedy and Johnson, with whom I was very close.... We were *not* opposed to an independent, unified Vietnam. We were *not!* I want to make that very, very clear. I don't think you understood it then, and I'm not sure you understand it today."[28] In other words, McNamara belatedly claimed that the Kennedy and Johnson administrations had been open to a compromise like what Hoffmann had outlined in 1966 for a negotiated peace settlement. That was not apparent to Hoffmann or other U.S. observers at the time, nor to the Vietnamese. Nor have historians of the Vietnam War, who have studied the records, found the evidence for McNamara's claim. On the contrary, historians have found abundant documentation that the Kennedy and Johnson administrations, including McNamara, resisted the kind of compromise that Hoffmann suggested in 1966, and that the U.S. government pursued the broad rather than narrow interpretation of its goals, as Morgenthau noted in 1968.[29]

Nor did McNamara offer any documentation in *Argument Without End* for his claim that the Kennedy and Johnson administrations had pursued minimal goals, although this claim was central to his thesis about "missed opportunities." In fact, on the contrary, evidence in this book supported the opposite conclusion. In assessing the possibility of a neutral solution in South Vietnam, like that in Laos in 1962, McNamara dismissed the public endorsements by the National Liberation Front (NFL) and Hanoi for such a compromise as "pure propaganda." He also noted that "throughout the Kennedy administration and well into the Johnson administration, my colleagues and I—and, as the polls showed, the vast majority of the American public—believed that there was no neutral solution to the governance of South Vietnam because Hanoi and the NLF would not permit it. We believed we had no choice, therefore, but to continue to pursue the original goal of the Eisenhower administration: preserving an anticommunist bulwark in Saigon."[30]

Moreover, as McNamara recounted, President Johnson had reiterated this position in his New Year's greeting to General Duong Van Minh, who had replaced President Ngo Dinh Diem in the Saigon government after the U.S.-backed coup on November 1, 1963. Johnson told Saigon's new leader: "We shall maintain in Vietnam American personnel and material as needed to assist you in achieving victory.... Neutralization of South Vietnam is unacceptable [and] would only be another name for a communist take-over."[31] This quotation from Johnson contradicted McNamara's revisionist claim that the United States would have accepted "an independent, unified Vietnam" under Hanoi's leadership (and both Hanoi and the NLF would undoubtedly have rejected "an independent, unified Vietnam" under Saigon's leadership as the equivalent to military defeat) or his larger thesis about "missed opportunities." Even three decades after his tenure as secretary of defense, McNamara still refused to face the realities of the Vietnam War. He still preferred a fictionalized version of history.

Throughout *Argument Without End,* McNamara employed one stratagem after another to avoid any fundamental reconsideration of U.S. goals in Vietnam during the 1960s. Refusing to acknowledge that these might have been unrealistic, he rejected all arguments that America's pursuit of its goals had prolonged the war. Instead, he made the unsubstantiated claim that the Kennedy and Johnson administrations had been willing to negotiate an end to the war on terms that would have met Hanoi's essential requirements for peace. He stressed his own desire for peace, as if good intentions were enough to justify his statecraft. He was still seeking to shed moral and political responsibility for the power he had wielded as secretary of defense in the 1960s and for the consequences in Vietnam.

In his account of the origins and escalation of the war, McNamara seemed genuinely perplexed that the Vietnamese people, including Hanoi's leaders, had not understood in the 1960s—and still could not in the 1990s—that the United States did not want to be their enemy. From his Wilsonian perspective, he believed that Americans were proponents of national self-determination. Unlike the French, they had never sought a colonial empire. They had not wanted a war with the Vietnamese people. This outlook, he recounted, had characterized Kennedy, Johnson, and their advisers. "In their view," explained McNamara, "a great revolution was occurring—the births of new nations, whose constituents would have to choose between totalitarian communism and U.S.-style democracy. Given accurate information and a free choice, they believed, rational people would never choose communism over 'freedom'—to use Kennedy's favorite idiom. The problem was that the communists knew this too and sought at every opportunity to seize power by force of arms and to exercise control over people in the developing world, in part by brainwashing them with Marxist-Leninist dogma."[32] If the Hanoi and NLF leaders regarded the United States as their enemy, as they did in the 1960s, this confirmed for McNamara and other American policymakers in that decade that these communists were not representative of the Vietnamese people, and therefore that they were agents of the Soviet Union or the People's Republic of China. As communists, by definition, they could not also be nationalists.

U.S. officials who held this perspective were unable to escape the exceptionalism of American political culture, which appeared in their Wilsonianism. McNamara still could not in the 1990s. He still seemed genuinely perplexed—more than disingenuous—in his inability to comprehend how the Vietnamese people might have regarded the United States as their enemy. This myopic view of history—his belief that the Kennedy and Johnson administrations had adhered to the Wilsonian principle of national self-determination and that genuine Vietnamese nationalists should have understood this at the time—was fundamental to his thesis about "missed opportunities."

Loren Baritz identified the cultural assumptions that prevented Americans such as McNamara from understanding the Vietnamese perspective. In *Backfire* (1985), he noted:

> The myth of the city on a hill combined with solipsism in the assumptions about Vietnam made by the American war planners. In other words, we assumed that we had a superior moral claim to be in Vietnam, and because, despite their quite queer ways of doing things, the Vietnamese shared our values, they would applaud our intentions and embrace our physical presence.... Our claim to virtue was based on the often announced purity of our intentions. It was said, perhaps thousands of times, that all we wanted was freedom for other people, not land, not resources, and not domination. Because we believed that our intentions were virtuous, we could learn nothing from the French experience in Vietnam. After all, they had fought only to maintain their Southeast Asian colonies and as imperialists deserved to lose.... America's moral authority was so clear to us that we assumed that it also had to be clear to the Vietnamese.[33]

Thus, American exceptionalism had blinded U.S. policymakers from seeing how others, outside the ideological framework of Wilsonianism, might view reality from different perspectives.

McNamara's myopic view of history appeared in his account of the evolution of Washington's and Hanoi's mindsets from 1945 to 1960. At first, he did not intend to review the U.S.–Vietnamese relationship during this era, presupposing that one could understand the tragic war of the 1960s by focusing on events beginning with Kennedy's presidency. During the first meeting in Hanoi, however, the Vietnamese insisted on including the earlier years in the conversations. It was important to them, for example, that President Truman had decided in 1950 to help the French finance their war in Indochina. Yet, McNamara could not understand why the Vietnamese had viewed the United States as their enemy. Unable to comprehend why Ho Chi Minh had seen American involvement as an indication that "U.S. imperialists" were seeking to replace France and "gain complete control over Indochina" for themselves, McNamara characterized the Vietnamese leader's view of the United States as "a doomsday conclusion."[34] McNamara discounted the evidence, even when he included it in *Argument Without End*, that contradicted his thesis about "missed opportunities." Despite Ho Chi Minh's critique of Truman's decision and other similar Vietnamese condemnations of "U.S. neocolonialism" and "U.S. imperialism" in the 1950s, McNamara still denied in the 1990s any real conflict of interests between Hanoi and Washington. He saw only "fundamental misunderstandings."[35] Defining differences between Hanoi and Washington in this way, he sought to explain the origins of the tragic war without ever reconsidering U.S. goals toward Vietnam. He dismissed Vietnamese views as simply wrong, when these challenged his preconceived judgments.

McNamara argued that the war had resulted from mutual ignorance. He kept the focus on failures of knowledge and misperception, thereby avoiding more probing questions about responsibility for the war and its consequences. In his summary he stated: "Washington just could *not* bring itself to believe Hanoi was *not* a communist puppet bent on conquering all of Southeast Asia, beginning with South Vietnam. And Hanoi could *not* bring itself to believe that Washington was *not* a neoimperialist bent on destroying the Hanoi government and, with it, any possibility of a unified Vietnam. Erroneous mindsets drove the escalation. Misunderstandings facilitated it."[36] In his explanation of the war, McNamara did not ask how, even if all of Vietnam had fallen to Communism, it would have directly threatened U.S. security. He did not ask why the United States, as the world's most powerful nation, had been so afraid of such a small, relatively weak nation in Southeast Asia. He did not ask whether, given this vast disparity in power, Washington had been more responsible than Hanoi for the war and its consequences. Nor did he ask what answers to these questions might reveal about the Wilsonianism of American political culture. Rather than probing these questions, McNamara conceded only that "*Hanoi was no domino!*" He still maintained that "*Washington was no imperialist!*"[37] By focusing on "fundamental misunderstandings" and "missed opportunities" on both sides, he evaded any serious reassessment of his most basic, preconceived judgments.

McNamara refused to acknowledge that U.S. goals in Vietnam in the 1960s had been unrealistic. Although recognizing then that the United States probably could not achieve its goals by military means, he could not at the time—and still could not in the 1990s—bring himself to draw the logical conclusion that Washington policymakers needed to reconsider their goals. Even after he knew that the United States could not win the war at a bearable cost, he did not initiate a fundamental reassessment of its role in Vietnam. "Where did *we* go wrong?" McNamara later asked. "I'll speak first to what I'll call *Washington's* failure. It was clear to some of us as early as 1965, when the first significant peace initiatives occurred, that the United States might well fail to achieve its political objectives in Vietnam through military means." McNamara realized in the 1990s that the Johnson administration should have asked basic questions about its involvement in Vietnam, but it did not. "To this day," he acknowledged, "it is difficult to explain why I, and others, did not force the key issues to the surface, debate them fully, then proceed on the basis of our conclusions. Had we done so, our diplomatic effort would have been far more intense and far more effective. As it was, Hanoi believed it to be a trick." McNamara belatedly realized that Washington had failed to originate "a reliable channel to Hanoi, and a realistic message," which he described as "gestures toward some sort of compromise that would allow us to begin talking with each other directly."[38]

Even in the 1990s, McNamara evaded the fundamental questions that realists were asking in the 1960s. He referred to "some sort of compromise" without an honest and careful analysis of whether the most that Washington might have conceded would have been sufficient to match the least that Hanoi and the NLF might have accepted in a peace settlement. Without some kind of mutually acceptable compromise, no negotiations could have succeeded. The only alternative was continuation of the war. Given the reality that the United States could not win the war at a bearable cost, which some U.S. officials, including McNamara as early as 1965, had begun to grasp, the United States had faced a terrible dilemma in Vietnam. The Johnson administration's failure to seek a negotiated end to the war by reducing its goals revealed its political incompetence and moral bankruptcy. In the judgment of realists, it was utterly irresponsible for the United States to continue the killing for a hopeless cause. McNamara had sought to evade this dilemma in the 1960s, and he continued that evasion in *Argument Without End.*

In his account of peace initiatives from 1965 to 1967, McNamara revised the historical record to fit his predetermined thesis about "missed opportunities." This evasive technique appeared in his analysis of Hanoi's Four Points of April 8, 1965, and Washington's Fourteen Points of December 29, 1965. These conflicting sets of goals, which the two sides had outlined as their respective conditions for a peace settlement, he insisted, were not actually so different from each other. His fictionalized version of history on this crucial issue provided the basis for McNamara's unsubstantiated claim that the United States would have accepted "an independent, unified Vietnam" and therefore that Hanoi's failure to understand Washington's position was one of the "missed opportunities" for peace.

Hanoi's Four Points of April 8, 1965, McNamara noted, had called for the United States to recognize "the basic rights of the Vietnamese people—peace, independence, sovereignty, unity, and territorial integrity." This would have required the end of U.S. bombing of North Vietnam and the withdrawal of U.S. troops from South Vietnam. As stipulated in the 1954 Geneva Agreements, there should be no foreign troops in Vietnam or military alliances between either Hanoi or Saigon and other nations. The South Vietnamese people should settle their internal affairs in accordance with the NLF program. The people throughout Vietnam should determine the peaceful reunification of their own nation "without foreign interference."[39]

Washington's Fourteen Points, which Secretary of State Dean Rusk had outlined on December 29, 1965, were quite different from Hanoi's Four Points, despite McNamara's belated attempt to emphasize the similarities. The Fourteen Points had listed possible terms for a peace settlement, which might have included some future concessions, but that would have enabled the United States to achieve its essential goals. Rather than accepting Hanoi's points even as the basis for negotiations, the Johnson administration had welcomed only "negotiations without preconditions." The Geneva Agreements might provide the basis for peace. The negotiations should begin before the United States withdrew its troops, although it might stop the bombing under certain conditions. The cessation of hostilities could be placed on the agenda. If Hanoi were to "cease aggression" against South Vietnam, the NLF (or the Vietcong, as

Americans called the southern Vietnamese resistance) could participate in the negotiations. Washington reaffirmed its support for "free elections" to give the people of South Vietnam a choice in their government. Presumably at some later time, "the question of reunification of Vietnam should be determined by the Vietnamese themselves."[40]

Rusk had understood that the Fourteen Points would not sacrifice the primary U.S. objective in the war. As he stated, "We put everything into the basket except the surrender of South Vietnam."[41] The secretary of state recognized that Washington's Fourteen Points were fundamentally different from Hanoi's Four Points. As he recalled, "The Four Point Program was quite deceptive; the third of those four points required the imposition of the program of the National Liberation Front upon all South Vietnam. To us this meant that Hanoi was never interested in talking seriously about peace."[42] In other words, there were irreconcilable differences between Hanoi's and Washington's goals in Vietnam.

George C. Herring, whose *America's Longest War* (1979) is the classic textbook on the U.S. role in Vietnam, agreed with Rusk that the Fourteen Points would not have sacrificed South Vietnam for the sake of peace. Herring summarized the Johnson administration's position:

> The United States indicated that it was willing to stop the bombing, but only after Hanoi took reciprocal steps of de-escalation. It would withdraw its troops from the south, but only after a satisfactory political settlement had been reached. The administration accepted the principle that the future of South Vietnam must be worked out by the South Vietnamese. At the same time, however, it made clear that it would not admit the Vietcong to the government, a move that would be like "putting the fox in the chicken coop," [Vice President Hubert H.] Humphrey declared publicly. The Fourteen Points conceded merely that the views of the Vietcong "would have no difficulty being represented," and this only after Hanoi had "ceased its aggression." Beneath these ambiguous words rested a firm determination to maintain an independent, non-Communist South Vietnam.[43]

Both during the 1960s and the 1990s, the Vietnamese saw the same differences between Hanoi's Four Points and Washington's Fourteen Points that Rusk and Herring did. Nguyen Khac Huynh, who had earlier coordinated Hanoi's peace initiatives and participated in peace talks, explained during the later conversations "why the Fourteen Points were so totally—absolutely—unacceptable to us, no matter how reasonable they may appear to you." He focused on Rusk's thirteenth point, which required Hanoi to "cease aggression" in South Vietnam. This presupposed that the Vietnamese were committing aggression against some other country, not fighting to defend themselves in their own land. He asked: "What are we supposed to make of this? I will tell you what we made of it: We called it an insult. It *was* an insult. From this fact alone, we could conclude—we *did* conclude—that this was not a serious proposal of anything realistic."[44] In agreement, Tran Quang Co drew the logical Vietnamese conclusion regarding McNamara's original thesis. "The question is: Were there 'missed opportunities' during this period to end the war via one or more of these contacts which were initiated by the U.S.? I think the answer is 'no,' " he concluded.[45]

However, McNamara minimized the differences between Hanoi's Four Points and Washington's Fourteen Points. Claiming that the two statements of peace conditions were "*not* irreconcilable," he summarized what "were" Hanoi's and Washington's "bottom lines" during the 1960s, as he understood them in the 1990s. This incredible version of history prompted Nguyen Khac Huynh to ask McNamara when he had gained his understanding of these "bottom lines." He asked him whether he had come to this: "Just recently or during the war? And within the U.S. leadership, while you were still within the leadership, had anyone considered these minimum objectives? As scholars, we are concerned with the real situation at the time—what people actually had in their minds at the time. Did you or others think of this then, in the middle 1960s, as we have been discussing?" McNamara's answer was one of the most telling revelations in *Argument Without End*. He replied: "I'll tell you the truth. I thought of them the night before last, on the basis of what I had heard in our discussions here at the conference." Yet, the fact that McNamara had just thought of them did not prevent him from presenting the "bottom lines" as if they "were" the peace conditions of Hanoi and Washington three decades earlier. In response to Nguyen Khac Huynh, however, McNamara conceded that "on Vietnam, we just never got our minds wrapped around the issues in the way that I presented them to you today, and that you say—and I thank you for telling me—is basically a correct view of what it would have taken to get our two sides together in—I'll say not later than 1965—and therefore prevent a lot of what happened later."[46]

This dialogue revealed the untrustworthiness of McNamara's fictionalized version of history, which presented the past as he thought it should have been rather than as it actually was. It discredited his central thesis about "missed opportunities," which depended on this fabrication. Nevertheless, McNamara repeated his thesis at the Hanoi conference and in *Argument Without End*. Apparently unembarrassed by what he was forced to admit about his fictionalized history, he reiterated during the discussions: "My belief is that there could have been negotiations between the end of '65 and '68 which would have led to a settlement that was roughly the same as the one that eventually occurred, but without that terrible loss of life."[47] He questioned why the Vietnamese leaders did not pursue peace negotiations with the United States in the 1960s, suggesting that they were indifferent to the suffering of their people. Apparently desperate to avoid his own responsibility for the war, McNamara tried to shift it to the Vietnamese. Tran Quang Co replied: "I must say that this question of Mr. McNamara's has allowed us to better understand the issue .... I believe we have learned still more about the U.S. We understand better now that the U.S. understands very little about Vietnam. Even now—in this conference—the U.S. understands very little about Vietnam."[48] Nguyen Khac Huyuh added that in 1965–1967 "the U.S. objective was twofold: to 'break the back of the Vietcong,' and to break the will of North Vietnam. We understood the Americans to be committed to a military victory .... This was war and each side was trying to win, according to its own definition of 'winning.' "[49]

This revealing dialogue, which, to his credit, McNamara included in *Argument Without End,* refuted his thesis about "missed opportunities." Nevertheless, he reiterated the thesis as if it expressed the mutual understanding of the Americans and the Vietnamese at the Hanoi conference. Unfortunately, the lessons of history that McNamara offered in this book were based on fabrication. His incredible version of history reflected the same regrettable qualities as his earlier statecraft.

President Johnson's recollection did not support McNamara's revisionist history. In his memoirs, *The Vantage Point* (1971), Johnson summarized the U.S. goals in the war:

> In the summer of 1965 I came to the painful conclusion that an independent South Vietnam could survive only if the United States and other nations went to its aid with their own fighting forces. From then until I left the Presidency, we had three principal goals: to insure that aggression did not succeed; to make it possible for the South Vietnamese to build their country and their future in their own way; and to convince Hanoi that working out a peaceful settlement was to the advantage of all concerned. Those three main strands of action—defeating aggression, building a nation, and searching for peace—were tightly braided together in all that we, the other allies, and the Vietnamese tried to accomplish over the next three and a half years.[50]

Johnson recalled that in November 1965 McNamara had advised him that, while the United States was not losing the war, it was not winning it either. To achieve U.S. goals in Vietnam, the secretary of defense thought that more U.S. troops and more aggressive bombing would be required. Johnson recounted:

> McNamara felt strongly that before we took either of these actions—sending more men and exerting more pressure on the North—we should try to find a way to peace, using a bombing halt to reinforce our diplomacy. He was persuaded that a bombing pause would give Ho Chi Minh a chance to move toward a solution if he wished to do so. If the pause failed to achieve that goal, McNamara argued, it would at least demonstrate our genuine desire for a peaceful settlement and thereby temper the criticism we were getting at home and abroad. He also thought that it would be easier for us to carry out necessary additional military measures in the future if we first made a serious peace move.[51]

In the context that Johnson described, McNamara had sent a memorandum to the president on November 7 to express his growing concerns. After visiting Vietnam, he submitted a second memorandum on November 30, 1965. In it, McNamara recalled, he had listed two alternatives. Either the United States might pursue "a compromise solution ... and hold further deployments to a minimum" or "stick with our stated objectives and with the war, and provide what it takes in men and material." He did not indicate his preference in the memorandum. In *Argument Without End,* he merely observed that "the first option—a compromise political solution—was not pursued."[52] Although by 1965 he was beginning to grasp that the United States might not win the war, McNamara did not advise Johnson to reconsider U.S. goals or even to shift from the broad to a narrow interpretation of them.

McNamara gave no indication, either in *Argument Without End* or in the source for the November 30 memorandum that he cited, of the kind of compromise he thought might have been necessary for a peace settlement. The source, a study prepared by William Conrad Gibbons for the Senate Foreign Relations Committee, did, however, provide more information about his attitude at the time. From Deborah Shapley's biography of McNamara, *Promise and Power* (1993), it quoted her conclusion that: "Robert McNamara looked into the abyss and saw three years of war leading only to stalemate, and he warned the President. He went through the motions of considering compromise but rejected this course. He saw his miscalculation but stuck with the war that winter; he was committed to it, politically, publicly, and emotionally. Giving up was not in his program or his temperament. And he believed the cause was just."[53] All he could bring himself to recommend under the circumstances was a temporary bombing halt for Christmas 1965, which provided the setting for Rusk's announcement of Washington's Fourteen Points. McNamara did not advise Johnson to reconsider U.S. goals despite his calculation that the chances of winning the war were no better than one in two or three. That he could find no way either to win or to end the war was his Vietnam tragedy.[54]

For two more years, McNamara played out this tragedy before quietly leaving the stage. Throughout that time, he failed to initiate a fundamental reconsideration of U.S. policy in Vietnam, only more temporary bombing halts. In retrospect, however, he claimed that both Hanoi and Washington had missed opportunities for ending the war sooner. In *Argument Without End,* he listed six peace initiatives that failed but that he now thought should have succeeded. One of them, in February 1967, had involved the British and Soviet prime ministers, Harold Wilson and Alexei Kosygin. McNamara's reconstruction of the U.S. position, which he shared with the Vietnamese during the Hanoi conference, followed the same lines as his interpretation of Washington's Fourteen Points. "What was our proposal?" he asked. "These were the major points: A cease-fire, troop withdrawals, elections, political participation by the NLF, reunification of North and South Vietnam. That sounds to me very close to your Four Points."[55]

Nguyen Co Thach, the Vietnamese foreign minister in the 1980s who had been deputy foreign minister in the 1960s, tried to explain the obstacle. He noted that the United States was still bombing North Vietnam at the time. McNamara protested: "But the cease-fire included what we took to be your central requirement—cessation of bombing in the North. I just don't understand why you weren't willing to discuss it, to pursue it, to see how far you could push us. What in the world did you have to lose?" Nguyen Co Thach replied: "We were willing to negotiate anything but our basic principles, contained in the Four Points." Only after the United States had changed its position on bombing in 1968 was Hanoi willing to enter negotiations. He explained that "in 1968, President Johnson agreed to abide by the Four Points and therefore cease the bombings of the North. Then we could begin to negotiate, and we did. But that is different than the Fourteen Points of [December 29, 1965] that you are talking about. Completely different."[56]

Nothing that the Vietnamese said during the Hanoi discussions in the 1990s convinced McNamara to change his original thesis. Without really comprehending how thoroughly Nguyen Co Thach and his colleagues had rejected it, McNamara reiterated: "The point I want to make is: *This is a missed opportunity!* In essence, the deal that was finally made six years later, after hundreds of thousands more people were killed—yours and ours—it was essentially the same deal."[57] Despite all the statements by the Vietnamese during the Hanoi conference to the contrary, McNamara concluded *Argument Without End* with a reaffirmation of his central thesis: "My general conclusion," he stated, "may strike some as obvious, but in light of the data in this chapter it cannot possibly be overemphasized: *There were a great many missed opportunities to move to a negotiated settlement of the Vietnam War between May 1965 and October 1967.* Now that we have the data to compare Washington's and Hanoi's views of each other's decisions and actions during the 1965–1967 period, the extent of missed opportunities is truly mind-boggling."[58]

What is truly mind-boggling was that McNamara, in the 1990s as in the 1960s, either would not or could not recognize the realities of the Vietnam War. He was consistently unwilling or unable to escape the preconceived judgments and erroneous assessments that had marred his statecraft in the 1960s and that discredited his revisionist history in the 1990s.

As secretary of defense, McNamara had entrapped himself in a crusade that, as he knew, was not likely to succeed. Yet, like President Wilson during the fight over the League of Nations after World War I, he would not compromise. He rigidly adhered to what he thought was "right." He expressed this mentality in a private conversation with President Johnson prior to his appearance in August 1967 before a Senate committee. McNamara recalled that "the president warned me about the heat I would face. 'I am not worried about the heat, as long as I know what we are doing is right,' I told him."[59] Robert J. Myers noted the larger significance of this statement: "So we have a situation in which the reasons for the intervention were faulty and the secretary of defense was fighting a crusade. The criterion was not strategy and success but 'right.' McNamara's statement accepts the validity of two dubious principles of Kantian philosophy: that reason is superior to experience and that principle is superior to consequences. One can elaborate at length on the dimensions of this folly."[60] While serving as secretary of defense, McNamara had not reassessed the experience in Vietnam or recognized the consequences of the war in such a way as to devise a realistic alternative. He failed to reconcile the ends and means of U.S. policy in Vietnam.

Not surprisingly, McNamara fled from his political and moral failure. In 1968, he left the Department of Defense to head the World Bank. Later, he sought a different form of evasion by returning to the Vietnam tragedy as author of *In Retrospect* (1995) and then of *Argument Without End*. He was still seeking an escape and believed he had finally found it. From the Vietnam War, he claimed to have derived lessons of history that would enable the twenty-first century to live in peace, thereby finally achieving the Wilsonian promise. There were "missed opportunities" for peace during the 1960s, he argued. Although this central thesis required McNamara to construct a fictionalized history to support it, he derived lessons from this experience for the future. What Hans Morgenthau stated with reference to McGeorge Bundy in the 1960s applied as well to McNamara both then and later: "Things are naturally more complicated for men who bear the responsibility for this misadventure [in Vietnam] and the evils, domestic and international, attendant to it. They cannot be expected to liquidate the war, nor is their counsel, so false in the past, worth listening to now."[61]

Accordingly, scholars should not rely on McNamara's revisionist history of the Vietnam War to understand the past. Nor should U.S. policymakers expect *Wilson's Ghost* to provide reliable guidelines for the future. In this book, McNamara and Blight prescribed "realistic empathy" as the antidote to global catastrophe. Understanding the enemy, they argued, would enable the United States to achieve its goals for a peaceful world in the twenty-first century without violating the Wilsonian moral and multilateral imperatives.[62] McNamara had shown no "realistic empathy" toward the Vietnamese during the 1960s. He still did not even in the 1990s, as he unwittingly revealed in *Argument Without End*. He now acknowledged, although without explicitly referring to himself, that: "President Johnson and his senior advisers had almost no realistic empathy during the escalation in Vietnam, especially between 1965 and 1968, when the war became an American war."[63] Despite that failure, McNamara still defended the morality of U.S. involvement in Vietnam, and, thus, his role in it. In his view, he and his colleagues perhaps neglected the Wilsonian multilateral imperative, but their goals were consistent with the Wilsonian moral imperative.

Rejecting Reinhold Niebuhr's earlier criticism of the immorality of U.S. statecraft in Vietnam, McNamara reasserted:

> We thought we were acting in the interests of mankind, but the cost in lives lost was far greater than we or others had predicted. What should we have done differently? I believe we should have elevated to the same level as other objectives our intention to keep human carnage to a minimum. Had we done so, we would have explored more fully other ways to achieve our goals. If we had, I now believe—and the available evidence strongly suggests—that we could have ended the war as early as 1962, and not later than 1967, without any significant loss in our strategic position worldwide. In that case, we might have "saved our soul," as Norman Thomas said, and protected our interests as well.[64]

Trying to save his soul without confessing his own moral responsibility for the Vietnam tragedy, McNamara missed Charles Dickens's essential point in *A Christmas Carol.* If Ebenezer Scrooge had empathized with Bob Cratchit and his family, but did not help them—if Scrooge had reaffirmed his good intentions, but still pursued his own selfish ambitions for dominance and wealth—if Scrooge had expressed only "realistic empathy," but relentlessly adhered to his goal of maximizing his profits at any cost to others—Dickens's tale would surely not have become a revered literary classic. Some of McNamara's ideas about both the past and the future are worthy of consideration, but they should be subjected to careful analysis and accepted only with great caution. Instead of relying on the fantastic history and unrealistic advice of McNamara or anyone else still haunted by "Wilson's ghost," it would be better to heed the wisdom of Dickens and listen to the ghost of Jacob Marley.

CHAPTER 13

POST–COLD WAR WILSONIANISM:
AMERICA'S MISSION?

Lloyd E. Ambrosius, "America's Mission?," in *Deutschland und der Westen: Internationale Beziehungen im 20. Jahrhundert,* ed. Guido Müller (Stuttgart: Franz Steiner Verlag, 1998), 85–91. Reprinted by permission of Franz Steiner Verlag Wiesbaden GmbH, Stuttgart.

In the post–Cold War era, U.S. policymakers and commentators on the role of the United States in world affairs focused once more on President Woodrow Wilson's legacy. Whether affirming or deploring his diplomatic leadership, they generally agreed that Wilsonian statecraft still offered compelling lessons for the United States at the end of the twentieth century. Wilson defined America's mission during World War I in such a way that his legacy continued to shape the debate over U.S. foreign policy.

In this ongoing debate over the history and future of American foreign relations, Klaus Schwabe's most important book, *Deutsche Revolution und Wilson-Frieden* (1971), translated as *Woodrow Wilson, Revolutionary Germany, and Peacemaking, 1918–1919* (1985),[1] remained a significant source for anyone who wanted to understand the global involvement of the United States. Just as President Wilson sought to reconcile his missionary diplomacy with the realities of power, so, too, did U.S. policymakers and commentators seek the appropriate balance for the United States between ideology and power politics in the post–Cold War world. In this renewed search for America's mission, few looked back to Wilson with Schwabe's scholarly sophistication.

The political scientist Tony Smith embraced the Wilsonian legacy for U.S. foreign policy in the post–Cold War world. In *America's Mission* (1994), he advocated "Wilsonianism," which he defined as "the conviction that American national interests could best be pursued by promoting democracy worldwide."[2] He affirmed, moreover, that the United States had wisely pursued this Wilsonian mission throughout the twentieth century. This nation had promoted "a world order of democratic states" that respected each other's right of national self-determination and a liberal international economic order. "Since Wilson's time," Smith claimed, "the most consistent tradition in American foreign policy with respect to this global change has been the belief that the nation's security is best protected by the expansion of democracy worldwide."[3]

Smith emphasized America's vital contribution to the global success of democracy. He thought that "it is difficult to escape the conclusion that since World War I, the fortunes of democracy worldwide have largely depended on American power."[4]

Through its intervention, not just its example, the United States had provided essential leadership in the global struggle for democracy. Smith argued that "liberal democratic internationalism, or Wilsonianism, has been the most important contribution of the United States to the international history of the twentieth century." This American contribution, he affirmed, had shaped the pattern of contemporary history and thus strengthened democratic government worldwide, notably by the end of the Cold War.[5]

Even Wilson's critics recognized his powerful legacy throughout the twentieth century. Henry Kissinger, President Richard Nixon's national security adviser and secretary of state, acknowledged in *Diplomacy* (1994) that the Wilsonian mission had continued to dominate American ideology and shape U.S. foreign policy: "The idea that peace depends above all on promoting democratic institutions has remained a staple of American thought to the present day."[6] Kissinger lamented that: "For three generations, critics have savaged Wilson's analysis and conclusions; and yet, in all this time, Wilson's principles have remained the bedrock of American foreign-policy thinking."[7] Kissinger added that "whenever America has faced the task of constructing a new world order, it has returned in one way or another to Woodrow Wilson's precepts."[8] That the United States would do so again after the Cold War was therefore not at all unique.

In the post–Cold War world, Kissinger emphasized that the United States must accept its continuing involvement abroad and also adjust to the limits of its power: "What *is* new about the emerging world order is that, for the first time, the United States can neither withdraw from the world nor dominate it."[9] Maybe Kissinger only recently recognized this dual reality, but it had shaped the history of U.S. foreign relations throughout the twentieth century, as Schwabe understood and I stressed in *Woodrow Wilson and the American Diplomatic Tradition* (1987).[10]

A self-proclaimed realist, Kissinger criticized his fellow Americans for their contradictory attitudes. Rather than pursuing a consistent approach to foreign affairs, they had shifted back and forth between "America as beacon" and "America as crusader." Not knowing whether the United States should passively serve as a model for the world or actively intervene overseas to impose its values and institutions, Americans had alternated between isolationism and internationalism. These were "two contradictory attitudes toward foreign policy," Kissinger noted. Under the first, "America serves its values best by perfecting democracy at home," but under the second, "America's values impose on it an obligation to crusade for them around the world."[11] He identified the first attitude with American isolationism and the second with Wilsonian internationalism.

In Kissinger's judgment, President Theodore Roosevelt had offered a more realistic approach than Wilson did to American involvement in the twentieth-century world. Praising him for embracing Old World diplomacy, Kissinger affirmed that: "With Roosevelt holding such European-style views, it was not surprising that he approached the global balance of power with a sophistication matched by no other American president and approached only by Richard Nixon."[12] Other presidents, certainly Wilson among them, were less adept at avoiding the extremes of either irresponsible withdrawal from or crusading involvement in world affairs.

In *America's Mission*, Tony Smith criticized the international relations theory of "realism"—including Kissinger's version—for concentrating on the power of states as rational actors in world affairs and focusing too narrowly on strategic and diplomatic issues. He emphasized the linkage between democracy within states and international security, given that the internal values and institutions of states profoundly shape their external behavior. Democratic governments, he believed, were more peaceful in international relations than nondemocratic ones. A realistic U.S. foreign policy, Smith therefore concluded, should promote democracy as the best way to achieve peace. He thus incorporated Wilsonian idealism into his view of America's mission.[13]

According to Smith, Wilsonian idealism provided ideological means for achieving realistic goals. He endorsed "the Wilsonian view that the promotion of democracy worldwide advances the national security of the United States ... and hence satisfies realist demands that the country think of its interests defined in terms of the international organization of power." Smith sought to reconcile the "realist and Wilsonian agendas for foreign policy" and thus to demonstrate that "the two agendas are compatible."[14] Smith offered this historical synthesis as his lesson for U.S. policymakers in the post–Cold War world.

Kissinger and Smith articulated apparently contrasting views, but they actually shared a great deal in common. Although the one condemned and the other extolled Wilson's legacy in U.S. foreign relations, they were ideologically closer than either of them would likely admit. Despite obvious differences, Kissinger's and Smith's ideas about the nature of democracy restricted their understanding of significant international developments, which appeared only on the periphery of their vision, if at all. Their common ideology prevented both Kissinger and Smith from comprehending important aspects of the twentieth-century world. This ideological affinity concerning the exclusive nature of democracy—like Wilson's conception of the liberal democratic state a century earlier—enabled both of them to applaud President Ronald Reagan's worldwide crusade for democracy. Understanding this remarkable consensus is the key to analyzing the intellectual confusion in Kissinger's and Smith's books and, even more important, in the current debate over Wilson's legacy in U.S. foreign policy during the post–Cold War world.

Among recent presidents, Smith thought that Ronald Reagan best exemplified the advantages of Wilsonianism in his crusading, yet realistic leadership in foreign affairs. "Seen from the century-old perspective of American efforts to promote democracy abroad," he asserted, "no administration since the presidency of Woodrow Wilson [1913–1921] has been so committed to the tenets of liberal democratic internationalism as that of Ronald Reagan." Smith noted that Reagan nominally rejected "liberalism" but was nevertheless a good Wilsonian. "When a president makes American leadership of a world community of democratic nations following free-market practices the core features of his foreign policy, then whatever he calls himself, he most certainly is a Wilsonian."[15]

Smith applauded Reagan's pursuit of democracy in Africa, Asia, and Latin America in the name of the Reagan Doctrine. He thought that even the president's support for undemocratic, anti-Communist "freedom fighters" promoted the Wilsonian mission of national self-determination. "In short, freedom fighters who were not democrats could still be nationalists, and the United States would support their quest for national self-determination, an appeal that had mattered greatly to liberals of Wilson's era."[16] In Smith's view, Reagan's "democratic revolution" thus fulfilled America's Wilsonian mission.

Kissinger's affirmation of Reagan's crusading foreign policy was, at first glance, at variance with his style of power politics, which placed reasons of state above morality. Moreover, as Nixon's national security adviser and secretary of state, and later as President Gerald Ford's secretary of state, Kissinger had suffered severe criticism from neoconservatives, including Reagan himself. Yet, Kissinger and all these Republican presidents shared the common ideology of anti-Communism that had characterized American attitudes during the entire history of the Cold War. They also agreed in blaming American liberals, mostly Democrats, for whatever went wrong at home and abroad in the 1960s and subsequent decades. Yet, Kissinger's own ideology embraced more tenets of Wilsonianism than he acknowledged. This became more apparent in his affirmation of Reagan's anti-Communist crusade for democracy with arguments that were remarkably similar to Smith's.

Even earlier, as national security adviser and secretary of state, Kissinger had pursued the Wilsonian mission in world affairs, despite his subsequent denunciation of Wilsonianism. His problems with the Vietnam War revealed this paradoxical pattern. Although he later blamed the war in Southeast Asia on liberals in the 1960s, he himself had supported U.S. military intervention in Vietnam at the time. He collaborated with the secretary of defense Robert S. McNamara as a consultant. Later, he interpreted this war as the tragic consequence of Wilson's legacy of idealism in U.S. foreign policy. He argued in *Diplomacy* that the United States had entered "the morass" of Vietnam because it had followed "a Wilsonian approach to foreign policy" rather than "a geopolitical approach geared to analysis of national interest." He explained that "the Wilsonian approach to foreign policy permitted no distinction to be made among the monsters to be slain. Universalist in its approach to world order, Wilsonianism did not lend itself to an analysis of the relative importance of various countries. America was obliged to fight for what was right, regardless of local circumstances, and independent of geopolitics."[17] By this account, the failure of Americans to recognize fundamental differences between Europe and Asia had resulted in their unrealistic pursuit of democracy as well as security in Vietnam.

In retrospect, Kissinger claimed that the domino theory, which expressed a universalist Wilsonian ideology, had trapped the United States in a war it could not win. The fundamental contradiction between its political and strategic goals doomed the United States to eventual failure: "The central dilemma became that America's political goal of introducing a stable democracy in South Vietnam could not be attained in time to head off a guerilla victory, which was America's strategic goal. America would have to modify either its military or its political objectives."[18] Failing to do either, the United States eventually lost the war.

In Kissinger's revisionist history, President John F. Kennedy had applied "Wilsonian assumptions" in Vietnam by seeking victory for democracy over Communism. "Ultimately," Kissinger argued, "the issue was not democracy so much as power."[19] American leaders had overlooked this geopolitical reality, which later seemed so clear to Kissinger. But they were not prepared to make such a realistic assessment of Vietnam in the 1960s. "In the post-World War II period, America had been fortunate to have never had to choose between its moral convictions and its strategic analysis," Kissinger explained. "All of its key decisions had been readily justified as both promoting democracy and resisting aggression."[20]

Ironically, Kissinger himself evidenced the same ideological confusion that he denounced as Wilsonianism in others. His own contradictory attitudes toward Vietnam reappeared in *Diplomacy*. He noted that, by the end of Lyndon Johnson's presidency: "The real choice before America was not between victory and compromise, but between victory and defeat."[21] Yet, as Nixon's national security adviser, Kissinger had not acted on the basis of this assessment. He did not confront the "real choice" that he recounted in his book, but sought instead "a negotiated compromise." Both at the time and in retrospect, Kissinger engaged in wishful thinking that the United States could pursue the "Vietnamization" of the war—a policy that would obviously abandon any future prospect of U.S. military victory—and yet somehow escape eventual defeat.[22] This approach to U.S. policy in Vietnam, a strange mixture of utopian thinking and of amoral, if not immoral, behavior, did not conform to the standards of classical realism that Kissinger proclaimed.

Moreover, both Nixon and Kissinger had espoused the domino theory that had shaped the Cold War ideology of U.S. policymakers and culminated in Vietnam. The historian Frank Ninkovich traced the internal logic of the domino theory from Woodrow Wilson to Nixon and Kissinger, all of whom embraced the American ideology of modernity. Emphasizing the importance of "credibility" in the modern world, in which public opinion defined power in international relations, both Nixon and Kissinger operated within the American tradition of Wilsonianism. The Nixon Doctrine, as Ninkovich observed, "amounted to only a minor emendation of the still regnant Wilsonian outlook. On balance, Nixonian realism was hardly a repudiation of cold-war strategy or neo-Wilsonian assumptions in favor of classical realpolitik."[23]

Far less than Kissinger acknowledged, for he was unwilling or unable to recognize that he, too, espoused an American ideology, his so-called realism actually shared much in common with Wilsonianism. Kissinger as well as Nixon retained key tenets of the Wilsonian worldview. Their idea of "linkage" as well as their emphasis on "credibility" betrayed an underlying universalism that had characterized Wilson's thinking during World War I and shaped American global anti-Communism during the Cold War. Their vision of a new "structure of peace" was not all that different from earlier or later ideals of a "new world order." Moreover, as I noted in *Woodrow Wilson and the American Diplomatic Tradition,* "they combined an ideological rigidity with practical flexibility. The so-called realism of Nixon and Kissinger was actually closer to the cynicism which the theologian Reinhold Niebuhr had recognized as the reverse side of idealism."[24] In other words, Wilsonianism also influenced their thinking about U.S. foreign policy.

Both Nixon and Kissinger acknowledged Nixon's ideological connection with Wilsonianism. Nixon looked back to Wilson rather than Theodore Roosevelt as his hero. "Wilson had the greatest vision of America's world role. But he wasn't practical enough," Nixon told Garry Wills.[25] Kissinger conceded that "Nixon often invoked standard Wilsonian rhetoric" in his pursuit of American national interests. He combined Wilsonian idealism and classical realism into "a novel synthesis of the American experience." Thus, Kissinger observed, "in Nixon's mind, Wilsonianism and *Realpolitik* would merge."[26]

At other times, however, Kissinger emphasized the contrast between Wilsonianism and Nixon's (or Kissinger's) approach to U.S. foreign relations. "Nixon did not accept the Wilsonian verities about the essential goodness of man or the underlying harmony among nations to be maintained by collective security," he explained in *Diplomacy*. "Wilson had perceived a world progressing inexorably toward peace and democracy; America's mission in it was to help the inevitable along."[27] According to Kissinger, Nixon's pessimistic view of human nature and international relations distinguished his (and Kissinger's) statecraft from Wilsonianism. "Because American thinking on foreign policy had been shaped by liberal ideas ever since Woodrow Wilson," Kissinger lamented, "there was no ready constituency for Nixon's style of diplomacy."[28] In other words, Wilson's legacy accounted for the resistance in the United States to Nixon's realism. From this perspective, too, Kissinger blamed Wilson's putative successors, the liberals, not only for the 1960s but also for the loss of Vietnam and other failures of statecraft during the Nixon-Kissinger era.

Yet, Kissinger himself embraced more of Wilson's legacy than he generally admitted. Reagan's global crusade for democracy against Communism won Kissinger's approval during the 1980s, which was not so surprising in view of his own anti-Communist ideology. Kissinger accused the Democrats of "making the world safe for anti-American radicals." As leader of Reagan's bipartisan commission on Central America, he participated directly in the president's crusade by insisting on viewing the Sandinista revolution in Nicaragua within the framework of the global East–West struggle.[29]

Kissinger recognized and even approved the Wilsonian mission in Reagan's foreign policy. In *Diplomacy*, he acknowledged: "Like Woodrow Wilson, Reagan understood that the American people, having marched throughout their history to the drumbeat of exceptionalism, would find their ultimate inspiration in historic ideals, not in geopolitical analysis .... Like Roosevelt, Nixon had had a far better understanding of the workings of international relations; like Wilson, Reagan had a much surer grasp of the workings of the American soul."[30] Wilson's legacy thus provided the ideological orientation for Reagan's global crusade for democracy. "In fact," Kissinger noted, "Reagan took Wilsonianism to its ultimate conclusion. America would not wait passively for free institutions to evolve, nor would it confine itself to resisting direct threats to its security. Instead, it would actively promote democracy, rewarding those countries which fulfilled its ideals and punishing those which fell short—even if they presented no other visible challenge or threat to America."[31]

One might have expected Kissinger, given his avowed anti-Wilsonianism, to have criticized Reagan's foreign policy. Instead, he praised the Reagan Doctrine and the worldwide anti-Communist crusade that it justified in such places as Afghanistan, Angola, and Nicaragua. Kissinger's rationale for this Wilsonian mission during Reagan's presidency coincided with Tony Smith's: "The high-flying Wilsonian language in support of freedom and democracy globally was leavened by an almost Machiavellian realism."[32] Thus, Kissinger, like Smith, combined Wilsonian idealism with classical realism in praising Reagan's foreign policy. Applauding this version of America's mission and its consequent worldwide success, Kissinger exulted: "By the 1990s, free peoples everywhere were again looking to America for guidance in constructing yet another new world order."[33]

Thus, both Kissinger and Smith—like both Wilson and Reagan during their presidencies—defined America's mission in the post–Cold War world in similar terms. This remarkable consensus among such different U.S. policymakers and commentators expressed their common ideology, and also their exclusive definitions of democracy. When Smith lauded America's historic struggle for democracy world-wide, including Wilson's and Reagan's roles, he noted the priority on the political rather than the socioeconomic dimensions of democracy. Thus, peoples in other countries outside the acceptable mainstream of "liberal democratic internationalism" were relegated to the margins. Kissinger showed even less interest than Smith in either the political or the socioeconomic dimensions of democracy in any country, including the United States, and even more Eurocentrism. Other peoples appeared on the periphery of his vision—or in the pages of *Diplomacy*—as the subjects of European, and subsequently American, foreign relations, but rarely as active partici-pants in their own right. Smith and Kissinger, no less than Wilson and Reagan, embraced the exclusive nature of American democracy that historian Robert H. Wiebe analyzed so perceptively in *Self-Rule*.[34]

Much of the ongoing debate over America's mission in the post–Cold War world, including Kissinger's and Smith's noteworthy books, remained within the ideologi-cal limits of Wilsonianism. Reagan's global crusade for democracy, epitomizing Wilson's legacy in U.S. foreign relations, had promised a bright future that seemed to emerge in the "new world order" of the post–Cold War era. What was often lack-ing in the debate over U.S. foreign policy after the Cold War—and certainly in Kissinger's and Smith's contributions to it—was a sophisticated understanding of Woodrow Wilson's statecraft and a recognition of the exclusive nature of democracy in traditional American ideology. The limited debate over which tenets of Wilsonianism to emphasize in a particular case neglected the larger questions about the adequacy of the Wilsonian tradition of liberal internationalism as the cultural foundation for U.S. foreign policy. U.S. policymakers and commentators needed to ask, as did the British political scientist Michael Cox, whether the United States was a "superpower without a mission?"[35] Adjustment to the real post–Cold War world required a more fundamental reassessment of America's mission, as defined by Wilson's legacy in U.S. foreign relations, than most Americans, including Kissinger and Smith, had yet imagined. In this ongoing debate, sophisticated scholarship on Woodrow Wilson, such as that by Klaus Schwabe, was still highly relevant.

Notes

Introduction

1. Lloyd E. Ambrosius, *Woodrow Wilson and the American Diplomatic Tradition: The Treaty Fight in Perspective* (Cambridge: Cambridge University Press, 1987).
2. Lloyd E. Ambrosius, *Wilsonian Statecraft: Theory and Practice of Liberal Internationalism during World War I* (Wilmington, DE: Scholarly Resources, 1991).
3. For a variety of articles on this subject, see "The American Century: A Roundtable (Part I)," *Diplomatic History* 23 (Spring 1999): 157–370, and "The American Century: A Roundtable (Part II)," ibid. (Summer 1999): 391–537.
4. Robert O. Keohane, ed., *Neorealism and Its Critics* (New York: Columbia University Press, 1986); Michael W. Doyle, *Ways of War and Peace: Realism, Liberalism, and Socialism* (New York: W. W. Norton, 1997).
5. David Steigerwald, "Reclamation of Woodrow Wilson," *Diplomatic History* 23 (Winter 1999): 79–99. See also Steven J. Bucklin, *Realism and American Foreign Policy: Wilsonians and the Kennan-Morgenthau Thesis* (Westport, CT: Praeger Publishers, 2001).
6. Ronald Steel, *Pax Americana* (New York: Viking Press, 1967), *Walter Lippmann and the American Century* (Boston: Little, Brown, 1980), and *Temptations of a Superpower* (Cambridge, MA: Harvard University Press, 1995).
7. Jack Donnelly, *Realism and International Relations* (Cambridge: Cambridge University Press, 2000), 6–11.
8. Keohane, *Neorealism,* 7, 160; Robert O. Keohane and Joseph S. Nye, *Power and Interdependence,* Second Edition (Glenview, IL: Scott, Foresman, 1989), 23–37.
9. Donnelly, *Realism,* 5.
10. Scholars have examined the combination of ideals and self-interest—or liberalism and realism—in the ideology and practice of U.S. foreign relations. See, for example, Robert Endicott Osgood, *Ideals and Self-Interest in America's Foreign Relations: The Great Transformation of the Twentieth Century* (Chicago: University of Chicago Press, 1953) and John Mearsheimer, *The Tragedy of Great Power Politics* (New York: W. W. Norton and Company, 2001).
11. John Ehrman, *Neoconservatism: Intellectuals and Foreign Affairs, 1945–1994* (New Haven, CT: Yale University Press, 1995).
12. Isaiah Bowman, *The New World: Problems in Political Geography* (Yonkers-on-Hudson, NY: World Book Company, 1921), 1.
13. Bowman, *New World,* 2–3.
14. Bowman, *New World,* 3.
15. Benjamin R. Barber, *Jihad vs. McWorld* (New York: Times Books, 1995), 5.
16. Barber, *Jihad vs. McWorld,* 6–7.
17. Francis Fukuyama, *The End of History and the Last Man* (New York: Free Press, 1992).
18. Samuel P. Huntington, *The Clash of Civilizations and the Remaking of World Order* (New York: Touchstone Book, 1996), 125.

19. Thomas L. Friedman, *The Lexus and the Olive Tree* (New York: Anchor Books, 2000), 31. For an excellent analysis of the theme of globalization and references to the extensive literature on the subject, see Thomas W. Zeiler, "Just Do It! Globalization for Diplomatic Historians," *Diplomatic History* 25 (Fall 2001): 529–51.
20. David Reynolds, *One World Divisible: A Global History Since 1945* (New York: W. W. Norton, 2000), 2.
21. Reynolds, *One World Divisible,* 3–6.
22. Ambrosius, *Woodrow Wilson,* xii–xiii, passim.
23. Robert Wohl, *The Generation of 1914* (Cambridge, MA: Harvard University Press, 1979); Paul Fussell, *The Great War and Modern Memory* (New York: Oxford University Press, 1975; Jay Winter, Geoffrey Parker, and Mary R. Habeck, *The Great War and the Twentieth Century* (New Haven, CT: Yale University Press, 2000).
24. Henry F. May, *The End of American Innocence: A Study of the First Years of Our Time, 1912–1917* (New York: Alfred A. Knopf, 1959); Meirion and Susie Harries, *The Last Days of Innocence: America at War, 1917–1918* (New York: Random House, 1997).
25. Ellen Glasgow, *A Certain Measure* (New York, 1938), 118, quoted in May, *End of American Innocence,* 85.
26. May, *End of American Innocence,* 355.
27. Randolph S. Bourne, *War and the Intellectuals: Essays by Randolph S. Bourne, 1915–1919,* ed. Carl Resek (New York: Harper and Row, 1964); Ambrosius, *Woodrow Wilson,* 6, 33, 297; Leslie J. Vaughan, *Randolph Bourne and the Politics of Cultural Radicalism* (Lawrence: University Press of Kansas, 1997).
28. Rogers M. Smith, *Civic Ideals: Conflicting Visions of Citizenship in U.S. History* (New Haven, CT: Yale University Press, 1997), 469.
29. Robert H. Wiebe, *Self-Rule: A Cultural History of American Democracy* (Chicago: University of Chicago Press, 1995), 180. See also Nell Irvin Painter, *Standing at Armageddon: The United States, 1877–1919* (New York: W. W. Norton, 1987) and Kevin Phillips, *The Cousins' Wars: Religion, Politics, and the Triumph of Anglo-America* (New York: Basic Books, 1999).
30. For a good example of deriving lessons from Wilson's legacy for current U.S. policymaking, see John Gerard Ruggie, *Winning the Peace: America and World Order in the New Era* (New York: Columbia University Press, 1995).
31. Steigerwald, "Reclamation of Woodrow Wilson," 79–99.
32. Ruggie, *Winning the Peace,* 2. See also Doyle, *Ways of War and Peace,* 205.
33. Henry Kissinger, *Diplomacy* (New York: Simon and Schuster, 1994), 52.
34. Kissinger, *Diplomacy,* 54. See also Henry Kissinger, *Does America Need a Foreign Policy? Toward a Diplomacy for the 21st Century* (New York: Simon and Schuster, 2001), 272–8.
35. Tony Smith, *America's Mission: The United States and the Worldwide Struggle for Democracy in the Twentieth Century* (Princeton, NJ: Princeton University Press, 1994), 9.
36. Smith, *America's Mission,* 6.
37. Amos Perlmutter, *Making the World Safe for Democracy: A Century of Wilsonianism and Its Totalitarian Challengers* (Chapel Hill: University of North Carolina Press, 1997), 134.
38. Perlmutter, *Making the World,* 44.
39. Perlmutter, *Making the World,* 165.
40. Perlmutter, *Making the World,* 166.
41. Frank Ninkovich, *The Wilsonian Century: U.S. Foreign Policy since 1900* (Chicago: University of Chicago Press, 1999), 5–6.
42. Akira Iriye, *The Cambridge History of American Foreign Relations,* vol. 3: *The Globalizing of America, 1913–1945* (Cambridge: Cambridge University Press, 1993), 45, 71–2.
43. "Address Before a Joint Session of the Congress on the Persian Gulf Crisis and the Federal Budget Deficit," September 11, 1990, George Bush, *Public Papers of the Presidents: 1990* (Washington, DC: Government Printing Office, 1991), 2: 1218–22.
44. "Address to the Nation Announcing Allied Military Action in the Persian Gulf," January 16, 1991, George Bush, *Public Papers of the Presidents: 1991* (Washington, DC: Government Printing Office, 1992), 1: 42–4.

45. "Remarks at the Annual Convention of the National Religious Broadcasters," January 28, 1991, Bush, *Public Papers,* 1: 70–2.
46. "Address to the Nation on the Suspension of Allied Offensive Combat Operations in the Persian Gulf," February 27, 1991, Bush, *Public Papers,* 1: 187–8.
47. "Address to the Nation on Airstrikes Against Serbian Targets in the Federal Republic of Yugoslavia (Serbia and Montenegro)," March 24, 1999, William J. Clinton, *Public Papers of the Presidents: 1999* (Washington, DC: Government Printing Office, 2000), 1: 451–2.
48. "Remarks at a North Atlantic Treaty Organization Commemorative Ceremony," April 23, 1999, Clinton, *Public Papers,* 1: 606–7.
49. "Joint Statement on Kosovo," April 23, 1999, Clinton, *Public Papers,* 1: 607–9.
50. "Address to the Nation on the Military Technical Agreement on Kosovo," June 10, 1999, Clinton, *Public Papers,* 1: 912–16.
51. David Halberstam, *War in a Time of Peace: Bush, Clinton, and the Generals* (New York: Scribner, 2001), 484.
52. Halberstam, *War in a Time of Peace,* 490.
53. "Commencement Address at the University of Chicago in Chicago, Illinois," June 12, 1999, Clinton, *Public Papers,* 1: 931–5.
54. "Remarks at a World Trade Organization Luncheon in Seattle," December 1, 1999, Clinton, *Public Papers,* 2: 2189–94.
55. "Remarks to the 54th Session of the United Nations General Assembly in New York City," September 21, 1999, Clinton, *Public Papers,* 2: 1563–7. See also Stephen D. Krasner, *Sovereignty: Organized Hypocrisy* (Princeton, NJ: Princeton University Press, 1999).
56. "President George W. Bush's Inaugural Address," January 20, 2001, <http://www.whitehouse.gov/news/print/inaugural-address.html>.
57. "Address to a Joint Session of Congress and the American People," September 20, 2001, <http://www.whitehouse.gov/news/releases/2001/09/print/20010920-8.html>.
58. "Presidential Address to the Nation," October 7, 2001, <http://www.whitehouse.gov/news/releases/2001/10/print/2001/20011007-8.html>.
59. "President Holds Prime Time News Conference," October 11, 2001, <http://white-house.gov/news/releases/2001/10/print/20011011-7.html>.
60. Hans J. Morgenthau, *Scientific Man vs. Power Politics* (Chicago: University of Chicago Press, 1946), 36.
61. Morgenthau, *Scientific Man,* 52.
62. Morgenthau, *Scientific Man,* 63.
63. "President Holds Prime Time News Conference," October 11, 2001.
64. For a comparable self-revelation of Wilson's inability to comprehend critical foreign views of the United States, see "Remarks to Mexican Editors," [June 7, 1918], *The Papers of Woodrow Wilson,* ed. Arthur S. Link (Princeton, NJ: Princeton University Press, 1985), 48: 255–9.
65. "President Bush Speaks to United Nations," November 10, 2001, <http://www.whitehouse.gov/releases/2001/11/print/20011110-3.html>.
66. Michael Hirsh, "America Adrift: Writing History of the Post Cold Wars," *Foreign Affairs* 80 (November/December 2001): 158–64. See also Fouad Ajami, "The Sentry's Solitude," ibid., 2–16, and Karen Armstrong, *Islam: A Short History* (New York: Modern Library, 2000), 141–87.
67. Sir Michael Howard, "Mistake to Declare this a 'War,'" Associated Newspapers Ltd., October 31, 2001. See also Michael Howard, "What's in a Name? How to Fight Terrorism," *Foreign Affairs* 81 (January/February 2002): 8–13.
68. For an excellent analysis of this problem, see G. John Ikenberry, *After Victory: Institutions, Strategic Restraint, and the Rebuilding of Order after Major Wars* (Princeton, NJ: Princeton University Press, 2001).
69. For a brief sketch of the president's life, see Lloyd E. Ambrosius, "Woodrow Wilson," *American National Biography,* ed. John A. Garraty and Mark C. Carnes, 24 vols. (New York: Oxford University Press, 1999), 23: 604–12.

Chapter 1   Woodrow Wilson and the Culture of Wilsonianism

1. Henry R. Luce, "The American Century," *Life* (Feb. 17, 1941): 61–5, reprinted in *Diplomatic History* 23 (Spring 1999): 159–71. See also Donald W. White, *The American Century: The Rise and Decline of the United States as a World Power* (New Haven, CT: Yale University Press, 1996).

2. Recent books that focus on Wilson's legacy or Wilsonianism include Frank Ninkovich, *Modernity and Power: A History of the Domino Theory in the Twentieth Century* (Chicago: University of Chicago Press, 1994), Tony Smith, *America's Mission: The United States and the Worldwide Struggle for Democracy in the Twentieth Century* (Princeton, NJ: Princeton University Press, 1994), Derek Heater, *National Self-Determination* (New York: St. Martin's Press, 1994), Henry Kissinger, *Diplomacy* (New York: Simon and Schuster, 1994), David Steigerwald, *Wilsonian Idealism in America* (Ithaca, NY: Cornell University Press, 1994), Walter A. McDougall, *Promised Land, Crusader State: The American Encounter with the World Since 1776* (Boston: Houghton Mifflin, 1997), Amos Perlmutter, *Making the World Safe for Democracy: A Century of Wilsonianism and Its Totalitarian Challengers* (Chapel Hill: University of North Carolina Press, 1997), and Frank Ninkovich, *The Wilsonian Century: U.S. Foreign Policy since 1900* (Chicago: University of Chicago Press, 1999).

3. Ray Stannard Baker and William E. Dodd, eds., *The Public Papers of Woodrow Wilson*, 6 vols. (New York: Harper and Brothers, 1925–7), 5: 8, 14.

4. Baker and Dodd, *Public Papers*, 5: 162.

5. Excellent studies of Wilson's political thought include Niels Aage Thorsen, *The Political Thought of Woodrow Wilson, 1875–1910* (Princeton, NJ: Princeton University Press, 1988), and Daniel D. Stid, *The President as Statesman: Woodrow Wilson and the Constitution* (Lawrence: University Press of Kansas, 1998).

6. Excellent introductions to the rich scholarship on nationalism include John Hutchinson and Anthony D. Smith, eds., *Nationalism* (Oxford: Oxford University Press, 1994), and Geoff Eley and Ronald Grigor, eds., *Becoming National: A Reader* (New York: Oxford University Press, 1996).

7. Woodrow Wilson, *Mere Literature and Other Essays* (Boston: Houghton, Mifflin, 1896), 199–200.

8. Some who erroneously identified Wilson's principle of national self-determination with ethnonationalism include Heater, *National Self-Determination;* Kissinger, *Diplomacy;* Daniel Patrick Moynihan, *Pandaemonium: Ethnicity in International Politics* (New York: Oxford University Press, 1993), and Walker Connor, *Ethnonationalism: The Quest for Understanding* (Princeton, NJ: Princeton University Press, 1994).

9. Baker and Dodd, *Public Papers*, 5: 155–62.

10. Woodrow Wilson, *A History of the American People*, 10 vols. (New York: Harper and Brothers, 1918). For an excellent inquiry into the relationship between history and ideology, including historicism and the modern idea of progress, see Hugh De Santis, *Beyond Progress: An Interpretive Odyssey to the Future* (Chicago: University of Chicago Press, 1996).

11. Wilson, *History,* 8: 57–8.

12. Wilson, *History,* 7: 28.

13. Wilson, *History,* 8: 58.

14. Baker and Dodd, *Public Papers,* 1: 43–59, 159–78.

15. Wilson, *History,* 8: 121.

16. Wilson, *History,* 10: 15.

17. Wilson, *History,* 10: 161–2.

18. Wilson, *History,* 10: 134–86.

19. Baker and Dodd, *Public Papers,* 5: 423.

20. Franz-Wilhelm Koch, *Die Konzeption des organischen Staates in der politischen Philosophie Woodrow Wilson: 1875–1912* (Ph.D. dissertation, Universität zu Köln, 1983).

21. Woodrow Wilson, *The State: Elements of Historical and Practical Politics* (Boston: D. C. Heath, 1889), 366.
22. Wilson, *The State,* 449.
23. Woodrow Wilson, *Division and Reunion: 1829–1889* (New York: Longmans, Green, 1893). For this transition in Wilson's thought, see Lloyd E. Ambrosius, *Wilsonian Statecraft: Theory and Practice of Liberal Internationalism* (Wilmington, DE: Scholarly Resources, 1991), 3–6.
24. Milton M. Gordon, "Assimilation in America," *Daedalus* 90 (Spring 1961): 263–85, reprinted in James R. M. Wilson, ed., *Forging the American Character,* 2 vols. (third edition; Upper Saddle River, NJ: Prentice Hall, 1997), 2: 71–90.
25. Michael H. Hunt, *Ideology and U.S. Foreign Policy* (New Haven, CT: Yale University Press, 1987), 46–91, 125–35.
26. Wilson, *History,* 1: 1–169, 2: 1–180.
27. Wilson, *History,* 2: 42.
28. Wilson, *History,* 3: 15.
29. Wilson, *History,* 4: 17.
30. Wilson, *History,* 5: 83.
31. Wilson, *History,* 6: 3.
32. Wilson, *History,* 6: 30; Woodrow Wilson, *George Washington* (New York: Harper and Brothers, 1896).
33. Wilson, *History,* 6: 12.
34. Wilson, *History,* 6: 131.
35. Some historians have recognized this point: Nell Irvin Painter, *Standing at Armageddon: The United States, 1877–1919* (New York: W. W. Norton, 1987), 216–390, and Robert H. Wiebe, *Self-Rule: A Cultural History of American Democracy* (Chicago: University of Chicago Press, 1995), 113–80.
36. Wilson, *History,* 7: 90.
37. Wilson, *History,* 7: 80.
38. Wilson, *History,* 9: 82.
39. Wilson, *History,* 9: 1–114.
40. Woodrow Wilson, *Congressional Government: A Study in American Politics* (Boston: Houghton Mifflin, 1885; Gloucester: Peter Smith, 1973), 28.
41. Wilson, *Congressional Government,* 39–40.
42. Wilson, *Congressional Government,* 53.
43. Arthur S. Link, ed., *The Papers of Woodrow Wilson* (Princeton, NJ: Princeton University Press, 1968), 5: 58–92.
44. Woodrow Wilson, *An Old Master and Other Political Essays* (New York: Charles Scribner's Sons, 1893), 80.
45. Woodrow Wilson, *Constitutional Government in the United States* (New York: Columbia University Press, 1908).
46. Jeffrey K. Tulis, *The Rhetorical Presidency* (Princeton, NJ: Princeton University Press, 1987).
47. Stockton Axson, *"Brother Woodrow": A Memoir of Woodrow Wilson,* ed. Arthur S. Link (Princeton, NJ: Princeton University Press, 1993), 231.
48. Baker and Dodd, *Public Papers,* 4: 410.
49. Baker and Dodd, *Public Papers,* 5: 621.
50. F. H. Hinsley, *Sovereignty* (Cambridge: Cambridge University Press, 1986), 210–11. For the idea of international social control and the rejection of pluralism in Wilson's vision of the League of Nations, see Lloyd E. Ambrosius, *Woodrow Wilson and the American Diplomatic Tradition: The Treaty Fight in Perspective* (Cambridge: Cambridge University Press, 1987).
51. Lloyd E. Ambrosius, "Dilemmas of National Self-Determination: Woodrow Wilson's Legacy," in *The Establishment of European Frontiers after the Two World Wars,* eds. Christian Baechler and Carole Fink (Bern: Peter Lang, 1996), 21–36.

52. Ambrosius, *Woodrow Wilson*, 51–135. See also Marc Gallicchio, *The African American Encounter with Japan and China: Black Internationalism in Asia, 1895–1945* (Chapel Hill: University of North Carolina Press, 2000), 15–29.

Chapter 2   Woodrow Wilson and the Quest for Orderly Progress

1. "Nature of Democracy in the United States," in Arthur S. Link, ed., *The Papers of Woodrow Wilson* (Princeton, NJ: Princeton University Press, 1969), 6: 238.
2. For a different interpretation that emphasizes order instead of control, see Robert H. Wiebe, *The Search for Order: 1877–1920* (New York: Hill and Wang, 1967).
3. On the inadequacy of Wilson's legacy of collective security, for example, see Roland N. Stromberg, *Collective Security and American Foreign Policy: From the League of Nations to NATO* (New York: Frederick A. Praeger, 1963).
4. For an excellent summary of the global transformation of the modern world, see Geoffrey Barraclough, *An Introduction to Contemporary History* (New York: Penguin Books, 1964).
5. C. Vann Woodward, "The Age of Reinterpretation," *American Historical Review* 66 (October 1960): 1–19.
6. Edward Alsworth Ross, *Social Control: A Survey of the Foundations of Order* (New York: Macmillan, 1901).
7. John Bates Clark, *The Control of Trusts: An Argument in Favor of Curbing the Power of Monopoly by a Natural Method* (New York: Macmillan, 1901).
8. Franklin Henry Giddings, *Democracy and Empire: Their Psychological Economic and Moral Foundations* (New York: Macmillan, 1900), v.
9. Woodrow Wilson, *Congressional Government: A Study of American Politics* (Boston: Houghton Mifflin, 1885; sixteenth edition, 1900), xi–xii.
10. Woodrow Wilson, *Constitutional Government in the United States* (New York: Columbia University Press, 1908), 77–8.
11. Edward S. Corwin, *The President's Control of Foreign Relations* (Princeton, NJ: Princeton University Press, 1917); Quincy Wright, "The Control of Foreign Relations," *American Political Science Review* 15 (February 1921): 1–26; Quincy Wright, *The Control of American Foreign Relations* (New York: Macmillan, 1922).
12. Herbert Croly, *The Promise of American Life* (New York: Capricorn Books, 1964; first edition, 1909), 22, 289–314.
13. Walter Lippmann, *Drift and Mastery: An Attempt to Diagnose the Current Unrest* (Englewood Cliffs, NJ: Prentice Hall, 1961; first edition, 1914), 148.
14. Lawrence E. Gelfand, *The Inquiry: American Preparations for Peace, 1917–1919* (New Haven, CT: Yale University Press, 1963).
15. Charles Forcey, *The Crossroads of Liberalism: Croly, Weyl Lippmann, and the Progressive Era, 1900–1925* (New York: Oxford University Press, 1961), 221–315; David W. Noble, *The Progressive Mind, 1890–1917* (Chicago: Rand McNally, 1970), 53–64, 165–79; John C. Farrell, "John Dewey and World War I: Armageddon Tests a Liberal's Faith," *Perspectives in American History* 9 (1975): 299–340.
16. Randolph S. Bourne, "A War Diary," *The Seven Arts* 2 (September 1917): 535–47, in *War and the Intellectuals: Essays by Randolph S. Bourne, 1915–1919*, ed. Carl Resek (New York: Harper and Row, 1964), 36–47.
17. Henry Adams, *The Education of Henry Adams: An Autobiography* (Boston: Houghton Mifflin, 1918), 401.
18. For other aspects of his views, see William C. Widenor, *Henry Cabot Lodge and the Search for an American Foreign Policy* (Berkeley: University of California Press, 1979).
19. "The Bible and Progress," in Ray Stannard Baker and William E. Dodd, eds., *The Public Papers of Woodrow Wilson*, 6 vols. (New York: Harper and Brothers, 1925–7), 2: 291–302; "Religion and Patriotism," in Arthur S. Link, ed., *The Papers of Woodrow Wilson* (Princeton, NJ: Princeton University Press, 1972), 12: 474–8.

20. George D. Herron, *Woodrow Wilson and the World's Peace* (New York: Mitchell Kennerley, 1917), 68–9, 76–7.

21. Mitchell Pirie Briggs, *George D, Herron and the European Settlement* (Stanford, CA: Stanford University Press, 1932), 249.

22. John M. Mulder, *Woodrow Wilson: The Years of Preparation* (Princeton, NJ: Princeton University Press, 1978), 229–77.

23. Arthur S. Link, *Wilson*, vol. 2: *The New Freedom* (Princeton, NJ: Princeton University Press, 1956), 320.

24. Baker and Dodd, *Public Papers*, 3: 64–9, 406–28.

25. Baker and Dodd, *Public Papers*, 3: 409, 439–45; Mark T. Gilderhus, "Pan-American Initiatives: The Wilson Presidency and 'Regional Integration,' 1914–1917," *Diplomatic History* 3 (Fall 1980): 409–23.

26. David Healy, *Gunboat Diplomacy in the Wilson Era: The U.S. Navy in Haiti, 1915–1916* (Madison: University of Wisconsin Press, 1976); Hans Schmidt, *The United States Occupation of Haiti, 1915–1934* (New Brunswick, NJ: Rutgers University Press, 1971), 3–107; Sumner Welles, *Naboth's Vinyard: The Dominican Republic, 1844–1924*, 2 vols. (New York: Payson and Clarke Ltd., 1928), 2: 700–835; Dana G. Munro, *Intervention and Dollar Diplomacy in the Caribbean, 1900–1921* (Princeton, NJ: Princeton University Press, 1964), 269–529.

27. Link, *Wilson*, 2: 375.

28. Robert E. Quirk, *An Affair of Honor: Woodrow Wilson and the Occupation of Veracruz* (Lexington: University of Kentucky Press, 1962); Friedrich Katz, *The Secret War in Mexico: Europe, the United States, and the Mexican Revolution* (Chicago: University of Chicago Press, 1981), 3–249; Lloyd C. Gardner, "Woodrow Wilson and the Mexican Revolution," in Arthur S. Link, ed., *Woodrow Wilson and a Revolutionary World, 1913–1921* (Chapel Hill: University of North Carolina Press, 1982), 3–48.

29. Katz, *Secret War*, 253–383; Barbara W. Tuchman, *The Zimmermann Telegram* (New York: Ballantine Books, 1958); Mark T. Gilderhus, "Wilson, Carranza, and the Monroe Doctrine: A Question in Regional Organization," *Diplomatic History* 7 (Spring 1983): 103–15.

30. Lansing to Gerard, Washington, July 21, 1915, U.S. Department of State, *Papers Relating to the Foreign Relations of the United States, 1915, Supplement: The World War* (Washington, DC: Government Printing Office, 1928), 481; Baker and Dodd, *Public Papers*, 3: 321.

31. Robert Lansing Diary, July 11, 1915, Jan. 9, 1916, Robert Lansing Papers, Manuscript Division, Library of Congress, Washington, DC.

32. Baker and Dodd, *Public Papers*, 3: 386.

33. Baker and Dodd, *Public Papers*, 4: 91.

34. Baker and Dodd, *Public Papers*, 4: 184–8.

35. Baker and Dodd, *Public Papers*, 4: 407–14.

36. Baker and Dodd, *Public Papers*, 5: 6–16.

37. For Wilson's transition from neutrality to intervention, see Edward H. Buehrig, *Woodrow Wilson and the Balance of Power* (Bloomington: Indiana University Press, 1955); Ernest R. May, *The World War and American Isolation 1914–1917* (Cambridge, MA: Harvard University Press, 1959); Daniel M. Smith, *The Great Departure: The United States and World War I, 1914–1920* (New York: John Wiley and Sons, 1965); Daniel M. Smith, "National Interest and American Intervention, 1917: An Historiographical Appraisal," *Journal of American History* 52 (June 1965): 5–24; Arthur S. Link, *Wilson*, vol. 3: *The Struggle for Neutrality, 1914–1915* (Princeton, NJ: Princeton University Press, 1960), vol. 4: *Confusions and Crisis, 1915–1916* (Princeton, NJ: Princeton University Press, 1964), and vol. 5: *Campaigns for Progressivism and Peace, 1916–1917* (Princeton, NJ: Princeton University Press, 1965).

38. Baker and Dodd, *Public Papers*, 5: 12–13.

39. Baker and Dodd, *Public Papers*, 5: 155–62; Arno J. Mayer, *Political Origins of the New Diplomacy, 1917–1918* (New Haven, CT: Yale University Press, 1959).

40. George F. Kennan, *Soviet–American Relations, 1917–1920*, vol. 1: *Russia Leaves the War* (Princeton, NJ: Princeton University Press, 1956); Edward M. Coffman, *The War To End All Wars: The American Military Experience in World War I* (New York: Oxford University Press, 1968); Edward M. Coffman, *The Hilt of the Sword: The Career of Peyton C. March* (Madison: University of Wisconsin Press, 1966); Daniel R. Beaver, *Newton D. Baker and the American War Effort, 1917–1919* (Lincoln: University of Nebraska Press, 1966).

41. Betty Miller Unterberger, "Woodrow Wilson and the Russian Revolution," in Link, *Wilson and Revolutionary World*, 49–104; George F. Kennan, *Soviet–American Relations, 1917–1920*, vol. 2: *The Decision to Intervene* (Princeton, NJ: Princeton University Press, 1958).

42. Baker and Dodd, *Public Papers*, 5: 253–61.

43. Roosevelt to Balfour, New York, Dec. 10, 1918, in Elting E. Morison, ed., *The Letters of Theodore Roosevelt* (Cambridge, MA: Harvard University Press, 1954), 8: 1414–15.

44. Gerhard Schulz, *Revolutions and Peace Treaties, 1917–1920* (London: Methuen, 1967); John M. Thompson, *Russia, Bolshevism and the Versailles Peace* (Princeton, NJ: Princeton University Press, 1967); Arno J. Mayer, *Politics and Diplomacy of Peacemaking: Containment and Counterrevolution at Versailles, 1918–1919* (New York: Alfred A. Knopf, 1967); N. Gordon Levin, Jr., *Woodrow Wilson and World Politics: America's Response to War and Revolution* (New York: Oxford University Press, 1968); Alan J. Ward, *Ireland and Anglo-American Relations, 1899–1921* (London: Wiedenfeld and Nicholson, 1969), 70–268.

45. U.S. Department of State, *Papers Relating to the Foreign Relations of the United States, 1919: The Paris Peace Conference*, 13 vols. (Washington, DC: Government Printing Office, 1942–7), 3: 177–201; Baker and Dodd, *Public Papers*, 5: 395–400.

46. *Foreign Relations: Paris Peace Conference*, 5: 85–6.

47. David Hunter Miller, *The Drafting of the Covenant*, 2 vols. (New York: G. P. Putnam's Sons, 1928), 1: 3–555; Lloyd E. Ambrosius, "Wilson, Clemenceau, and the German Problem at the Paris Peace Conference of 1919," *Rocky Mountain Social Science Journal* 12 (April 1975): 69–79; Lloyd E. Ambrosius, "Wilson, the Republicans, and French Security after World War I," *Journal of American History* 59 (September 1972): 341–52; Inga Floto, "Woodrow Wilson: War Aims, Peace Strategy, and the European Left," in Link, *Wilson and Revolutionary World*, 127–45.

48. Russell H. Fifield, *Woodrow Wilson and the Far East: The Diplomacy of the Shantung Question* (Hamden, CT: Archon Books, 1965); Raymond A. Esthus, "The Open Door and Integrity of China 1899–1922: Hazy Principles for Changing Policy," and David F. Trask, "Sino-Japanese-American Relations During the Paris Peace Conference of 1919," in Thomas H. Etzold, ed., *Aspects of Sino-American Relations since 1784* (New York: New Viewpoints, 1978), 48–101; Paul Gordon Lauren, "Human Rights in History: Diplomacy and Racial Equality at the Paris Peace Conference," *Diplomatic History* 2 (Summer 1978): 257–78.

49. Klaus Schwabe, *Deutsche Revolution und Wilson Frieden: Die amerikanische und deutsche Friedensstrategie zwischen Ideologie und Machtpolitik 1918/19* (Düsseldorf: Droste Verlag, 1971); Peter Berg, *Deutschland und Amerika, 1918–1929: Über das deutsche Amerikabild der zwanziger Jahre* (Lübeck: Matthiesen Verlag, 1963), 9–47; Lloyd E. Ambrosius, "The United States and the Weimar Republic: America's Response to the German Problem," in Jules Davids, ed., *Perspectives in American Diplomacy: Essays on Europe, Latin America, China, and the Cold War* (New York: Arno Press, 1976), 78–104; J. Joseph Huthmacher and Warren I. Susman, eds., *Wilson's Diplomacy: An International Symposium* (Cambridge, MA: Schenkman Publishing Company, 1973).

Chapter 3   Wilson's League of Nations: Collective Security and National Independence

1. For explicit statements of this thesis, see John Chalmers Vinson, *Referendum for Isolation: Defeat of Article Ten of the League of Nations Covenant* (Athens, GA: University of Georgia

Press, 1961), 1–2, 35, 96; Ruhl J. Bartlett, *The League to Enforce Peace* (Chapel Hill: University of North Carolina Press, 1944), 52–5; Selig Adler, *The Isolationist Impulse: Its Twentieth Century Reaction* (New York: Free Press, 1957), 92–5; Edward H. Buehrig, *Woodrow Wilson and the Balance of Power* (Bloomington: Indiana University Press, 1955), 210, 238–43; Edward H. Buehrig, ed., *Wilson's Foreign Policy in Perspective* (Bloomington: Indiana University Press, 1957), 42–53; Seth P. Tillman, *Anglo-American Relations at the Paris Peace Conference of 1919* (Princeton, NJ: Princeton University Press, 1961), 101–8; Arthur Walworth, *Woodrow Wilson,* 2 vols. (New York: Longmans, Green, 1958), 2: 27, 256–60; and Robert Endicott Osgood, *Ideals and Self-Interest in America's Foreign Relations: The Great Transformation of the Twentieth Century* (Chicago: University of Chicago Press, 1953), 189, 244, 284–5. The same thesis is implicit in other major works, including Denna Frank Fleming, *The United States and the League of Nations, 1918–1920* (New York: G. P. Putnam, 1932), 82–117; Arthur S. Link, *Wilson the Diplomatist: A Look at His Major Foreign Policies* (Baltimore: Johns Hopkins Press, 1957), 95, 119–20, 134–9; Thomas A. Bailey, *Woodrow Wilson and the Lost Peace* (New York: Macmillan, 1944), 179–93; Thomas A. Bailey, *Woodrow Wilson and the Great Betrayal* (New York: Macmillan, 1945), 30–1; Daniel M. Smith, *The Great Departure: The United States and World War I, 1914–1920* (New York: John Wiley and Sons, 1965), 123–9, 178–81; and Harley Notter, *The Origins of the Foreign Policy of Woodrow Wilson* (Baltimore: Johns Hopkins University Press, 1937), 521–9. Roland N. Stromberg, *Collective Security and American Foreign Policy: From the League of Nations to NATO* (New York: Frederick A. Praeger, 1963), 22–45, and N. Gordon Levin, Jr., *Woodrow Wilson and World Politics: America's Response to War and Revolution* (New York: Oxford University Press, 1968), 179–83, recognize some of the limits of Wilson's departure from isolationism. Despite his explicit references to the revolutionary character of the League, Robert Osgood argues persuasively in *Ideals and Self-Interest* that the "great transformation" of American foreign policy came not under Wilson's leadership but rather awaited World War II.

2. Walter Lippmann, *Men of Destiny* (New York: Macmillan, 1927), 122–3.

3. Ray Stannard Baker and William E. Dodd, eds., *The Public Papers of Woodrow Wilson,* 6 vols. (New York: Harper and Brothers, 1925–7), 5: 258.

4. Baker and Dodd, *Public Papers,* 5: 330.

5. Georges Clemenceau, *Grandeur and Misery of Victory* (New York: Harcourt, Brace, 1930), 171–2, 198–9; Diary of Edward M. House, Jan. 7, 1919, Edward M. House Papers, Yale University Library, New Haven, CT; Charles Seymour, ed., *The Intimate Papers of Colonel House,* 4 vols. (Boston: Houghton Mifflin, 1926–8), 4: 269–70, 306–7; David Hunter Miller, *My Diary at the Conference of Paris,* 21 vols. (New York: Appeal Printing Company, 1924), 1: 26, Dec. 3, 1918.

6. Pichon to Wilson, Paris, Feb. 4, 1919, Woodrow Wilson Papers, Library of Congress, Washington, DC; Léon Bourgeois, *Le Pacte de 1919 et la Société des Nations* (Paris: Bibliotheque Charpentier, 1919), 197–215.

7. David Hunter Miller, *The Drafting of the Covenant,* 2 vols. (New York: G. P. Putnam's Sons, 1928), 1: 168–9, and 2: 264, 430–1, 550; Robert Cecil, *A Great Experiment* (New York: Oxford University Press, 1941), 77; Ray Stannard Baker, *Woodrow Wilson and World Settlement,* 3 vols. (Garden City, NY: Doubleday, Page, 1922), 1: 214–15, 219–23, 231; Robert Lansing, *The Peace Negotiations: A Personal Narrative* (Boston: Houghton Mifflin Company, 1921), 34–54, 77–92, 106–7, 122–5; Lansing to Wilson, Paris, Dec. 23, 1918, Wilson Papers.

8. Miller, *Drafting the Covenant,* 1: 170.

9. Miller, *Drafting the Covenant,* 2: 296–7.

10. Baker, *World Settlement,* 1: 288; Stephen Bonsal, *Unfinished Business* (Garden City, NY: Doubleday, Doran, 1944), 29.

11. Baker and Dodd, *Public Papers,* 6: 351; for the relationship between Wilson's policy toward Eastern Europe and the League, see John M. Thompson, *Russia, Bolshevism, and*

the Versailles Peace (Princeton, NJ: Princeton University Press, 1966), 240–1, and Address of the President to the Democratic National Committee, Feb. 28, 1919, Joseph P. Tumulty Papers, Library of Congress, Washington, DC.

12. Cecil, *Great Experiment,* 75.
13. Miller, *Drafting the Covenant,* 1: 173–5.
14. Miller, *Drafting the Covenant,* 1: 173–6, and 2: 268–9.
15. Miller, *Drafting the Covenant,* 1: 179–80, 192–5, and 2: 268–9, 282.
16. Miller, *Drafting the Covenant,* 1: 290–2, 331, and 2: 350; Miller, *Diary,* 1: 176–88, March 18, 1919.
17. Miller, *Drafting the Covenant,* 1: 176–82, and 2: 269–70.
18. Baker, *World Settlement,* 1: 219, 223, 344–59.
19. David Lloyd George, *Memoirs of the Peace Conference,* 2 vols. (New Haven, CT: Yale University Press, 1939), 1: 420–1.
20. Miller, *Drafting the Covenant,* 1: 207, and 2: 291–2; Bourgeois, *Le Pacte de 1919,* 205–8; Baker, *World Settlement,* 1: 362.
21. Miller, *Drafting the Covenant,* 1: 209–10, and 2: 293–7; Lloyd George, *Memoirs,* 1: 424–5; Baker, *World Settlement,* 1: 268–369.
22. Miller, *Drafting the Covenant,* 1: 216–17, and 2: 296; Miller, *Diary,* 1: 119–20, Feb. 12, 1919; Cecil, *Great Experiment,* 78–9; Baker, *World Settlement,* 1: 374–5.
23. Miller, *Drafting the Covenant,* 2: 319.
24. Miller, *Drafting the Covenant,* 1: 243–53, and 2: 317–19; Cecil, *Great Experiment,* 78–9; Bonsal, *Unfinished Business,* 52–3.
25. Miller, *Drafting the Covenant,* 1: 253–4.
26. Miller, *Drafting the Covenant,* 1: 253–60, and 2: 320–1; Bonsal, *Unfinished Business,* 54–5.
27. U.S. Department of State, *Papers Relating to the Foreign Relations of the United States: The Paris Peace Conference, 1919,* 13 vols. (Washington, DC: Government Printing Office 1942–7), 3: 212–13.
28. *Foreign Relations: Paris Peace Conference,* 3: 219–24; Diary of Edward M. House, Feb. 14, 1919.
29. André Tardieu, *The Truth about the Treaty* (Indianapolis: Bobbs-Merrill Co., 1921), 158–61; Rhineland Question, Feb. 26, 1919, Wilson Papers.
30. Miller, *Drafting the Covenant,* 1: 444.
31. Miller, *Drafting the Covenant,* 1: 442–61, and 2: 369–74, 381–4; Miller, *Diary,* 1: 234–9, Apr. 10, 1919; Bonsal, *Unfinished Business,* 182–5; Diary of Edward M House, Apr. 11–12, 1919; Seymour, *Intimate Papers,* 4: 424–5.
32. Diary of Edward M. House, March 16, 1919.
33. Diary of Edward M. House, March 24, 1919.
34. Miller, *Drafting the Covenant,* 1: 324–5, 350–1, and 2: 537–8; Bonsal, *Unfinished Business,* 161–7.
35. *Foreign Relations: Paris Peace Conference,* 3: 294–5.
36. *Foreign Relations: Paris Peace Conference,* 3: 285–332; Miller, *Drafting the Covenant,* 1: 495–8, and 2: 695–743; Miller, *Diary,* 1: 278, Apr. 28, 1919; Bonsal, *Unfinished Business,* 210–14; Cecil, *Great Experiment,* 99–100; Diary of Edward M. House, Apr. 28, 1919.
37. White to Countess Seherr-Thoss, Aug. 6, 1922, quoted in Allan Nevins, *Henry White: Thirty Years of American Diplomacy* (New York: Harper and Brothers, 1930), 487; see also White to J. W. Davis, Paris, March 18, 1919, John W. Davis Papers, Yale University Library, New Haven, CT.
38. Diary of Robert Lansing, May 6, 1919, Library of Congress.
39. Lansing, *Peace Negotiations,* 166–7.
40. Bliss to Newton D. Baker, March 19, 1919, quoted in David F. Trask, "General Tasker Howard Bliss and the 'Sessions of the World,' 1919," *Transactions* of the American Philosophical Society, New Series, 56, Part 8 (1966): 33; see also Bliss to American Peace Commission, Paris, Feb. 26, 1919, Tasker Howard Bliss Papers, Library of Congress, Washington, DC.

41. Bliss to Sidney Mezes, Paris, Dec. 26, 1918, Bliss Papers.
42. U.S. Senate, *Congressional Record,* 66 Congress, 1 Session, 58: 2338 (July 10, 1919).
43. *Congressional Record,* 66 Cong., 1 Sess., 58: 3310 (July 29, 1919).
44. *Congressional Record,* 66 Cong., 1 Sess., 58: 4014 (Aug. 20, 1919).
45. *Congressional Record,* 66 Cong., 1 Sess., 58: 4017–19, 4025–7 (Aug. 20, 1919).
46. *Congressional Record,* 66 Cong., 1 Sess., 58: 4030 (Aug. 20, 1919).

Chapter 4 Wilson, Clemenceau, and the German Problem at the Paris Peace Conference of 1919

1. William E. Dodd, *Woodrow Wilson and His Work* (Garden City, NY: Doubleday, Page, 1920), 302, 331.
2. Ray Stannard Baker, *Woodrow Wilson and World Settlement,* 3 vols. (Garden City, NY: Doubleday, Page, 1922), 1: 1–421, and 2: 1–123.
3. George Bernard Noble, *Policies and Opinions at Paris, 1919: Wilsonian Diplomacy, the Versailles Peace and French Public Opinion* (New York: Macmillan, 1935), 181, 420, 422.
4. Paul Birdsall, *Versailles Twenty Years After* (New York: Reynal and Hitchcock, 1941), xi.
5. Thomas A. Bailey, *Woodrow Wilson and the Lost Peace* (New York: Macmillan, 1944), 324.
6. Arthur S. Link, *Wilson the Diplomatist: A Look at His Major Foreign Policies* (Baltimore: Johns Hopkins Press, 1957), 109.
7. Arthur Walworth, *Woodrow Wilson,* vol. 2: *World Prophet* (New York: Longmans, Green, 1958), 216–35.
8. Seth P. Tillman, *Anglo-American Relations at the Paris Peace Conference of 1919* (Princeton, NJ: Princeton University Press, 1961), 401–2.
9. Arno J. Mayer, *Political Origins of the New Diplomacy, 1917–1918* (New Haven, CT: Yale University Press, 1959), 34; Arno J. Mayer, *Politics and Diplomacy of Peacemaking: Containment and Counterrevolution at Versailles, 1918–1919* (New York: Alfred A. Knopf, 1967), 168, 462, 563.
10. N. Gordon Levin, Jr., *Woodrow Wilson and World Politics: America's Response to War and Revolution* (New York: Oxford University Press, 1968), 2–3, 123, 129, 137, 146, 151.
11. Klaus Schwabe, *Deutsche Revolution und Wilson-Frieden: Die amerikanische und deutsche Friedensstrategie zwischen Ideologie und Machtpolitik, 1918/19* (Düsseldorf: Droste Verlag, 1971), 12–13, 39, 191–5, 226, 312–22, 652–9. See also Ernst Fraenkel, "Das deutsche Wilsonbild," *Jahrbuch für Amerikastudien* 5 (Heidelberg: Carl Winter-Universitätsverlag, 1960): 66–120; and Peter Berg, "Deutschland und Amerika, 1918–1929: Über das deutsche Amerikabild der zwanziger Jahre," *Historische Studien* 385 (Lübeck and Hamburg: Matthiesen Verlag, 1963): 9–47.
12. Hans W. Gatzke, *Germany's Drive to the West: A Study of Germany's Western War Aims during the First World War* (Baltimore: Johns Hopkins Press, 1950); Fritz Fischer, *Griff nach der Weltmacht* (Düsseldorf: Droste Verlag, 1961), trans. *Germany's Aims in the First World War* (New York: W. W. Norton, 1967).
13. Wolfgang J. Mommsen, "The Debate on German War Aims," and Klaus Epstein, "Gerhard Ritter and the First World War," in *1914: The Coming of the First World War,* ed. Walter Laqueur and George L. Mosse (New York: Harper and Row, 1966), 45–70, 186–203.
14. Gerhard L. Weinberg, "The Defeat of Germany in 1918 and the European Balance of Power," *Central European History* 2 (Sept. 1969): 248–60.
15. Ray Stannard Baker and William E. Dodd, eds., *The Public Papers of Woodrow Wilson,* 6 vols. (New York: Harper and Brothers, 1925–7), 5: 330.
16. U.S. Department of State, *Papers Relating to the Foreign Relations of the United States: The Paris Peace Conference, 1919,* 13 vols. (Washington, DC: Government Printing Office, 1942–7), 3: 212–13.
17. U.S. Senate, *Congressional Record,* 66 Congress, 1 Session, 58: 4014 (Aug. 20, 1919).
18. *Congressional Record,* 66 Cong., 1 Sess., 58: 3310 (July 10, 1919).

19. Diary of Edward M. House, Mar. 16, 1919, Edward M. House Papers, Yale University Library, New Haven, CT.
20. Lloyd E. Ambrosius, "Wilson's League of Nations," *Maryland Historical Magazine* 65 (Winter 1970): 369–93.
21. Benson to Wilson, March 14, 1919, Woodrow Wilson Papers, Library of Congress, Washington, DC.
22. Bliss to Wilson, March 14, 1919, Wilson Papers and Tasker Howard Bliss Papers, Library of Congress, Washington, DC.
23. *Foreign Relations: Paris Peace Conference,* 4: 356–79, 385–403.
24. André Tardieu, *The Truth About the Treaty* (Indianapolis, IN: Bobbs-Merrill, 1921), 147–67; Great Britain, *House of Commons Sessional Papers,* vol. 26 (London: His Majesty's Stationery Office, 1924), "Papers Respecting Negotiations for an Anglo-French Pact," Cmd. 2169, 25–57; Rhineland Question, [Feb. 26, 1919], Wilson Papers.
25. Diary of Edward M. House, March 12, 1919; David Lloyd George, *Memoirs of the Peace Conference,* 2 vols. (New Haven, CT: Yale University Press, 1939), 1: 265–6; Tardieu, *Truth,* 176–8; David Hunter Miller, *The Drafting of the Covenant,* 2 vols. (New York: G. P. Putnam's Sons, 1928), 2: 296–7; David Hunter Miller, *My Diary at the Conference of Paris,* 21 vols. (New York: Appeal Printing Co., 1924), 1: 293–4; newspaper interview, July 10, 1919, Wilson Papers.
26. Clemenceau to Wilson, March 17, 1919, Wilson Papers; "Negotiations for an Anglo-French Pact," 69–76; Tardieu, *Truth,* 177–82; Georges Clemenceau, *Grandeur and Misery of Victory* (New York: Harcourt, Brace, 1930), 232–7.
27. Some Considerations for the Peace Conference, [March 25, 1919], Wilson Papers; Lloyd George, *Memoirs,* 1: 266–73; "Negotiations for an Anglo-French Pact," 76–85.
28. Paul Mantoux, *Les Délibérations du Conseil des Quatre: 24 mars–28 juin 1919,* 2 vols. (Paris: Éditions du Centre national de la recherche scientifique, 1953), 1: 39–51.
29. President Wilson's Proposition, [March 28, 1919], Amendments Proposed by France, Apr. 12, 1919, House Papers; Diary of Edward M. House, Apr. 2–4, 1919; Mantoux, *Délibérations,* 1: 144–5; Tardieu, *Truth,* 138, 205.
30. Wilson to House, Apr. 12, 1919, House Papers and Wilson Papers.
31. Diary of Edward M. House, Apr. 12, 14–15, 1919; Tardieu, *Truth,* 209.
32. *Foreign Relations: Paris Peace Conference,* 5: 113–14,117–18; Mantoux, *Délibérations,* 1: 318–19; Lloyd George, *Memoirs,* 1: 280–1; Tardieu, *Truth,* 139–40, 186.
33. *Foreign Relations: Paris Peace Conference,* 5: 474–6, 494–5; Mantoux, *Délibérations,* 1: 492–3; Miller, *Diary,* 1: 293–4; Wilson to Clemenceau, May 6, 1919, Lloyd George to Clemenceau, May 6, 1919, Wilson to White, Apr. 17, 1919, Wilson Papers.
34. Lloyd E. Ambrosius, "Wilson, the Republicans, and French Security after World War l," *Journal of American History* 59 (Sept. 1972): 341–52.
35. Bailey, *Wilson and Lost Peace,* 312.

Chapter 5   Secret German–American Negotiations during the
Paris Peace Conference

1. Morton H. Halperin, Jerry J. Berman, Robert L. Borosage, and Christine M. Marwick, *The Lawless State: The Crimes of the U.S. Intelligence Agencies* (New York: Penguin Books, 1976); David Wise, *The American Police State: The Government Against the People* (New York: Random House, 1976); J. Anthony Lukas, *Nightmare: The Underside of the Nixon Years* (New York: Viking Press, 1976); Graham Allison and Peter Szanton, *Remaking Foreign Policy: The Organizational Connection* (New York: Basic Books, 1976), 188–210; Graham T. Allison, *Essence of Decision: Explaining the Cuban Missile Crisis* (Boston: Little, Brown, 1971); Morton H. Halperin, *Bureaucratic Politics and Foreign Policy* (Washington, DC: Brookings Institution, 1974). Other studies of bureaucratic politics and executive-legislative relations concerning national security policy include John Newhouse, *Cold*

Dawn: The Story of SALT (New York: Holt, Rinehart, and Winston, 1973) and Alton Frye, *A Responsible Congress: The Politics of National Security* (New York: McGraw-Hill, 1975).

2. For summaries and critiques of the New Left historiography, see Charles S. Maier, "Revisionism and the Interpretation of Cold War Origins," *Perspectives in American History* 4 (1970): 311–47; Robert W. Tucker, *The Radical Left and American Foreign Policy* (Baltimore: Johns Hopkins Press, 1971); Robert James Maddox, *The New Left and the Origins of the Cold War* (Princeton, NJ: Princeton University Press, 1973); Selig Adler, "Hoover's Foreign Policy and the New Left," in Martin L. Fausold, ed., *The Hoover Presidency: A Reappraisal* (Albany: State University of New York Press, 1974), 153–63; Lloyd E. Ambrosius, "The Orthodoxy of Revisionism: Woodrow Wilson and the New Left," *Diplomatic History* 1 (Summer 1977): 199–214.

3. Samuel P. Huntington, *The Soldier and the State: The Theory and Politics of Civil–Military Relations* (Cambridge, MA: Harvard University Press, 1957), 80–97, 313–466; Morris Janowitz, *The Professional Soldier: A Social and Political Portrait* (New York: Free Press, 1971), 19–74, 345–413. On the industrial and managerial revolutions, see Walter Millis, *Arms and Men: A Study in American Military History* (New York: Putnam, 1956), 72–210, and James E. Hewes, Jr., *From Root to McNamara: Army Organization and Administration, 1900–1963* (Washington, DC: Center of Military History, U.S. Army, 1975).

4. George F. Kennan, *Memoirs, 1925–1950* (Boston: Little, Brown, 1967), 372.

5. Fritz T. Epstein, "Zwischen Compiègne und Versailles: Geheime amerikanische Militär-diplomatie in der Periode des Waffenstillstandes 1918/19: Die Rolle des Obersten Arthur L. Conger," *Vierteljahrshefte für Zeitgeschichte* 3 (October 1955): 412–45; Klaus Schwabe, *Deutsche Revolution und Wilson-Frieden: Die amerikanische und deutsche Friedensstrategie zwischen Ideologie und Machtpolitik 1918/19* (Düsseldorf: Droste Verlag, 1971).

6. Walter Loeb, Bericht über die Unterredung mit Oberst Conger, Frankfurt, Dec. 4, 1918, and Walter Loeb, Bericht über unsere Fahrt in das amerikanische Hauptquartier an die Reichs-Regierung, Frankfurt, Dec. 13, 1918, Kassette III, Mappe 14 (Nachlass Carl Giebel, Friedrich-Ebert-Stiftung, Bonn-Bad Godesberg); Walter Loeb, Bericht über die Unterredung mit Oberst Conger, Frankfurt, Dec. 4, 1918, and Walter Loeb, Bericht über unsere Fahrt in das amerikanische Hauptquartier an die Reichs-Regierung, Frankfurt, Dec. 13, 1918, A. A. Weimar, III (Politisches Archiv des Auswärtigen Amts, Bonn; Microcopy T120, Roll 2411, Series 4665/Frames E218929–936, National Archives, Washington, DC).

7. Statement of Paul Freiherr von Eltz Rübenach to A. L. Conger, Treves, Dec. 30, 1918, General Headquarters, G-2, File 091, Record Group 120, Series 7, Box 5164 (Records of the American Expeditionary Forces, National Archives, Washington, DC); Wilhelm Groener, *Lebenserinnerungen* (Göttingen: Vandenhoeck and Ruprecht, 1957), 484–7.

8. Walter Loeb and Norbert Einstein, Bericht über die Unterredung mit Oberst Conger im grossen Hauptquartier zu Trier am 4. und 5. Januar 1919, Frankfurt, Jan. 9, 1919, A. A. Weimar, III (Politisches Archiv des Auswärtigen Amts; T120, Roll 2411, 4665/E218937–943).

9. Holtzendorff to Brockdorff-Rantzau, Berlin, Jan. 24, 1919, Weltkrieg 30, Bd. 17 (Politisches Archiv des Auswärtigen Amts; T120, Roll 2032–33, 4080/D921121–127); Groener, *Lebenserinnerungen*, 48; Heineken, Stapelfeldt and Peltzer to Pershing, Treves, Jan. 14, 1919, General Headquarters, G-2, File 091, RG 120, Ser. 7, Box 5164 (Records of the American Expeditionary Forces).

10. Conger to Nolan, Treves, Jan. 16, 1919, Conger to Nolan, Treves, Jan. 17, 1919, Nolan to McAndrew, [Chaumont], Jan. 19, 1919, and Collins to Boyd, [Chaumont], Jan. 21, 1919, General Headquarters, G-2, File 091 (RG 120, Ser. 7, Box 5164 (Records of the American Expeditionary Forces).

11. Nolan to McAndrew, [Chaumont], Jan. 27, 1919, and Statement by Baron von Eltz to Colonel Conger, at Advanced G.H.Q., Treves, Jan. 26, 1919, General Headquarters, G-2, File 091, RG 120, Ser. 7, Box 5164 (Records of the American Expeditionary Forces); Groener, *Lebenserinnerungen*, 487–8.

12. Loeb to Brockdorff-Rantzau, Frankfurt, Jan. 27, 1919, and Walter Loeb, Bericht über den Aufenthalt im amerikanischen Hauptquartier am 25. und 26. Januar 1919, und die Unterredung mit Herrn Oberst Conger, Frankfurt, Jan. 27, 1919, Weltkrieg 30, Bd. 17 (Politisches Archiv des Auswärtigen Amts; T120, Roll 2032–33, 4080/D921294–299).

13. Meeting between Mr. Loeb and Dr. Einstein and a General Staff Officer, Feb. 2, 1919, and Nolan to Pershing, Paris, Feb. 7, 1919, General Headquarters, G-2, File 091, RG 120, Ser. 7, Box 5164 (Records of the American Expeditionary Forces); Pershing to House, [Chaumont], Feb. 10, 1919, and Nolan to Pershing, Paris, Feb. 7, 1919, Box 97 (John J. Pershing Papers, Library of Congress, Washington, DC); Pershing to House, [Chaumont], Feb. 10, 1919, and [Nolan] to Pershing, Paris, Feb. 7, 1919, Drawer 15, File 45 (Edward M. House Papers, Yale University Library, New Haven, CT).

14. Walter Loeb, Bericht über den Aufenthalt im Amerikanischen Hauptquartier und die Unterredung mit Oberst Conger am 8. und 9. Februar 1919, Frankfurt, Feb. 10, 1919, A. A. Weimar, III (Politisches Archiv des Auswärtigen Amts; T120, Roll 2411, 4665/E218971–975); Aufzeichnung über Mitteilungen des Herrn Loeb aus Frankfurt an den Staatssekretär des Auswärtigen Amts, Feb. 9, 1919, Weltkrieg 30, Bd. 19 (Politisches Archiv des Auswärtigen Amts; T120, Roll 2034–35, 4080/D921930–931); Conger to Nolan, Treves, Feb. 9, 1919, General Headquarters, G-2, File 091, RG 120, Ser. 7, Box 5164 (Records of the American Expeditionary Forces); Pershing to House, Chaumont, Feb. 10, 1919, and Extract, and Conger to Nolan, Treves, Feb. 9, 1919, Box 97 (Pershing Papers).

15. Conger to Nolan, Treves, Feb. 12, 1919, General Headquarters, G-2, File 091, RG 120, Ser. 7, Box 5164 (Records of the American Expeditionary Forces); Seelinger to Auswärtiges Amt, Trier, Feb. 15, 1919, and Besprechung zwischen Oberst Conger, Geheimrat Cuno und Generaldirektor Heineken am 13. Februar 1919 morgens 10 Uhr im Regierungsgebäude zu Trier, Trier, Feb. 13, 1919, Weltkrieg 30, Bd. 24 (Politisches Archiv des Auswärtigen Amts; T120, Roll 2036–37, 4080/ D922815–818).

16. Conger to Nolan, Treves, Feb. 15, 1919, General Headquarters, G-3, File 1035, RG 120, Set. 268, Box 3163 (Records of the American Expeditionary Forces); M[atthias] Erzberger, *Erlebnisse im Weltkrieg* (Stuttgart and Berlin: Deutsche Verlags-Anstalt, 1920), 362.

17. Walter Loeb, Bericht über den Aufenthalt im amerikanischen Hauptquartier in Trier am 23. Feb. 1919, Frankfurt, Feb. 24, 1919 (Kleine Erwerbungen 328–3, Nachlass Otto Landsberg, Bundesarchiv, Koblenz); Erzberger to Scheidemann, Berlin, Feb. 24, 1919, and Loeb telegram, Frankfurt, Feb. 24, 1919, R431/164 (Akten der Reichskanzlei, Bundesarchiv, Koblenz); Erzberger to Brockdorff-Rantzau, Weimar, Feb. 24, 1919, and Loeb telegram, Frankfurt, Feb. 24, 1919 (Nachlass Brockdorff-Rantzau, Politisches Archiv des Auswärtigen Amts, Bonn; T120, Roll 3441, 9105/H234280–282); Loeb to Auswärtiges Amt, Frankfurt, Feb. 24, 1919, Weltkrieg 30 Geh., Bd. 1 (Politisches Archiv des Auswärtigen Amts; T120, Roll 2063, 4099/D931029–030); Conger to Nolan, Treves, Feb. 23, 1919, General Headquarters, G-2, File 388.3, RG 120, Ser. 7, Box 5175 (Records of the American Expeditionary Forces); Loeb to Roediger, Frankfurt, Feb. 19, 1919, and Roediger to Loeb, Weimar, Feb. 20, 1919, A. A. Weimar, V. 9 (Politisches Archiv des Auswärtigen Amts; T120, Roll 2413, 4665/E220602–604); Pershing to Foch, Paris, Feb. 21, 1919, G-3, File 1038, RG 120, Ser. 268, Box 3172 (Records of the American Expeditionary Forces).

18. Gherardi to American Commission to Negotiate Peace, Berlin, Feb. 10, 1919, File 184.01202/33, RG 256 (Records of the American Commission to Negotiate Peace, National Archives, Washington, DC; M820, Roll 217, Frame 163); U.S. Department of State, *Papers Relating to the Foreign Relations of the United States: The Paris Peace Conference, 1919*, 13 vols. (Washington, DC: Government Printing Office, 1942–7), 11: 46–9; Loeb to Brockdorff-Rantzau, Weimar, Feb. 13, 1919, A. A. Weimar, III (Politisches Archiv des Auswärtigen Amts; T120, Roll 2411, 4665/E218928).

19. Churchill to Nolan, Paris, Feb. 21, 1919, and Gherardi to American Commission to Negotiate Peace, Berlin, Feb. 10, 1919, General Headquarters, G-2, File 388.3, RG 120, Ser. 7, Box 5175 (Records of the American Expeditionary Forces).

20. Moreno to Conger, [Chaumont], Feb. 25, 1919, Conger to Moreno, Treves, Feb. 27, 1919, Nolan to Churchill, [Chaumont], March 1, 1919, Churchill to Grew, Paris, March 4, 1919, and Churchill to Nolan, Paris, March 4, 1919, General Headquarters, G-2, File 388.3, RG 120, Ser. 7, Box 5174 (Records of the American Expeditionary Forces).

21. U.S. Senate, *Foreign and Military Intelligence: Final Report of the Select Committee to Study Governmental Operations with Respect to Intelligence Activities* (Washington, DC: Government Printing Office, 1976), Book I, 7, 9; Taylor Branch, "The Trial of the C.I.A.," *New York Times Magazine* (Sept. 12, 1976), 35, 115–26.

22. Loeb to Scheidemann, Frankfurt, March 10, 1919, and Walter Loeb, Bericht über die Unterredung im Amerikanischen-Grossen-Hauptquartier in Trier am 8. und 9. März 1919, Frankfurt, March 10, 1919, R431/164 (Akten der Reichskanzlei); Hagen Schulze, ed., *Akten der Reichskanzlei, Weimarer Republik: Das Kabinett Scheidemann, 13. Februar bis 20. Juni 1919* (Boppard: H. Boldt, 1971), 27–32; Loeb to Bernstorff, Frankfurt, March 11, 1919, and Walter Loeb, Bericht über die Unterredung im Amerikanischen-Grossen-Hauptquartier in Trier am 8. und 9. März 1919, Frankfurt, March 10, 1919, Geschäftsstelle für die Friedensverhandlungen, P100318 (Politisches Archiv des Auswärtigen Amts; T120, Roll 3909, 9935/E695047–054); Loeb to Brockdorff-Rantzau, Frankfurt, March 10, 1919 (Nachlass Brockdorff-Rantzau; T120, Roll 3441, 9105/H234055–056).

23. Conger to Nolan, [Trier], March 22, 1919, Eltz to Conger (Coblenz, 15 March), No. 1, Treves, March 21, 1919, Eltz to Conger (Coblenz, 15 March), No. 2, Treves, March 21, 1919, and Eltz to Conger (Coblenz, 15 March), No. 3, Treves, March 21, 1919, General and Special Staffs, M.I.D., RG 165, Folder 124–424 (Records of the War Department, National Archives, Washington, DC); Eltz to Conger (Coblenz, 15 March), Treves, March 21, 1919, General Headquarters, G-2-B, Advance G.H.Q., General File, Folder T-134 1/2, RG 120, Ser. 753, Box 6022 (Records of the American Expeditionary Forces).

24. Noske to Conger, March 18, 1919, Statement of strength of the German army, No. 12, March 22, 1919, Henrotin and A. L. Conger, Interview with Herr Noske, Minister of War and Colonel Reinhardt, Minister of War for Prussia, No. 9, Treves, March 21, 1919, A. L. Conger, Impressions of the German General Staff, No. 8, Treves, March 21, 1919, A. L. Conger, Interviews with General Groener, Chief of Staff of the German Army, No. 7, Treves, March 21, 1919, A. L. Conger, Interview with Field Marshal Hindenburg at his Headquarters, Kolberg on March 19, 1919, No. 6, Treves, March 21, 1919, and A. L. Conger, Interview with Professor Hans Delbrück, of the University of Berlin, at Berlin, on March 20, No. 5, Treves, March 21, 1919, General and Special Staffs, M.I.D., RG 165, Folder 124–424 (Records of the War Department); Henrotin and A. L. Conger, Interview with Herr Noske, Minister of War and Colonel Reinhardt, Minister of War for Prussia, Treves, March 21, 1919, and A. L. Conger, Interviews with General Groener, Chief of Staff of the German Army, Treves, March 21, 1919, General Headquarters, G-2-B, Advance G. H. Q., General File, Folder T-134 1/2, RG 120, Ser. 753, Box 6022 (Records of the American Expeditionary Forces); Groener, *Lebenserinnerungen,* 489–91; Epstein, "Zwischen Compiègne und Versailles," 418.

25. A. L. Conger and Frederick Henrotin, General Conclusions, No. 11, Treves, March 21, 1919, General and Special Staffs, M.I.D., RG 165, Folder 124–424 (Records of the War Department); General Pershing's Diary, March 22, 1919, Box 4–5 (Pershing Papers).

26. Memorandum No. 171, March 21, 1919, File 184.012/50, RG 256 (Records of the American Commission to Negotiate Peace; M820, Roll 217, 88–89); *Foreign Relations: Paris Peace Conference,* 11: 132.

27. Bliss to Pershing, Paris, March 23, 1919, Nolan to Bliss, [Chaumont], March 24, 1919, and Nolan to Coxe [Chaumont], March 27, 1919, General Headquarters, G-2, American Commission to Negotiate Peace, RG 120, Ser. 1621, Box 5887 (Records of the American Expeditionary Forces); Nolan to Bliss, [Chaumont], March 24, 1919, Box 71 (Tasker Howard Bliss Papers, Library of Congress, Washington, DC); Bliss to House, Paris, March 28, 1919, and Bliss to White, Paris, March 28, 1919, Box 69 (Bliss Papers);

Bliss to White, Paris, March 28, 1919, Box 41 (Henry White Papers, Library of Congress, Washington, DC).

28. Loeb to Brockdorff-Rantzau, Frankfurt, March 28, 1919, and Walter Loeb, Bericht über die Unterredung mit Herrn Oberst Conger im Hotel Preussischer Hof in Limburg a. d. L. in der Nacht vom 27. auf 28. März 1919, Frankfurt, March 28, 1919, Weltkrieg 30 Geh., Bd. I (Politisches Archiv des Auswärtigen Amts; T120, Roll 2063, 4099/D931086–094); Loeb to Bernstorff, Frankfurt, March 28, 1919, and Walter Loeb, Bericht über die Unterredung mit Herrn Oberst Conger im Hotel Preussischer Hof in Limburg a. d. L. in der Nacht vom 27. auf 28. März 1919, Frankfurt, March 28, 1919, Geschäftsstelle für Friedensverhandlungen, P100318 (Politisches Archiv des Auswärtigen Amts; T120, Roll 3909, 9935/E695033–040); Walter Loeb, Bericht über die Unterredung mit Herrn Oberst Conger im Hotel Preussischer Hof in Limburg a. d. L. in der Nacht vom 27. auf 28. März 1919, Frankfurt, March 28, 1919 (Kleine Erwerbungen 328–3, Nachlass Landsberg); Erzberger to Brockdorff-Rantzau, Berlin, Apr. 1, 1919, and Bericht über die Unterredung mit Oberst Conger im Hotel Preussischer Hof in Limburg a. d. L. in der Nacht vom 27. auf 28. März 1919, Frankfurt, March 28, 1919 (Nachlass Brockdorff-Rantzau; T120, Roll 3441, 9105/H234779–785).

29. Loeb to Auswärtiges Amt, Telegramm aus Frankfurt, March 28, 1919, Weltkrieg 30 Geh., Bd. 1 (Politisches Archiv des Auswätigen Amts; T120, Roll 2063, 4099/D931084–085); Reichsminister to Ebert, Weimar, March 28, 1919, and Telegramm aus Frankfurt, 28 March 1919, R43I/1 (Akten der Reichskanzlei); Loeb to Scheidemann, Frankfurt, March 4, 1919, and Loeb to Scheidemann, March 24, 1919, R43I/164 (Akten der Reichskanzlei); Epstein, "Zwischen Compiègne und Versailles," 419–20.

30. *Akten der Reichskanzlei: Kabinett Scheidemann,* 109–16; Loeb to Brockdorff-Rantzau, Frankfurt, March 24, 1919 (Nachlass Brockdorff-Rantzau; T120, Roll 3441, 9105/H234313–314); Loeb to Bernstorff, Frankfurt, March 24, 1919, Loeb to Bernstorff, Frankfurt, Apr. 1, 1919, W. E. L[oeb], memorandum, Treves, March 30, 1919, and Walter Loeb, Peace Conditions Acceptable to Germany, Weltkrieg 30 Geh., Bd. 1 (Politisches Archiv des Auswärtigen Amts; T120, Roll 2063, 4099/D931095–100); Epstein, "Zwischen Compiègne und Versailles," 420–2.

31. W. E. L[oeb], memorandum, Treves, March 30, 1919, and W. E. L[oeb], Peace Conditions Acceptable to Germany, General and Special Staffs, M.I.D., RG 165, Folder 124–424 (Records of the War Department); Nolan to Coxe, [Chaumont], March 31, 1919, and Peace Conditions Acceptable to Germany, General Headquarters, G-2, American Commission to Negotiate Peace, RG 120, Ser. 1621, Box 5887 (Records of the American Expeditionary Forces); Nolan to Bliss [Chaumont], March 31, 1919, No. 5, General Headquarters, G-2, American Commission to Negotiate Peace, RG 120, Ser. 1622, Box 5889 (Records of the American Expeditionary Forces); Nolan to Bliss, [Chaumont], March 31, 1919, No. 5, Box 41 (White Papers); *Foreign Relations: Paris Peace Conference,* 11: 142; Bliss to Wilson, Paris, Apr. 1, 1919, Box 70 (Bliss Papers); Bliss to Wilson, Paris, Apr. 1, 1919, Nolan to Bliss [Chaumont], March 31, 1919, and Nolan to Bliss, [Chaumont], March 31, 1919, No. 5, Series 5B (Woodrow Wilson Papers, Library of Congress, Washington, DC); Epstein, "Zwischen Compiègne und Versailles," 422–4.

32. Paul Mantoux, *Les Délibérations du Conseil des Quatre (24 mars–28 juin 1919),* 2 vols. (Paris: Éditions du Centre national de la recherche scientifique, 1955), 1: 105–8, 115–19; *Akten der Reichskanzlei: Kabinett Scheidemann,* 116–17, 121, 129–31; Report on the Negotiations of April 3rd and 4th at Spa, Ser. 5B (Wilson Papers).

33. Walter Loeb, Telegramm aus Mannheim, Apr. 7, 1919, R43I/164 (Akten der Reichskanzlei); Loeb to Auswärtiges Amt, Telegramm aus Mannheim, Apr. 7, 1919, Loeb to Brockdorff-Rantzau, Frankfurt, Apr. 8, 1919, and Walter Loeb, Bericht über die Unterredung vom 5. auf 6. April 1919 im amerikanischen Grossen-Hauptquartier in Trier, Frankfurt, Apr. 8, 1919, Weltkrieg 30 Geh., Bd. 1 (Politisches Archiv des Auswärtigen Amts; T120, Roll 2063, 4099/D931109–116); Loeb to Bernstorff,

Frankfurt, Apr. 8, 1919, and Walter Loeb, Bericht über die Unterredung vom 5. auf 6. April 1919 im amerikanischen Grossen-Hauptquartier in Trier, Frankfurt, Apr. 8, 1919, Geschäftsstelle für die Friedensverhandlungen, P100318 (Politisches Archiv des Auswätigen Amts; T120, Roll 3909, 9935/E695017–023); Walter Loeb, Bericht über die Unterredung vom 5. auf 6. April 1919 im amerikanischen Grossen-Hauptquartier in Trier, Frankfurt, Apr. 8, 1919 (Kleine Erwerbungen 328–3, Nachlass Landsberg); *Akten der Reichskanzlei: Kabinett Scheidemann,* 150.

34. Loeb to Auswärtiges Amt, Telegramm aus Frankfurt, Apr. 14, 1919, Erzberger's Entwurf, Apr. 14, 1919, Haniel to Brockdorff-Rantzau, Weimar, Apr. 15, 1919, Loeb to Brockdorff-Rantzau, Frankfurt, Apr. 14, 1919, and Walter Loeb, Bericht über die Unterredung vom 12. auf 13. April 1919 im Amerikanischen Grossen-Hauptquartier in Trier, Frankfurt, Apr. 14, 1919, Weltkrieg 30 Geh., Bd. I (Politisches Archiv des Auswärtigen Amts; T120, Roll 2063, 4099/D931120–136); Loeb to Bernstorff, Frankfurt, Apr. 14, 1919, and Walter Loeb, Bericht über die Unterredung vom 12. auf 13. April 1919 im Amerikanischen Grossen-Hauptquartier in Trier, Frankfurt, Apr. 14, 1919, Geschäftsstelle für die Friedensverhandlungen, P100318 (Politisches Archiv des Auswärtigen Amts; T120, Roll 3909, 9935/E695009–013); Walter Loeb, Bericht über die Unterredung vom 12. auf 13. April 1919 im Amerikanischen Grossen-Hauptquartier in Trier, Frankfurt, Apr. 14, 1919 (Kleine Erwerbungen 328–3, Nachlass Landsberg); *Akten der Reichskanzlei: Kabinett Scheidemann,* 159–60; Loeb to Scheidemann, Frankfurt, Apr. 10, 1919, and Albert to Loeb, Weimar, Apr. 14, 1919, R431/164 (Akten der Reichskanzlei); Nolan to McAndrew, [Chaumont], Apr. 23, 1919, General Headquarters, G-3 Reports, General Correspondence, RG 120, Ser. 268, Box 3125 (Records of the American Expeditionary Forces).

35. Geheime Aufzeichnung, Berlin, Apr. 19, 1919 (Nachlass Brockdorff-Rantzau; T120, Roll 3441, 9105/H234180–192); Dresel to American Commission to Negotiate Peace, [Berlin], Apr. 20, 1919, and Lansing to Wilson, Paris, Apr. 23, 1919, Ser. 5B (Wilson Papers); *Foreign Relations: Paris Peace Conference,* 12: 82–83; *Foreign Relations: Paris Peace Conference,* 5: 204–5; Mantoux, *Les Délibérations,* 1: 350–1. Because Wilson identified Dresel's report as originating "from an Officer in the United States 3rd Army, who had had a talk with Brockdorff-Rantzau," Klaus Schwabe assumed he referred to Conger and that this mistake was "perhaps a sign that he was more familiar with his activities than with those of Dresel"; Schwabe, *Deutsche Revolution,* 562. Wilson referred instead to Colonel R. H. Williams, Third Army, AEF, who had transmitted Dresel's report to the American Commission to Negotiate Peace and whose name and identification appeared on the copy Wilson received from Lansing.

36. Conger to Nolan, Treves, Apr. 14, 1919, General and Special Staffs, M.I.D., RG 165, Folder 124–424 (Records of the War Department); Loeb to Brockdorff-Rantzau, Frankfurt, Apr. 16, 1919, Weltkrieg 30 Geh., Bd. I (Politisches Archiv des Auswärtigen Amts; T120, Roll 2063, 4099/D931137–138); Walter Loeb, Bericht über die Unterredung mit Herrn Major Henrotin, Major und Generalstab, geheime Abteilung II, Spezial-Abteilung der Armee, 4.5.1919, Trier, Frankfurt, May 5, 1919, Lfd. Nr. 14 (Nachlass Matthias Erzberger, Bundesarchiv, Koblenz).

37. Geheime Aufzeichnung vom 29. April 1919 (Nachlass Brockdorff-Rantzau; T120, Roll 3443, 9105/H235251–256); Bliss to Wilson, Paris, May 1, 1919, Conger to Bliss, Treves, Apr. 30, 1919, Interview with Count Brockdorff-Rantzau (April 28), and Interviews of a Confidential Agent with Members of the German Government (Berlin, April 26 and 27, 1919), Treves, Apr. 30, 1919, Ser. 5B (Wilson Papers); Epstein, "Zwischen Compègne und Versailles," 426; Interviews of a Confidential Agent with Members of the German Government (Berlin, April 26 and 27, 1919), Treves, Apr. 30, 1919, General and Special Staffs, M.I.D., RG 165, Folder 124–424 (Records of the War Department); *Foreign Relations: Paris Peace Conference,* 5: 405; Mantoux, *Les Délibérations,* 1: 446–7; Walter Loeb, Bericht über die Unterredung im Amerikanischen-Grossen-Hauptquartier in Trier am 4.

Mai 1919, Frankfurt, May 5, 1919 (Kleine Erwerbungen 328–3, Nachlass Landsberg); Walter Loeb, Bericht über die Unterredung im Amerikanischen-Grossen-Hauptquartier in Trier am 4. Mai 1919, Frankfurt, May 5, 1919, Lfd. Nr. 14 (Nachlass Erzberger); Walter Loeb, Bericht über die Unterredung im Amerikanischen-Grossen-Hauptquartier in Trier am 4. Mai 1919, Frankfurt, 5 May 1919, Geschäftsstelle für die Friedensverhandlungen, P100318 (Politisches Archiv des Auswärtigen Amts; T120, Roll 3909, 9935/E695007–008); Dieckhoff to Haniel, Berlin, May 7, 1919, and Bericht über die Unterredung im Amerikanischen Grossen-Hauptquartier in Trier am 4. Mai 1919, Frankfurt, May 5, 1919, Deutsche Friedensdelegation in Versailles, Pol 13 (Politisches Archiv des Auswärtigen Amts; T120, Roll 2407, 4663/E215433–435). For his argument that Conger operated under Wilson's instructions, see Schwabe, *Deutsche Revolution*, 561–2.

38. Loeb to Erzberger, Frankfurt, May 14, 1919, Walter Loeb, Bericht über die Unterredung mit Oberst Conger am 10. Mai 1919 im Hotel Preussischer Hof in Limburg, Frankfurt, May 14, 1919, Lfd. Nr. 46 (Nachlass Erzberger); Loeb to Bernstorff, Frankfurt, May 14, 1919, and Walter Loeb, Bericht über die Unterredung mit Oberst Conger am 10. Mai 1919 im Hotel Pressischer Hof in Limburg, Frankfurt, May 14, 1919, Deutsche Friedensdelegation in Versailles, Pol 4 (Politisches Archiv des Auswärtigen Amts; T120, Roll 2403, 4662/E212880–889); Loeb to Scheidemann, Frankfurt, May 14, 1919, and Walter Loeb, Bericht über die Unterredung mit Oberst Conger am 10. Mai 1919 im Hotel Preussischer Hof in Limburg, Frankfurt, May 14, 1919, R43I/2 (Akten der Reichskanzlei); *Akten der Reichskanzlei: Kabinett Scheidemann*, 325–30; Walter Loeb, Bericht über die Unterredung mit Oberst Conger am 10. Mai 1919 im Hotel Preussischer Hof in Limburg, Frankfurt, May 14, 1919 (Kleine Erwerbungen 328–3, Nachlass Landsberg); Loeb to [Roediger], Frankfurt, May 14, 1919, Bericht über die Unterredung mit Oberst Conger am 10. Mai 1919 im Hotel Preussischer Hof in Limburg, and Translation, General Headquarters, G-2-B, Advance G.H.Q., General File, Folder T-134 1/2, RG 120, Ser. 753, Box 6022 (Records of the American Expeditionary Forces).

39. Aufzeichnung von Prof. Delbrück, May 18, 1919, and Langwerth to Brockdorff-Rantzau, Berlin, May 18, 1919, Deutsche Friedensdelegation in Versailles, Pol 4 (Politisches Archiv des Auswärtigen Amts; T120, Roll 2403, 4662/E212875–877, E292896–899); Bernstorff to Friedensdelegation, Berlin, May 19, 1919, Deutsche Friedensdelegation in Versailles, Pol 13, Bd. 2 (Politisches Archiv des Auswärtigen Amts; T120, Roll 2407, 4663/F215776–777); Frederick Henrotin, Memorandum, Trier, May 20, 1919, F. Henrotin, Impressions in Germany, Trier, May 20, 1919, A. L. Conger, Memorandum for A. C. of S. G-2 [Nolan]: Report of Trip to Berlin, Treves, May 20, 1919, Interview with Herr Erzberger, Trier, May 20, 1919, and F. Henrotin, Impressions of Interview with Herr Erzberger, Trier, May 20, 1919, General Headquarters, G-2-B, Advance G.H.Q., General File, Folder T-134 1/2, RG 120, Ser. 753, Box 6022 (Records of the American Expeditionary Forces); *Foreign Relations: Paris Peace Conference*, 12: 124–35; Epstein, "Zwischen Compiègne und Versailles," 429–42; Groener, *Lebenserinnerungen*, 496–7; *Akten der Reichskanzlei: Kabinett Scheidemann*, 345–7.

40. Lansing to Wilson, Paris, May 21, 1919, A. L. Conger, Memorandum for A. C. of S. G-2 [Nolan]: Report of Trip to Berlin, Treves, May 20, 1919, A. L. Conger, memorandum, May 20, 1919, Frederick Henrotin, memorandum, Trier, May 20, 1919, Frederick Henrotin, Memorandum for Assistant Chief of Staff: Impressions in Germany, Trier, May 20, 1919, Interview with Herr Erzberger, Trier, May 20, 1919, and Frederick Henrotin, Impressions of Interview with Herr Erzberger, Trier, May 20, 1919, Ser. 5B (Wilson Papers); General Pershing's Diary, May 22, 1919, Box 4–5 (Pershing Papers); *Foreign Relations: Paris Peace Conference*, 11: 182; Epstein, "Zwischen Compiègne und Versailles," 442–3.

41. Janowitz, *Professional Soldier*, viii.

42. Dieckhoff to Albert, Berlin, May 26, 1919, Loeb to Bernstorff, Telegramm aus Frankfurt, May 26, 1919, Loeb to Scheidemann, Frankfurt, May 27, 1919, and Walter Loeb, Bericht über die Unterredung im amerikanischen Hauptquartier am 24. und 25. Mai 1919 in

Trier, Frankfurt, May 27, 1919, R431/3 (Akten der Reichskanzlei); Loeb to Erzberger, Telegamm aus Frankfurt, May 25, 1919, Loeb to Erzberger, Frankfurt, May 27, 1919, and Walter Loeb, Bericht über die Unterredung im amerikanischen Hauptquartier am 24. und 25. Mai 1919 in Trier, Frankfurt, May 27, 1919, Lfd. Nr. 46 (Nachlass Erzberger); Walter Loeb, Bericht über die Unterredung im amerikanischen Hauptquartier am 24. und 25. Mai 1919 in Trier, Frankfurt, May 27, 1919 (Kleine Erwerbungen 328–3, Nachlass Landsberg); Roediger to Loeb, Versailles, May 22, 1919, Bernstorff [Loeb] to Brockdorff-Rantzau, Berlin, May 26, 1919, Bernstorff to Brockdorff-Rantzau, Berlin, May 28, 1919, Loeb to Bernstorff, Telegramm aus Frankfurt, May 26, 1919, Loeb to Brockdorff-Rantzau, Frankfurt, May 27, 1919, and Walter Loeb, Bericht über die Unterredung im amerikanischen Hauptquartier am 24. und 25. Mai 1919 in Trier, Frankfurt, May 27, 1919, Deutsche Friedensdelegation in Versailles, Pol 4 (Politisches Archiv des Auswärtigen Amts; T120, Roll 2403, 4662/E212894–895, Roll 2404, 4662/E212922–926, E212936–941).

43. Loeb to Erzberger, Frankfurt, June 6, 1919, and Walter Loeb, Bericht über die Verhandlung im amerikanischen Hauptquartier in der Nacht vom 3. auf den 4. Juni 1919, Frankfurt, June 6, 1919, Lfd. Nr. 46 (Nachlass Erzberger); Bernstorff to Brockdorff-Rantzau, Berlin, June 8, 1919, Walter Loeb, Bericht über the Verhandlung im amerikanischen Hauptquartier in der Nacht vom 3. auf den 4. Juni 1919, Frankfurt, June 6, 1919, Brockdorff-Rantzau to Bernstorff, Versailles, June 10, 1919, Brockdorff-Rantzau to Langwerth, Versailles, June 10, 1919, Bernstorff and Langwerth to Friedensdelegation, Weimar, June 13, 1919, Loeb to Brockdorff-Rantzau, Frankfurt, June 6, 1919, Walter Loeb, Bericht über die Verhandlung im amerikanischen Hauptquartier in der Nacht vom 3. auf den 4. Juni 1919, Frankfurt, June 6, 1919, Romberg, Aufzeichnung, Berlin, June 12, 1919, and Loeb to Bernstorff, Frankfurt, June 14, 1919, Deutsche Friedensdelegation in Versailles, Pol 4 (Politisches Archiv des Auswärtigen Amts; T120, Roll 2404, 4662/E212983–994, E213006, E213009, E213016017, E213054); Bernstorff to Loeb, June 8, 1919, and Loeb to Bernstorff, Frankfurt, June 6, 1919, Geschäftsstelle für Friedensverhandlungen, P100318 (Politisches Archiv des Auswärtigen Amts; T120, Roll 3909, 9935/E695003, E695006); Erzberger to Langwerth, Berlin, June 13, 1919, Weltkrieg 30 Geh., Bd. I (Politisches Archiv des Auswärtigen Amts; T120, Roll 2063, 4099/D931228); Loeb to Scheidemann, Frankfurt, June 6, 1919, Walter Loeb, Bericht über die Verhandlung im amerikanischen Hauptquartier in der Nacht vom 3. auf den 4. Juni 1919, Frankfurt, June 6, 1919, and Rhomberg to Langwerth, Berlin, June 12, 1919, R431/4 (Akten der Reichskanzlei); Romberg, Aufzeichnung, Berlin, June 12, 1919, R431/8 (Akten der Reichskanzlei); *Akten der Reichskanzki: Kabinett Scheidemann,* 427–31; Walter Loeb, Bericht über die Verhandlung irn amerikanischen Hauptquartier in der Nacht vom 3. auf den 4. Juni 1919, Frankfurt, June 6, 1919 (Kleine Erwerbungen 328–3, Nachlass Landsberg); Groener, *Lebenserinnerungen,* 497–9.

44. Baker to Pershing, Washington, May 26, 1917, in John J. Pershing, *My Experiences in the World War,* 2 vols. (New York: Harper and Row, 1931), 1: 38–9, and Frederick Palmer, *Newton D. Baker, America at War,* 2 vols. (New York: Dodd, Mead, 1931), 1: 170–2; Confidential Cablegrams From GHQ, AEF, to the War Department, 1918–1919, and Confidential Cablegrams From the War Department to GHQ AEF, 1918–1919, RG 120 (Records of the American Expeditionary Forces; M930, Rolls 7 and 18); Historical Division, Department of the Army, *United States Army in the World War, 1917–1919: Reports of Commander-in-Chief. A.E.F., Staff Sections and Services,* 17 vols. (Washington, DC: Center of Military History, U.S. Army, 1948), 13: 10–11.

45. Loeb to Ebert, Frankfurt, Aug. 5, 1919, Weltkrieg 30 Geh., Bd. I (Politisches Archiv des Auswärtigen Amts; T120, Roll 2063, 4099/D931232–233); General Pershing's Diary, Dec. 20, 1918, Jan. 16–17, Feb. 10–13, 22–23, March 22–23, Apr. 17–18 and 23, May 4 and 22, 1919, Box 4–5 (Pershing Papers).

46. Richard D. Challener, *Admirals, Generals, and American Foreign Policy, 1898–1914* (Princeton, NJ: Princeton University Press, 1973), 364–7; Pershing, *My Experiences,* 1: 37.

For a perceptive discussion of the wartime relations between Wilson and Pershing, see Ernest R. May, *The Ultimate Decision: The President as Commander in Chief* (New York: G. Braziller, 1960), 109–31. For critical information on the wartime activities of the Military Intelligence Division within the United States, see Joan M. Jensen, *The Price of Vigilance* (Chicago: Rand McNally, 1968).

Chapter 6   Wilson, the Republicans, and French Security after World War I

1. Denna Frank Fleming, *The United States and the League of Nations: 1918–1920* (New York: G. P. Putnam, 1932); W. Stull Holt, *Treaties Defeated by the Senate* (Baltimore, MD: Johns Hopkins University Press, 1933), 249–308; Ruhl J. Bartlett, *The League to Enforce Peace* (Chapel Hill: University of North Carolina Press, 1944); Thomas A. Bailey, *Woodrow Wilson and the Great Betrayal* (New York: Macmillan, 1945); Selig Adler, *The Isolationist Impulse: Its Twentieth-Century Reaction* (New York: Free Press, 1957), 15–111; John Chalmers Vinson, *Referendum for Isolation: Defeat of Article Ten of the League of Nations Covenant* (Athens: University of Georgia Press, 1961); Arno J. Mayer, *Politics and Diplomacy of Peacemaking: Containment and Counterrevolution at Versailles, 1918–1919* (New York: Alfred A. Knopf, 1967), 167.

2. John Milton Cooper, Jr., *The Vanity of Power: American Isolationism and the First World War, 1914–1917* (Westport, CT: Greenwood Press, 1969).

3. Warren F. Kuehl, *Seeking World Order: The United States and International Organization to 1920* (Nashville, TN: Vanderbilt University Press, 1969); Sondra R. Herman, *Eleven Against War: Studies in American Internationalist Thought, 1898–1921* (Stanford, CA: Hoover Institution Press, 1969), 1–85, 179–229.

4. John A. Garraty, *Henry Cabot Lodge: A Biography* (New York: Alfred A. Knopf, 1953), 342–82; Karl Schriftgiesser, *The Gentleman from Massachusetts: Henry Cabot Lodge* (Boston: Little, Brown, 1944), 299–351; Philip C. Jessup, *Elihu Root: 1905–1937* (New York: Dodd, Mead, 1938), 372–417; Henry F. Pringle, *The Life and Times of William Howard Taft: A Biography*, 2 vols. (New York: Farrar and Rinehart, 1939), 2: 926–50; Allan Nevins, *Henry White: Thirty Years of American Diplomacy* (New York: Harper and Brothers, 1930), 350–478.

5. Memorandum [Dec. 2, 1918], Henry Cabot Lodge Papers (Massachusetts Historical Society, Boston); U.S. Senate, *Congressional Record,* 65 Congress, 3 Session, 57: 724–8 (Dec. 21, 1918).

6. Henry L. Stimson to Will H. Hays, Feb. 18, 1919, Hays to Ernest Bross, Feb. 22, 1919, Will H. Hays Papers (Indiana State Library, Indianapolis); Stimson to Elihu Root, March 19, 1919, Hays to Root, March 20, 24, 1919, Elihu Root Papers (Manuscript Division, Library of Congress, Washington, DC).

7. Root to Hays, March 29, 1919, Root to Moorfield Storey, March 20, 1919, Root Papers.

8. Henry Cabot Lodge to Root, April 29, 1919, Root to Lodge, June 19, July 24, 1919, Root Papers; Root to Lodge, June 19, July 24, 1919, Lodge to W. S. Bigelow, June 23, 26, 1919, Lodge Papers.

9. *Congressional Record,* 66 Cong., 1 Sess., 58: 3310–12 (July 29, 1919); David Hunter Miller, *My Diary at the Conference of Paris,* 21 vols. (New York: Appeal Printing Company, 1924), 1: 293–4; newspaper interview, July 10, 1919, Woodrow Wilson Papers (Manuscript Division, Library of Congress, Washington, DC). For an account of the French security treaties with Great Britain and the United States, see Louis A. R. Yates, *United States and French Security: 1917–1921* (New York: Twayne Publishers, 1957).

10. Albert J. Beveridge to Lodge, Aug. 9, 1919, Lodge Papers; Lodge to Beveridge, Aug. 11, 1919, Albert J. Beveridge Papers (Manuscript Division, Library of Congress, Washington, DC).

11. Ralph A. Stone includes in this group Philander C. Knox, Frank B. Brandegee, Albert B. Fall, Joseph Medill McCormick, George H. Moses, Miles Poindexter, Lawrence Y.

Sherman, Bert M. Fernald, and Charles S. Thomas. Ralph A. Stone, "The Irreconcilables' Alternatives to the League of Nations," *Mid-America* 49 (July 1967): 163–73; Ralph Stone, *The Irreconcilables: The Fight against the League of Nations* (Lexington: University Press of Kentucky, 1970), 26–7, 41, 44–8, 55, 180.

12. *Congressional Record,* 65 Cong., 3 Sess., 57: 603–6 (Dec. 18, 1918), 4687–94 (March 1, 1919); ibid., 66 Cong., 1 Sess., 58: 894 (June 10, 1919).

13. *Congressional Record,* 66 Cong., 1 Sess., 58: 8777 (Nov. 19, 1919), 3075–83 (July 24, 1919), 3230–6 (July 28, 1919), 4028–9 (Aug. 20, 1919).

14. *Congressional Record,* 66 Cong., 1 Sess., 58: 330–1 (May 28, 1919), 4053 (Aug. 20, 1919); Stone, "The Irreconcilables' Alternatives to the League of Nations," 168.

15. *Congressional Record,* 66 Cong., 1 Sess., 58: 508 (June 2, 1919); Hiram W. Johnson to Beveridge, Nov. 24, 1919, Beveridge Papers.

16. Beveridge to William E Borah, April 19, Nov. 24, 1919, William E. Borah Papers (Manuscript Division, Library of Congress, Washington, DC); Borah to Beveridge, April 22, Nov. 28, 1919, Beveridge Papers.

17. *Congressional Record,* 66 Cong., 1 Sess., 58: 3143–4 (July 25, 1919).

18. James M. Beck to Borah, July 22, 1919, Borah to Beck, July 23, 1919, Borah Papers.

19. Knox to Beveridge, June 18, 1919, Beveridge Papers and Philander C. Knox Papers (Manuscript Division, Library of Congress, Washington, DC).

20. Lodge to Henry White, May 20, 1919, Lodge Papers.

21. Lodge to William Astor Chanler, June 23, 1919, Oct. 14, 1919, Lodge Papers.

22. Root to Lodge, Nov. 1, 1919, Lodge Papers.

23. Lodge to Root, Nov. 3, 1919, Root Papers.

24. Lodge to H. St. George Tucker, Dec. 17, 1919, Lodge Papers. See also Lodge to White, Aug. 19, 1919, Lodge Papers.

25. Brandegee to Beveridge, Dec. 9, 1919, Beveridge Papers. The observations of Lodge and Brandegee were accurate; no references to any attempts by the administration to gain support for the French security treaty appear in the papers of Woodrow Wilson, Joseph P. Tumulty, or Gilbert M. Hitchcock (Manuscript Division, Library of Congress, Washington, DC).

26. Henry Cabot Lodge, *The Senate and the League of Nations* (New York: Charles Scribner's Sons, 1925), 156.

27. Lodge to White, Jan. 3, 1922, Henry White Papers (Manuscript Division, Library of Congress, Washington, DC).

28. White to Root, March 7, 19, 1919, White to Lodge, March 19, April 29, 1919, Root Papers; White to Lodge, April 29, 1919, Lodge Papers.

29. William Howard Taft to LeBaron B. Colt, July 17, 1919, Taft to Hays, July 17, 20, 1919, Taft to William H. Short, July 18, 1919, William Howard Taft Papers (Manuscript Division, Library of Congress, Washington, DC). No references to the French security treaty appear in the Frank B. Kellogg Papers (Minnesota Historical Society, St. Paul).

30. George F. Kennan, *American Diplomacy, 1900–1950* (Chicago: University of Chicago Press, 1951); Hans J. Morgenthau, *In Defense of the National Interest: A Critical Examination of American Foreign Policy* (New York: Alfred A. Knopf, 1951); Robert Endicott Osgood, *Ideals and Self-Interest in America's Foreign Relations: The Great Transformation of the Twentieth Century* (Chicago: University of Chicago Press, 1953).

Chapter 7   The United States and the Weimar Republic: America's
Response to the German Problem

1. Ray Stannard Baker and William E. Dodd, eds., *The Public Papers of Woodrow Wilson* (New York: Harper and Brothers, 1925–7), 5: 257.

2. David Hunter Miller, *The Drafting of the Covenant,* 2 vols. (New York: G. P. Putnam's Sons, 1928), 2: 727, 735. Most historians have emphasized Article 10; see, for example,

John Chalmers Vinson, *Referendum for Isolation: Defeat of Article Ten of the League of Nations Covenant* (Athens: University of Georgia Press, 1961). Some also have noted Article 19; see especially Edward H. Buehrig, "Woodrow Wilson and Collective Security," in Edward H. Buehrig, ed., *Wilson's Foreign Policy in Perspective* (Bloomington: Indiana University Press, 1957), 34–60.

3. Paul Mantoux, *Paris Peace Conference 1919: Proceedings of the Council of Four, March 24–April 18* (Genève: Institut universitaire de hautes études internationales, 1964), 45. For evidence of Wilson's misunderstanding of French public opinion, see George Bernard Noble, *Policies and Opinions at Paris, 1919: Wilsonian Diplomacy, the Versailles Peace, and French Public Opinion* (New York: Macmillan, 1935).

4. U.S. Department of State, *Papers Relating to the Foreign Relations of the United States: The Paris Peace Conference, 1919,* 13 vols. (Washington, DC: Government Printing Office, 1942–7), 4: 543–7.

5. Lloyd E. Ambrosius, "Wilson's League of Nations," *Maryland Historical Magazine* 65 (Winter 1970): 369–93.

6. W. R. Gherardi to American Commission to Negotiate Peace, Berlin, February 8, 1919, Department of State, Record Group 256, File No. 184.01202/18, National Archives, Washington, DC. See also D. K. Buse, "Ebert and the German Crisis, 1917–1920," *Central European History* 5 (September 1972): 234–55; Klaus Schwabe, "Woodrow Wilson and Germany's Membership in the League of Nations, 1918–19," *Central European History* 8 (March 1975): 3–22.

7. Dresel to Joseph Grew, Berlin, April 23, 1919, Department of State, RG 256, #189.013102/4, National Archives; Sally Marks and Denis Dulude, "German–American Relations, 1918–1921," *Mid-America* 53 (October 1971): 211–26.

8. Charles B. Dyar to A.C.N.P., Berlin, May 10, 1919, Department of State, RG 256, #184.013202/4, National Archives.

9. Alma Luckau, *The German Delegation at the Paris Peace Conference* (New York: Columbia University Press, 1941); Otto-Ernst Schüddekopf, "German Foreign Policy between Compiègne and Versailles," *Journal of Contemporary History* 4 (April 1969): 481–97; Peter Berg, "Deutschland und Amerika, 1918–1929: Über das deutsche Amerikabild der zwanziger Jahre," *Historische Studien* 385 (Lübeck and Hamburg: Matthiesen Verlag, 1963): 9–47; Ernst Fraenkel, "Das deutsche Wilsonbild," *Jahrbuch für Amerikastudien* 5 (1960): 66–120; Klaus Schwabe, *Deutsche Revolution und Wilson-Frieden: Die amerikanische und deutsche Friedensstrategie zwischen Ideologie und Machtpolitik, 1918/19* (Düsseldorf: Droste Verlag, 1971).

10. Lloyd E. Ambrosius, "The United States and the Weimar Republic, 1918–1923: From the Armistice to the Ruhr Occupation" (Ph.D. dissertation, University of Illinois, Urbana, 1967), 134–218; Lloyd E. Ambrosius, "Wilson, Clemenceau, and the German Problem at the Paris Peace Conference of 1919," *Rocky Mountain Social Science Journal* 12 (April 1975): 69–79.

11. U.S. Senate, *Congressional Record,* 66 Congress, 1 Session, 58: 2336–9 (July 10, 1919).

12. W. M. Jordan, *Great Britain, France and the German Problem, 1918–1939: A Study of Anglo-French Relations in the Making and Maintenance of the Versailles Settlement* (London: Oxford University Press, 1943); Arnold Wolfers, *Britain and France between Two Wars: Conflicting Strategies of Peace from Versailles to World War II* (New York: Harcourt, Brace, 1940); Martin Gilbert, *The Roots of Appeasement* (New York: New American Library, 1966).

13. Ambrosius, "The United States and the Weimar Republic," 236–59. For accounts of the abortive French security treaties with Great Britain and the United States, see J. Paul Selsam, *The Attempts to Form an Anglo-French Alliance, 1919–1924* (Philadelphia: University of Pennsylvania Press, 1936); Louis A. R. Yates, *United States and French Security, 1917–1921* (New York: Twayne Publishers, 1957); Lloyd E. Ambrosius, "Wilson, the Republicans, and French Security after World War I," *Journal of American History* 59 (September 1972): 341–52.

14. Kurt and Sarah Wimer, "The Harding Administration, the League of Nations, and the Separate Peace Treaty," *Review of Politics* 29 (January 1967): 13–24; Robert K. Murray, *The Harding Era: Warren G. Harding and His Administration* (Minneapolis: University of Minnesota Press, 1969), 135–40.

15. Wilson to Edward M. House, Washington, October 31, 1918, U.S. Department of State, *Papers Relating to the Foreign Relations of the United States, 1918,* Supplement 1, *The World War* (Washington, DC: Government Printing Office, 1933), 1: 427–8.

16. Ronald W. Pruessen, "John Foster Dulles and Reparations at the Paris Peace Conference, 1919: Early Patterns of a Life," *Perspectives in American History* 8 (1974): 381–410; Philip Mason Burnett, *Reparation at the Paris Peace Conference: From the Standpoint of the American Delegation* (New York: Columbia University Press, 1940), 1: 66–70, 142–57.

17. John Maynard Keynes, *The Economic Consequences of the Peace* (New York:. Harcourt, Brace, and Howe, 1920); John Maynard Keynes, *A Revision of the Treaty: Being a Sequel to the Economic Consequences of the Peace* (New York: Harcourt, Brace, 1922); Sally Marks, "Reparations Reconsidered: A Reminder," *Central European History* 2 (December 1969): 356–65; David Felix, "Reparations Reconsidered with a Vengeance," *Central European History* 4 (June 1971): 171–9; Sally Marks, "Reparations Reconsidered: A Rejoinder," *Central European History* 5 (December 1972): 358–61; David Felix, *Walther Rathenau and the Weimar Republic: The Politics of Reparations* (Baltimore: Johns Hopkins Press, 1971).

18. Hughes to Myron T. Herrick, Washington, October 17, 1922, Department of State, RG 59, #462.00R296/1, National Archives, Washington, DC.

19. Keith L. Nelson, *Victors Divided: America and the Allies in Germany, 1918–1923* (Berkeley: University of California Press, 1975); Ambrosius, "The United States and the Weimar Republic," 329–77, 397–411; Jolyon P. Girard, "Congress and Presidential Military Policy: The Occupation of Germany," *Mid-America* 56 (October 1974): 211–20; Royal J. Schmidt, *Versailles and the Ruhr: Seedbed of World War II* (The Hague: Martinus Nijhoff, 1968).

20. Joan Hoff Wilson, *American Business and Foreign Policy, 1920–1933* (Lexington: University Press of Kentucky, 1971), x. On American isolationism, see Selig Adler, *The Isolationist Impulse: Its Twentieth-Century Reaction* (New York: Free Press, 1957); Alexander DeConde, "On Twentieth-Century Isolationism," in Alexander DeConde, ed., *Isolation and Security: Ideas and Interests in Twentieth-Century American Foreign Policy* (Durham, NC: Duke University Press, 1957), 3–32; Klaus Schwabe, "Der amerikanische Isolationismus im 20. Jahrhundert: Legende und Wirklichkeit," *Frankfurter Historische Vorträge* 1 (Wiesbaden: Franz Steiner Verlag, 1975).

21. Wilson, *American Business and Foreign Policy,* 65–100, 123–56; Harold G. Moulton and Leo Pasvolsky, *War Debts and World Prosperity* (New York: Brookings Institution, 1932); Dieter Bruno Gescher, *Die Vereinigten Staaten von Nordamerika und die Reparationen, 1920–1924* (Bonn: Ludwig Rohrscheid Verlag, 1956).

22. Howard H. Quint and Robert H. Ferrell, eds., *The Talkative President: The Off-the-Record Press Conferences of Calvin Coolidge* (Amherst: University of Massachusetts Press, 1964), 181, 184–5.

23. Kellogg to Norman Armour, Washington, October 31, 1928, U.S. Department of State, *Papers Relating to the Foreign Relations of the United States, 1928* (Washington, DC: Government Printing Office, 1943), 2: 874.

24. Hughes to Coolidge, November 8, 1923, in David J. Danelski and Joseph S. Tulchin, eds., *The Autobiographical Notes of Charles Evans Hughes* (Cambridge, MA: Harvard University Press, 1973), 256.

25. Carl P. Parrini, *Heir to Empire: United States Economic Diplomacy* (Pittsburgh, PA: University of Pittsburgh Press, 1969), 212–47; Melvyn P. Leffler, "The Struggle for Stability: American Policy toward France, 1921–1933" (Ph.D. dissertation, Ohio State University, 1972), 278–355.

26. William Appleman Williams, "The Legend of Isolationism in the 1920's," *Science and Society* (Winter 1954), reprinted in William Appleman Williams, *History as a Way of*

Learning (New York: New Viewpoints, 1973), 115–34; William Appleman Williams, *The Tragedy of American Diplomacy* (New York: Dell Pub. Co., 1962), 104–59, William Appleman Williams, "A Note on American Foreign Policy in Europe in the Nineteen Twenties," *Science and Society* 22 (Winter 1958): 1–20.

27. Werner Link, *Die amerikanische Stabilisierungspolitik in Deutschland, 1921–32* (Düsseldorf: Droste Verlag, 1970).

28. Lionel Kochan, *Russia and the Weimar Republic* (Cambridge, UK: Bowes and Bowes, 1954); Josef Korbel, *Poland between East and West: Soviet and German Diplomacy toward Poland, 1919–1933* (Princeton, NJ: Princeton University Press, 1963); Piotr S. Wandycz, *France and Her Eastern Allies, 1919–1925: French-Czechoslovak-Polish Relations from the Paris Peace Conference to Locarno* (Minneapolis: University of Minnesota Press, 1962); Jon Jacobson, *Locarno Diplomacy: Germany and the West, 1925–1929* (Princeton, NJ: Princeton University Press, 1972); Gaines Post, Jr., *The Civil-Military Fabric of Weimar Foreign Policy* (Princeton, NJ: Princeton University Press, 1973), 3–262; F. L. Carsten, *The Reichswehr and Politics, 1918–1933* (Berkeley: University of California Press, 1973), 3–308; Henry L. Bretton, *Stresemann and the Revision of Versailles: A Fight for Reason* (Stanford, CA: Stanford University Press, 1953); Hans W. Gatzke, *Stresemann and the Rearmament of Germany* (Baltimore, MD: Johns Hopkins Press, 1954); Henry Ashby Turner, Jr., *Stresemann and the Politics of the Weimar Republic* (Princeton, NJ: Princeton University Press, 1963); Robert Gottwald, *Die deutsch-amerikanischen Beziehungen in der Ära Stresemann* (Berlin: Colloquium Verlag, 1965).

29. Robert H. Ferrell, *Peace in Their Time: The Origins of the Kellogg-Briand Pact* (New Haven, CT: Yale University Press, 1952). For contrary arguments that Republican policy was realistic, see L. Ethan Ellis, *Republican Foreign Policy, 1921–1933* (New Brunswick, NJ: Rutgers University Press, 1968), and Melvyn P. Leffler, "Political Isolationism, Economic Expansionism, or Diplomatic Realism: American Policy toward Western Europe, 1921–1933," *Perspectives in American History* 8 (1974): 411–61.

30. Hoover to Wilson, April 11, 1919, Herbert Hoover, *The Ordeal of Woodrow Wilson* (London: Museum Press Ltd., 1958), 202.

31. Hoover, *Ordeal,* 267.

32. Hoover, *Ordeal,* 233–52.

33. Stimson Diary, March 30, 1931, quoted in Jefferson Davis Futch, "The United States and the Fall of the Weimar Republic: German–American Relations, 1930–1933" (Ph.D. dissertation, Johns Hopkins University, 1962), 77–8.

34. Futch, "The United States and the Fall of the Weimar Republic," 1–213; Edward W. Bennett, *Germany and the Diplomacy of the Financial Crisis, 1931* (Cambridge, MA: Harvard University Press, 1962); Bernard V. Burke, "American Economic Diplomacy and the Weimar Republic," *Mid-America* 54 (October 1972): 211–33; F. G. Stambrook, "The German–Austrian Customs Union Project of 1931: A Study of German Methods and Motives," *Journal of Central European Affairs* 21 (April 1961): 15–44; Stanley Suval, *The Anschluss Question in the Weimar Era: A Study of Nationalism in Germany and Austria, 1919–1932* (Baltimore, MD: Johns Hopkins University Press, 1974), 75–165; Charles P. Kindleberger, *The World in Depression, 1929–1939* (Berkeley: University of California Press, 1973), 128–98; Robert H. Ferrell, *American Diplomacy in the Great Depression: Hoover-Stimson Foreign Policy, 1929–1933* (New Haven, CT: Yale University Press, 1957), 106–19; Louis P. Lochner, *Herbert Hoover and Germany* (New York: Macmillan, 1960), 68–131; Leffler, "The Struggle for Stability," 356–92.

35. F. P. Walters, *A History of the League of Nations* (London: Oxford University Press, 1952), 500–516; Ferrell, *American Diplomacy in the Great Depression,* 194–214; Post, *The Civil-Military Fabric of Weimar Foreign Policy,* 265–358; Carsten, *The Reichswehr and Politics,* 309–405; Leffler, "The Struggle for Stability," 614–31.

36. Hugh R. Wilson, *Diplomat Between Wars* (New York: Longmans, Green, 1941); Hugh R. Wilson, Jr., *A Career Diplomat, The Third Chapter: The Third Reich* (New York: Vantage Press, 1960).

37. William Edward Dodd, *Woodrow Wilson, 1918–1920 and the World Situation, 1938* [Address before the Democratic Women's Luncheon Club of Philadelphia, December 28, 1938] (Philadelphia, 1938); Arnold Offner, *American Appeasement: United States Foreign Policy and Germany, 1933–1938* (Cambridge, MA: Harvard University Press, 1969); Robert Dallek, *Democrat and Diplomat: The Life of William E. Dodd* (New York: Oxford University Press, 1968), 171–317.

38. Robert A. Divine, *Second Chance: The Triumph of Internationalism in America during World War II* (New York: Atheneum, 1967); Bruce Kuklick, "History as a Way of Learning," *American Quarterly* 22 (Fall 1970): 609–28.

39. William E. Dodd, *Woodrow Wilson and His Work* (Garden City, NY: Doubleday, Page, 1920); Ray Stannard Baker, *Woodrow Wilson and World Settlement*, 3 vols. (Garden City, NY: Doubleday, Page, 1922); Paul Birdsall, *Versailles Twenty Years After* (New York: Reynal and Hitchcock, 1941); Arthur S. Link, *Wilson the Diplomatist: A Look at His Major Foreign Policies* (Baltimore, MD: Johns Hopkins Press, 1957); Seth P. Tillman, *Anglo-American Relations at the Paris Peace Conference of 1919* (Princeton, NJ: Princeton University Press, 1961).

40. Warren I. Cohen, *The American Revisionists: The Lessons of Intervention in World War I* (Chicago: University of Chicago Press, 1967), 65–6; Harry Elmer Barnes, "Woodrow Wilson," *American Mercury* 1 (April 1924): 479–90; Selig Adler, "The War-Guilt Question and American Disillusionment, 1918–1928," *Journal of Modern History* 23 (March 1951): 1–28.

41. Arno J. Mayer, *Political Origins of the New Diplomacy, 1917–1918* (New Haven, CT: Yale University Press, 1959); Arno J. Mayer, *Politics and Diplomacy of Peacemaking: Containment and Counterrevolution at Versailles, 1918–1919* (New York: Alfred A. Knopf, 1967); N. Gordon Levin, Jr., *Woodrow Wilson and World Politics: America's Response to War and Revolution* (New York: Oxford University Press, 1968).

42. Schwabe, *Deutsche Revolution und Wilson-Frieden*.

Map of Germany (1919–1923) that appears between Part II and Part III: U.S. Department of State, *Papers Relating to the Foreign Relations of the United States: Paris Peace Conference, 1919* (Washington, D.C.: U.S. Government Printing Office, 1947), Volume XIII (after page 1018). The map was compiled and drawn in the Department of State, Division of Geography and Cartography in February 1945.

Chapter 8   Ethnic Politics and German–American Relations after World War I: The Fight over the Versailles Treaty in the United States

1. Ray Stannard Baker and William E. Dodd, eds. *The Public Papers of Woodrow Wilson*, 6 vols. (New York: Harper and Brothers, 1925–7), 6: 78–9, 82–3, 368, 389, 399–400.

2. George Creel, *The War, the World, and Wilson* (New York: Harper and Brothers, 1920), 201–12, 328–46, 362.

3. Joseph P. Tumulty, *Woodrow Wilson as I Know Him* (Garden City, NY: Doubleday, Page, 1921), 214, 344–9; John F. Duff, "German–Americans and the Peace, 1918–1920," *American Jewish Historical Quarterly* 59 (June 1970): 439–40.

4. William E. Dodd, *Woodrow Wilson and His Work* (Garden City, NY: Doubleday, Page, 1920), 321–5. See also Denna Frank Fleming, *The United States and the League of Nations, 1918–1920* (New York: G. P. Putnam, 1932), 467–8.

5. Wiseman to Eric Drummond, May 30, 1918; Wiseman, "The Attitude of the United States and of President Wilson towards the Peace Conference," [c. 20 October 1918], W. B. Fowler, *British–American Relations, 1917–1918: The Role of Sir William Wiseman* (Princeton, NJ: Princeton University Press, 1969), 275, 292; *The Gaelic American* (New York), June 1, 1918, 1, 5; Great Britain, *Documents Relative to the Sinn Fein Movement* (London: His Majesty's Stationery Office, 1921), Cmd. 1108.

6. Wiseman to Ian Malcolm, July 1, 1919, to Arthur Balfour, July 18, 1919, E. L. Woodward and Rohan Butler, eds., *Documents on British Foreign Policy, 1919–1939,* First Series (London: His Majesty's Stationery Office, 1954), 5: 980–5.

7. Earl Curzon to Grey, Sept. 9, 1919; Grey to Curzon, Oct. 5, 1919, *Documents on British Foreign Policy,* 5: 977, 1000, 1003–4. Grey to Lloyd George, Oct. 5, 1919; Geddes to Lloyd George, June 8, 1920; Geddes to Curzon, June 29, 1920, David Lloyd George Papers (Beaverbrook Library, London), F/60/3/7, F/60/4/2, and 4.

8. *Viereck's The American Monthly* (New York), 11: Nov. 1919, 78, 83; 12: March 1920, 5–6, 20; May 1920, 69–70; June 1920, 101–2; July 1920, 133–4; Aug. 1920, 165; Sept. 1920, 197–9, 210; Dec. 1920, 269–97; Jeremiah A. O'Leary to Viereck, Dec. 18, 1919, George Sylvester Viereck Papers (Special Collections Department, University of Iowa Libraries, Iowa City), Box 1. See also Niel M. Johnson, *George Sylvester Viereck: German–American Propagandist* (Urbana: University of Illinois Press, 1972), 57–108; Joan M. Jensen, *The Price of Vigilance* (Chicago: Rand McNally, 1968), 174–5, 293; Carl Wittke, *German–Americans and the World War* (Columbus: Ohio State Archeological and Historical Society, 1936), 197–209; Wittke, *The German-Language Press in America* (Lexington: University of Kentucky Press, 1957), 262–78; Frederick C. Luebke, *Bonds of Loyalty: German–Americans and World War I* (DeKalb: Northern Illinois University Press, 1974), 309–31.

9. John Sharp Williams to Viereck, July 9, 1917, March 29, 1921, Viereck Papers, Box 1; George Coleman Osborn, *John Sharp Williams: Planter-Statesman of the Deep South* (Baton Rouge: Louisiana State University Press, 1943), 330–80.

10. *The Gaelic American* (New York), Jan. 12, 1918, 4; Oct. 5, 1918, 4; Oct. 19, 1918, 4; Dec. 21, 1918, 4; Jan. 18, 1919, 4; Feb. 22, 1919, 1, 4; March 8, 1919, 4; March 15, 1919, 1, 7; Apr. 5, 1919, 3, 11; Apr. 12, 1919, 1; Apr. 19, 1919, 10; Apr. 26, 1919, 2, 4; May 3, 1919, 4; May 10, 1919, 2, 4; May 17, 1919, 4; May 24, 1919, 4; May 31, 1919, 4; June 14, 1919, 1. Diarmuid Lynch to Friends of Irish Freedom, Nov. 19, 1920, Joseph McGarrity Papers (National Library of Ireland, Dublin, Ms. 17, 523); Rossa F. Downing to Daniel F. Cohalan, July 24, 1919, John Devoy Papers (National Library of Ireland, Dublin, Ms. 18, 007). See also Ralph Stone, *The Irreconcilables: The Fight against the League of Nations* (Lexington: University Press of Kentucky, 1970), 102–7; Robert James Maddox, *William E. Borah and American Foreign Policy* (Baton Rouge: Louisiana State University Press, 1969), 58–9.

11. *The Gaelic American* (New York), Aug. 30, 1919, 4; Sept. 13, 1919, 4; Nov. 29, 1919, 1; Dec. 6, 1919, 4; Jan. 17, 1920, 4; Feb. 14, 1920, 4; March 27, 1920, 4; William E. Borah to Daniel F. Cohalan, Nov. 22, 1919, William E. Borah Papers (Library of Congress, Washington, DC), Box 551.

12. Louis L. Gerson, *The Hyphenate in Recent American Politics and Diplomacy* (Lawrence: University of Kansas Press, 1964), 47–108.

13. Thomas A. Bailey, *Woodrow Wilson and the Great Betrayal* (New York: Macmillan, 1945), 22–9; Selig Adler, *The Isolationist Impulse: Its Twentieth Century Reaction* (New York: Free Press, 1957), 73–89; Selig Adler, *The Uncertain Giant: American Foreign Policy between the Wars, 1921–1941* (New York: Macmillan, 1965), 4–13; Julius W. Pratt, *Challenge and Rejection: The United States and World Leadership, 1900–1921* (New York: Macmillan, 1967), 197–8; Arthur S. Link, *Wilson the Diplomatist: A Look at His Major Foreign Policies* (Baltimore, MD: Johns Hopkins Press, 1957), 133–4; Link, *Woodrow Wilson: Revolution, War, and Peace* (Arlington Heights, IL: AHM Publishing Corporation, 1979), 108.

14. Charles Callan Tansill, *America and the Fight for Irish Freedom: 1866–1922* (New York: Devin-Adair, 1957), 284–339; John Patrick Buckley, *The New York Irish: Their View of American Foreign Policy, 1914–1921* (New York: Arno Press, 1976), 189–282; Joseph Edward Cuddy, *Irish–America and National Isolationism, 1914–1920* (New York: Arno Press, 1976), 158–245; Lawrence J. McCaffrey, *The Irish Diaspora in America* (Bloomington: Indiana University Press, 1976), 135–7; Donald Harman Akenson, *The United States and Ireland* (Cambridge, MA: Harvard University Press, 1973), 43–5.

15. John B. Duff, "The Versailles Treaty and the Irish–Americans," *Journal of American History* 15 (Dec. 1968): 582–98; Alan J. Ward, *Ireland and Anglo-American Relations, 1899–1921* (London: Wiedenfeld and Nicholson, 1969), 166–213; Joseph P. O'Grady, *The Immigrants' Influence on Wilson's Peace Policies* (Lexington: University Press of Kentucky, 1967). The New Left historians, although focusing on the domestic origins of foreign policy, have ignored ethnic politics while concentrating on political economy; see William Appleman Williams, *The Tragedy of American Diplomacy* (New York: Dell Publishing Company, 1962), 86–159; Arno J. Mayer, *Politics and Diplomacy of Peacemaking: Containment and Counterrevolution at Versailles, 1918–1919* (New York: Alfred A. Knopf, 1967), 875–93; N. Gordon Levin, Jr., *Woodrow Wilson and World Politics: America's Response to War and Revolution* (New York: Oxford University Press, 1968), 253–60.

16. Henry Cabot Lodge to Samuel P. Nobbs, Dec. 16, 1919, Henry Cabot Lodge Papers (Massachusetts Historical Society, Boston), File 1919, Peace, League, Political, I–Z.

17. *The American Monthly,* 12: Oct. 1920, 229–34, 238; Nov. 1920, 261–2, 270; Dec. 1920, 293–4; Randolph C. Downes, *The Rise of Warren Gamaliel Harding, 1865–1920* (Columbus: Ohio State University Press, 1970), 477–85; James M. Cox, *Journey Through My Years* (New York: Simon and Schuster, 1946), 225–87; Wesley M. Bagby, *The Road to Normalcy: The Presidential Campaign and Election of 1920* (Baltimore, MD: Johns Hopkins University Press, 1962), 153–5. The 1920 election posed a dilemma for the Devoy-Cohalan faction of Irish–Americans: The Democratic party endorsed Wilson and the League of Nations, and Harding refused to court its support; see Devoy to Cohalan, July 4, 1920, Oct. 31, 1920, John Devoy-D. F. Cohalan Letters (National Library of Ireland, Dublin, Ms. 15,416); *The Gaelic American* (New York), Oct. 9, 1920, 4; Oct. 30, 1920, 4; Nov. 13, 1920, 4.

18. *The Gaelic American* (New York), July 26, 1919, 4; Aug. 2, 1919, 4; Oct. 18, 1919, 1; Oct. 25, 1919, 1; Oct. 25, 1919, 4; Nov. 1, 1919, 4; Nov. 29, 1919, 4; Feb. 21, 1920, 4; Mar. 27, 1920, 4.

19. Patrick McCartan to William Maloney, March 10, 1919, Patrick McCartan Papers (National Library of Ireland, Dublin, Ms. 17,675); McCartan to Harry [Boland], Oct. 4, 1919; McCartan to Arthur Griffith, Oct. 29, 1919; McCartan to Michael J. Gallagher, Aug. 7, 1920 (McCartan Papers, Ms. 17,677); McCartan to O'Connell, Nov. 7, 1919; Devoy to Michael Collins, Feb. 16, 1922, Devoy-Cohalan Letters (Ms. 15,416); *The Gaelic American* (New York), Aug. 9, 1919, 1; Aug. 23, 1919, 1; Sept. 13, 1919, 6–7; Nov. 8, 1919, 1; March 13, 1920, 5; Patrick McCartan, *With De Valera in America* (New York: Brentano, 1932), 133–88; Marie Veronica Tarpey, *The Role of Joseph McGarrity in the Struggle for Irish Independence* (New York: Arno Press, 1976), 96–161.

20. Thomas M. Henderson, *Tammany Hall and the New Immigrants: The Progressive Years* (New York: Arno Press, 1976), 300–310. The major studies of the political behavior of various ethnic groups in the 1920 election have lumped "ethnic groups with a pro-German or anti-British bias" or all "immigrant districts" together, thereby blurring the diversity among ethnic voters and the possibility that Irish–American voters may have remained substantially loyal to the Democratic party, as they did in 1916, while German–American, Italian–American, and other voters defected; see Samuel Lubell, *The Future of American Politics* (Garden City, NY: Doubleday, 1955), 137–43; David Burner, *The Politics of Provincialism: The Democratic Party in Transition, 1918–1932* (New York: Alfred A. Knopf, 1967), 28–73.

21. These conclusions are based on my Guttman scale analysis of Senate roll-call votes in 1919–20. In the 1910 census, 10 percent or more of the white population was of German birth or parentage in 14 states (Illinois, Indiana, Iowa, Maryland, Michigan, Minnesota, Missouri, Nebraska, New Jersey, New York, North Dakota, Ohio, South Dakota, Wisconsin). Senators from these states ranked 1 (La Follette), 7, 8, 9, 10, 11, 13, 16, 19, 25, 26, 28, 32, 33, 36, 37, 41, 42, 43, 44, 46, 50, 51, 53, 64, 72, 80 (Hitchcock), and 89. See also Clifford L. Nelson, *German-American Political Behavior in Nebraska and Wisconsin, 1916–1920* (Lincoln: University of Nebraska Press, 1972).

22. On the idea of cultural pluralism, see Randolph S. Bourne, "Trans-National America," in *War and the Intellectuals: Essays by Randolph S. Bourne, 1915–1919,* ed. Carl Resek (New

York: Harper and Row, 1964), 107–23; Milton M. Gordon, "Assimilation in America: Theory and Reality," *Daedalus* 90 (Spring 1961): 263–85.

Chapter 9   Dilemmas of National Self-Determination:
Woodrow Wilson's Legacy

1. Alfred Cobban, *The Nation State and National Self-Determination* (London: Collins, 1969), 104.
2. Daniel Patrick Moynihan, *Pandaemonium: Ethnicity in International Politics* (New York: Oxford University Press, 1993), 81.
3. Walker Connor, *Ethnonationalism: The Quest for Understanding* (Princeton, NJ: Princeton University Press, 1994).
4. Moynihan, *Pandaemonium*, 14.
5. Ray Stannard Baker and William E. Dodd, eds., *The Public Papers of Woodrow Wilson* (New York: Harper and Brothers, 1925–7), 1: 60–2, 336–7, 360–7.
6. G. R. Conyne, *Woodrow Wilson: British Perspectives, 1912–21* (London: Macmillan, 1992).
7. Henry Kissinger, *Diplomacy* (New York: Simon and Schuster, 1994), 30, 54.
8. Tony Smith, *America's Mission: The United States and the Worldwide Struggle for Democracy in the Twentieth Century* (Princeton, NJ: Princeton University Press, 1994), 3–13.
9. Kissinger, *Diplomacy*, 19; Moynihan, *Pandaemonium*, 78–80.
10. Smith, *America's Mission*, 87.
11. Derek Heater, *National Self-Determination: Woodrow Wilson and His Legacy* (New York: St. Martin's Press, 1994), 212.
12. Heater, *National Self-Determination*, 26.
13. Lloyd E. Ambrosius, *Woodrow Wilson and the American Diplomatic Tradition: The Treaty Fight in Perspective* (Cambridge: Cambridge University Press, 1987), 119–22, 137, 167; Michael H. Hunt, *Ideology and U.S. Foreign Policy* (New Haven, CT: Yale University Press, 1987), 130–1.
14. Baker and Dodd, *Public Papers*, 1: 159–78; Niels Aage Thorsen, *The Political Thought of Woodrow Wilson, 1870–1910* (Princeton, NJ: Princeton University Press, 1988).
15. Garry Wills, *Lincoln at Gettysburg: The Words That Remade America* (New York: Simon and Schuster, 1992), 263.
16. Baker and Dodd, *Public Papers*, 1: 43–59; Thomas J. Pressly, *Americans Interpret Their Civil War* (New York: Free Press, 1962), 196–226.
17. Baker and Dodd, *Public Papers*, 1: 368–95.
18. Baker and Dodd, *Public Papers*, 1: 416–42; Smith, *America's Mission*, 37–65.
19. Baker and Dodd, *Public Papers*, 1: 437–8.
20. Baker and Dodd, *Public Papers*, 1: 310–59, 396–415; 2: 1–23. For various theories of nationalism, see John Hutchinson and Anthony D. Smith, *Nationalism* (Oxford: Oxford University Press, 1994), 3–131.
21. Baker and Dodd, *Public Papers*, 2: 187.
22. Baker and Dodd, *Public Papers*, 4: 407–14.
23. Baker and Dodd, *Public Papers*, 5: 6–16.
24. For a critique of Wilson's response to Bolshevism, see Lloyd C. Gardner, *Safe for Democracy: The Anglo-American Response to Revolution, 1913–1923* (New York: Oxford University Press, 1984).
25. David W. McFadden, *Alternative Paths: Soviets and Americans, 1917–1920* (New York: Oxford University Press, 1993); Georg Schild, *Between Ideology and Realpolitik: Woodrow Wilson and the Russian Revolution, 1917–1921* (Westport, CT: Greenwood Press, 1995); David Foglesong, *America's Secret War Against Bolshevism: United States Intervention in the Russian Civil War, 1917–1920* (Chapel Hill: University of North Carolina Press, 1995).
26. Baker and Dodd, *Public Papers*, 5: 155–62.

27. Betty Miller Unterberger, *The United States, Revolutionary Russia, and the Rise of Czechoslovakia* (Chapel Hill: University of North Carolina Press, 1989); Lloyd E. Ambrosius, "Wilsonian Self-Determination," *Diplomatic History* 16 (Winter 1992): 141–8.

28. David Steigerwald, *Wilsonian Idealism in America* (Ithaca, NY: Cornell University Press, 1994), 67.

29. Paul Mantoux, *The Deliberations of the Council of Four (March 24–June 28, 1919)*, ed. Arthur S. Link with the assistance of Manfred F. Boemeke, 2 vols. (Princeton, NJ: Princeton University Press, 1992), 1: 479–80, 496–9; Ambrosius, *Woodrow Wilson and the American Diplomatic Tradition*, 11, 51–79, 107–35.

30. Important studies on Wilson's peacemaking include Klaus Schwabe, *Woodrow Wilson, Revolutionary Germany, and Peacemaking, 1918–1919: Missionary Diplomacy and the Realities of Power* (Chapel Hill: University of North Carolina Press, 1985); Arthur Walworth, *Wilson and His Peacemakers: American Diplomacy at the Paris Peace Conference, 1919* (New York: W. W. Norton, 1986); and Jan Willem Schulte Nordholt, *Woodrow Wilson: A Life for World Peace* (Berkeley: University of California Press, 1991).

31. Mantoux, *Deliberations*, 1: 31.

32. Mantoux, *Deliberations*, 1: 55–68, 83–5.

33. Mantoux, *Deliberations*, 1: 185–6, 195–9, 204–8, 210–17.

34. Mantoux, *Deliberations*, 1: 256–63, 272.

35. Mantoux, *Deliberations*, 1: 459.

36. Mantoux, *Deliberations*, 1: 106–9, 123–4; 2: 282.

37. Mantoux, *Deliberations*, 2: 269–86, 307–14, 352–3, 388–93, 452–5.

38. Mantoux, *Deliberations*, 1: 144–5, 234; 2: 392, 422.

39. Mantoux, *Deliberations*, 1: 458–60.

40. Mantoux, *Deliberations*, 2: 312.

41. Mantoux, *Deliberations*, 2: 527.

42. Mantoux, *Deliberations*, 1: 439–41, 472–3; 2: 88–91, 330–3, 341, 481–3, 524–7, 578–81.

43. Mantoux, *Deliberations*, 2: 222–4.

44. Mantoux, *Deliberations*, 2: 226.

45. Heater, *National Self-Determination*, 53–176.

46. Robert A. Dahl, *Democracy and Its Critics* (New Haven, CT: Yale University Press, 1989), 207.

Chapter 10   Woodrow Wilson's Health and the Treaty Fight, 1919–1920

1. Thomas A. Bailey, *Woodrow Wilson and the Great Betrayal* (New York: Macmillan, 1943), 145, 173, 243, 277.

2. David M. Kennedy suggested the argument that "a vigorous President might well have succeeded in rallying public support for his unamended version of the treaty, and in bringing Lodge to heel," but he did not provide any evidence to substantiate it. See David M. Kennedy, "The Wilson Wars," *New Republic* (March 17, 1982), 36–8, and *Over Here: The First World War and American Society* (New York: Oxford University Press, 1980), 359–63.

3. Sigmund Freud and William C. Bullitt, *Thomas Woodrow Wilson: A Psychological Study* (Boston: Houghton Mifflin, 1966), 261, 281–3, 289, 291. For a condensed version of this study, see Sigmund Freud and W. C. Bullitt, "Woodrow Wilson (I)," *Encounter* 28 (Jan. 1967): 3–24, and "Woodrow Wilson (II)," ibid., 28 (Feb. 1967): 3–24.

4. Freud and Bullitt, *Thomas Woodrow Wilson*, 259, 263–4. For an alternative, and much more realistic, interpretation of Wilson's role during the peace conference, see Klaus Schwabe, *Woodrow Wilson, Revolutionary Germany, and Peacemaking, 1918–1919: Missionary Diplomacy and the Realities of Power* (Chapel Hill: University of North Carolina Press, 1985).

5. Other factual errors are outlined by Arthur S. Link, "The Case for Woodrow Wilson," in *The Higher Realism of Woodrow Wilson and Other Essays* (Nashville, TN: Vanderbilt University Press, 1971), 140–54. For other critiques of the Freud-Bullitt study, see Erik H. Erickson, "The Strange Case of Freud, Bullitt, and Woodrow Wilson: I," and Richard Hofstadter, "The Strange Case: II," *New York Review of Books* 8 (Feb. 9, 1967): 3–8; Joshua A. Hoffs, "Comments on Psychoanalytic Biography with Special Reference to Freud's Interest in Woodrow Wilson," *Psychoanalytic Review* 56 (1969): 402–14; and Paul Roazen, *Freud: Political and Social Thought* (New York: Alfred A. Knopf, 1968), 300–322.

6. Alexander L. George and Juliette L. George, *Woodrow Wilson and Colonel House: A Personality Study* (New York: Dover, 1964; 1st edition, 1956), 196, 311; Alexander L. George, "Power As a Compensatory Value for Political Leaders," *Journal of Social Issues* 24 (1968): 29–49.

7. James David Barber, *The Presidential Character: Predicting Performance in the White House* (Englewood Cliffs, NJ: Prentice Hall, 1972), 63.

8. Freud and Bullitt, *Thomas Woodrow Wilson,* 284. For Wilson's stronger motivation for power than achievement, see David G. Winter, *The Power Motive* (New York: Free Press, 1973), 212–16.

9. Edwin A. Weinstein, "Woodrow Wilson's Neurological Illness," *Journal of American History* 57 (1970): 397, 346. See also Edwin A. Weinstein, "Denial of Presidential Disability: A Case Study of Woodrow Wilson," *Psychiatry* 30 (1967): 376–90, and Walter J. Friedlander, "About Three Old Men: An Inquiry into how Cerebral Arteriosclerosis has altered World Politics," *Stroke* 3 (1972): 467–9.

10. John A. Garraty, *Interpreting American History: Conversations with Historians,* 2 vols. (New York: Macmillan, 1970), 2: 140.

11. Edwin A. Weinstein, James William Anderson, and Arthur S. Link, "Woodrow Wilson's Political Personality: A Reappraisal," *Political Science Quarterly* 93 (1978): 585–98.

12. Edwin A. Weinstein, *Woodrow Wilson: A Medical and Psychological Biography* (Princeton, NJ: Princeton University Press, 1981), 363.

13. Charles E. Neu, "The Search for Woodrow Wilson," *Reviews in American History* 10 (1982): 223–8; John Milton Cooper, Jr., *The Warrior and the Priest: Woodrow Wilson and Theodore Roosevelt* (Cambridge, MA: Harvard University Press, 1983), 339–42. For a somewhat more skeptical assessment, see Robert H. Ferrell, *Woodrow Wilson and World War I, 1917–1920* (New York: Harper and Row, 1985), 161, 273–4.

14. Juliette L. George and Alexander L. George, "Woodrow Wilson and Colonel House: A Reply to Weinstein, Anderson, and Link," *Political Science Quarterly* 96 (1981–2): 641–65; Michael F. Marmor, "Wilson, Strokes, and Zebras," *New England Journal of Medicine* 307 (Aug. 26, 1982): 528–35.

15. For the basis of this judgment, see Lloyd E. Ambrosius, *Woodrow Wilson and the American Diplomatic Tradition: The Treaty Fight in Perspective* (Cambridge: Cambridge University Press, 1987).

16. See, for example, John A. Garraty, *Henry Cabot Lodge: A Biography* (New York: Alfred A. Knopf, 1968), 294–401, and William C. Widenor, *Henry Cabot Lodge and the Search for an American Foreign Policy* (Berkeley: University of California Press, 1979), 171–348.

17. Bernard Brodie, "A Psychoanalytic Interpretation of Woodrow Wilson," *World Politics* 9 (1957): 416.

18. Jerrold M. Post, "Woodrow Wilson Re-examined: [The Mind-Body Controversy Redux and Other Disputations]"; Juliette L. George and Alexander L. George, "Comments on 'Woodrow Wilson Re-examined'"; Edwin A. Weinstein, "Comments on 'Woodrow Wilson Re-examined'"; Michael Marmor, "Comments on 'Woodrow Wilson Re-examined'"; and Jerrold M. Post, "Reply to the Three Comments on 'Woodrow Wilson Re-examined,'" *Political Psychology* 4 (1983): 289–331; Juliette L. George, Michael F. Marmor, and Alexander L. George, "Issues in Wilson Scholarship: References to Early 'Strokes' in the *Papers of Woodrow Wilson,*" and Arthur S. Link, David W. Hirst,

John Wells Davidson, and John E. Little to the Editor, *Journal of American History* 70 (1984): 845–53, 945–55. For a good summary of the controversy, see Thomas T. Lewis, "Alternative Psychological Interpretations of Woodrow Wilson," *Mid-America* 65 (1983): 71–85.

19. George D. Herron, *Woodrow Wilson and the World's Peace* (New York: Mitchell Kennerley, 1917), 68–77; Mitchell Pirie Briggs, *George D. Herron and the European Settlement* (Stanford, CA: Stanford University Press, 1932), 249.

20. For the importance of religion in Wilson's life and its influence on his foreign policy, see Arthur S. Link, "Woodrow Wilson and his Presbyterian Inheritance" and "The Higher Realism of Woodrow Wilson," in *Higher Realism of Woodrow Wilson*, 3–20, 127–39; John M. Mulder, *Woodrow Wilson: The Years of Preparation* (Princeton, NJ: Princeton University Press, 1978), and Robert M. Crunden, *Ministers of Reform: The Progressives' Achievement in American Civilization, 1889–1920* (New York: Basic Books, 1982), 225–73.

21. George and George, *Woodrow Wilson and Colonel House*, 273; Arthur S. Link, *Woodrow Wilson: Revolution, War, and Peace* (Arlington Heights, IL: AHM Publishing Corporation, 1979), 107; Weinstein, *Woodrow Wilson*, 349.

22. Freud and Bullitt, *Thomas Woodrow Wilson*, 288.

23. Lloyd Ambrosius, "Woodrow Wilson and the Quest for Orderly Progress," in *Traditions and Values: American Diplomacy, 1865–1945,* ed. Norman A. Graebner (Lanham, MD: University Press of America, 1983), 73–100.

24. This point is suggested, but not developed, by Robert Dallek, *The American Style of Foreign Policy: Cultural Politics and Foreign Affairs* (New York: Alfred A. Knopf, 1983), 91.

Chapter 11   The Orthodoxy of Revisionism:
Woodrow Wilson and the New Left

1. Robert A. Divine, *Second Chance: The Triumph of Internationalism in America during World War II* (New York: Atheneum, 1967); Bruce Kuklick, "History as a Way of Learning," *American Quarterly* 22 (Fall 1970): 609–28.

2. Harry S. Truman, *Public Papers of the Presidents of the United States: Harry S. Truman, 1945* (Washington, DC: Government Printing Office, 1961), 138–44.

3. Seyom Brown, *The Faces of Power: Constancy and Change in United States Foreign Policy from Truman to Johnson* (New York: Columbia University Press, 1968), 1–372; Richard J. Barnet, *Intervention and Revolution: The United States in the Third World* (Cleveland: World Publishing Company, 1968), 80–1, 154, passim; Ernest R. May, *"Lessons" of the Past: The Use and Misuse of History in American Foreign Policy* (New York: Oxford University Press, 1973), 19–121; Robert E. Osgood and others, *Retreat from Empire? The First Nixon Administration* (Baltimore, MD: Johns Hopkins University Press, 1973), 1–108, 207–39; Marvin Kalb and Bernard Kalb, *Kissinger* (Boston: Little, Brown, 1974), 6–7, 45–8, 169, 192, 224, 296, 426–30.

4. Garry Wills, *Nixon Agonistes: The Crisis of the Self-Made Man* (Boston: Houghton Mifflin, 1970), 20. For a remarkably similar evaluation of Wilson's presidency by historians, see Gary M. Maranell, "The Evaluation of Presidents: An Extension of the Schlesinger Polls," *Journal of American History* 57 (June 1970): 104–13.

5. Townsend Hoopes, *The Devil and John Foster Dulles* (Boston: Little, Brown, 1973), 17–21, 26–32, passim. Eisenhower was less inclined than Dulles to engage in military crusades against communism; Herbert S. Parmet, *Eisenhower and the American Crusades* (New York: Macmillan, 1972), 120–5, 184–9, 193–200, 268–74, 298–9, 357–72, 375–81, 388–405, 531–3, 574.

6. Reinhold Niebuhr, *The Children of Light and the Children of Darkness: A Vindication of Democracy and a Critique of Its Traditional Defense* (New York: Charles Scribner's Sons, 1944); Reinhold Niebuhr, *The Irony of American History* (New York: Charles Scribner's

Sons, 1952); Donald B. Meyer, *The Protestant Search for Political Realism, 1919–1941* (Berkeley: University of California Press, 1960); Hans J. Morgenthau, "The Influence of Reinhold Niebuhr in American Political Life and Thought," in *Reinhold Niebuhr: A Prophetic Voice in Our Time,* ed. Harold R. Landon (Greenwich, CT: Seabury Press, 1962), 97–116.

7. Hans J. Morgenthau, *In Defense of the National Interest: A Critical Examination of American Foreign Policy* (New York: Alfred A. Knopf, 1951); Hans J. Morgenthau, *A New Foreign Policy for the United States* (New York: Frederick A. Praeger, 1969); George F. Kennan, *American Diplomacy, 1900–1950* (Chicago: University of Chicago Press, 1951); George F. Kennan, *On Dealing with the Communist World* (New York: Harper and Row, 1964); Norman A. Graebner, ed., *Ideas and Diplomacy: Readings in the Intellectual Tradition of American Foreign Policy* (New York: Oxford University Press, 1964).

8. David Halberstam, *The Best and the Brightest* (New York: Random House, 1969), 72, 77, 404, passim; McGeorge Bundy, *The Pattern of Responsibility* (Boston: Houghton Mifflin, 1952); McGeorge Bundy, "Foreign Policy: From Innocence to Engagement," in *Paths of American Thought,* ed. Arthur M. Schlesinger, Jr. and Morton White (Boston: Houghton Mifflin, 1963), 293–308; W. W. Rostow, *The United States in the World Arena: An Essay in Recent History* (New York: Harper, 1960).

9. Lloyd C. Gardner, "American Foreign Policy 1900–1921: A Second Look at the Realist Critique of American Diplomacy," in *Towards a New Past: Dissenting Essays in American History,* ed. Barton J. Bernstein (New York: Pantheon Books, 1967), 202–31; Lloyd C. Gardner, *Architects of Illusion: Men and Ideas in American Foreign Policy, 1941–1949* (Chicago: Quadrangle Books, 1970), 202–31, 270–320; Thomas G. Paterson, "The Search for Meaning: George F. Kennan and American Foreign Policy," in *Makers of American Diplomacy: From Theodore Roosevelt to Henry Kissinger,* ed. Frank J. Merli and Theodore A. Wilson (New York: Scribner, 1974), 249–84.

10. For critiques of the New Left historiography, see Charles S. Maier, "Revisionism and the Interpretation of Cold War Origins," *Perspectives in American History* 4 (1970): 311–47; Robert W. Tucker, *The Radical Left and American Foreign Policy* (Baltimore, MD: Johns Hopkins Press, 1971); Robert James Maddox, *The New Left and the Origins of the Cold War* (Princeton, NJ: Princeton University Press, 1973).

11. D. F. Fleming, *The Cold War and Its Origins, 1917–1960,* 2 vols. (Garden City, NY: Doubleday, 1961), 1: xi, xiv, 58, 69–83, 270, 433–76, passim.

12. Selig Adler, "Hoover's Foreign Policy and the New Left," and Joan Hoff Wilson, "A Reevaluation of Herbert Hoover's Foreign Policy," in *The Hoover Presidency: A Reappraisal,* ed. Martin L. Fausold (Albany: State University of New York Press, 1974), 153–86; Joan Hoff Wilson, *Herbert Hoover: Forgotten Progressive* (Boston: Little, Brown, 1975), 269–82; Herbert Hoover, *The Ordeal of Woodrow Wilson* (London: Museum Press Ltd., 1958).

13. Robert James Maddox, *William E. Borah and American Foreign Policy* (Baton Rouge: Louisiana State University Press, 1969), 4–5, 32, 44; Ralph Stone, *The Irreconcilables: The Fight Against the League of Nations* (Lexington: University of Kentucky Press, 1970), 93, passim. William Appleman Williams favorably viewed Borah's critique of Wilson's diplomacy in *The Tragedy of American Diplomacy* (rev. ed., New York: Dell Pub. Co., 1962), 113, 118–22, and "The Legend of Isolationism in the 1920's," *Science and Society* (Winter 1954), reprinted in William Appleman Williams, *History as a Way of Learning* (New York: New Viewpoints, 1973), 120, 125–7, 134.

14. Arthur S. Link, "Special Mission," *New York Times Book Review* (April 28, 1968), 40.

15. N. Gordon Levin, Jr., *Woodrow Wilson and World Politics: America's Response to War and Revolution* (New York: Oxford University Press, 1968), 1–6, 32–49, 92–113, 183–220.

16. Levin, *World Politics,* 125–55. As principal sources on the punitive theme in Allied peace plans, Levin cited Harold I. Nelson, *Land and Power: British and Allied Policy on Germany's Frontiers, 1916–19* (Toronto: University of Toronto Press, 1963) and

George Bernard Noble, *Policies and Opinions at Paris, 1919: Wilsonian Diplomacy, the Versailles Peace, and French Public Opinion* (New York: Macmillan, 1935).

17. Levin, *World Politics*, 162, 177.
18. Levin, *World Politics*, 154; William E. Dodd, *Woodrow Wilson and His Work* (Garden City, NY: Doubleday, Page, 1920), 302, 334.
19. Ray Stannard Baker, *Woodrow Wilson and World Settlement: Written From His Unpublished and Personal Materials*, 3 vols. (Garden City, NY: Doubleday, Page, 1922), 2: 11, 22.
20. Paul Birdsall, *Versailles Twenty Years After* (New York: Reynal and Hitchcock, 1941), xi.
21. Thomas A. Bailey, *Woodrow Wilson and the Lost Peace* (New York: Macmillan, 1944), 312.
22. Seth P. Tillman, *Anglo-American Relations at the Paris Peace Conference of 1919* (Princeton, NJ: Princeton University Press, 1961), 401–2, 408. For my critique of this dualistic, anti-French interpretation, see Lloyd E. Ambrosius, "Wilson, Clemenceau, and the German Problem at the Paris Peace Conference of 1919," *Rocky Mountain Social Science Journal* 12 (April 1975): 69–79.
23. Ray Stannard Baker and William E. Dodd, eds., *The Public Papers of Woodrow Wilson*, 6 vols. (New York: Harper and Brothers, 1925–7), 4: 344–9; Woodrow Wilson, "Mr. Goldwin Smith's 'Views' on Our Political History," *The Forum* 16 (December 1893): 488–99; Arthur S. Link, ed., *The Papers of Woodrow Wilson* (Princeton, NJ: Princeton University Press, 1970), 8: 346–57; George C. Osborn, "Woodrow Wilson and Frederick Jackson Turner," New Jersey Historical Society *Proceedings* 74 (July 1956): 208–29.
24. Woodrow Wilson, *The State: Elements of Historical and Practical Politics* (Boston: D. C. Heath, 1889); Louis Hartz, *The Liberal Tradition in America: An Interpretation of American Political Thought since the Revolution* (New York: Harcourt, Brace, 1955); Louis Hartz, *The Founding of New Societies: Studies in the History of the United States, Latin America, South Africa, Canada, and Australia* (New York: Harcourt, Brace, and World, 1964).
25. Levin, *World Politics*, 134–5, 155, 158.
26. Eckart Kehr, *Der Primat der Innenpolitik: Gesammelte Aufsätze zur preussisch-deutschen Sozialgeschichte im 19. und 20. Jahrhundert* (Berlin: de Gruyter, 1965); Charles A. Beard, "Making a Bigger and Better Navy," *New Republic* 68 (October 14, 1931): 223–6; Charles A. Beard, *The Idea of National Interest: An Analytical Study in American Foreign Policy* (New York: Macmillan, 1934), 142, 198; Charles A. Beard, *The Open Door at Home: A Trial Philosophy of National Interest* (New York: Macmillan, 1935), 172; Arthur Lloyd Skop, "The Primacy of Domestic Politics: Eckart Kehr and the Intellectual Development of Charles A. Beard," *History and Theory* 13 (1974): 119–31.
27. William Appleman Williams, "A Note on Charles Austin Beard's Search for a General Theory of Causation," *American Historical Review* 62 (October 1956): 59–80, and "Charles Austin Beard: The Intellectual as Tory-Radical," in *American Radicals: Some Problems and Personalities*, ed. Harvey Goldberg (New York: Monthly Review Press, 1957), 295–308.
28. Levin, *World Politics*, 24, 36, 84, 113–15, 202, 237–8, 245–6; Carl P. Parrini, *Heir to Empire: United States Economic Diplomacy, 1916–1923* (Pittsburgh, PA: University of Pittsburgh Press, 1969).
29. Arno J. Mayer, *Dynamics of Counterrevolution in Europe, 1870–1956: An Analytical Framework* (New York: Alfred A. Knopf, 1971), 160, passim; Arno J. Mayer, "Domestic Causes of the First World War," in *The Responsibility of Power*, ed. Leonard Krieger and Fritz Stern (Garden City, NY: Doubleday, 1967), 308–24; Arno J. Mayer, *Political Origins of the New Diplomacy, 1917–1918* (New Haven, CT: Yale University Press, 1959); Arno J. Mayer, *Politics and Diplomacy of Peacemaking: Containment and Counterrevolution at Versailles, 1918–1919* (New York: Alfred A. Knopf, 1967), 10–11, 17, 29, 175–7, 211, 491, 515, 566–8, 570–5, 699–700, 877.
30. Mayer, *Political Origins*, 4, 329.
31. Mayer, *Politics and Diplomacy*, 168, 462, 563.

32. Woodrow Wilson, "Nature of Democracy in the United States," in *The Papers of Woodrow Wilson,* ed. Arthur S. Link (Princeton, NJ: Princeton University Press, 1969), 6: 238.

33. *Congressional Record,* 66 Congress, 1 Session, 58: 2339 (July 10, 1919).

34. Becker to Dodd, June 17, 1920, Phil L. Snyder, "Carl L. Becker and the Great War: A Crisis for Humane Intelligence," *Western Political Quarterly* 9 (March 1956): 1–10; Carl Becker, "Mr. Wilson at the Peace Conference," *Nation* 116 (February 14, 1923): 186–8.

35. Wilson to Coolidge, November 5, 1919, Joseph P. Tumulty Papers, Manuscript Division, Library of Congress, Washington, DC.

36. Warren F. Kuehl, *Seeking World Order: The United States and International Organization to 1920* (Nashville, TN: Vanderbilt University Press, 1969), 200–345.

37. Mayer, *Politics and Diplomacy,* 55.

38. Levin, *World Politics,* 137.

39. Dodd, *Woodrow Wilson,* 297.

40. Denna Frank Fleming, *The United States and the League of Nations, 1918–1920* (New York: G. P. Putnam, 1932), 63.

41. Thomas A. Bailey, *Woodrow Wilson and the Great Betrayal* (New York: Macmillan, 1945), 67, 70–1, 169, 277.

42. For my critique of this traditional (and revisionist) interpretation, see Lloyd E. Ambrosius, "Wilson, the Republicans, and French Security after World War I," *Journal of American History* 59 (September 1972): 341–52.

43. Alexander L. George and Juliette L. George, *Woodrow Wilson and Colonel House: A Personality Study* (Boston: Houghton Mifflin, 1966; 1st edition, 1956); Ernest Lee Tuveson, *Redeemer Nation: The Idea of America's Millennial Role* (Chicago: University of Chicago Press, 1968), 115, 173–5, 209–13, 224–5; Sigmund Freud and William C. Bullitt, *Thomas Woodrow Wilson: A Psychological Study* (Boston: Houghton Mifflin, 1967); Arthur S. Link, *The Higher Realism of Woodrow Wilson and Other Essays* (Nashville, TN: Vanderbilt University Press, 1971), 127–54; Samuel F. Wells, Jr., "New Perspectives on Wilsonian Diplomacy: The Secular Evangelism of American Political Economy," *Perspectives in American History* 6 (1972): 389–419.

44. Walter Millis, *Road to War: America, 1914–1917* (Boston: Houghton Mifflin, 1935); George F. Kennan, *Soviet–American Relations, 1917–1920,* vol. 1: *Russia Leaves the War* (Princeton, NJ: Princeton University Press, 1956), and vol. 2: *The Decision to Intervene* (Princeton, NJ: Princeton University Press, 1958).

45. William Appleman Williams, "American Intervention in Russia, 1917–1920," *Studies on the Left* 3 (Fall 1963): 24–48; ibid., 4 (Spring 1964): 39–57. For the variety in American responses, see Peter G. Filene, *Americans and the Soviet Experiment, 1917–1933* (Cambridge, MA: Harvard University Press, 1967); Christopher Lasch, *The American Liberals and the Russian Revolution* (New York: Columbia University Press, 1962); John M. Thompson, *Russia, Bolshevism, and the Versailles Peace* (Princeton, NJ: Princeton University Press, 1966).

46. Edward H. Buehrig, *Woodrow Wilson and the Balance of Power* (Bloomington: Indiana University Press, 1955); Ernest R. May, *The World War and American Isolation, 1914–1917* (Cambridge, MA: Harvard University Press, 1959); Arthur S. Link, *Wilson,* vol. 3: *The Struggle for Neutrality, 1914–1915* (Princeton, NJ: Princeton University Press, 1960), vol. 4: *Confusions and Crises, 1915–1916* (Princeton, NJ: Princeton University Press, 1964), and vol. 5: *Campaigns for Progressivism and Peace, 1916–1917* (Princeton, NJ: Princeton University Press, 1965); Daniel M. Smith, "National Interest and American Intervention, 1917: An Historiographical Appraisal," *Journal of American History* 52 (June 1965): 5–24.

47. Link, *Higher Realism,* 127–54.

48. May, *World War and American Isolation,* 436–7.

49. Buehrig, *Woodrow Wilson,* 274.

50. For the manifold dimensions of German–American relations in 1918–1919, see Klaus Schwabe, *Deutsche Revolution und Wilson-Frieden: Die amerikanische und deutsche Friedensstrategie zwischen Ideologie und Machtpolitik, 1918/19* (Düsseldorf: Droste Verlag, 1971).

51. Ronald Steel, *Pax Americana* (New York: Viking Press, 1967); David P. Calleo, *The Atlantic Fantasy: The U.S., NATO, and Europe* (Baltimore, MD: Johns Hopkins Press, 1970); David P. Calleo and Benjamin M. Rowland, *America and the World Political Economy: Atlantic Dreams and National Realities* (Bloomington: Indiana University Press, 1973); Richard J. Barnet, *Roots of War: The Men and Institutions Behind U.S. Foreign Policy* (Baltimore, MD: Penguin Books, 1971); Robert W. Tucker, *Nation or Empire? The Debate Over American Foreign Policy* (Baltimore, MD: Johns Hopkins Press, 1968); Robert W. Tucker, *A New Isolationism: Threat or Promise?* (New York: Universe Books, 1972).

Chapter 12   Vietnam Revisited: Wilson's Ghost

1. Robert S. McNamara, James G. Blight, and Robert K. Brigham, *Argument Without End: In Search of Answers to the Vietnam Tragedy* (New York: Public Affairs, 1999), 1.
2. McNamara, *Argument Without End*, 2.
3. McNamara, *Argument Without End*, 4–5.
4. Robert S. McNamara and James G. Blight, *Wilson's Ghost: Reducing the Risk of Conflict, Killing, and Catastrophe in the 21st Century* (New York: Public Affairs, 2001).
5. McNamara and Blight, *Wilson's Ghost*, 17.
6. Lloyd E. Ambrosius, *Woodrow Wilson and the American Diplomatic Tradition: The Treaty Fight in Perspective* (Cambridge: Cambridge University Press, 1987), 294–5.
7. Ronald H. Stone, *Reinhold Niebuhr: Prophet to Politicians* (Washington, DC: University Press of America, 1981), 191–204; Richard Fox, *Reinhold Niebuhr: A Biography* (New York: Pantheon Books, 1985), 283–5; Ronald Steel, *Walter Lippmann and the American Century* (Boston: Little, Brown, 1980), 557–84; Hans J. Morgenthau, *Truth and Power: Essays of a Decade, 1960–1970* (New York: Praeger Publishers, 1970); George F. Kennan, *Memoirs, 1950–1963* (Boston: Little, Brown, 1972), 59–60, 95, 99; Norman A. Graebner, *Ideas and Diplomacy: Readings in the Intellectual Tradition of American Foreign Policy* (New York: Oxford University Press, 1964), 791–7.
8. George F. Kennan, *At a Century's Ending: Reflections, 1982–1995* (New York: W. W. Norton, 1996), 276. For connections between ethics and political philosophy in realist thought, see, for example, George F. Kennan, *Around the Cragged Hill* (New York: W. W. Norton, 1993), Christoph Frei, *Hans J. Morgenthau: An Intellectual Biography* (Baton Rouge: Louisiana State University Press, 2001), and Stanley Hoffmann, *Duties Beyond Borders: On the Limits and Possibilities of Ethical International Politics* (Syracuse, NY: Syracuse University Press, 1981).
9. Morgenthau, *Truth and Power,* 409–10.
10. Morgenthau, *Truth and Power,* 415.
11. McNamara, *Argument Without End,* 381.
12. McNamara, *Argument Without End,* 22.
13. McNamara, *Argument Without End,* 23.
14. McNamara, *Argument Without End,* 24.
15. McNamara, *Argument Without End,* 387.
16. McNamara, *Argument Without End,* 26.
17. McNamara, *Argument Without End,* 40.
18. McNamara, *Argument Without End,* 40–1.
19. McNamara, *Argument Without End,* 379.
20. McNamara, *Argument Without End,* 49.
21. McNamara, *Argument Without End,* 49.

22. McNamara, *Argument Without End*, 50.
23. Stanley Hoffmann, *Gulliver's Troubles, Or the Setting of American Foreign Policy* (New York: McGraw-Hill Book Co., 1968), 384.
24. Hoffmann, *Gulliver's Troubles*, 385.
25. Hoffmann, *Gulliver's Troubles*, 191–4.
26. Morgenthau, *Truth and Power*, 421–3.
27. McNamara, *Argument Without End*, 171–2.
28. McNamara, *Argument Without End*, 56–7.
29. Robert Buzzanco, *Masters of War: Military Dissent and Politics in the Vietnam Era* (Cambridge: Cambridge University Press, 1996); Robert D. Schulzinger, *A Time for War: The United States and Vietnam, 1941–1975* (New York: Oxford University Press, 1997); Frederik Logevall, *Choosing War: The Lost Chance for Peace and the Escalation of War in Vietnam* (Berkeley: University of California Press, 1999); Richard H. Shultz, Jr., *The Secret War Against Hanoi: Kennedy's and Johnson's Use of Spies, Saboteurs, and Covert Warriors in North Vietnam* (New York: HarperCollins Publishers, 1999).
30. McNamara, *Argument Without End*, 101.
31. McNamara, *Argument Without End*, 113.
32. McNamara, *Argument Without End*, 30.
33. Loren Baritz, *Backfire: A History of How American Culture Led Us into Vietnam and Made Us Fight the Way We Did* (New York: William Morrow, 1985), 33.
34. McNamara, *Argument Without End*, 70.
35. McNamara, *Argument Without End*, 74, 95.
36. McNamara, *Argument Without End*, 217.
37. McNamara, *Argument Without End*, 95.
38. McNamara, *Argument Without End*, 221.
39. McNamara, *Argument Without End*, 223–4.
40. McNamara, *Argument Without End*, 236.
41. McNamara, *Argument Without End*, 237.
42. McNamara, *Argument Without End*, 225.
43. George C. Herring, *America's Longest War: The United States and Vietnam, 1950–1975* (New York: John Wiley and Sons, 1979), 166.
44. McNamara, *Argument Without End*, 237.
45. McNamara, *Argument Without End*, 245.
46. McNamara, *Argument Without End*, 248–50.
47. McNamara, *Argument Without End*, 254.
48. McNamara, *Argument Without End*, 255.
49. McNamara, *Argument Without End*, 258–9.
50. Lyndon Baines Johnson, *The Vantage Point: Perspectives of the Presidency, 1963–1969* (New York: Holt, Rinehart, and Winston, 1971), 232.
51. Johnson, *Vantage Point*, 234.
52. McNamara, *Argument Without End*, 273–4.
53. William Conrad Gibbons, *The U.S. Government and the Vietnam War: Executive and Legislative Roles and Relationships*, 4 vols. (Washington, DC: Government Printing Office, 1994), 4: 107–8; Deborah Shapley, *Promise and Power: The Life and Times of Robert McNamara* (Boston: Little, Brown, 1993), 359.
54. McNamara, *Argument Without End*, 278.
55. McNamara, *Argument Without End*, 289.
56. McNamara, *Argument Without End*, 290–1.
57. McNamara, *Argument Without End*, 291.
58. McNamara, *Argument Without End*, 301.
59. Robert S. McNamara, *In Retrospect: The Tragedy and Lessons of Vietnam* (New York: Vintage Books, 1995), 284.

60. Robert J. Myers, *U.S. Foreign Policy in the Twenty-First Century: The Relevance of Realism* (Baton Rouge: Louisiana State University Press, 1999), 92–3.
61. Morgenthau, *Truth and Power,* 425.
62. McNamara and Blight, *Wilson's Ghost,* 64–73.
63. McNamara and Blight, *Wilson's Ghost,* 67.
64. McNamara and Blight, *Wilson's Ghost,* 44.

Chapter 13   Post-Cold War Wilsonianism: America's Mission?

1. Klaus Schwabe, *Deutsche Revolution und Wilson-Frieden: Die amerikanische und deutsche Friedensstrategie zwischen Ideologie und Machtpolitik 1918/19* (Düsseldorf: Droste Verlag, 1971); Klaus Schwabe, *Woodrow Wilson, Revolutionary Germany, and Peacemaking, 1918–1919: Missionary Diplomacy and the Realities of Power* (Chapel Hill: University of North Carolina Press, 1985).
2. Tony Smith, *America's Mission: The United States and the Worldwide Struggle for Democracy in the Twentieth Century* (Princeton, NJ: Princeton University Press, 1994), xv.
3. Smith, *America's Mission,* 9.
4. Smith, *America's Mission,* 10.
5. Smith, *America's Mission,* 12–13.
6. Henry Kissinger, *Diplomacy* (New York: Simon and Schuster, 1994), 33.
7. Kissinger, *Diplomacy,* 52.
8. Kissinger, *Diplomacy,* 54.
9. Kissinger, *Diplomacy,* 19.
10. Lloyd E. Ambrosius, *Woodrow Wilson and the American Diplomatic Tradition: The Treaty Fight in Perspective* (Cambridge: Cambridge University Press, 1987).
11. Kissinger, *Diplomacy,* 18.
12. Kissinger, *Diplomacy,* 41.
13. Smith, *America's Mission,* 30–1; Tony Smith, "In Defense of Intervention," *Foreign Affairs* 73 (Nov./Dec. 1994): 34–46.
14. Smith, *America's Mission,* 32.
15. Smith, *America's Mission,* 268.
16. Smith, *America's Mission,* 299.
17. Kissinger, *Diplomacy,* 621.
18. Kissinger, *Diplomacy,* 649.
19. Kissinger, *Diplomacy,* 654.
20. Kissinger, *Diplomacy,* 667.
21. Kissinger, *Diplomacy,* 670.
22. Kissinger, *Diplomacy,* 669. See also Walter Isaacson, *Kissinger* (New York: Simon and Schuster, 1992), 117–20, 157–82.
23. Frank Ninkovich, *Modernity and Power: A History of the Domino Theory in the Twentieth Century* (Chicago: University of Chicago Press, 1994), 316. See also Isaacson, *Kissinger,* 234–354, 399–490.
24. Ambrosius, *Woodrow Wilson,* 295.
25. Garry Wills, *Nixon Agonistes: The Crisis of the Self-Made Man* (Boston: Houghton Mifflin, 1970), 20.
26. Kissinger, *Diplomacy,* 706–7.
27. Kissinger, *Diplomacy,* 705.
28. Kissinger, *Diplomacy,* 743.
29. Isaacson, *Kissinger,* 718, 723–6.
30. Kissinger, *Diplomacy,* 767.
31. Kissinger, *Diplomacy,* 773.
32. Kissinger, *Diplomacy,* 774.

33. Kissinger, *Diplomacy,* 702.
34. Robert H. Wiebe, *Self-Rule: A Cultural History of American Democracy* (Chicago: University of Chicago Press, 1995). See also David Steigerwald, *Wilsonian Idealism in America* (Ithaca, NY: Cornell University Press, 1994).
35. Michael Cox, *US Foreign Policy after the Cold War: Superpower Without a Mission?* (London: Pinter, 1995).

For Further Reading

Ambrosius, Lloyd E. *Wilsonian Statecraft: Theory and Practice of Liberal Internationalism during World War I.* Wilmington, DE: Scholarly Resources, 1991.

———. *Woodrow Wilson and the American Diplomatic Tradition: The Treaty Fight in Perspective.* Cambridge: Cambridge University Press, 1987.

Axson, Stockton. *"Brother Woodrow": A Memoir of Woodrow Wilson.* Princeton, NJ: Princeton University Press, 1993.

Bacino, Leo J. *Reconstructing Russia: U.S. Policy in Revolutionary Russia, 1917–1922.* Kent, OH: Kent State University Press, 1999.

Boemeke, Manfred F., Gerald D. Feldman, and Elisabeth Glaser, eds. *The Treaty of Versailles: A Reassessment after 75 Years.* Cambridge: Cambridge University Press, 1998.

Boyle, Francis Anthony. *Foundations of World Order: The Legalist Approach to International Relations, 1898–1922.* Durham, NC: Duke University Press, 1999.

Buckley, Thomas H., and Edwin B. Strong, Jr. *American Foreign and National Security Policies, 1914–1945.* Knoxville: University of Tennessee Press, 1987.

Calhoun, Frederick S. *Power and Principle: Armed Intervention in Wilsonian Foreign Policy.* Kent, OH: Kent State University Press, 1986.

Chickering, Roger, and Stig Forster, eds. *Great War, Total War: Combat and Mobilization on the Western Front.* Cambridge: Cambridge University Press, 2000.

Clements, Kendrick A. *The Presidency of Woodrow Wilson.* Lawrence: University Press of Kansas, 1992.

———. *William Jennings Bryan: Missionary Isolationist.* Knoxville: University of Tennessee Press, 1982.

———. *Woodrow Wilson: World Statesman.* Boston: Twayne Publishers, 1987.

Cohen, Warren I. *The American Revisionists: The Lessons of Intervention in World War I.* Chicago: University of Chicago Press, 1967.

Conyne, G. R. *Woodrow Wilson: British Perspectives, 1912–21.* London: Macmillan, 1992.

Coogan, John W. *The End of Neutrality: The United States, Britain, and Maritime Rights, 1899–1915.* Ithaca, NY: Cornell University Press, 1981.

Cooper, John Milton, Jr. *Breaking the Heart of the World: Woodrow Wilson and the Fight for the League of Nations.* Cambridge: Cambridge University Press, 2001.

———. *Walter Hines Page: The Southerner as American, 1855–1918.* Chapel Hill: University of North Carolina Press, 1977.

———. *The Warrior and the Priest: Theodore Roosevelt and Woodrow Wilson.* Cambridge, MA: Harvard University Press, 1983.

Cooper, John Milton, Jr., and Charles E. Neu. *The Wilson Era: Essays in Honor of Arthur S. Link.* Arlington Heights, IL: Harlan Davidson, 1991.

Doerries, Reinhard R. *Imperial Challenge: Ambassador Count Bernstorff and German–American Relations, 1908–1917.* Chapel Hill: University of North Carolina Press, 1989.

Doyle, Michael W. *Ways of War and Peace: Realism, Liberalism, and Socialism.* New York: W. W. Norton, 1997.

Esposito, David M. *The Legacy of Woodrow Wilson: American War Aims in World War I.* Westport, CT: Praeger, 1996.

Ferrell, Robert H. *Woodrow Wilson and World War I, 1917–1921.* New York: Harper and Row, 1985.

Floto, Inga. *Colonel House in Paris: A Study of American Policy at the Paris Peace Conference 1919.* Princeton, NJ: Princeton University Press, 1980.

Fogelsong, David S. *America's Secret War Against Bolshevism: U.S. Intervention in the Russian Civil War, 1917–1920.* Chapel Hill: University of North Carolina Press, 1995.

Fox, Richard. *Reinhold Niebuhr: A Biography.* New York: Pantheon Books, 1985.

Frei, Christoph. *Hans J. Morgenthau: An Intellectual Biography.* Baton Rouge: Louisiana State University Press, 2001.

Gardner, Lloyd C. *Safe for Democracy: The Anglo-American Response to Revolution, 1913–1923.* New York: Oxford University Press, 1984.

Gilderhus, Mark T. *Pan American Visions: Woodrow Wilson in the Western Hemisphere, 1913–1921.* Tucson: University of Arizona Press, 1986.

Graebner, Norman A. *Ideas and Diplomacy: Readings in the Intellectual Tradition of American Foreign Policy.* New York: Oxford University Press, 1964.

Hall, Linda B. *Oil, Banks, and Politics: The United States and Postrevolutionary Mexico, 1917–1924.* Austin: University of Texas Press, 1995.

Heater, Derek. *National Self-Determination: Woodrow Wilson and His Legacy.* New York: St. Martin's Press, 1994.

Heckscher, August. *Woodrow Wilson: A Biography.* New York: Charles Scribner's Sons, 1991.

Hilderbrand, Robert C. *Power and the People: Executive Management of Public Opinion in Foreign Affairs, 1897–1921.* Chapel Hill: University of North Carolina Press, 1981.

Hunt, Michael H. *Ideology and U.S. Foreign Policy.* New Haven, CT: Yale University Press, 1987.

Ikenberry, G. John. *After Victory: Institutions, Strategic Restraint, and the Rebuilding of Order after Major Wars.* Princeton, NJ: Princeton University Press, 2001.

Iriye, Akira. *The Cambridge History of American Foreign Relations,* vol. 3: *The Globalizing of America, 1913–1945.* Cambridge: Cambridge University Press, 1993.

Johnson, Robert David. *The Peace Progressives and American Foreign Relations.* Cambridge, MA: Harvard University Press, 1995.

Katz, Frederick. *The Secret War in Mexico: Europe, the United States, and the Mexican Revolution.* Chicago: University of Chicago Press, 1981.

Kawamura, Noriko. *Turbulence in the Pacific: Japanese–U.S. Relations during World War I.* Westport, CT: Praeger, 2000.

Kennan, George F. *Around the Cragged Hill.* New York: W. W. Norton, 1993.

———. *Soviet–American Relations, 1917–1920,* 2 vols. Princeton, NJ: Princeton University Press, 1956–8.

Kennedy, David M. *Over Here: The First World War and American Society.* New York: Oxford University Press, 1980.

Killen, Linda. *The Russian Bureau: A Case Study in Wilsonian Diplomacy.* Lexington: University Press of Kentucky, 1983.

Kissinger, Henry. *Diplomacy.* New York: Simon and Schuster, 1994.

Levin, N. Gordon, Jr. *Woodrow Wilson and World Politics: America's Response to War and Revolution.* New York: Oxford University Press, 1968.

Link, Arthur S. *The Higher Realism of Woodrow Wilson and Other Essays.* Nashville, TN: Vanderbilt University Press, 1971.

———. *Wilson,* 5 vols. Princeton, NJ: Princeton University Press, 1947–65.

———. *Woodrow Wilson: Revolution, War, and Peace.* Arlington Heights, IL: AHM Publishing Corporation, 1979.

———, ed. *Woodrow Wilson and a Revolutionary World, 1913–1921.* Chapel Hill: University of North Carolina Press, 1982.

Knock, Thomas J. *To End All Wars: Woodrow Wilson and the Quest for a New World Order.* New York: Oxford University Press, 1992.

Mayer, Arno J. *Political Origins of the New Diplomacy, 1917–1918.* New Haven, CT: Yale University Press, 1959.

————. *Politics and Diplomacy of Peacemaking: Containment and Counterrevolution at Versailles, 1918–1919.* New York: Alfred A. Knopf, 1967.

McDougall, Walter A. *Promised Land, Crusader State: The American Encounter with the World Since 1776.* Boston: Houghton Mifflin, 1997.

McFadden, David W. *Alternative Paths: Soviets and Americans, 1917–1920.* New York: Oxford University Press, 1993.

McNamara, Robert S., and James G. Blight. *Wilson's Ghost: Reducing the Risk of Conflict, Killing, and Catastrophe in the 21st Century.* New York: Public Affairs, 2001.

Mitchell, Nancy. *The Danger of Dreams: German and American Imperialism in Latin America.* Chapel Hill: University of North Carolina Press, 1999.

Moynihan, Daniel Patrick. *Pandaemonium: Ethnicity in International Politics.* New York: Oxford University Press, 1993.

Mulder, John M. *Woodrow Wilson: The Years of Preparation.* Princeton, NJ: Princeton University Press, 1978.

Ninkovich, Frank. *Modernity and Power: A History of the Domino Theory in the Twentieth Century.* Chicago: University of Chicago Press, 1994.

————. *The Wilsonian Century: U.S. Foreign Policy since 1900.* Chicago: University of Chicago Press, 1999.

Nordholt, Jan Willem Schulte. *Woodrow Wilson: A Life for World Peace.* Berkeley: University of California Press, 1991.

Perlmutter, Amos. *Making the World Safe for Democracy: A Century of Wilsonianism and Its Totalitarian Challengers.* Chapel Hill: University of North Carolina Press, 1997.

Rosenberg, Emily S. *Financial Missionaries to the World: The Politics and Culture of Dollar Diplomacy, 1900–1930.* Cambridge, MA: Harvard University Press, 1999.

Schwabe, Klaus. *Woodrow Wilson, Revolutionary Germany, and Peacemaking, 1918–1919: Missionary Diplomacy and the Realities of Power.* Chapel Hill: University of North Carolina Press, 1985.

Smith, Tony. *America's Mission: The United States and the Worldwide Struggle for Democracy in the Twentieth Century.* Princeton, NJ: Princeton University Press, 1994.

Steel, Ronald. *Walter Lippmann and the American Century.* Boston: Little, Brown, 1980.

Steigerwald, David. *Wilsonian Idealism in America.* Ithaca, NY: Cornell University Press, 1994.

Stid, Daniel D. *The President as Statesman: Woodrow Wilson and the Constitution.* Lawrence: University Press of Kansas, 1998.

Thorsen, Niels Aage. *The Political Thought of Woodrow Wilson, 1870–1910.* Princeton, NJ: Princeton University Press, 1988.

Trask, David F. *The AEF and Coalition Warmaking, 1917–1918.* Lawrence: University Press of Kansas, 1993.

Unterberger, Betty Miller. *The United States, Revolutionary Russia, and the Rise of Czechoslovakia.* Chapel Hill: University of North Carolina Press, 1989.

Vaughan, Leslie J. *Randolph Bourne and the Politics of Cultural Radicalism.* Lawrence: University Press of Kansas, 1997.

Walworth, Arthur. *Wilson and His Peacemakers: American Diplomacy at the Paris Peace Conference, 1919.* New York: W. W. Norton, 1986.

Weinstein, Edwin A. *Woodrow Wilson: A Medical and Psychological Biography.* Princeton, NJ: Princeton University Press, 1981.

Widenor, William C. *Henry Cabot Lodge and the Search for an American Foreign Policy.* Berkeley: University of California Press, 1979.

Winter, Jay, Geoffrey Parker, and Mary R. Habeck, eds. *The Great War and the Twentieth Century.* New Haven, CT: Yale University Press, 2000.

Woodward, David R. *Trial by Friendship: Anglo-American Relations, 1917–1918.* Lexington: University Press of Kentucky, 1993.

INDEX